Crime And Civil Society

Crime And Civil Society

Can We Become A
More Law-Abiding People?

David G. Green
Emma Grove
Nadia A. Martin

Foreword by
His Honour Judge Alan Taylor

Additional Essay by
Norman Dennis

Civitas: Institute for the Study of Civil Society
London
Registered Charity No. 1085494

First published February 2005

ISBN 1-903 386-36 5

Typeset by Civitas
in Palatino

Printed in Great Britain by
St Edmundsbury Press Ltd
Blenheim Industrial Park, Newmarket Road
Bury St Edmunds, Suffolk

Contents

Authors

David G. Green is the Director of Civitas. His books include *The New Right: The Counter Revolution in Political, Economic and Social Thought*, Wheatsheaf, 1987; *Reinventing Civil Society*, IEA, 1993; *Community Without Politics: A Market Approach to Welfare Reform*, IEA, 1996; *Benefit Dependency: How Welfare Undermines Independence*, IEA, 1998; *An End to Welfare Rights: The Rediscovery of Independence*, 1999; *Delay, Denial and Dilution*, 1999 (with Laura Casper); *Stakeholder Health Insurance*, Civitas, 2000; *Health Care in France and Germany: Lessons for the UK*, Civitas, 2001 (with Ben Irvine). He wrote the chapter on 'The Neo-Liberal Perspective' in Blackwell's *The Student's Companion to Social Policy*, (2nd edn) 2003.

He writes occasionally for newspapers, including in recent years pieces in the *Guardian* and *The Sunday Times* (on health reform), *The Times* (on race, NHS reform and crime) and the *Daily Telegraph* (on crime).

Emma Grove grew up in London. She was educated at the City of London School for Girls and the University of Edinburgh, graduating with a First in Sociology in 2003. She was a crime researcher at Civitas and is now working at *The Times*.

Nadia A. Martin was raised in Massachusetts where she attended the Groton School. She earned her BSc degree at the Walsh School of Foreign Service at Georgetown University. At Civitas, Nadia has worked on crime, family and healthcare policy. Her previous works include *Marriage on MARS*, a study of the Government's support of marriage and family, published by Civitas in 2002. She has appeared as a commentator on the BBC and Sky as well as in newspaper articles. Now based at the Stockholm School of Economics, she is pursuing further studies and research in economics and finance.

Preface

Our aim is to understand how best to encourage a more law-abiding society. The study is organised as follows. The first chapter describes the current crime problem and Chapter 2 goes on to discuss the main standpoints in today's public debate.

Part I, comprising Chapters 3-12, examines the various measures taken to reduce offending, drawing a good deal on North American evidence, where efforts to evaluate programmes have been far more rigorous than here. Policing plays a major role in reducing crime, but is the subject of a separate study by Norman Dennis, *Cultures and Crimes: Policing in Four Nations*.[1] Here we focus on the role of the criminal justice authorities in reducing reoffending by convicted criminals.

Part II, comprising Chapters 13-15, focuses on public policy recommendations. Chapter 13 looks at the latest American thinking, Chapter 14 sets out the guiding principles for reform and Chapter 15 appraises the policies of the British Government.

The authors are grateful to Rosie Milner, Josie Cluer, James Cave and Ian Ginsberg for their research assistance during their time at Civitas.

The study received funding from Reform and from the Esmée Fairbairn Foundation's Rethinking Crime and Punishment initiative, each allowing a full-time researcher to be employed.

David G. Green

Foreword

There is widespread public concern about the high level of crime in this country. Although the statistics fluctuate a little year on year, the picture is clear: over the past two generations crime has increased enormously. A great deal of crime goes unrecorded, and much of the crime that is reported to the police is not adjudicated upon by our criminal courts. The result is that there is a substantial cost to the community and many people go about in fear of being the victims of crime. People ask, quite reasonably, how this has come about. In an age of great technological advances, when so many people enjoy a prosperous lifestyle far beyond that of their parents and grandparents, why is it that so much crime and anti-social behaviour are ruining it all? In short, what are the causes of crime?

Many excuses or explanations are offered. 'It is the price of a free society', we are told. 'You cannot turn the clock back.' There is a widespread feeling that nothing can be done about the situation and that, if one is the victim of crime, it is a misfortunate like falling ill. More and more people despair as successive governments fail to stem the tide despite considerable numbers of initiatives and policy changes. We are left with the feeling that nothing works.

A large amount of time and money is spent in dealing with the results of criminal and anti-social behaviour, and even more is spent on protecting society from further conduct of the same kind. There is a continual detailed debate about what to do with those who are convicted in our courts, but this book shows that whatever type of sentence is imposed by judges and magistrates, whether it be custodial or non-custodial, the re-offending rate is depressingly high. However, we should not forget that, although many defendants go on offending, there are some who do not appear to do so. Whether that is because they have learned the error of their ways as a result of the sentence of the court, or for any other reason, is usually not known.

As every judge and magistrate knows, the typical occupant of the dock in a criminal court is male (a small but increasing number are female) and less than 30 years of age. He is likely to have started offending in his teenage years, and it is likely that he had no father-figure present for the majority of his formative years. He will almost certainly be unemployed and his educational achievements will have been well below average. He will have become addicted to alcohol or other drugs. The level of premeditation or lack of self-control associated with his offending will have increased with time.

Consequently, the efforts of the criminal justice system to stop him offending will have failed conspicuously. However, many young men of this kind cease to offend or offend much less often after the age of 30. By that time they will have matured sufficiently to realise that crime does not pay and that, if they do not alter their lifestyle, they will spend longer and longer periods of time in prison.

This is, of course, a generalisation, but sadly most defendants do fit the profile.

Many mothers cope adequately, even admirably, without the help of a child's father, but unfortunately the sixfold increase in divorce over the past 30 or so years coincides with the enormous increase in crime. It is foolish to ignore the obvious correlation.

Not only is the preponderance of divorce a facet of the past generation, the rate of illegitimacy has soared too. One of the most startling statistics of the age is that during the first 60 years of the twentieth century the rate of illegitimacy was five per cent. Now it is 40 per cent and rising. Thus, nearly half of children these days are born out of wedlock. It is accepted that some of them are born to parents who, whilst not married, are cohabiting. Nevertheless the rate of breakdown between cohabiting couples is much greater than that between married couples. Hence the alarming statistic that over a quarter of all children in the country, some three million of them, have experienced for at least part of their lives the absence of a parent, overwhelmingly the father.

Any person who is aware of these facts cannot help but see the link between upbringing and crime. Disadvantage and deprivation lead to delinquency and dishonesty and produce damaged lives. Yet so little seems to be said or done to seek to restore the benefits of a stable home life to children. It is hardly surprising, therefore, that so many succumb to the influences that lead to poor education (both intellectual and moral) and criminal behaviour. Efforts made by a multitude of agencies to prevent young people from re-offending are like trying to 'close the gate after the horse has bolted'. We have got to increase our efforts to prevent crime happening in the first place, because, as research carried out on the North American continent and in the United Kingdom shows, it is so difficult to redress the downward spiral of disadvantage, delinquency, addiction and crime once it has begun.

The message of this book is that crime and anti-social activity are so rife that a holistic and expensive campaign over a long period of time has to be started. Short-term, isolated and unconnected experiments and initiatives are unlikely to produce lasting improvements. We are dealing with young men who have been brought up badly for, say, 16 years. We cannot hope to correct that in 16 weeks or even 16 months of custodial or community sentences. The criminal justice system can only change those who wish to be changed, and there are not many of them.

The important thing is to deflect and deter young people from starting a life of crime, to catch those who do commit a crime and to deal with them appropriately. The task can be summed up by three Ps: parenting, policing and punishment. (Many would add a fourth: piety. Selfishness is the forerunner of every criminal act.)

First of all let us consider parenting. Relationships are pre-eminent in a child's upbringing and there is none closer than that with his or her parents. If one parent is missing, the result is often catastrophic. It can be said that parental relationships on the one hand and marriage on the other hand have no obvious connection as everything depends on the actual as opposed to the formal bond. An argument in support of that can be mounted, but the truth is that children of happily married parents, on the whole, do much better in life than those less advantaged. What does a child need from his or her parents? The answer can be put succinctly: a child needs to know what it is to be loved and provided for, and to be taught the difference between right and wrong. This is absorbed by example as much as in any other way. Children brought up without the good influence of their fathers are likely to be adversely influenced by their peers.

Parenting should be seen not only in the context of a happy and stable home life but in a wider sphere too. Schools, churches and other social and sporting institutions have their part to play in a child's moral upbringing. The need is great for good male role models for children. However, teachers seem to be wary of befriending disadvantaged children in case such friendships are misinterpreted; many churches have no young people; and constructive activities outside these areas seem to be decreasing. The cry 'There is nothing for them to do in this neighbourhood' is heard all too often. Should we not try to cultivate on a national level a method of teaching young people about marriage, parenting and staying together, 'for better for worse, in sickness and in health, till death do us part'? At all levels of society there is an erosion of support for marriage, which is depicted as merely one lifestyle option. Yet the connection between the breakdown of family life and crime is there for all to see.

Alongside parenting we must have policing. The courts (acting on behalf of society) can do nothing with those who commit crime unless they are caught by the police and brought before them. When the call is made for more police officers, and that their presence should be more visible, the phrase 'nanny state' is used as an objection. But what is the alternative? Are we going to go on as we are? Policing should, of course, be personal as well as public. We all have a responsibility to look after ourselves and our property. The more frequent use of burglar alarms and car alarms has helped in a limited way to reduce acquisitive crime, but other crime, particularly acts of violence, possession and supply of drugs, and commercial fraud will only be avoided by constant vigilance and sensible precautions. Regrettably we will have to put up with inconvenience in order to avoid being victims as innocent members of the public. Criminals can be deterred for a time, but the real deterrent is the likelihood of being caught. Many offenders who are brought before the courts have committed many crimes before eventually being apprehended.

Policing is redundant without punishment. The purpose of establishing the guilt of a defendant in court must be in order to apply some appropriate sanction. But why? And what is the appropriate sanction anyway? The clear objective is to stop people committing crime. However, this is where the divergent views emerge and research is used to support a particular approach, yet crime continues at a high level. There are the STADs (Send Them All Down) and the ABCs (Anything But Custody). The judges and magistrates have the unenviable task of passing sentence against the background of these competing approaches and various shades of opinion. Meanwhile, the attitudes of some protagonists in the debate leads one almost to the view that the courts themselves are to blame for the volume of crime!

By far the most clear-cut form of punishment in our criminal law is custody. To send a person to prison is not intended to consign him to a period of degradation but to deprive him of his liberty. The nature of the punishment is the loss of freedom for the offender to move about as he pleases, and thus to prevent him from committing further crimes in the public arena. But is that all? It is hoped that others of like mind will be deterred from offending in the future in the knowledge of what happens to those who are caught, and it is hoped that the offender himself will be deterred from re-offending. But they will not be deterred if the likelihood of being caught is not very high. So no matter what rehabilitative measures are adopted and resettlement plans are made while they are in custody, the temptation to re-offend is more likely to be assuaged if the outside arena is more closely policed when they are released. That does not mean that rehabilitative measures have no value. It is acknowledged that some are successful for some offenders, for a while at least, but the re-conviction rate, whatever is tried, is very depressing.

The effect of imprisonment is, therefore, the deprivation of liberty for a time in the hope that the offender and others will be deterred. In the meantime, the public is protected from the offender for that period. The question is then asked whether the effect could be the same without sending him to prison. The argument is put as follows: if efforts are allowed to be made to correct the offender's behaviour without sending him to prison, and thus depriving him of all the positive and non-criminal aspects of his life, would not that tend to be better for him? The argument appears to ignore the deterrent aspect of punishment, but, be that as it may, the answer is, of course, that if as a result of that approach crime went down considerably, support would be forthcoming on all sides. But this book shows that the re-conviction rates following non-custodial sentences are on the whole similar to those following custodial sentences, bearing in mind that those sentenced to custody are bound to be guilty of more serious offending.

Regrettably, this study shows that the courts have little effect when it comes to preventing people from reoffending. Crime will only be reduced by a vastly increased rate of detection and by targeting children in deprived and vulnerable situations in order to compensate for the absent role models in their lives. Let us by all means save some.

His Honour Judge Alan Taylor

Understanding and the Social Sciences
Norman Dennis

In examining an encyclopædic range of programmes aimed at reducing offending and reoffending, and particularly the research assessments of them, *Crime and Civil Society* is primarily interested in the question of what works, what does not work and what is promising for public policy. But it is always alert to three other questions about each programme, of less immediate interest to policy-makers, but just as important to them in the long run. When we look at a programme that appeared to work, how certain can we be that it was the treatment programme itself that had been responsible for the effects, and not something else? When we see that a programme had worked in one set of circumstances, what confidence can we have that it would have worked in a different set of circumstances? These are both aspects of the question: Where we know that it did work, why did it work? Running through the whole volume, therefore, is the authors' explicit or implicit 'assessment of the assessments'.

Many of the evaluations of whether programmes work, do not work, or possibly might work, especially the evaluations of American programmes, follow to a greater or lesser degree the protocols of statistical methodology in the social sciences. Lawrence Sherman and his colleagues re-evaluated, using their Maryland scientific methods scale (SMS), more than 600 programmes intended to prevent crime. The SMS rated on a five-point scale how closely the original evaluations corresponded to the protocols of sound social-scientific research. Sherman and his colleagues discarded studies that were rated 2 or lower on the 5-point scale of the SMS.[1]

In outline, a study of the impact of a treatment programme of offenders is said to be more or less scientific in the Sherman sense to the extent that it meets the following requirements. There are two populations of offenders. Each is exactly the same in composition as the other. There is the same distribution of ages, of educational histories, of the number, type and severity of previous offences committed, of number of convictions, of ethnicity, of social class, of family stability or breakdown, and so on—in principle, endlessly. One of these two identical populations is exposed to a new element, the treatment programme. The other is not. Differences (however small) that then appear between the two groups in, say, the proportion reconvicted after a stated period can then be attributed to the programme.

In practice, limitation of resources of money and research staff mean that any actual study is only a very rough and ready approximation to this. In practice, also, populations of offenders are so large that the full populations are rarely studied. A sample is drawn from each population. So long as the two samples are *random* samples in the strict statistical sense of the word random, then the certainty with which one can say that the programme has made the difference (in the example here) in the proportion of offenders reconvicted, can be read off from mathematical tables that deal with the properties of *all* random samples, random samples as such. If the total populations are not investigated, then random sampling is essential for the purpose of establishing the measurable uncertainty of the figures given by the samples as estimates of the figures for the populations being sampled.

Random sampling is essential to scientific method in sample studies. It is a useful and almost universally used tool of the social sciences. But random sampling is nevertheless a subsidiary matter. What is essential is the study of identical populations, one of which is exposed to a new variable, the other not.

As *Crime and Civil Society* shows, the lay usage of words like sample and population is often confused with the words as they are used in the social sciences. To take one example from many, the evaluation of the On-Side project (p. 183) talks about a 'sample' of offenders who were the beneficiaries of the On-Side programme. Yet the beneficiaries were not a sample in the statistical sense at all. They were a population of young offenders at the Young Offenders Institution at Portland, who were specially selected as being deemed to be highly motivated to avoid reoffending when they were released. The proportions who did reoffend in this population were compared with the proportions who reoffended in the population of all young offenders in institutions countrywide.

But conclusions about the effectiveness of the programme could only be drawn by comparing two identical populations of young offenders, both populations being composed of offenders deemed to be highly motivated not to reoffend, one population being subjected to the On-Side programme, and the other not subject to it. Practically, random samples of the populations are drawn, and the proportions reoffending in the sample exposed to the programme and not exposed to the programme are used to estimate the proportions in the populations with a degree of confidence that can be stated on the basis of what is known about the characteristics of random samples as such.

Because of confusion about what constitutes 'evidence-based crime prevention' even the Portland On-Side study can be—has been—

'hailed as a turning point for prison resettlement strategies' (p. 183). Dr Green and his co-authors do not disparage the scheme itself. Common sense tells us that the programme content of On-Side was highly likely to be beneficial to those who were selected for it, and probably on the figures did lower the offending rate, though to an unknown extent—but that is about as much as can be said of it as *generalisable evidence* for policy purposes.

There is an important downside to an emphasis on 'evidence-based' policy. The idea that On-Side or any other programme should be disregarded because it does not come anywhere on, say, the SMS scale is a pernicious one. It is highly desirable that there should be a body of experts in academia or elsewhere whose mind-set is obsessively scientific; who will accept nothing as evidence in their own field that has not been subjected to the strictest controlled scrutiny in a carefully designed research project, and has survived so far the tests-to-destruction of their equally science-obsessed colleagues working in the same field. It is the mind-set that believes nothing until it has been tested anew. But it is highly undesirable if this mind-set comes to be that of the general community. Members of the general community —the ordinary citizen, father, mother and teacher—do not start with knowing nothing about 'what works', waiting as social know-nothings for the scientific community to disclose its latest findings. What the general community 'knows'—the German phrase for common sense is strikingly apt, *gesunder Menschenverstand*, 'healthy understanding'—is in effect an amalgam of the results of an infinite number of experiments that have taken place in the history of humanity. Some of it is wrong, and scientific social experiments can help in identifying where and why and to what extent common sense is common nonsense. But much of it is right. In focusing on his or her own programme and assessing whether it works, the 'experimental' social scientist, as a basic professional commitment, abandons common sense as a guide to what is true and false, and consigns the answer to experiments with treatment groups and control groups. In focusing on the particular programme, the scientist is right take the background culture for granted. He deliberately ignores the wood in order to have a clear view of his tree. The results of this mind-set, however, can be disastrous for public policy. Yet this is what has characterised public policy on a large scale for the past 40 years. ('Scientific' social research has only been present on any scale in this country since the expansion of the universities in the 1960s.) The broad facts of a largely crime-free England during the hundred years from, say, 1855 to 1955, and the religious, familial, educational, recreational and other institutions that created and sustained it, are treated as of no consequence. This is appropriate in the case of the scientific observer as he conducts his own experiment, but it is not appropriate that the general public should lose all confidence in what generations have found to be 'what works'. 'Post-modernism', which has the distinction of being a philosophy that is identical with its own *reductio ad absurdum*, carries this mind-set to its limits. In the modish form in which it is prevalent in the contemporary arts and media, and in a surprisingly wide range of subjects taught in the universities—from the social sciences to English and religious studies —it maintains that no one can say with any more confidence than anyone else what is true or what is good. According to post-modernist doctrine, what is more, there is *no way* by which one person can get to know better than anybody else what is true or good; thereby rejecting scientific discovery as the basis for sound knowledge, as well as common sense, religion, or anything else as the basis for valid knowledge and sound morality. An increasingly bemused general public is thus 'dazzled by science' into a state of apathetic uncertainty—they are inducted into the post-modernist state of mind—and, with their confidence in common sense weakened, policy makers are led by the nose by fund-seekers and pressure groups to place an exaggerated faith in one or other of the lengthening parade of 'schemes' of treatment and assessment, none of which even at its best could possibly, in fact, greatly affect offending rates when the basic structure of a crime-free society has been and continues to be dismantled. The very phrase 'what works' avoids the raising of post-modernist hackles that an expression containing the words 'what does some good' would occasion. What good do these schemes do? They are generally likely to do some marginal good for the offenders subject to them. They always do some substantial good for the people who are employed to design, administer, analyse and publicise them.

Crime and Civil Society uses Sherman's work extensively on the quality of the *design* of evaluation studies of programmes designed to reduce offending. But a peculiarity of work in the social sciences is that, however perfect the scientific design of an evaluation or social experiment, implementing that design introduces far more difficulties than arise in evaluations and experiments in the natural sciences. Power-plays, warring cliques, considerations of prestige and loss of face notoriously play their part there too. But only the researchers and the people who are going to use their research (the latter often as anxious and able to put a spin on findings as any politician) are in a position consciously to bias the design, findings, and interpretation of the research. The 'research material' of the natural scientist, whether it is inanimate or animate, is non-human. In the social sciences, here, in the scientific evaluation of treatment programmes for offenders, vested interests lurk in every nook and cranny at all stages of the evaluation process, from the initial design to the final spin put on the findings in their presentation to the general public through the media.

Social scientists attempting to evaluate the success, failure or promise of programmes designed to prevent people offending are immediately immersed in an area of research which is highly charged with ideology. *Crime and Civil Society* deals with the radically different world-views from which these ideologies spring. The ideological preconceptions that researchers bring into social science are far more important in the effect on their work than is the case with the natural sciences. They are beset on every side with vociferous pressure groups whose own world-views lead them to take the side of the offender or the side of the offender's victims, and with vague and mainly dormant community opinion that sometimes manifests itself as the defender of the victim, but can also manifest itself in glorifying the criminal—that is to say, sometimes one section of the public shouts loudest, sometimes the other, with the 'fickleness' of any crowd or mob. To take two examples almost at random, we can think of the access the Kray brothers were accorded to high society in the later 1960s[2] and the applause that greeted the archetypal lovable rogue, Howard Marks, 'Mr Nice', around college campuses and in television appearances in the 1990s. Incorporated in the title of the paperback edition of Howard Marks's autobiography are the words: 'He was Britain's most wanted man. He has just spent seven years in America's toughest penitentiary. You'll like him'.[3] Strong passions are sometimes roused, but more rarely, in favour of or against the 'raw material' of the research in the natural sciences, though much more so in the twenty-first century than in the nineteenth and twentieth (for example, campaigns in opposition to research involving pain to animals, and in opposition to research concerning genetically modified crops).

Most of the possible sources of funding for social research, to a markedly greater extent than funding bodies in the natural sciences (which are not free from these strictures), are controlled by organisations with their own *ideological* agenda. In the field of criminology these funding organisations predominantly supported research that sided or would side in some way with the offender. They did not fund research that would potentially help the offender's victim, or help preserve the institutions of society that had demonstrably made Britain for at least the century from the 1850s to the 1950s a low-crime society. For many years after the 1960s, for example, the chances were very low that anyone would be funded whose research programme hinted that it might end in findings favourable to the case that the rise in crime was connected with the rise in the number and proportion of unmarried parents and the number of children from broken families. 'The family was not deteriorating, it was only changing', and there was no further light that research could throw on that unchallengeable fact. Even when the particular piece of grant-aided research work was well designed, therefore, it was part of an overall production of biased research.

In some kinds of social research, access is accorded to each individual subject by the subject himself or herself, as the researcher stops him or her in the street or knocks on the house door. The researcher needs nobody else's permission. But what social researchers call *entrée* is frequently essential if research is to be carried out on their human subjects. Those who can grant or refuse *entrée* have a vested interest in putting their own work and that of their organisation in a good light. Researchers whose reputations threaten a critical report, or an independent and therefore potentially critical report, find it more difficult than do 'sound' researchers to gain access to organisations the work of which they want to evaluate, including access to the details of the work of previous evaluators. Hardly any work on the abuse of illicit drugs, for example, is assessed by researchers who are suspected of scepticism about the received wisdom. The received wisdom is that the legalisation of the use of at present illicit drugs would solve most of the problems of drug misuse and drug-related criminality. Still less are funds allocated, and access granted, to researchers who start with the notion that taking illicit drugs is a bad thing, period. The open question for those who predominantly control research into illicit drug use is whether illicit drug use *is* a bad thing, not the open question of how the bad thing, drug taking, can be reduced. The very words good and bad disappeared from the non-judgemental dictionaries of post-modernism and multiculturalism, unless flagged as 'obsolete'. The appearance of the term 'abuse', or even 'misuse' of drugs, would itself handicap a research submission that contained it. It is almost unknown for any organisation or any individual researcher to be allocated a research grant to, say, assess the efficacy of any 'just say no to drugs' campaign in schools. Griffith Edwards, of the Addiction Research Unit of the Institute of Psychiatry, traced the trajectory of the growth of

Britain's drug problem from the time of the Rolleston report of 1926 up to the early 1980s.[4] 'In the years that followed Rolleston and right up to the beginning of the 1960s', Edwards writes, 'drug problems in Britain remained both in pattern and extent much as Rolleston had perceived them in 1926. Putting the matter in its simplest terms, Britain's drug problem was of interest exactly and only because of its trivial size. ... The first official statistics furnished in 1934 to the League of Nations gave a total of 300 addicts for the whole country. The breakdown of this long-established equilibrium came in the early 1960s, and when it came it was dramatic. ... In 1962 only three opiate addicts aged under 20 were on the index, while by 1967 the numbers in this age group had risen to 395.'

In starkest contrast, Joanne Condon and Nicola Smith's analysis of the findings from the 2002-03 British Crime Survey (BCS) showed that on the *low* estimate of the BCS, 16,000 young people aged 16 to 24 had used crack cocaine in the year before they were interviewed and 6,000 had used heroin. The low estimate of the use by young people in this age group of any Class A drugs—the most dangerous of the illicit drugs, and the most strictly prohibited—was 419,000. Those taking any illicit drug were numbered on the low estimate at 1,608,000.[5]

At the beginning of the 1960s Britain was a country in which the use of illicit drugs was restricted to a few artists, musicians, doctors and iatrogenic addicts. From the 1960s, she rapidly became a country where the use of recreational drugs was widespread, and in the research and treatment field only known advocates of 'informed choice' and 'harm prevention' were realistic contenders for funds.

Similarly, in the field of the treatment of offenders, the 'gatekeepers' to grant allocation and research contracts for the evaluation of prog-rammes have been predominantly individuals and groups whose humanitarian interests have directed them to look favourably on only applications for funds or for *entrée* that promised results favourable to 'treatment in the community' and unfavourable to prison.

As compared with its scale in the natural sciences, the problem of controlling the process of data collection is more severe in the social sciences. The natural scientist may be passionate about his subject, but it is a qualitatively different relationship than that which can develop between a social researcher, senior or junior, and the population or sample he or she is studying. It is relatively easy for someone working on a research project, including part-timers employed to carry out routine questionnaire work, to begin to see the world from the point of view of the people with whom he or she is in contact—in the field of research under discussion here, offenders. The average difference between offenders and non-offenders is not, say, that offenders misbehave 90 per cent of the time, and non-offenders misbehave 0.9 per cent of the time. It is much nearer the mark, though the figure is arbitrary, to say that offenders misbehave five per cent of the time, and non-offenders 0.5 per cent of the time. As the Gilbert and Sullivan verse has it, 'When a villain's not engaged in his employment/And concocting his felonious little plans/His capacity for innocent enjoyment/Is just as great as any other man's'.

While it is not easy to feel sympathy for genetically modified maize, and to come to feel that you really ought to put the best case for it you can, it is easy to feel sympathy for probably the vast majority of offenders, and to come to feel that you should put the best case for them. Howard Marks is, no doubt, one of the most personable men you could possibly meet. When they say that they have done no harm, or that they are not to blame for what circumstances have driven them to do, or they have reformed, or that they are drug-free, or that they have committed no offences in the previous six months and so on, the tendency is to fill in the questionnaire or submit the report in a way that gives the offender every benefit of every doubt. This well-known phenomenon for long had a label in social sciences which has now dropped out of use: 'going native'. That is, there is an inbuilt tendency to bias the results in favour of successful outcomes of programmes.

Statistical methodology can be misused either naïvely or intentionally. Sometimes it is misused by using formulæ and technical terms to gloss over omissions and errors. Sometimes it is misused by ostensibly strict adherence to inappropriate statistical protocols.

An example of naïvely strict adherence to statistical protocol is an unwillingness to accept that in very many cases correlation for all practical purposes *does* mean causation. It is true that we must always keep an open mind to the possibility that some proof will be produced that what we have known since the beginning of time happens not to be true. The earth does, after all, move round the sun. Given that caveat, the famous—very high—correlation between the rate of venereal disease (as STDs were called at the time) in Tokyo and the production of steel in Pittsburgh could not by any stretch of the imagination of a present-day Galileo be supposed to run in the direction of more VD in Japan leading to busier steel mills to the United States. In fact a link was shown to exist—a so-called tertiary correlation—namely, the increase in sexual activities of sailors and Japanese prostitutes with the increase of American steel imports into Japan.

'Correlation does not mean causation' is a fundamental and sound dictum. The paradox is that it is sometimes used *against* accepting strong correlations, confirmed by time-sequence studies that establish which variable was introduced first, and used *for* accepting on weak grounds that the direction of causation was in the other direction. Such a reversal of common sense and established knowledge is the stock-in-trade of, for example, certain offender-oriented pressure groups whose humane motives are not impugned by pointing to their proclivity for misunderstanding statistics. Dr Green and his co-authors give a number of examples of arbitrary reversals of emphasis of this kind in the assessment of criminal-justice treatment programmes. Of more interest to the media than any well-based finding that merely confirms what common sense says, on the model of 'man bites dog' these reversals of emphasis gain a public circulation out of all proportion to their scientific worth.

Misused statistical methods give a spurious credibility to the claim, for example, that the correlation between the number of prisoners and the number of crimes is evidence that 'prison causes crime'. Another example—there are many—is 'labelling theory' (brought over from its extremely widespread popularity in the sociology of education from the 1970s onwards) that claims that calling people criminals causes them to become criminals—contrary to the common-sense belief that the cause of calling people criminals is that they have committed crimes.

Of course there are small negative feedback effects of both prison and labelling. The experience of prison does reinforce the criminal propensity of some offenders to commit more crimes. Give a dog a bad name and you give it a licence to behave badly. But these effects are much weaker than society's reaction to an increase in the number of criminals by incarcerating more of them, or somebody being called an offender for the very good reason that he has offended. The error and damage lie in presenting them as the whole or the main story of causation.

An example of the naïve overestimation of the importance of statistical findings is the 'fiddling while Rome burns' effect. By concentrating on a particular intervention intended to reform the offender or reduce his reoffending by some other means, sight is lost of the importance of broad cultural and institutional arrangements of proven historical worth in preventing crime, but which continue to fall into decay. As Edmund Burke said of the liberty newly won in the French Revolution, he would suspend his congratulations until he was informed on how it had been combined 'with morality and religion;

with solidity and prosperity; with peace and order; with civil and social manners'. Liberty is a good thing, Burke wrote, but all these things are good things also, 'and without them, liberty is not a benefit that lasts, and is not likely to continue long'.[6]

A prime example of the 'fiddling while Rome burns' syndrome was the progressive dismemberment from the 1960s of the institution of life-long monogamy as the social framework for rearing children, in the belief that the liberty of people to make their own sexual arrangements, and ever-more perfect schemes for government-funded care from university-trained social workers and other experts, would more than make up for any losses in family stability.[7] Another example was the gradual disappearance of schools that conceived their function as being, to use the words of Matthew Arnold, to make prevail, to carry from one end of society to another, the *best* knowledge and the *best* ideas of their time, and the best that had been known and done in the world in the past—to diffuse the 'sweetness and light' endowed by a culture that, as compared with most other societies in the history of humankind, from its diverse origins and current openness to the world had had the good fortune to be on the whole benign. This was not in order that the person and the society might rest on their laurels, but to ensure that they constantly learned the lessons of '*all* the voices of human experience' in order to give a greater fullness and certainty to the solution of the problem of what they ought to strive to become.[8]

The idea that, when someone has committed a crime, expert interventions can accomplish what the family, the school, the church, and the ambience of the narrower and wider community influences have failed to accomplish, appeared in an extreme form in the earlier idealistic programmes of the Bolsheviks in the USSR. The rotten structures of personality produced by marriage, the mir, the church, the nobility, the factory and other cultural forms of the Russian Empire had created criminals. Society, not the criminal, was to blame for criminality. The rotten structures could and should be stripped out, and sound structures installed. Offenders' institutions, to use the striking title of a famous book of the time, would be 'the smithies of the new man'.[9]

The wholesale attack in the West on its cultural assumptions about the broadly benign role of the family of married parents and their children; of religious organisations; of community standards; of schools that transmitted their society's cultural heritage; of a protective police force; of local and parliamentary politics and so forth, occurred much later. Western social-affairs intellectuals from the late 1950s propagated the view that these institutions corrupted, that they did not civilise the child, on a large scale. Society is mad, so the mentally ill are the only sane people. Its laws are biased against the poor and the bold, so the people who break them are the pathfinders to justice. The guidance and control of fathers, mothers, schoolteachers, the clergy, neighbours, are not prophylactics against crime. They are the generators of crime. The criminal is society's victim.[10]

The 1960s produced a spate of competing ideological schools that were entitled 'anti-' this (e.g. anti-psychiatry) or 'post-' that (e.g. postmodernism) and the 'neo-' or 'new-' other (e.g. the new left, the new criminology). They agreed only in their hostility to the 'hegemonic' culture. They attacked the faith in the victory of reason over ignorance. This was deconstructed as 'the myth of truth'. Faith in social order was deconstructed as class, then increasingly as gender and racial oppression. Faith in moral standards was deconstructed in favour of the moral equivalence of all lifestyle choices. The stacks of Foucaults and Derridas, the Lyotards and Feyerabends were still to be found piled high in bookstores that serviced university courses in 2004.

These views gradually found acceptance in the general population after the 1960s, and by the end of the century permeated popular culture. Society could do without the type of father, mother, neighbour, teacher, priest, police officer, novelist, soldier, reporter, entertainer, poet, footballer and so forth who did an effective job, either directly or by example, of socialising children into law-abiding conduct and into an inbuilt commitment to duties owed to others. Society could do without the mechanisms of control that took the form of condemning and controlling the sort of conduct that was consensually defined as bad behaviour. And during the period of transition to the problem-free harmony of a society conscientiously following the maxim 'every man for himself', the deficits could be made up, and the difficulties presented by the existence of ever more 'offenders who are society's victims' could be mitigated, by ever-more numerous, ever more variegated, and ever more assiduously assessed and researched remedial programmes provided by teams of expert professionals paid for by the state.

There is another way in which statistical findings are overestimated as reasons for either accepting or rejecting the hypothesis that a particular form of intervention is efficacious in either reforming an offender or by some other means preventing offences being committed by him or her. The 'statistical significance' is a technical term that refers to an essential starting point, but by no means the end point of assessing a finding's importance for public policy.

In taking a sample of a variable from a population of items—in this book mainly a population of offenders—the statement of the degree of statistical significance of a finding about the variable from the sample merely says that, with the essential proviso that it is in technical statistical terms a 'random' sample, that in an infinite number of samples from the population, there is a certain chance, say one chance in 20 or one chance in 100—'significance at the 0.05 level' or 'significance at the 0.01 level' respectively—that the result is due to random chance whatever the distribution of the variable in the population. When the term 'the finding is statistically significant' is used without further information being given, it usually means 'significant at the 0.05 level'.

A common design of statistical methodology is to take two statistically random samples from a single population. One of the pair of random samples is then subject to 'the intervention', the 'treatment' or to 'the experimental variable'. (All the terms mean the same thing.) This is the 'experimental group'. The other random sample is not subject to the treatment. This is the control group. The chances at the end of the treatment that differences between the treatment group and the control group are not due to the treatment but due to the fact that the figures are for two samples, and not from the population from which they have been drawn, can be read from general statistical tables. The difference that the treatment makes between the two groups is expressible as a type of correlation. A correlation calculated on a different basis from that above, the Pearsonian correlation coefficient, is so commonly found to be statistically significant at plus or minus 0.35 (where +1 is a perfect positive correlation between the two variables and minus 1 is a perfect inverse correlation) that it has been called 'God's own correlation'. Plus or minus 0.35, however statistically safe, accounts for only ten per cent of the relationship between the two variables (ten per cent of the 'variance'). To be *important for policy*, the difference that the intervention makes in the experimental group as compared with the control group, has to be *worth it* in terms of the unit expenditure of money spent on treatment and research staff, administration, premises, and other resources per unit of the benefit to society derived from the difference it has made to those who have received the treatment. Correlations can thus be *statistically* significant at levels at which they are distinctly *not* 'significant' for policy. This is so much the case that it is an iconoclastic dictum of statistical analysis that what is important is not the statistical significance of a finding but its magnitude.

This assessment of assessments shows, finally, that nearly all interventions with a therapeutic, training or educational intention require large personal inputs from leaders, teachers and other practitioners. In principle it is essential, but in practice extremely difficult, to separate the general, theorised, effects of any programme of intervention from the idiosyncratic effects of the staff employed to administer it. Father Edward Flanagan set up his Boys' Home in Omaha in 1917 for five boys on a borrowed $90. His work became famous as Boys' Town, and it continues today in several Boys' and Girls' Towns in the United States. Within a wide range of programmes the effect of his charismatic personality would have been of benefit to the boys. (The impact of charismatic leadership was emphasised in a major Hollywood film of 1938, *Boys' Town*, with Spencer Tracey as Father Flanagan.) The discrepancy between the design and theory of a programme, and the way in which it is delivered in practice, has long been recognised as a quite general possibility—classically encapsulated in Pope's 'Essay on Man': 'For Forms of Government let fools contest/Whate'er is best administer'd is best'. In research it is very difficult to disentangle the two, and therefore, for all the sophistication and excellence of research design, to prevent *parti pris* exaggeration of the success of the featured programme.

Conversely, any strong programme can fail to produce beneficial results if it comes to be administered by jobsworths who inflexibly implement only its documented rules, or by ideologues who implement it with regard only to a utopian vision. The purpose of assessing programmes is to discover which of them are generally applicable, and it is always essential, therefore, not to confuse the achievements of particular persons administering a programme with the achievements of the programme itself. Separating out these two effects, as many of the studies in this book reveal, is not always attempted, and often not even recognised as a necessity.

Norman Dennis

Summary

Chapter 1: There is currently a dispute about the nature of the crime problem. Some say that we have too much crime and need resolute measures to reduce it. Others contend that we have too many people in prison because of the vindictiveness of judges and the punitive mentality of the public. We examine the crime figures and find that the crime rate in England and Wales is high, compared with our own history and with other countries.

We then look at the imprisonment rate compared with other countries per 100,000 population and per 1,000 crimes. England and Wales have a large prison population compared to population size, but not compared to the number of crimes. Among EU members we have a below-average imprisonment rate per 1,000 crimes. Our problem is not that we have too many people in prison, but that we have too much crime.

Chapter 2: When disputing parties are at loggerheads, it is often because unspoken assumptions are being made about human nature or the human condition. Sometimes clarifying what these assumptions are can lead to a new consensus. One important division is between determinists, who see human behaviour as the outcome of forces outside individual control, and others who believe that, while we often find ourselves in unwanted situations, we are always responsible for making the most of any predicament.

Three world-views guide the debate: the view that people are inherently good, but corrupted by society; the belief that people are rational calculators who weigh up the costs and benefits of alternative courses of action; and the belief that we are moral agents, guided by conscience, shaped by social institutions. Our approach rejects the first and combines the second and third.

Chapter 3: We examine the evidence that incapacitation and deterrence reduce crime and present the findings that both are effective. Professor Nagin has surveyed deterrence research up to 1998 and identified three main approaches: interrupted time series, 'ecological' approaches and perceptual studies. Interrupted time series examine the impact of specific interventions, such as police crack-downs on drug dealing in a particular street or drink-driving in a locality. Such measures have been found to have an effect, but there may be some displacement. Ecological studies compare statistics of criminal sanctions and crime in large areas (whole countries or US states) across time. Nagin concludes that 'a number of studies have been successful in isolating a deterrent effect'. Perceptual studies, with 'few exceptions', found that self-reported crime was lower among people who perceived that 'sanction risks and costs' were higher.

Professor David Farrington of the University of Cambridge, in conjunction with Patrick Langan of the US Department of Justice, compared the USA with England and Wales between 1981 and 1996. A negative correlation between the risk of punishment and the rate of crime was taken as support for the theory that increasing the risk of punishment is linked to falling crime. In England and Wales they found strong support for the theory that 'links falling risk of punishment to rising crime'. After 1981 the conviction rate in England and Wales fell and the crime rate rose. Similarly, the incarceration rate fell and the crime rate rose. However, the correlations between the severity of punishment and the crime rate were mixed. Nevertheless, there was a strong link between the severity of punishment of car thieves and the rate of vehicle theft. After 1981, in England and Wales, the proportion of car thieves sentenced to prison, their average sentence, the time served and the percentage of sentence served, as well as the number of days of actual incarceration, all fell. During this time, vehicle theft rose according to both the British Crime Survey and police records.

Chapter 4: We examine evidence that cognitive-behavioural schemes for rehabilitating offenders are effective. We find that they have had only a weak effect on criminal behaviour. There are two landmark studies: one is a meta-analysis by Mark Lipsey and a large-scale primary study by David Robinson.

Lipsey's study appraised nearly 400 schemes, mainly for juveniles, and covered rehabilitation of all types. But he was studying other studies, not adding to primary knowledge. He found an overall reduction in reoffending of five percentage points (from 50 per cent to 45 per cent), sometimes expressed as a ten per cent reduction.

David Robinson's study of 2,125 prisoners in Canada was the first large-scale primary study of cognitive behavioural therapy. Taking re-admission to prison as the measure: 44.5 per cent of the treatment group were readmitted; and 50 per cent of the control group. Again, a change of about five percentage points.

If some rehabilitation schemes have a small impact on reoffending some of the time, what sort of rehabilitation programmes work best? This question is not easy to answer. In some ways it is easier to say what does not work. Raising self-esteem on its own makes no difference to reoffending, and nor does non-directive counselling, such as sharing feelings with others. Lipsey says that there are three influences on outcomes: researcher involvement; type of treatment; and amount of treatment. Researcher involvement could mean that the results are biased, but it could also mean that these schemes require a high level, perhaps an exceptional level, of commitment by staff. Two kinds of treatment stood out: those involving skills and employment; and those focusing on overt behaviour, often using behavioural methods. For example, staff would apply the rules strictly: not turning up for all sessions would be punished, and compliance would be rewarded. The amount of treatment needed to be substantial. Lipsey says courses should last at least six months, with at least 100 hours of contact at the rate of two contacts per week.

The Home Office has put considerable effort into cognitive behavioural therapy, including schemes such as Reasoning and Rehabilitation, and Enhanced Thinking Skills. They have not been successful. A Home Office study (*Findings 226*) covering adult males from 1998-2000 found that the reconviction rate for the treatment group was 75.4 per cent and the control group 75.7 per cent.

Chapter 5: The offenders most difficult to reform are those on drugs. Studies have found that the most effective approach so far is the in-prison therapeutic community, but that the impact only lasts if followed through by intensive support and supervision on release.

Key-Crest in Delaware has been carefully studied by James Inciardi. After three years, only five per cent of the control group were free of drugs, whereas 22 per cent of those who took part in the prison therapeutic community were drug-free. A similar proportion (23 per cent) of offenders who took part in a comparable programme at a halfway-house were also drug-free, but if they completed the halfway-house programme and a further six months of aftercare, 35 per cent were drug-free. Arrest rates were also lower.

The results of the Amity project in California were similar. The control group received no drug treatment and 75 per cent had been reincarcerated after three years. Of those who completed the prison-based therapeutic community treatment, 79 per cent had been sent back to prison after three years, but when offenders completed the prison therapeutic community course plus aftercare, only 27 per cent had been jailed three years later.

Chapter 6: We examine prison education and work programmes. They are found to be among the most effective methods of encouraging prisoners to lead a law-abiding life on release. There are only a few large-scale studies. William Saylor and Gerald Gaes studied 7,000 American prisoners who performed work in a prison industry or

---

workshop, or who underwent vocational training or both. Twelve months after release 86.5 per cent of the experimental group had a job as did 62 per cent of the control group. They were followed up eight years later, when the authors tried to distinguish between prisoners who had taken part in prison work and those who had studied for vocational qualifications. Those involved in prison industries reoffended 24 per cent less than the control group and those who had acquired vocational qualifications 33 per cent less.

Chapter 7: We look at intensive supervision in the community and find that it has not made much difference to offending behaviour. US studies found that it allowed more breaches to be detected but did not bring about lasting changes of behaviour. The RAND corporation (Joan Petersilia and Susan Turner) evaluated 14 intensive supervision programmes (ISPs) in nine states in 1993. They measured re-arrests after one year and violations of court orders after one year. Of those on ISP, 37 per cent had been arrested after one year, compared with 33 per cent of the control group. And, of those on ISP, 65 per cent had committed technical violations, compared with 38 per cent of the control group.

Not all these schemes involved tagging but several did. A Home Office study of tagging in England looked at over 21,000 offenders released early under Home Detention Curfew (HDC): five per cent were recalled and the reconviction rate while tagged was 2.1 per cent.

Offenders selected for early release were those considered by prison governors to present a low risk to the public. The evidence is that these appraisals were reasonably accurate. While they were tagged (up to 60 days at the time of the study) the monitoring appeared to exercise a restraining effect on their offending behaviour.

However, there was no evidence of any continuing impact on reoffending. The Home Office compared two groups: (a) those eligible for HDC and released in May and June 1999, some tagged and some not; and (b) prisoners eligible for HDC and discharged in October and November 1998, but not tagged because the scheme had not started. Reconvictions were measured after six months: 30.8 per cent of the 1999 experimental group had been reconvicted, compared with 30.0 per cent of the 1998 control group. The Home Office conclusion was that tagging had a 'broadly neutral' effect on behaviour.

Moreover, HDC applies to selected prisoners believed to present a low risk to the public, whereas the Intensive Supervision and Surveillance Programme applies to the most serious young offenders. This makes the American evidence more relevant than the study of the

British HDC, and American studies found that intensive supervision had no significant behavioural impact. At the time of writing, only the initial report on ISSP was available. The reoffending rate after 12 months confirms American experience.

Chapter 8: Community-based drug treatments, including Drug Treatment and Testing Orders, have made only a small difference to drug taking in either the US or England. Efforts to reduce drug-related crime typically depend on rehabilitative treatment to reduce dependency and heightened supervision to increase compliance with sentences. Those interventions that emphasised treatment had some success. For example, offenders receiving treatment combined with urine testing in Baltimore City had a conviction rate of 14 per cent compared to 21 per cent for two control groups. Drug courts in the US have also been found to reduce reoffending slightly, but the evaluations undertaken so far are not considered robust enough to draw definite conclusions.

Drug Treatment and Testing Orders in the UK have been found to have little impact on both drug taking and reoffending. The results of a two-year reconviction study showed that reconviction rates were 80 per cent, and completion rates were low: only 30 per cent of those whose whereabouts were known at the end of the study finished the order and 67 per cent had the order revoked, mainly for non-compliance.

Chapter 9: Evidence indicates that boot camps have had mixed results. The militaristic element appears to have made little difference to offending behaviour, but whether it is beneficial in combination with other measures remains unproven. A multi-site study in the US by Mackenzie showed that programmes emphasising military discipline had no real impact on reoffending. Others that combined military drill or routine with constructive activity and more rehabilitative elements were found to have slightly more encouraging results.

High Intensity Training at Thorn Cross, a UK juvenile boot camp that focused on giving offenders rounded treatment, including drug treatment, vocational skills, enhanced thinking skills and aftercare, was shown by a UK study to reduce reoffending by about ten per cent after one year. However, the effect had disappeared after two years.

The effectiveness of 'shock tactics' in reducing reoffending was examined by only one American study. It found that presenting offenders with the 'horrors' of prison life and 'scaring' them away from criminal lifestyles had a negative impact on participants, producing a far higher rate of reoffending among the experimental group than among controls.

Chapter 10: Financial penalties have not been evaluated to the same rigorous standards as rehabilitation. Evidence from the US, compiled by Turner and Greene, indicates that fines may be an appropriate sanction for low-risk offenders who would otherwise be sentenced to routine probation.

The main problem in England and Wales is inadequate enforcement. The National Audit Office reported that in 2000-01 the 42 magistrates' courts committees collected only 63 per cent of the year's financial penalties. Fine enforcement in England and Wales has been inadequate for some time, but the collaboration of the courts in Merseyside with the private sector has suggested a possible solution.

Chapter 11: It has long been argued that greater efforts should be made to provide throughcare to ex-prisoners, that is, support and supervision in the community. We provide examples of some worthwhile schemes but there is little convincing evidence of any significant impact on reoffending. One of the most carefully evaluated American schemes was the Skillman aftercare initiative. It found that increased supervision and services, including counselling and job advocacy, had little impact on arrest rates and self-reported offending.

Some evaluations are underway in England, but as yet reconviction data have not been gathered. Smaller evaluations of throughcare programmes are not rigorous enough to judge whether properly-administered throughcare can significantly reduce reoffending. The provision of effective throughcare is dogged by the difficulty of maintaining contact with released prisoners. Post-release contact with throughcare agencies in the UK programmes was voluntary and there was little incentive for participants to keep in contact beyond their own personal preferences. The chapter concludes that concerted efforts to help prisoners to resettle into the community after release can have beneficial effects, and we argue that the potential for harnessing those benefits should be expoited in a prison setting.

Chapter 12: We examine traditional probation and restorative justice. We find little evidence that probation is effective in reducing reoffending compared with alternatives. While minimal research has been devoted to probation, Petersilia and Turner compared reoffending rates between two groups: those sentenced to prison alone and those sentenced to a short prison-term, followed by probation. When including the incapacitation effect in their calculations, Petersilia and Turner found evidence that prisoners reoffended 20 per cent less than probationers. The chapter goes on to explore a reform movement calling for 'broken windows' probation, which advocates placing probation officers in the community working with local groups, not conducting office-based interviews.

The Re-integrated Shaming Experiments (RISE) conducted in Canberra, Australia, offer the most reliable evidence about restorative justice. However, Sherman, Strang and Woods found a crime-reduction effect in the case of youth violence only.

Community justice, which goes further than restorative justice, suggests a 'broken windows' approach to restoring order within the community, by combining efforts by the courts, police and probation authorities with those of local charities and groups. It is too early to say whether such schemes reduce offending.

Chapter 13: We ask whether we can learn from America, in particular from the strategy of the Office for Juvenile Justice and Delinquency Prevention (OJJDP). The OJJDP emphasises several areas of public policy—not just the administration of punishment. First, it emphasises the importance of the early socialisation of children in the family. Public policies can only achieve so much, but England and Wales urgently needs a public debate to encourage a new consensus about the family, parenting and marriage. Second, the OJJDP emphasises the impact of the wider society on the expectations we have of each other and, in particular, the influence of the media and all those who contribute to opinion formation through writing and broadcasting. Third, the OJJDP highlights the important influence on crime of local communities. Where there is strong local attachment and mutual confidence that neighbours will support one another, crime is lower. Fourth, the OJJDP does not avoid tough questions about what should be done with recalcitrant offenders. Many crime reformers have a romantic view of human nature and emphasise the importance of rehabilitation and early prevention. The OJJDP makes it clear that persistent offenders should be removed from the community and detained in secure facilities to prevent further harm to the public.

Chapter 14: We define the guiding principles for reform. Recommended solutions are placed in four categories: social investment (both public and private) in institutions that encourage a law-abiding lifestyle, especially the family; reducing the net advantages of crime through 'situational' change; reducing the net benefits of crime by increasing the risk of detection and punishment; and personalised programmes to reduce reoffending by convicted criminals.

Policy recommendations include:

• Increase social investment in early socialisation and combating disorder in schools. Most people do not commit crimes because they have been brought up to share the community's standards. No crime policy will be able to alter beliefs and attitudes if the institutions for encouraging social cohesion—especially the family, schools and churches—are in a weakened state.

- Increase police numbers and switch police effort to primary prevention (broken windows policing).

- Do not put any more public funds into intensive supervision programmes as an alternative to prison. However, they could be the basis for post-release supervision, if the new variable sentence (below) is implemented.

- Scrap cognitive-behavioural therapy and transfer the money to basic and vocational education. There is good evidence that vocational and work-related skills are beneficial and a significant increase in investment would be justified.

- Extend the use of prison-based therapeutic communities for drug users combined with intensive aftercare.

- Increase prison capacity. The aim should be to lower the prison population once we have a lower crime rate; not a small prison population regardless of the crime rate.

- Improve prison régimes by assessing prisoners immediately on arrival and treat their stay in jail as a preparation for release from Day 1. Get them off alcohol and drugs (a problem affecting the majority) and give them educational and vocational skills.

- Reform parole so that the release date depends on demonstrated good behaviour. At present release at the half-way stage is automatic and can be even earlier under Home Detention Curfew. The normal rule should be that the whole sentence is served unless offenders earn up to one-third off for good behaviour, subject to their agreement to be supervised in the community for the remainder of the original sentence, plus at least six months afterwards.

- Increase the supervision of prisoners on release from jail.

- Introduce a graduated approach to juvenile offending. A 'welfare' approach should be attempted initially. However, if serious offences continue to be committed, the level of intervention by the authorities should escalate. The more recalcitrant the offender, the more determined the response should be. Our system fails to react with sufficient resilience when dealing with persistent offenders. After providing every opportunity to change, an effective system must be willing to punish individuals who continue to commit crimes. We suggest that once offenders have been convicted three times for an indictable offence, there is such overwhelming evidence that they are likely to spend the next several years committing offences that they should be sent to secure institutions for a significant period. The detention and training order, the main custodial sentence that is applied after three convictions (fewer for serious offences) should be a minimum of 12 months and a maximum of four years, followed by intensive supervision for 12 months or more after release. Release after 12 months should depend on a prolonged period of demonstrated good behaviour.

- Radically improve the collection rate of fines.

- Establish a pilot scheme under which the same organisation would run a prison and supervise offenders after their release, to ensure continuity.

Chapter 15: As the situation stands in early 2005, the Government is failing to get even the simple things right. It has too few police on the streets and fails to imprison the majority of serious and persistent offenders. The Prison Service neglects to take the most basic steps needed to encourage a law-abiding life on release. It does not adequately combat drug dependency in prison and fails to provide many prisoners with employment skills. When prisoners are released it does not provide adequate supervision, leading to frequent relapses into criminal habits.

1

Introduction

The Nature of the Problem

Opinion at present is divided between rival accounts of the problem we face. The first is that we have too many people in prison. As a result, Lord Chief Justice Woolf and others have called for fewer criminals to be sent to jail. The second view is that we have too much crime. And, by implication, we have failed to learn from overseas experience of effective crime reduction. Which of these interpretations is closer to the truth?

Too many people in prison?

A major grant-giving foundation, the Esmée Fairbairn Foundation, has established a commission of enquiry (the Coulsfield Inquiry) to explore how to reduce the use of prison. The starting point for its inquiry is concern about the number of people in prison. In similar vein, the Prison Reform Trust regularly claims that there are too many people in prison.

This approach has received some encouragement from a recent Home Office report showing that in England and Wales we have more prisoners per 100,000 population than any other EU country. The *Guardian* account of the Home Office document began with the headline: 'UK now Europe's jail capital' and continued with, 'Incarceration rate outstrips Libya and Malaysia'. Statistics confirm, it said, that British courts are 'far more punitive than those of Canada and Australia, and beat all those of its closest European neighbours', including France, Germany and Spain.[1]

This line of criticism has been going on for some time. Another example from the *Guardian*[2] referred to the 'primordial British love of punishment' and called on the government to 'bite the bullet and face down public ignorance and vindictiveness'. And it quoted Churchill saying that we must never give up believing in the capacity of the human heart to change.

We are presented with a contrast between belief in the capacity of the human heart to change, and prison, which is thought to imply giving up on people, or throwing away the key.

How do we compare with Europe? In 2002, concern about prison overcrowding led Britain's senior judge, Lord Woolf, to discourage judges and magistrates from sending criminals to jail. When he made his statement, the BBC television news announced that the prison population was rising when crime was falling and Britain already had more people in jail per head of population than the rest of Europe. The implication is that judges and magistrates are deploying a rather barbaric instrument when everyone else in Europe prefers a more gentle approach.

But a closer look at the figures suggests a different interpretation. The proper comparison is not between the number of prison inmates and the total population, but between the number of prisoners and the volume of crime. A country with a high level of crime would expect to have to put more people in jail. And England and Wales have one of the highest crime rates among industrialised countries.

Table 1.1 (see p. 3) shows the rate of imprisonment in the EU in 2000. In the EU the average number of prisoners per 100,000 population (unweighted) in 2000 was 87, compared with 124 in England and Wales. But if we compare the number of prisoners to the number of recorded crimes, the EU average was 17.7 and the figure for England and Wales was 12.7. In fact, 9 out of 15 EU countries had rates of imprisonment for every 1,000 crimes that were the same or higher. France was higher, Spain much higher and Germany the same.

Comparison with countries outside Europe reveals a similar pattern. In 1999, Canada had 123 prisoners per 100,000 population compared with England and Wales, but 15.9 prisoners per 1,000 recorded crimes. Japan had only 43 prisoners per 100,000 population but 25.3 per 1,000 recorded crimes. Australia, which had the worst crime victimisation rate out of the 17 countries in the International Crime Victim Survey, had 108 prisoners per 100,000 population and 15.4 per 1,000 crimes.

On this evidence prison in England and Wales is under-used. Compared to our population we have a high proportion of prisoners, but when compared with the amount of crime we have relatively few prisoners. Our prison population, therefore, reflects the amount of crime, not the vindictiveness of either the public or judges.

This brings us to the second approach, which begins with the claim that we have too much crime. How serious is the UK's crime problem? How do we compare with other countries? Has crime got worse over time? And, at the moment, is the crime rate going up or down?

Table 1.1
Prison population in EU countries, per 100,000 population and per 1,000 recorded crimes, 2000

Country	Prison population	Prisoners per 100,000 population	Estimated country population (millions)	Recorded crimes	Prisoners per 1,000 recorded crimes	Crimes per 100,000 population
EU average		87			17.7	6,625
England & Wales	65,666	124	52,939,000	5,170,843	12.7	9,762
N. Ireland	1,011	60	1,697,800	119,912	8.4	7,095
Scotland	5,868	115	5,114,600	423,172	13.9	8,297
Austria	6,861	84	8,127,024	560,306	12.2	6,909
Belgium	8,524	83	10,239,085	848,648	10.0	8,279
Denmark	3,240	61	5,330,020	504,231	6.4	9,443
Finland	2,887	56	5,181,115	385,797	7.5	7,448
France	48,835	80	58,746,500	3,771,849	12.9	6,405
Germany	79,507	97	82,142,684	6,264,723	12.7	7,620
Greece	8,038	76	10,521,669	369,137	21.8	3,502
Ireland (Eire)	2,887	76	3,790,000	73,276	39.4	1,933
Italy	54,579	94	57,679,895	2,205,782	24.7	3,819
Luxembourg	400	92	435,700	22,816	17.5	5,185
Netherlands	13,847	87	15,940,815	1,173,688	11.8	7,368
Portugal	12,728	124	9,997,590	363,294	35.0	3,558
Spain	45,309	114	39,852,651	923,269	49.1	2,339
Sweden	5,678	64	8,882,800	1,214,968	4.7	13,678

Sources: Home Office Statistical Bulletin 5/02, July 2002; OECD Health Data; EU averages unweighted

International comparisons

First, how do England and Wales compare with other similar countries?[3] Among the most reliable surveys is the International Crime Victim Survey (ICVS) of 2000, which covers 17 countries.

The latest ICVS found that England and Wales in 1999 had the second highest risk of crime. Australia was bottom of the league with 30 per cent of people reporting that they had been a victim of crime, and England and Wales came next with 26 per cent. In the USA the figure was only 21 per cent. In Europe, the Netherlands and Sweden were not much better than England and Wales with figures of 25 per cent, but in France only 21 per cent reported that they had suffered from crime. Based on crimes reported to the British Crime Survey in 2000, if the French figure had applied to England and Wales, there would have been nearly three million fewer crimes. The ICVS also found that:

- People in England and Wales experienced more crime per head than any other country in the survey, 54.5 crimes per 100 inhabitants compared with an average of 35.2 per 100.

- England and Wales had the worst record for 'very serious' offences, scoring 18 for every hundred inhabitants, followed by Australia with 16.

- The second highest level of contact crime, defined as robbery, sexual assault, and assault with force, was recorded in England and Wales (3.6 per cent of those surveyed). The highest figure was for Australia, where it was 4.1 per cent. The figure for the USA was 1.9 per cent and for Japan, 0.4 per cent.

The long-term crime rate

How much of a crime problem do we have today compared with the last 100 years? In the year ending March 2001, 5.2 million offences were recorded by the police in England and Wales. This was about 50 times the rate per 10,000 population in 1921 (when there were 103,258 crimes and when the population was only 37 million compared with 53 million today). It was about 35 times the rate in 1931 (159,278 crimes) and about ten times the rate in 1951, when 524,506 crimes were recorded by the police and the population was 44 million. Crime did not pass the million mark until 1964 and climbed steadily until it reached a peak of nearly 5.6 million in 1992. It currently seems to have reached a plateau of about ten times the rate in the early 1950s.

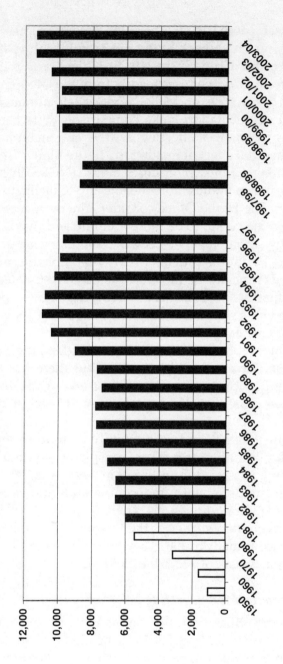

Figure 1.1
Recorded Crimes Per 100,000 Population
England and Wales, 1950 - 2003/04

Historical comparison: There are two measures of crime: police records, which go back to the nineteenth century (see Appendix 7); and the British Crime Survey (BCS), which starts in 1981. According to police records, crime rose steadily from the late 1950s but surged to a peak in about 1992 and 1993. Then it fell, although changes in the method of calculation make comparison more complex after 1998. There were changes affecting 1998-99 and again in 2002-03, both of which had the effect of making the figure higher. The introduction of the National Crime Recording Standard (NCRS) in 2002 was intended to make police figures more reliable and to facilitate comparison with the BCS. The Home Office considers the more recent (higher) figure based on the NCRS to be more accurate and that it increased overall crime by about ten per cent in the first year of implementation compared with the previous year. This probably means that police-recorded crime during the 1990s was underestimated by that amount.

The first BCS figures are for 1981 and show a peak in 1995, also followed by a significant fall, so that in 2002-03 it is now at the same rate as in the early to mid-1980s.

The high-volume crimes such as burglary, theft of cars, and theft from cars have fallen significantly but there has been a worrying increase in violent crime in the last few years. Total violent crime increased more than three times from 265,085 in 1991 to 991,800 in 2002-03.

During the 1990s and subsequently the more serious violent crimes, including murder, threat or conspiracy to murder and serious wounding increased from 15,829 in 1991 to 38,291 in 2002-03. Sexual offences, predominantly indecent assault and rape, also increased: from 29,423 in 1991 to 48,654. There were 45,323 robberies (defined as thefts involving violence or the threat of violence) in 1991, and more than twice as many in 2002-03, when there were 108,045, having fallen back from a peak of 121,370 in 2001-02.

Is the problem today getting better or worse?

The Home Office typically claims that crime is currently stable—a press release in January 2004 was headed 'Crime Remains Stable'.[4]

The most revealing measure of crime over the long term is crime per 100,000 population. Figure 1.1 (see p. 5) shows the Home Office estimates of recorded crime from 1950 until 2003-04. The Government naturally wants to put its policies in a good light and emphasises the large fall in crime, according to the BCS since 1995. It has often pointed out that public perceptions of the crime rate do not reflect this large fall. However, anyone reading the Government's press releases could be forgiven for being unclear. The press release announcing the publication of *Crime in England and Wales, 2002-03* was headed 'Crime down two per cent'.[5] However, a glance at the bullet points shows that crime recorded by the police was both down three per cent and up seven per cent (under the NCRS). The BCS showed a fall of two per cent.

The danger is that we will settle down to being a high-crime society, taking comfort from the fact that crime has fallen since the mid-1990s, when it was nearly eleven times the rate in 1950, to only ten times that rate today. In 1950 there were 1,048 recorded crimes per 100,000 population. As Figure 1.1 shows, from the late 1950s crime rose to a peak of 10,905 per 100,000 in 1992 and then fell to a low of 8,739 in 1997-98. Since then it has increased to 11,327 per 100,000 (partly as a result of the NCRS).

The overall trend since the 1950s has been steadily upwards.

How can the long-term trend be explained? Despite the heated nature of debates about the causes of crime, there is a good deal of consensus. The best evidence comes from longitudinal and cross-sectional surveys which suggest strong links between crime and changes in the socialisation of children. This evidence is discussed below.

However, these long-term changes in socialisation cannot explain the surge in crime in the late 1980s and early 1990s, nor the subsequent fall. It turns out that some particularly counter-productive measures were introduced during the 1970s and 1980s. Some of these reforms were reversed from 1993 onwards.

Why did crime peak in the 1990s?

Some especially unwise measures were taken during the late 1980s and early 1990s. The prevailing beliefs are summed up by a 1988 green paper which was followed by a white paper in 1990 which, in turn, led to the Criminal Justice Act of 1991. The intention of policy was to reduce the use of prison. The green paper shows how 'labelling theory' was accepted in the Home Office. If the authorities treat individuals like criminals they will behave according to expectations:

> Most young offenders grow out of crime as they become more mature and responsible. They need encouragement and help to become law-abiding. Even a short period of custody is quite likely to confirm them as criminals, particularly if they acquire new criminal skills from more sophisticated offenders. They see themselves labelled as criminals and behave accordingly.[6]

The white paper rejected the idea that criminals could be deterred:

...much crime is committed on impulse ... and is committed by offenders who live from moment to moment. It is unrealistic to construct sentencing arrangements on the assumption that most offenders will weigh up the possibilities in advance and base their conduct on rational calculation. Often they do not.[7]

We can identify eight significant developments that encouraged crime in the period under discussion.

- The importance of previous convictions was diminished by the Criminal Justice Act of 1991. Under section 29, courts were discouraged from giving a more severe sentence because of the number of previous convictions. Sentences were to be proportionate to the current offence only. Moreover, in cases where an offender was found guilty of more than one crime, judges were to take into account only the combined seriousness of any two offences. These limitations were repealed in 1993, but the harm had been done.[8]

- Between 1985 and 1994 cautions were particularly heavily used. Circular 14/1985 was based on labelling theory, as a Home Office Research Findings of 1997 acknowledged. Young offenders were at 'particular risk of becoming labelled as criminals if brought into the criminal justice system at a young age'.[9] Circular 18/1994 explicitly discouraged repeat cautioning but by then the wrong message had been sent for the best part of a decade. Repeat cautioning was reduced but continued at a high level. A Home Office survey found that 14 per cent of those cautioned in one week in November 1994 had been cautioned previously. In 1991 it had been 20 per cent. Moreover, there was considerable variation between police areas even for the most serious (indictable only) offences. In 21 forces out of 42 repeat cautions comprised more than 20 per cent of total cautions.[10]

- The use of informal warnings had also increased since 1987. Thirty-one out of 42 forces said that informal warnings did not influence future decisions about an offender.[11]

- The Criminal Justice Act of 1988 downgraded the unauthorised taking of a motor vehicle to a non-indictable offence, encouraging courts to use non-custodial sentences.[12] Common assault and criminal damage over £400 but under £2,000 were also downgraded. It was not until after 1993 that some sentences were increased. From December 1999, for example, a third conviction for domestic burglary was to lead to a minimum sentence of three years. Convictions had to have taken place after 1st December 1999.

- The Police and Criminal Evidence Act of 1984 increased the procedural safeguards for the accused and weakened the ability of the police to gather evidence. Some of the most harmful changes were not repealed until 2003.

- The Crown Prosecution Service was established in 1986, leading to an increased tendency to drop cases.[13]

- Parole reforms also sent the wrong message. Before the 1967 Criminal Justice Act prisoners were allowed one-third off their sentence for good behaviour. Afterwards, they could apply for release after serving only one-third of their sentence. A local review committee would consider their case and the final decision lay with the Parole Board, so that the sentence was indeterminate from the one-third stage up to the two-thirds stage. In 1983 the Government altered the rules to allow anyone serving a sentence of 12 months or more to be released after six months or one-third of their sentence, whichever was longer. As a result about 78 per cent of prisoners serving two years or less were released before serving two-thirds of their sentence.[14] The Criminal Justice Act 1991 changed the system again and created an automatic release at the half-way stage for all criminals serving under four years.

- The 1967 Criminal Justice Act introduced suspended sentences. However, they were not considered a success and were abolished for offenders under 21 in 1982. They continued to be available for adults, but the 1991 Criminal Justice Act laid down that a suspended sentence should only be passed if custody was justified and there were exceptional circumstances in favour of suspension.

The cumulative effect of these measures was to give the impression that crime paid.

Are the crime figures reliable?

To speak about the crime rate is not as straightforward as it might initially seem. Trying to establish the true facts proved to be a formidable task and raised some deeper questions about the viability of democratic government in the absence of independent and reliable sources of information.

When the new-style crime figures were published in 2002, Home Secretary David Blunkett claimed they were the 'most accurate measure' of crime ever. The report was also said to be the most comprehensive ever. But when you check the small print, it turns out that the Home Office itself thinks that there were far more than the

11.7 million crimes discovered by the British Crime Survey in 2003-04—perhaps four times as many.

Arriving at the true figure is not easy because police figures are notoriously unreliable, but the Home Office has made 'best estimates' of the extent of police under-recording of some offences. Even on the most cautious assumptions, at least another 10.9 million crimes should be added to the 11.7 million acknowledged crimes, a total of 22.6 million in 2003-04. According to another Home Office research study, *The Economic and Social Costs of Crime*, in 2000 there were at least 60 million crimes. On these estimates, the real figure lies somewhere between 22.6 million and 60 million in one year.

Why the huge disparity? Has there been a cover-up? Is any of this found only in a secret report? No, there is no secret report. It's partly a case of 'If you don't ask, you don't get'. And until members of the public do ask—and keep on asking—the Government has every intention of pretending that the crime problem is under control. The Government has become notorious for spin, and publication of the crime figures is no exception. No objective observer would say that the British Crime Survey is comprehensive when it misses out murder, sexual offences, crimes against people under 16, and crimes against commercial premises, including thefts of trucks, vans and shoplifting. And no independent statistician would claim that the British Crime Survey was the 'most accurate' measure of crime.

The central issue is the independence of the government statistical service. There cannot be a proper public debate about how best to deal with crime unless the full facts are made readily available for all. But as things stand, it is simply too tempting for any political party to have control of the release of information about crime—if the next election result might depend on public perception of the Government's effectiveness, it is not going to give easy 'ammunition' to opponents. The street crime initiative, prompted by Tony Blair's promise to get street crime 'under control' by the end of September 2002, revealed the nature of the problem. The figures published by the Government to prove its success were so widely perceived to be suspect that even the most steadfast loyalists doubted them.

The underlying problem is that many, if not all, statistical reports are still being submitted to ministers for approval of their content and the timing of their release. In an open society, there is no justification for the involvement of party politicians in regulating public access to information. Inevitably they use their control of the flow of facts to gain advantage over their opponents.

The independence of the Bank of England provides a parallel. The Government accepted that fixing interest rates was too tempting a party-political weapon and, to its credit, it handed authority to the independent Bank of England. Similarly, the independence of the National Audit Office and the Audit Commission has been accepted. But Home Office statisticians and the Office for National Statistics (ONS) lack full autonomy. The Office for National Statistics is supposed to be independent, but it too needs to be made wholly autonomous, perhaps accountable to Parliament as a whole rather than to the Government of the day.

In the September 2002 issue of *Horizons*, the official publication of the Office for National Statistics (ONS), Len Cook, the National Statistician, defends the impartiality of ONS. There have been 'one or two rumblings recently', he admits, about the extent to which ONS is free from political interference. The ONS, he insists, is thoroughly objective and acts with integrity under all circumstances. But does it? In the same issue of *Horizons*, the catchline for an article about the crime figures was: 'Looking at recent newspaper reports, you could be forgiven for thinking that crime is spiralling out of control. But the figures behind the headlines tell a different story.' The article goes on to attack newspapers for using headlines to sell papers and insists that, when you 'look at the long-term picture', crime has fallen by 22 per cent since 1997. The chances of being a victim of crime are 'at around their lowest since the BCS began in 1981—so don't have nightmares, do sleep well!'

Whilst using phrases like 'looking at the long-term-picture' and taking 'a closer look at the figures' the author of the article disregards both the long-term picture and the facts that any objective observer would see upon taking a closer look. Statistical analysis is notoriously open to interpretation and, for this very reason, we need a genuinely independent statistical service whose officials see themselves as servants of democracy, not the instruments of the party in power.

The official line

The Government is anxious to claim that it has got crime under control and Government press releases regularly emphasise the fall in crime since 1997. The Government is particularly anxious to encourage the public to rely on the British Crime Survey (BCS). In the press release (STAT026/2002) accompanying the 20001-02 crime figures David Blunkett claimed that: 'The largest ever BCS is now widely seen as the most accurate measure of people's experience of crime'.

In truth the British Crime Survey misses out a large amount of crime. The Preface to the annual Home Office report on crime, *Crime in England and Wales 2001/2002*, declares that the intention is to make available the 'most comprehensive picture of crime'. However, later in the document, significant omissions are acknowledged: illegal drug use, murder, sexual offences, offences against businesses, those living in institutions, and those under 16.

Crimes omitted from the British Crime Survey
Crimes with child victims

When comparing the BCS and recorded crime, the following adjustments were made by the Home Office in 2001-02 to allow for the exclusion of under-16s. The calculations are contained in a document obtainable from the Home Office, 'Comparing BCS and police counts of crime'. The Home Office assumed that 11 per cent of woundings were against under 16s, and reduced the recorded crime total by 24,381. Robbery was reduced by 20 per cent, or 18,968 offences. Theft from the person was reduced by nine per cent or 9,150 offences. And assault was reduced by 20 per cent or 44,396 offences. In total 96,895 recorded crimes were carried out against under 16s, but excluded for the purpose of comparison with the BCS figures.

We can get a little closer to the true figure by using BCS estimates of the crimes not reported to the police and, if reported, not recorded. The Home Office has produced a 'best estimate' of the proportion of crimes recorded by the police.

Table 1.2
Best estimate of crimes against victims aged 11-15,
excluded from the BCS

	Home Office estimates of crimes with victims aged 11-15	Best estimate of % of crimes recorded by police	Best estimate of actual crimes against victims aged 11-15
Woundings	24,381	30%	81,270
Robbery	18,968	21%	90,324
Theft from the person	9,150	15%	61,000
Assault	44,396	12%	369,967
Total			602,561

Source: Crime in England and Wales 2001/2002, Table 2.01

In other words, when the Government claimed that the BCS provided the most reliable picture of crime in 2001-02, it missed out 602,561 offences against children under 16. It also missed out offences against shops, offices and manufacturers. How many crimes against these victims are excluded?

Crimes against shops and offices

We can make similar calculations to those for the under-16s. The Home Office estimated that, in 2001-02, 50 per cent of vandalism (which includes arson and criminal damage to buildings) was against commercial premises, that is 507,375 offences. Similarly, 12 per cent of thefts from motor vehicles were against commercial victims, 64,898 offences; ten per cent of thefts of motor vehicles, 24,609 offences; ten per cent of attempted thefts of motor vehicles, 11,811 offences; ten per cent of attempted thefts from motor vehicles, 8,500 offences; and seven per cent of vehicle interference and tampering, 4,054 offences. Altogether this produces a total of 621,247 recorded offences, excluded for the purpose of comparison with the British Crime Survey.

These figures make no allowance for theft from commercial premises. In the *Economic and Social Costs of Crime*, published by the Home Office in 2000, the authors estimated the real number of thefts from shops by multiplying the number of recorded offences by 100. Why did they choose 100? The figure was based on a study by Professor Farrington of Cambridge University who has estimated that the multiplier should be between 100 and 1,000. The Home Office opted for the lowest figure in the range, 100, which produced an estimate of nearly 31 million instances of shoplifting. The report acknowledges that this figure may be on the low side and suggests another formula, also based on the work of Professor Farrington. He has estimated that for every criminal cautioned for or convicted of shoplifting, about 150 offences have actually been carried out. The Home Office further assumes that each offender in the official figures has been convicted for two acts of shoplifting. In 1998 120,000 individuals were cautioned for or convicted of theft from a shop. Using the Farrington formula the Home Office estimated that the total number of offences was 36 million.[15]

Professor Farrington's estimate is based on a detailed study of shoplifting, but to multiply recorded crime by 100 may strike many observers as rather arbitrary. Another indicator that could be used is the *Commercial Victimisation Survey* (CVS) carried out by the Home Office in 1994 to discover crime in 1993. The survey found 6,932,000 thefts by retailers' customers or unknown persons (but not counting employees or 'outsiders') in 1993. In that year only 275,607 acts of shoplifting were recorded by the police. If that ratio of recorded crime to actual crime is used, then the multiplier would be 25.2. In 2001-02 306,308 thefts from shops were recorded by the police. If multiplied by 25.2 the total is 7,718,961.

Table 1.3
***Best estimate of crimes against commercial victims,
excluded from the BCS***

	Recorded crimes against commercial victims	Best estimate of % of real crimes recorded by police	Best estimate of actual crimes against commercial victims
Vandalism	507,375	19%	2,670,395
Theft from motor vehicle	64,898	31%	209,348
Theft of motor vehicles	24,609	67%	36,730
Attempted theft of motor vehicle	11,811	32%	36,909
Attempted theft from motor vehicle	8,500	32%	26,563
Vehicle interference and tampering	4,054	32%	15,191
Total			2,995,136

Source: Crime in England and Wales 2001-02, Table 2.01.

This means that the amount of shoplifting not counted by the BCS in 2002/02 was somewhere between 7.7 million and 31 million, depending on which Home Office report is preferred.

On the most cautious of assumptions, therefore, there were 602,561 offences against people under 16 and, on similarly cautious assumptions, there were 2,995,135 offences against commercial victims, not including shoplifting. If shoplifting is included, based on the CVS and again making only the most cautious of assumptions, another 7,718,961 should be added, producing a grand total of 11,316,657 offences.

To this total should be added crimes that were recorded by the police but not covered by the BCS, including 121,332 drug offences, 317,399 cases of fraud and forgery, 41,425 sexual offences (including rape and sexual assault) and 850 homicides. They add up to 481,006, producing a grand total of 11,797,663.

That is, even on the most cautious assumptions, at least another 11.8 million crimes should be added to the 13 million acknowledged crimes, a grand total of 24.8 million.[16]

Reducing youth crime: a long record of failure

The high crime rate of the early 1990s led to a major investigation by the Audit Commission which published *Misspent Youth* in 1996, with a follow-up in 1998. Crime against individuals had increased by 73 per cent from 1981 to 1995. The total cost to the public services and victims was thought to be at least £16 billion.[17]

In 1994 two-fifths of known offenders were under 21 and a quarter were under 18. However, between 1983 and 1994 the annual number of convictions of young people aged 10-17 fell from about 200,000 to 150,000. According to the Audit Commission, this was because of a reduction in the proportion found guilty and the greater use of informal warnings. The latter trend was reinforced by the (already mentioned) reclassification as summary offences by the Criminal Justice Act 1988 of three major crimes: common assault, taking a motor vehicle without consent and criminal damage.

When these changes were taken into account, the Audit Commission concluded that offending by young people had not declined.[18] Moreover, the Audit Commission challenged the assumption of the Home Office that young offenders would soon 'grow out' of their offending. The commission found that they were not doing so. The peak age of offending had risen from 15 in 1986 to 18 in 1994.

The commission documented the appalling inadequacy of the system. Only three per cent of crimes reported to the BCS in 1994 led to police arrest and action and, of these, three in five offenders were only cautioned by the police.[19] The Audit Commission accepted that cautions could be effective for first-time offenders, acknowledging that about seven out of ten were not reconvicted within two years. However, repeat cautioning brought the system into disrepute, and it urged that no more than three cautions should be administered.

The police prosecuted the other two in every five of those arrested (1.3 per cent of offences). However, the Audit Commission found that 14 per cent of cases against young offenders were discontinued by the CPS and a further 11 per cent dismissed by the court, a total of 25 per cent. Many of the offenders had admitted guilt and a few were cautioned at this stage.[20] Of the cases in the youth court observed by the Audit Commission, four out of five were adjourned. Offenders often had to appear four times before a decision was taken. Many were bailed and in Gloucester in 1994 one-third reoffended on bail.[21]

The legal profession was not only criticised for causing delays, some lawyers were thought to have manipulated the system to increase their incomes. In 1993 legal aid reform gave lawyers higher fees if their client pleaded not guilty and, shortly afterwards, the proportion pleading guilty fell from 65 per cent in 1989 to 55 per cent in 1994.[22]

The Audit Commission commented that, 'Surprisingly, little or nothing happens to half the young people proceeded against by the police'.[23] A quarter of cases were discontinued or dismissed and a further 28 per cent were given an absolute or conditional discharge. As a result, the overall use of custody fell during the 1980s. For those aged 10-17 it fell from two per 1,000 in the age group in 1984 to one per 1,000 in 1994. Sentences were also shorter, with 95 per cent for less than 12 months.[24]

This sorry state of affairs was the result of a long period of conflict and indecision about the best way to deal with juvenile crime.

The background

Since the late 1960s there has been no real consensus about the best way to cope with juvenile offending and this uncertainty has tended to make the problem worse. The 1997 white paper *No More Excuses* was among the early signs that a corner might have been turned. However, the great bulk of today's probation officers and social workers who deal from day to day with young offenders formed their beliefs in the period criticised by Home Secretary, Jack Straw, as the era of excuse-making. How did we reach our current predicament?

The Children Act 1908 set up juvenile courts and abolished prison for juveniles. Previously they had been sent to adult prisons. The 1908 Prevention of Crime Act introduced preventive detention for 'habitual criminals' who led 'persistently a dishonest or criminal life' and had been convicted three times since the age of 16. Sentences could be from 5-10 years.[25] The same Act set up the Borstal system for 16-21 year-olds, which emphasised discipline and training, modelled on public schools. The sentence was from 1-3 years followed by six months supervision after release. The date of release after 12 months was determined by the authorities and depended on the behaviour of the offender.

The next major landmark was the 1933 Children and Young Persons Act which set up a special panel of magistrates for juveniles and required them to have regard to the welfare of the child. Courts were also permitted to act *in loco parentis*. Also from 1933 approved schools were established. They were usually run by charities whose aim was to help youngsters back onto the 'straight and narrow'. Attendance centres were founded, usually run by the police on a Saturday afternoon, and detention centres were also established to provide a short period under a tough, disciplined régime. The Home Secretary at the time said they would provide a 'short, but sharp reminder', remarkably similar language to the announcement of another Home Secretary, William Whitelaw, in the 1980s.

The 1948 Children Act tried to end the practice of placing neglected or unwanted children with delinquents. Local authority children's departments were set up to deal separately with fostering and adoption and local authorities were permitted to take children into care, if they were in need of care and protection.

The next round of measures came in the late 1960s. Preventive detention was replaced by the extended sentence under the 1967 Criminal Justice Act. Criminals could be sentenced to an additional 5-10 years on top of the original sentence. This provision lasted until the 1991 Criminal Justice Act and allowed violent or sex offenders to be subject to an additional period of detention if they presented a risk of serious harm to the public.

The 1969 Children and Young Persons Act was probably the high point of welfarist legislation. It was preceded by the white paper *Children in Trouble*. The intention was to deal with all offenders under 14 'in care', not through criminal proceedings, and increasingly social workers, rather than magistrates, decided whether children remained at home or were sent to a residential institution. The Act provided 'care and protection' proceedings for children aged 10-14 but only when it could be 'established that the child was not receiving such care, protection and guidance as a good parent might reasonably be expected to give'. Older children, up to the age of 17 could face prosecution but the police had to consult the local authority children's department.[26] Magistrates were often critical of the way in which local councils used their powers, believing that youths who needed to be controlled were not. Care orders were not abolished until the 1989 Children Act (implemented in 1991).

However, the 1969 Act also abolished approved schools and replaced them with community homes, which had the unfortunate consequence that delinquents were mixed with neglected or unwanted children, reversing the 1948 policy. It had been intended to phase out Borstals, but this hope was not realised until January 1983.

During the 1970s there was no consensus about juvenile justice and not all the measures in the 1969 Act were fully implemented following the change of government in 1970. There was also growing public awareness of rising juvenile crime. The ambiguity in official reactions is revealed by the increased use of police cautions combined with the greater use of custody for juveniles from 3,000 to over 7,000 between 1970 and 1978.[27]

The community homes came under criticism because they had become 'schools of crime', a claim not without truth, since criminal youths often had a bad influence on young people who had been taken into care because of parental neglect. There was also much concern about bullying. Critics called for community sentences instead of placing 'in care', arguing that they were no less effective at reducing offending and did not encourage the mixing of offenders with neglected children who had broken no law.

During the 1980s there were many changes to the law, mostly to little advantage. The 1979 Tory manifesto promised to strengthen sentencing and the 1980 white paper *Young Offenders* proposed to establish detention centres with 'tough' régimes. Two experimental centres were set up following William Whitelaw's 'short, sharp shock' announcement. However, the 1982 Criminal Justice Act tried to reduce the use of custody. Borstals were abolished and replaced by fixed terms of youth custody and the detention-centre sentence available since 1948 was shortened from 3-6 months to a minimum of 21 days and a maximum of four months.

In 1983 a determinate sentence of youth custody for 15-20 year-olds was introduced, with a maximum of 12 months for those under 17. (However, the possibility of custody for life was introduced for very serious offenders aged 17-20.) The Criminal Justice Act of 1988 then abolished the detention sentence and youth custody and introduced detention in a Young Offender Institution.

During the 1980s informal warnings and cautions were being used heavily, encouraged by Home Office circulars in 1978, 1985 and 1990. The 1990 circular accepted repeat cautioning. Under the 1991 Criminal Justice Act, Youth Courts had replaced the old juvenile courts and extended their jurisdiction to 17-year-olds. No public attendance was allowed and children under 16 had to be accompanied by their parents.

But, by the early 1990s there was rising concern about juveniles being out of control and the courts being ineffective. *The Times* reported one case in 1993 involving a teenager who was fined £1.60 by the Inner London Youth Court for going equipped to break into a car. There were six witnesses; the boy had 22 previous convictions or cautions and was on bail at the time.[28]

There had been urban riots in 1991 in Blackburn Leys (Oxford), Ely (Cardiff) and Meadowell (North Shields), leading to a Home Affairs Committee inquiry in late 1992. The Association of Chief Police Officers (ACPO) presented evidence that between 1980 and 1990 juvenile crime had increased by 54 per cent. Yet there had been fewer convictions because of the increased use, not only of cautions, but also of informal warnings. ACPO identified a 'small hard core' who had 'absolutely no fears whatsoever' of the criminal justice system.[29] In February 1993 public concern was still further aroused when James Bulger was murdered at the age of nearly three by two ten-year-olds.

Measures were gradually strengthened. The 1994 Criminal Justice and Public Order Act introduced secure training orders for children aged 12-14, with a minimum of six months and a maximum of two years. Half the time was to be spent in secure training and half in the community. Training was to involve 25 hours per week. It doubled the maximum sentence for 15-17 year-olds from one to two years. Courts were allowed to draw an inference from the silence of the accused and pilots for curfews and tagging were started.

Michael Howard, Home Secretary from 1993, also tried to increase police effectiveness with the Police and Magistrates Courts Act. Smaller police authorities were created, plans to combat crime had to be produced, and the use of performance targets was introduced. The Crime (Sentencing) Act of 1997 introduced tagging for 10-15 year-olds.

Labour came into power in 1997 and continued many Conservative policies. Jack Straw's 1997 white paper, *No More Excuses*, signalled the end of labelling theory and the idea that young offenders would 'grow out of it':

> An excuse culture has developed within the youth justice system. It excuses itself for its inefficiency, and too often excuses the young offenders before it, implying that they cannot help their behaviour because of their social circumstances. Rarely are they confronted with their behaviour and helped to take more personal responsibility for their actions.[30]

The principal aim of the system, he said, should be to prevent offending. The resultant 1998 Crime and Disorder Act introduced a number of useful measures.

The Audit Commission report of 1998 had wanted three main changes: offending behaviour programmes; multi-agency working; and a reduction of delays in handling young offenders.

The advocacy of multi-agency working led to the establishment of Youth Offending Teams (YOTs), based especially on the Northamptonshire Diversion Unit.[31] However, social services and probation often had different objectives and the creation of YOTs did not really overcome the difficulty. Social services departments continue to be the dominant influence in YOTs. Offending behaviour programmes were enthusiastically introduced, but as Chapter 2 shows, they have failed to reduce offending. Delays for young offenders have been cut, although, because total resources have not been increased, other cases have had to wait longer.

On the other hand, the Labour Government initially tried to prevent the prison population from rising and held it constant during 1999, 2000 and 2001. When David Blunkett became Home Secretary in June 2001 the prison population began to increase again. Nevertheless, police cautioning continues at a high rate and alternatives to custody continue to be preferred despite their demonstrated failure to provide the same level of public protection as prison.

The evidence and how we approached it

There is a huge academic literature evaluating the effectiveness of overseas strategies for reducing crime, particularly in the United States. The great merit of this body of work is that it obliges practitioners to examine whether or not their programmes are truly effective methods of reducing offending. The chief measure of success is reconviction after a given period, usually one or two years, although arrest data are also used.

The most systematic survey of the US evidence so far was carried out for the US Congress in 1997. The study was produced for the National Institute of Justice by a team led by Lawrence Sherman, then at the University of Maryland, and surveyed over 500 scientifically evaluated crime prevention practices. This study was updated in 2002 to embrace 675 programmes, including some UK evidence.[32]

The group developed the Maryland Scientific Methods Scale to assess the quality of evidence. The scale had five levels, each illustrated by an example programme to test the impact of CCTV on crime:

Level 1: Correlation between a prevention programme and a measure of crime at one point in time (e.g. 'areas with CCTV have lower crime rates than areas without CCTV'). This approach fails to rule out many potential inconsistencies (such as key differences between the areas compared) and also fails to establish causal order. (Is A causing B or

B causing A or is a third factor causing both?) For example, one area might have far greater concentrations of young males or drug users than the other.

Level 2: Measures of crime before and after the programme, with no comparable control condition (e.g. 'crime decreased after CCTV was installed in an area'). This method may establish causal order but fails to rule out other possible explanations for a reduction in crime.

Level 3: Measures of crime before and after the programme in experimental and comparable control conditions (e.g. 'crime decreased after CCTV was installed in an experimental area, but there was no decrease in crime in a comparable control area without CCTV'). This approach was regarded by Sherman's team as the minimum design adequate for drawing conclusions about 'what works'. However, there can still be problems with the sizes of control and experimental groups, and with selection effects (e.g. CCTV was installed in areas with strong residents associations who had campaigned for its installation; whereas areas without CCTV had no such groups).

Level 4: Measures of crime before and after the programme in multiple experimental and control units, controlling for other variables that influence crime, such as frequency of police patrols (e.g. 'victimisation of premises under CCTV surveillance decreased compared to victimisation of control premises without CCTV, after controlling for features of premises that influenced their victimisation').

Level 5: Random assignment to programme and control groups (e.g. 'victimisation of premises randomly assigned to have CCTV surveillance decreased compared to victimisation of control premises randomly assigned to be without it'). Providing that a sufficiently large number of units are randomly assigned, those in the experimental condition should be equivalent to those in the control condition on all possible external variables that could influence the outcome. Hence, this design deals with selection problems and has the highest possible explanatory power.

However, while randomised experiments in principle offer the highest validity, in practice they are relatively uncommon in criminology and also often have implementation problems (such as a high attrition rate). Consequently—as the authors acknowledge—if randomised controlled trials were the sole test, there would be 'very little to say about crime prevention, based on the existing science'. Consequently, they chose a middle course between 'reaching very few conclusions with great certainty and reaching very many conclusions with very little certainty'.[33]

The scale was used to select studies that threw light on the effectiveness of policy interventions. Schemes were put into four categories: 'what works', 'what doesn't work', 'what looks promising' and 'what we do not yet know'. (They found a large amount of experimentation about which no final conclusions could be drawn.)

For a programme to be classified as effective, there had to be at least two level 3-5 evaluations showing statistically significant results with the preponderance of all available evidence showing effectiveness. Essentially, they only counted schemes where there was a control group of some kind to permit comparison. Similarly, for a scheme to be classified as *in*effective there had to be at least two level 3-5 evaluations showing that crime was *not* reduced and passing statistical significance tests. To be classified as 'promising' a single level 3 or higher study was sufficient. Everything else was said to have 'unknown' effects.[34]

When describing findings we will report whether or not they were 'statistically significant'. Statistical significance is a way of estimating whether the findings from any sample of a total population are likely to accurately reflect the true situation for that total population. To make this judgement, statisticians calculate the likelihood that the findings would have occurred by sheer chance. If there is no more than a 1-in-20 chance of a random result, the findings are said to be statistically significant at the five per cent (or 0.05) confidence interval. If there is a 1-in-100 chance of a random result, the findings are statistically significant at the one per cent (0.01) level.

The results reported as statistically significant in this publication are significant at the five per cent level, unless otherwise stated. When researchers are trying to discover whether a particular programme reduced offending or made no difference to behaviour, then to say that the results were statistically significant at the five per cent confidence interval means that there is a 1-in-20 chance that the programme made no difference. This level of confidence in the findings is the lowest acceptable and most scientists aspire to the one per cent level of confidence or higher.

2

Rival Explanations of Crime

Why are most people law-abiding and some people criminals? Why do some societies experience more crime than others? Why do England and Wales have more crime than most comparable countries? Confronted by these questions, most common-sense observers would look at the impact of the criminal justice system. What are the chances of being caught, convicted and punished in England and Wales compared with elsewhere? Such comparisons are not easy to make, but the US Department of Justice has published a comparison of England and Wales with the US from 1981-1996.

It will be discussed in more detail below, but the findings may be summarised as follows. From 1981 to 1996 the risk of imprisonment increased in the USA and the crime rate fell. In England and Wales the opposite happened: the risk of imprisonment fell and the crime rate increased. Take one example: in the USA the number of imprisoned burglars for every 1,000 alleged burglars increased from 5.5 in 1981 to 8.4 in 1994. In England and Wales the number of imprisoned burglars per 1,000 alleged burglars fell from 7.8 in 1981 to only 2.2 in 1995. What happened to the burglary rate? In the USA, burglaries per 1,000 households fell by about half from 105.9 in 1981 to 54.4 in 1994. In England and Wales, burglaries per 1,000 households increased from 40.9 in 1981 to 82.9 in 1995. The study was carried out by Patrick Langan at the US Department of Justice and Cambridge University's Professor David Farrington, one of Britain's most respected criminologists.

However, some commentators are reluctant to draw the conclusion that crime can be deterred by increasing the risk of punishment. They believe there are underlying causes of crime, such as poverty or unemployment, and conclude that punishment is irrelevant. Among the landmark books was Karl Menninger's *The Crime of Punishment* in 1968. He was a psychiatrist who thought that the social sciences had proved that individuals were not responsible for their conduct. In his view, our actions are determined by circumstances, some of which are visible and some hidden (except to the psychologist). To punish someone, therefore, was to penalise them for something beyond their control, no different from punishing someone who had caught a common cold. Offenders should be seen as having a medical problem and receive treatment in order to rehabilitate them. He accepted that wrongdoers should make amends for losses suffered by victims but argued that no further penalty should be exacted. Any sanction that was not purely compensatory was vengeance or retaliation.

Psychologists tend to focus on the individual, but other criminologists prefer to focus on social circumstances. They share Menninger's view that criminals are not responsible for their conduct but believe that the solution lies, not in the rehabilitation of individuals, but in political action to change social conditions. The circumstances thought to be especially important are material, variously seen as social class, poverty, social exclusion or unemployment.

One of the most famous political slogans of recent times—tough on crime, tough on the causes of crime—was intended by its inventor, Tony Blair, to satisfy the two main contenders in the debate: those who want to hold criminals responsible for their actions, and those who deny personal responsibility because they believe that individuals are forced to commit crimes by a variety of 'underlying causes'. Mr Blair knew that voters in areas vulnerable to crime wanted action taken to apprehend and jail criminals. He would be tough on crime to please them, and, in order to accommodate the social and psychological determinists, he would continue to tackle 'underlying causes', particularly poverty.

However, Mr Blair's dichotomy still fails to get to the heart of the matter. There are important underlying causes, but until recently we have tended to focus on the wrong ones.

Underlying Causes

One of the most exhaustive studies of the causes of crime in recent times was published in 1985 by James Q. Wilson and Richard Herrnstein, *Crime and Human Nature: the Definitive Study of the Causes of Crime*. It brings together what we have learnt from criminal justice practice and academic disciplines, including economics, sociology, political philosophy and psychology. The authors argue that the long-term rate of crime is affected by three main factors.

1. The age structure of the population, specifically the proportion of young males. In each generation a proportion of the young males have proved to be predisposed to crime. They are characterised by low intelligence, a short time horizon and an aggressive temperament. If that proportion goes up, other things being equal, crime is likely to rise.

2. The net benefits of crime, including the number of criminal opportunities, and the costs if caught. The actual risk of punishment may rise or fall over time and may or may not correspond to the perceived risk of punishment. Other things being equal, if crime pays, a society is likely to experience more of it, and vice versa.

3. Social or cultural changes that reduce or increase 'social investment' in institutions that encourage law-abiding behaviour. Schools, churches and families can play an especially important role in encouraging individuals to think ahead, consider the feelings and interests of other people, and accept common rules. In ordinary language, if children are brought up to have a conscience, they will not commit a crime even if they think they can get away with it.

According to Wilson and Herrnstein, changes in material conditions often cited by criminologists as an underlying cause of crime—especially poverty and social exclusion—do not seem to have been important. During the twentieth century periods of recession and economic growth were both associated with increased crime.

Is poverty an underlying cause of crime?

Farrington's longitudinal study of South London found that the peak age of offending was 17-18, but it was also the peak age of affluence for many convicted males. Those who had been convicted tended to come from low-income families at age eight and had low-incomes themselves at age 32, but at age 18 they were well-off compared with their contemporaries. Convicted delinquents tended to be unskilled labourers, for example on building sites, and on a full adult wage, whereas non-delinquents tended to be students or in low-paid jobs with good prospects, such as bank clerks.[1] A direct attack on poverty as a risk factor when these youths were aged 18—by transferring money to the least affluent—would have passed money to non-offenders and disregarded deeper explanations of their behaviour.

The crime debate has been strongly influenced by criminologists who have contended that changes in material conditions are an underlying cause of crime—especially poverty and social exclusion. However, during the twentieth century periods of recession and economic growth were both associated with increased crime.

David Pyle and Derek Deadman studied burglary and robbery between 1946 and 1991. They found that personal consumption was negatively correlated with changes in crime (increasing personal consumption led to falling crime). Unemployment, however, was positively correlated with crime.[2]

Robert Witt and colleagues found that between 1988 and 1996 year-to-year changes in burglary and vehicle crime were positively correlated with year-to-year changes in the unemployment rate and the number of cars per head.[3]

Simon Field had earlier found that from 1950 to 1987 year-to-year changes in burglary, robbery and theft of vehicles were negatively correlated with year-to-year changes in personal consumption. He had also found that year-to-year increases in beer consumption were positively correlated with year-to-year increases in violent crime.[4]

Farrington and Jolliffe found that from 1981-1999 inflation-adjusted personal consumption per head was positively correlated with all types of crime except vehicle theft (measured by the BCS) and burglary and vehicle theft (recorded by the police). Inflation-adjusted GDP per capita was positively correlated with all types of crime except survey vehicle theft. In fact in the 1980s and 1990s personal consumption and GDP per head increased over time, whereas survey vehicle theft increased considerably and then fell sharply. To their surprise, beer consumption per head was negatively correlated with all types of crime. In addition, vehicle theft did not increase with the number of vehicles available to be stolen.[5]

These inconsistent results suggest that such theories offer only weak explanations for crime. The fact that in some periods personal consumption is positively correlated with crime (Farrington and Jolliffe) and in others (Field) negatively correlated, suggests that it was not the most important influence on behaviour. Similarly, beer consumption was positively correlated with crime in Field's study. He thought that increased income allowed greater beer consumption which, in turn, led to violence. However, Farrington and Jolliffe discovered a negative correlation.

From the late 1950s until the mid-1990s there was a constant increase in crime, despite ups and downs in the economic cycle. During the same period, social trends such as divorce, out-of-wedlock births, and alcohol and drug abuse were also increasing. Wilson and Herrnstein argue that changes in 'social investment' in moral education, especially in schools and in the family, offer a more convincing explanation of the increases in all these trends, including crime. In essence, our culture reduced the amount of collective effort it put into declaring and upholding community standards.

Moreover, we should not forget that a principal driver of behaviour is personal attitudes or beliefs. At any one time some people may have no job and want the money a job would provide. Indeed, at all levels of income there will be people who want more than they have got. But, whether they seek to satisfy their wants by legal or illegal means is always a personal choice. They will be influenced by community standards—some internalised, some consciously accepted as a personal guide, and others obeyed out of fear of the consequences of non-compliance. If there are some opinion leaders who say that unrequited material wants are acceptable grounds for crime, some potential law breakers will take that as an indication of prevailing public opinion. To avoid ambiguity, it is very important that accepted community standards should be openly discussed and made clear for all to see.

In denying or disregarding the importance of such influences, deterministic theories neglect one of the most important qualities of the human race: our capacity to be influenced by one another and to change our beliefs and practices in the light of experience.

We will need to return to these questions later, but first we need to get behind the most visible differences of opinion to the underlying assumptions being made by various protagonists—especially their beliefs about human nature, the human condition, and the appropriate scope and role of government.

Left-wing and right-wing

Contemporary discussion continues to be bedevilled by misleading contrasts, not least the tendency to classify policies as 'left-wing' or 'right-wing'. It is usually assumed that the left believe crime to be the result of social conditions and advocate changing those conditions through political action. The right are assumed to oppose this view and to argue that some people are bad and that their wrongdoing is only tenuously connected with their social conditions. Right-wing policies should, therefore, aim to deter offending by detecting, convicting and punishing criminals.

A book by David Wilson and John Ashton, *What Everyone in Britain Should Know About Crime and Punishment*, published in 1998, sums up the assumptions made by many criminologists:

> Right-wing theories tend to blame human wickedness and greed, permissive social policies, sexual freedom, the media, family breakdown and lack of respect for authority. In contrast, left-wing theories emphasise the role of social and economic factors, materialism and lack of support.[6]

David Wilson and Ashton go on to define the differences between the main political parties in these terms:

> Conservatism is an individualist doctrine which holds the individual to be free and rational, and therefore entirely responsible for his or her own actions. The parties of the left and centre, by contrast, believe that individual actions are shaped not

only by individual will, but also by the broader social and economic context in which they occur.[7]

These assertions embody many unstated assumptions. The claim that conservatives believe that individuals are 'entirely responsible for' their own actions confuses two notions: the idea that individuals are in fact the cause of events that affect them; and the idea that individuals are responsible for making the most of the situation in which they find themselves. A consistent defender of personal responsibility would argue that we often find ourselves in situations neither of our choosing nor of our making, but that we nonetheless remain responsible for discovering the best way forward. Whether or not our earlier actions contributed to any given predicament is always an open question.

Wilson and Ashton also claim that the left believe that individual actions are shaped by social conditions, whereas the right emphasise individual choice. However, when we look more deeply into the attitudes associated by Wilson and Ashton with the left, the list of acknowledged 'social conditions' is restricted. Moreover, their list of favoured 'right-wing' explanations includes permissive social policies and family breakdown. If these are not 'social', then Wilson and Ashton must be using the term in a highly idiosyncratic manner. In truth, thinkers of the right invariably attach considerable weight to changes in social conditions as methods of reducing crime, including the support of schools in which children are given a clear moral lead, and the fostering of stable families because they are held to provide the best environment for raising children.

Typically the left focuses on economic circumstances, especially poverty and unemployment, and advocates public policies to change the income distribution. At the same time, intellectuals who identify with the left tend to disregard analyses that focus on other social conditions, like family breakdown, discipline in schools and the role of religion. They are particularly reluctant to acknowledge that some families and certain family types—particularly step-families and single-parent families—are more frequently associated with crime. And typically they do not want to see changes in social conditions that would restore the prominence of the family based on lifelong marriage, despite clearly demonstrated links between family breakdown and crime. Moreover, some on the political left do not want to see schools made more orderly and are often suspicious of religion.

Thus, the division is not between those who emphasise underlying social causes and those who do not; it is more a debate about which underlying social causes are important.

Rival views of the human condition

One of the main divisions of opinion is between deterministic explanations of behaviour and those which emphasise personal responsibility. Among the former are Marxist economic determinism; genetic determinism which contends that paedophiles, for instance, will always be a risk to children; loose theories that 'crime is caused by poverty'; and situational theories, including those claiming that we have more crime today compared with 50 years ago because there is more to steal.

Among the theories emphasising personal responsibility two approaches stand out: those that see man as a rational calculator, guided by self-interest; and those that see man as a moral agent, guided by a conscience shaped by the wider society.

Man as a rational self-interested calculator

Hobbes was a keen observer of the human condition and lived through the bitter religious wars of the seventeenth century. He noted that people were inclined to fight each other for the things they wanted, including material gain, personal safety, prestige, and to impose their favourite beliefs on others. However, to avoid constant conflict, the right to use private violence had been surrendered to rulers whose task was to protect everyone from foreign attack and from criminals at home. At its simplest, Hobbes thought that people were inherently bad, from which it followed that it was necessary to erect institutions to control them. Without government to maintain law and order, life would famously be 'solitary, poor, nasty, brutish, and short'.

Hobbes saw people as capable of rationally calculating their own advantage, a view later developed by the utilitarians, especially Bentham. This meant that public policy towards crime should be based on ensuring that the punishment for a crime exceeded any advantage the offender might gain. When people compare the benefit of their crime 'with the harm of their punishment', said Hobbes, they will 'choose that which appeareth best for themselves'. This view continues to be strongly supported today.

Man as a moral agent, guided by conscience shaped by society

The tradition of the early liberals such as David Hume and Adam Smith owes much to Aristotle. It rests on the view that people are inherently predisposed to acquire a conscience. In this view, people are naturally social creatures and have an innate disposition to please other people and avoid their disapproval. To be sure, people are capable of selfishness but the challenge is, not only to check self-interest, but also to harness those natural moral sentiments which enable us to put ourselves in other people's shoes and develop a shared sense of right and wrong. The human challenge, therefore, is to devise or nurture the institutions that encourage mutual sympathy and concern. This means that families and schools are of special importance, as well as all those institutions of civil society that bring people together for common purposes without anyone commanding them to do so.

In this tradition of thought it makes no sense to think of people in a pre-social condition. No such state of affairs has ever been the reality. From the beginning people lived together in families, and later in tribes, villages, towns and wider social groupings for mutual support and protection. Functioning families, above all, prepare children for an adult life of personal responsibility. To understand the human condition as if nothing is going on but the calculation of pains and pleasures is insufficient. It is of particular relevance to any discussion of crime to recognise that most people do not commit offences even when they can be certain of avoiding punishment. They are guided by conscience. Human beings are born with a capacity to develop an internal sense of right and wrong, but whether they grow up with a well-developed conscience or not depends most of all on their family, and also on the reinforcements provided by the wider society, including schools, churches and intellectuals (including criminologists).

Man as a natural altruist, corrupted by society

So far we have contrasted deterministic theories with those emphasising individual responsibility, especially within a shared culture in which a particular sense of right and wrong is upheld. There is another influential group of modern thinkers who derive their ideas from Rousseau, with modifications. The essential idea is that 'society' causes self-serving or aggressive behaviour. The political remedy is not to uphold common standards but to release individuals from their grip —to sweep away intrusive institutions and emancipate man's true nature. According to Rousseau:

> It is then certain that compassion is a natural feeling, which by moderating the activity of love of self in each individual, contributes to the preservation of the whole species. It is this compassion ... which in a state of nature supplies the place of laws, morals, and virtues.[8]

In *Émile*, he writes:

Our wisdom is slavish prejudice, our customs consist in control, constraint, compulsion. Civilised man is born and dies a slave... All his life long man is imprisoned by our institutions.[9]

Such thinking does not necessarily deny the importance of individual responsibility in all cases, but it repudiates Adam Smith's view that upholding community standards is central to a civilised society.

Rousseau regarded Hobbes' arguments as pernicious. People are not naturally wicked, or scheming, or selfish. They are inherently good. They will not attack other people, unless taught to do so; and they will naturally sympathise with the misfortunes of others, unless they are urged by their society to be callous or uncaring. The corruption of people began with the formation of societies. Property played a central part in Rousseau's demonology: 'The first man, who having enclosed a piece of ground, bethought himself of saying, "This is mine," and found people simple enough to believe him' was the real founder of society. Property led to wars and inequality. For Hobbes, seeking glory and gain were natural, but for Rousseau they were the result of social convention. Rousseau's influence, especially the belief that people are not really responsible for their actions (because society has corrupted them) is still prevalent today, especially among criminologists. Many such theories boil down to the assertion that 'society made me do it'. However, Rousseau was not an economic determinist. His belief that 'society' corrupted individuals belongs in the deterministic camp, but his belief that raw human nature was essentially compassionate was not consistent with the claim that poverty causes crime.

One version of Rousseau's doctrine led to demands for individuals to be 'true to themselves'. But if it is true, for instance, that a paedophile has a genetic desire to have sex with young children, then he is being true to himself. Most people think he should *not* be true to himself. Instead he should be *un*true, or rather true to the prevailing community standards of right and wrong.

Today, Rousseau's theories tend to underpin the thinking of people who see themselves as 'progressives'. For example, an *Observer* leader in April 2003 said this: 'Home Secretary David Blunkett has, whatever some critics might say, a progressive agenda on crime. He has long expressed his desire to reduce the prison population'. Yet, the leader writer notes, the prison population has risen to record levels.

In the assumption that it is 'progressive' to reduce the prison population, we can see the hand of Rousseau. Human nature is held to be essentially good and so, in an ideal society, few people would be in prison. Most people would agree that it would be better to have a smaller prison population, but only so long as the reason why few people are in prison is that there is very little crime. To have few people in prison whilst there is a high level of crime is not a sign of a civilised society. It may be an indication that the leaders of society have lost their nerve, or perhaps the capacity to separate facts from personal preferences. Moreover, in failing to combat crime, such leaders are more likely to increase it.

The underlying mistake is to confuse hopes for human nature with assumptions about the current reality of human conduct. To confront human behaviour as we find it, is not to abandon hope for a better world, it is simply being realistic about what needs to be done to change the behaviour of known offenders and about the measures necessary to protect the public while the behaviour of offenders is changing.

Our assumptions

We accept that there is evidence that some people have innate tendencies. But, we do not claim that some people are born criminals. It is true that individuals who are impulsive (will not defer rewards or plan ahead) and of below average intelligence are more likely to be criminals, but much hinges on the early years when parents can either modify or encourage any natural predispositions. Failure at this stage can influence children to display little regard for the feelings of others—and such children are more likely to be the ones who turn to crime at an early age.

In *Crime and Human Nature*, Wilson and Herrnstein take pains to explain the style of parenting that most effectively diminishes criminal tendencies. The interaction with parents takes place on three levels.[10] First there is the development of 'attachment', a word used by Wilson and Herrnstein in a slightly wider sense than is common among psychologists. They mean the encouragement of a desire to win the approval of others and a sense that the child can count on receiving that approval when it is merited. Second, there is the development of a 'time horizon', an ability to think ahead and defer pleasures. And third, is the development of 'conscience', that is internalised constraints on certain actions. People with a strong conscience will feel anxious or uneasy—bad about themselves—when they flout the standards they have come to accept.

Effective parents tend to be warm rather than cold, and consistent in applying restrictions, not erratic. Warm and consistent parenting typically produces children with a strong conscience. To avoid confusion with utilitarianism, Wilson and Herrnstein emphasise that conscience is not about the calculation of advantage, that is merely seeking the approval or avoiding the disapproval of others. They accept that behaviour patterns are reinforced by rewards and punishments but deny that individuals are controlled by external factors. Children learn, not only how to gain rewards from others, but to internalise principles of conduct so that they share the same sense of right and wrong. Such beliefs and habits become part of their character to such a degree that they may be 'incapable' of committing crimes. This interpretation is caricatured by some sociologists as 'authoritarian', because values have been taught by society (mainly parents). In doing so they reveal their debt to Rousseau, who regarded moral education as a departure from built-in goodness.

If the interpretation of Wilson and Herrnstein is true, parental skills matter a great deal. It also explains why broken homes are important. Because parenting is a difficult task, if one parent must do the job of two it becomes more difficult still. Single parents, therefore, have less chance of success, particularly when confronted by an inherently difficult child, and still more so when they live in a disorderly neighbourhood where mutual support may be hard to come by. By the same token, a lone parent may be able to raise a child successfully if he or she is not naturally pre-disposed to crime, and the school and wider community are supportive.

Schools can play an important role in encouraging a shared sense of right and wrong, but since the Second World War there has been a fundamental dispute about the purposes of education. The critics of the established system, who had become dominant by the 1960s and 1970s, disliked schools that emphasised discipline, orderly classrooms and teachers imparting knowledge to pupils. Schools characterised by rules (symbolised by children sitting in rows listening), an emphasis on good character and the teaching of basic skills and knowledge, came to be despised. The emphasis on 'manners maketh man' was nothing but a disguise for hypocrisy and, anyway, it was all about imposing middle-class values on the masses (automatically assumed to be a bad thing, as Rousseau had taught).

Old fashioned schools were to be replaced by less formal institutions in which children would sit, not in rows, but in groups, theoretically working together. Teachers should not transmit knowledge but help pupils to discover it for themselves, a doctrine also straight out of Rousseau's *Émile*. This is how the back cover of the 1993 Everyman edition described its influence: 'Rousseau was certain of man's natural goodness, yet he perceived a world in which that benevolence was obliterated: from birth to death, men were fashioned by artificial social constraints into conditions of servitude, mutual distrust and alienation. Changes had to be made, allowing this natural goodness unhindered development.' The blurb goes on accurately to sum up the influence of Rousseau on education: 'Such is the impact of this doctrine upon educational practice that it seems today mere commonsense'.

Champions of traditional schooling were put on the defensive. Their counter-criticism was that schools should prepare pupils for life in a free society in which basic skills, such as reading, writing and numeracy would be an invaluable asset. No less important, a free society also rested on personal responsibility and co-operation with others and so a school should play its part in encouraging children to assert self-control and consider the feelings of other people. They understood from historical experience that the alternative to *self* control was *social* control and so, a society that wished to live under limited government must comprise individuals who imposed a voluntary check on their own wants for the good of all.

Moreover, defenders of a free society know that people who grow up without basic skills and without a sense of personal responsibility for their own conduct offer easy pickings for political wire-pullers. In reality, the followers of Rousseau were demanding the emancipation of pupils from the school rules that prepared them, not to be obedient to hated 'middle-class' authority, but to be capable of criticising it from a position of strength based on careful thought and sound knowledge, acquired in a shared process of open, public discussion.

To sum up: we accept that natural endowments and psychiatric imperatives make a difference, but contend that socialisation within the family and other key face-to-face institutions is the vital formative influence. We further contend, contrary to the followers of Rousseau, who regard social institutions as harmful, that the raising of children capable of exercising responsible and unselfish choices in a free society depends on the careful maintenance of institutions such as marriage. We do not deny that people often find themselves in circumstances not of their choosing but, contrary to determinists, we claim that how individuals respond, once in a given situation, is a matter of choice. To say this is not to accept that people are utilitarian calculators who do nothing but weigh the costs and benefits of actions, but it is to claim that we adapt our behaviour depending on the positive and negative consequences of which we are aware—guided at the same time by conscience shaped by our immediate family and the wider society.

We contend that man is best understood as a moral agent. The challenge, we might say, is to understand the institutions that work with the grain of human nature, not to get back to raw nature, which may lead us astray. Often, success in creating peaceful and stable societies depends on ignoring or overcoming nature—especially aggression and self-interest. What we call civilisation is partly a triumph over nature (our worst instincts) and partly working with the grain of our nature, by upholding institutions such as marriage that protect children and encourage concern for others.

The human challenge is how best to organise a coherent society despite human limitations. Having few people in jail is a legitimate measure of a good society, but only if there is little crime, which would imply that most people were guided by a strong sense that harming others is wrong. The aim of policy should be a low rate of imprisonment *because* we have a low crime rate, not a low rate of imprisonment, *whatever* the crime rate.

Where do justice and equity fit in?

So far we have considered rival theories of human nature and what they imply for public policy towards punishment and rehabilitation. But where does 'justice' fit in? Some enthusiasts for rehabilitation are actively disdainful towards the champions of 'just deserts'. Two of the leading enthusiasts, Don Andrews and James Bonta, for example, claim that just-deserts theorists believe that 'being held accountable for one's behaviour through judicial processing somehow makes one more responsible'. And they go on to accuse such theorists of dismissing 'human diversity' and 'direct human treatment services' in favour of 'big picture' concerns of 'justice' and 'preventing the breakdown of society'.[11]

Their dismissal of 'justice' as a 'big picture' concern suggests that they have failed to make a distinction which has played a prominent part in the post-war crime debate at least since H.L.A. Hart's 'Prolegomenon to the Principles of Punishment' of 1959.[12]

According to Hart, the battle between champions of rehabilitation, justice and utilitarianism failed to distinguish between, on the one hand, the overall justifying aim of the system of law and, on the other, the distribution or allocation of punishments. A system of law backed by threats of punishment must be understood as part of a communal effort to make rules for everyone to live by, usually in the belief that they are to the benefit of all.[13] The idea of an implicit social contract captures some of what is meant. As we all go about the daily business of earning a living, buying, selling and entering into agreements with others, it would often be a great advantage to break the rules—so long as everyone else was obeying them. But this would give the law-breaker an unfair advantage which had been deliberately foregone by the majority of law-abiding people out of a half-conscious sense that we all need to take 'the rough with the smooth' or that 'what you lose on the swings you gain on the roundabouts'. Punishment is necessary as retribution to restore balance. For this reason we speak of a criminal's 'debt' to society. We restore equity when the debt is discharged. There could be no equity while some people—the least scrupulous or most selfish—were able to gain advantage by ignoring the rules obeyed by everyone else, often to their own immediate *dis*advantage.

According to Hart, a society can be seen as:

> *offering* individuals including the criminal the protection of the laws on terms which are fair, because they not only consist of a framework of reciprocal rights and duties, but because within this framework each individual is given a *fair* opportunity to choose between keeping the law required for society's protection or paying the penalty.[14]

Criminal punishment, he says:

> defers action till harm has been done; its primary operation consists simply in announcing certain standards of behaviour and attaching penalties for deviation, making it less eligible, and then leaving individuals to choose.[15]

This system maximises individual freedom. Individuals can 'obey or pay'. They can identify beforehand when they will be punished and plan accordingly.

Rehabilitation is intended to strengthen an offender's disposition to keep within the law by methods other than fear of punishment, perhaps by encouraging repentance, recognition of moral guilt, or greater awareness of social responsibility; or perhaps offering education, vocational training, or psychological treatment. Hart finds it paradoxical that rehabilitation should be considered the dominant aim 'as if the main purpose of providing punishment for murder was to reform the murderer not to prevent murder.'[16]

Rehabilitation, he says, is a remedial step, the opportunity for which arises when the criminal law has 'failed in its primary task of securing society from the evil which breach of the law involves'. There are two groups of people in any society: those who have broken a law, and those who have not so far, but might. To treat rehabilitation as the dominant aim would, according to Hart, be to forgo hope of influencing the majority of non-offenders.[17]

In Hart's terminology, the possibility of reforming a criminal is an important consideration during the *allocation* of judicial sanctions, but it cannot serve as the paramount objective without disregarding the main purpose of any system of law, that of using moral re-affirmation and the threat of punishment to influence people who have not offended—so far.

Responsibility and blame

One further line of criticism should be attended to. We have defended the idea that individuals are personally responsible for dealing justly with others, but some critics claim that crime is an illness in need of curative treatment. The psychiatrist Willard Gaylin, for example, wrote in 1982 that: 'Psychiatrically speaking, nothing is wrong—only sick. If an act is not a choice but merely the inevitable product of a series of past experiences, a man can be no more guilty of a crime than he is guilty of an abscess'.[18]

In an earlier and more famous book to which reference has already been made, *The Crime of Punishment*, another psychiatrist, Karl Menninger, wrote that it was 'simply not true' that most offenders were 'fully aware' of what they had done. Officials should replace 'the punitive attitude with a therapeutic attitude'. Crime should be seen as an illness: 'It should be treated, and it could be.'[19]

We do not accept this point of view. Crime is behaviour to which there is an alternative and it is up to each of us to make the right choice or take the consequences.

To sum up: the remainder of the study will examine two main explanations for crime. First, that crime increases when the net benefits outweigh the net disadvantages. And second, that crime will increase or decrease depending on the collective effort made by members of society to declare and uphold shared standards of right and wrong. This second explanation directs our attention to the primary socialisation of children, especially in the family.

Part I
How to Reduce Reoffending: The Evidence

3

Incapacitation and Deterrence

Deterrence

What is known about the ability of the criminal justice system to influence the amount of crime? Some critics claim that there is no deterrent effect. Criminals, they say, do not calculate the risk of being caught and punished. They are impulsive or opportunist or driven to crime by circumstances.

Professor Daniel Nagin is one of the most respected authorities on deterrence. He has surveyed deterrence research up to 1998 and identified three main approaches: interrupted time series, 'ecological approaches' and perceptual studies. Interrupted time series examine the impact of specific interventions, such as police crack-downs on drug dealing in a particular street or drink-driving in a locality. Such measures have been found to have an effect, but there may be a displacement effect and the impact on behaviour may decay with time.

Ecological studies, in his use of the term, compare statistics of criminal sanctions and crime in large areas (whole countries or US states) across time. They aim to discover whether or not there are negative correlations between changes in criminal sanctions or the risk of punishment and the crime rate. A negative correlation would suggest that raising either the risk or severity of punishment would reduce crime. Nagin concludes that 'a number of studies have been successful in isolating a deterrent effect'.[1]

A third type of study focuses on personal perceptions of the risk of punishment and self-reported crime. Nagin found that with 'few exceptions' these studies discovered that self-reported crime was lower among people who perceived that 'sanction risks and costs' were higher.[2] Self-reports may be derived from three types of survey. Cross-sectional surveys interview a sample at a given time; longitudinal studies interview the same panel of people over time; and scenario-based studies present people with particular situations and ask how they would respond.

Cross-sectional and scenario-based studies have consistently found that perceptions of the risk of detection and punishment have 'negative, deterrent-like associations' with self-reported offending.[3]

Panel studies have typically involved a time lag. Interviewers try to understand the perception of risk at one point and then to examine criminal conduct a year later. The intention is to clarify whether the perception was causing criminal behaviour or vice versa. However, the time lag may be too long to establish any causal link at all and the scenario method was devised to overcome this problem. In general, such studies have found that people who perceived that sanctions were more certain or more severe were less likely to engage in crimes such as drink-driving. According to Nagin, 'a consensus has emerged among perceptual deterrence researchers that the negative association between sanction risk perceptions and offending behaviour or intentions is measuring deterrence'.[4]

Deterrence in England and Wales

We might begin with what criminals and potential criminals themselves say about their reasons for committing or not committing offences.

Interviews with both offenders and non-offenders suggest that many individuals take the risk of being caught into account. The Home Office has carried out two Youth Lifestyles Surveys (YLS) based on interviews with 12-30 year-olds living in private households. The first study was in 1992/93 and the second in 1998/99. Here we draw on the second survey which asked about factors that would prevent individuals from committing certain types of crime (a scenario-based study in Nagin's terminology).

Respondents were asked: 'Sometimes people see the chance to take money or an expensive object from a SHOP OR AN OFFICE. If you were ever tempted to take something , which one of these things would be most likely to stop you doing it?' They were shown a card with the following choices:

- The feeling that it is wrong.
- Because of the chances of getting caught.
- The fear of what other people would think of me if I were found out.
- It would harm/shame members of my family.
- The problems of having a criminal record (like not being able to get a job).
- The punishment which I might get (e.g. going to prison, having to pay a fine).
- Fear of hurting other person/don't like to hurt people.

- Someone else (friends/wife/etc.) would stop/hold me back.
- Fear of losing friendship with the person.
- Self-control.
- Other.
- Nothing would stop me.
- Would never be tempted.

They were then asked about the factors that would cause them not to steal from someone they knew. ('Sometimes people see the chance to take money or an expensive object BELONGING TO SOMEONE THEY KNOW. If you yourself were ever tempted to take something, which one of these things would be most likely to stop you doing it?') They were then presented with the same options.

Finally, they were asked a similar question about crimes of violence. ('Sometimes people get very angry with each other and feel like hitting them or using some form of violence. If you yourself felt like hitting someone, which one of these things would be most likely to stop you doing it?')

How important was the risk of punishment compared with other factors? When asked about shoplifting, the biggest single reason for not committing the crime was 'the feeling that it is wrong' (45 per cent). Those who answered that they 'would never be tempted' (23.7 per cent) were offering a similar kind of explanation, but they had internalised opposition to crime so much that it was 'unthinkable'. Also closely related were some other answers. Fear of what other people would think if they were found out (2.6 per cent of respondents) reflects both the risk of punishment and awareness of moral pressure, but those who answered that it would harm or shame members of their family (5.2 per cent) were largely reflecting the moral pressure they felt. We have, therefore, added together 'the feeling that it was wrong', 'would never be tempted' and belief that it would 'shame the family' (45.0 + 23.7 + 5.2) producing a total of 73.9 per cent. These answers all reflect moral pressure or conscience and suggest that early socialisation was effective for these respondents.

To arrive at a measure of the fear of detection, conviction and punishment we added together three answers: the 'chances of getting caught', 'problems of having a criminal record' and 'fear of the punishment' (11.2 + 6.2 + 5.1), a total of 22.5 per cent. We conjecture that these respondents were people whose offending could be reduced by increasing the risk of punishment.

Does the same apply to theft from a known person? In such cases, moral influence seems to be substantially stronger. Adding together the 'feeling that it is wrong', 'would never be tempted' and belief that it would 'shame the family' (46.1 + 34.6 + 4.6) produces a total 'moral influence' of 85.3 per cent. And if we add the 'chances of getting caught', 'problems of having a criminal record' and 'fear of the punishment' (3.7 + 1.8 + 1.2) then only 6.7 per cent were likely to be deterred by increasing the risk of punishment.

The findings for violence, however, suggest a different pattern of motivation. Adding together the 'feeling that it is wrong', 'would never be tempted' and belief that it would 'shame the family' (43.2 + 17.4 + 5.0) produces a total of 65.6 per cent. The total of those who feared the consequences was 17.1 per cent but 7.7 per cent said 'nothing would stop me', reflecting the impulsiveness of some crimes of violence.

We are able to compare youths who had committed offences with those who had not. For all youths (offenders and non-offenders), the fear of legal punishment was more of a deterrent for theft from a shop (22.5 per cent named this as the thing that would stop them from committing the offence), than for theft from an individual they knew (6.7 per cent) and the use of violence (17.1 per cent).

When youths who have committed crimes are compared to those who have not committed crimes, a pattern emerges. Among those who had *never* shoplifted, 79.4 per cent (46.8 + 28.1 + 4.5) said they would not commit the offence for moral reasons, and 17.9 per cent (8.8 + 3.8 + 5.3) because of fear of the consequences.

However, among those who had shoplifted, socialisation appears to have been less effective: 57.6 per cent (38.4 + 7.8 + 11.4) said they would not do so because of effective socialisation and 36.2 per cent (18.1 + 10.0 + 8.1) because of the risk of punishment.

Likewise, the fear of legal punishment for stealing from an individual they knew seems to have had more of a deterrent effect on people who had snatched a bag (29 per cent) compared with those who had never committed this crime (6.5 per cent). And people who had pick-pocketed were more deterred from stealing from an individual by legal punishment (18.6 per cent) than those who had not (6.6 per cent).

People who had committed severe violence against a non-family member were also more deterred from using violence by fear of legal punishment than those who had never committed this crime (30.3 per cent compared to 16 per cent).

However, 20 per cent of those who admitted that they had used severe violence against a non-family member said that 'nothing would ever stop them' from using violence. Their claim that 'nothing would stop them' suggests an awareness that they were capable of irrational conduct, or at least of losing control for a time. The attitude to property crime was very different. When questioned about stealing either from a shop or someone they knew, under one per cent of all those interviewed said that 'nothing would stop them'.

These findings are consistent with the hypothesis that the more rational the motivation for crime, the more likely the individual is to weigh the risk of detection against the benefits. If true, then individuals committing calculative crimes, especially when money is involved, are more likely to be deterred by the possibility of punishment.

Perceived likelihood of getting caught

The Youth Lifestyles Survey also allows us to understand perceptions of risk. Those who had shoplifted before tended to view the likelihood of getting caught shoplifting as lower than those who had never shoplifted: 35 per cent of those who had shoplifted believed that capture was likely, and 63.9 per cent thought it unlikely.[5] Of those who had never shoplifted, 42.1 per cent thought capture was likely, and 55.5 per cent thought capture unlikely. How realistic were their estimates? The police clear-up rate for theft and handling, which includes shoplifting, was about 14 per cent in the years before the survey was carried out. Thus, those with concrete experience were more accurate, but both groups over-estimated the risk.

How does burglary compare? People who had committed burglary before tended to view the likelihood of getting caught breaking into a house and stealing a VCR as a little lower than those who had never committed this crime. Of those who had burgled, 21.1 per cent thought capture likely, and 77.5 per cent thought capture unlikely; whereas 25.3 per cent of those who had never burgled thought capture likely, and 72.7 per cent thought capture unlikely. In 1995 and 1996 the police clear-up rate for burglary was 21 per cent, and in 1997/98 it was 23 per cent, all uncannily close to the perceived figure in 1998/99.[6]

To summarise the evidence: the differences between offenders and non-offenders suggest that the criminals had been less effectively socialised. In addition, the importance of early socialisation is confirmed by surveys of convicted offenders. The 1991 Prison Offenders Survey interviewed ten per cent of the male prison population and 20 per cent of the female, excluding those aged under 17.[7] It asked about family background and found that 19 per cent of prison inmates had spent most the time up to the age of 16 with one parent; eight per cent had spent most of the time in an institution; 26 per cent had been taken into local authority care at some time before the age of 16; and, of those aged under 21, 38 per cent had been in care (compared with only two per cent of the general population above or below 21 who had been in care).[8]

We draw two conclusions. First, that institutions for primary socialisation play a pivotal role and that, therefore, a society wanting little crime should ensure the good health of these institutions. The child's experience in the family is the most important, followed (at some distance) by schools and the other face-to-face institutions in each locality. Second, fear of punishment discourages potential offenders. It follows that, if the risk of punishment falls, then crime is likely to increase.

There is also a substantial body of academic work supporting this conclusion. A recent survey of the evidence for deterrence carried out by criminologists at the University of Cambridge concluded: 'The studies plainly suggest that when potential offenders are made aware of substantial risks of being punished, many of them are induced to desist'. They shared the view of other scholars that criminal punishment has now been shown capable of having deterrent effects.[9]

Incapacitation

To ask whether prison works is itself a controversial question. When we ask whether prison works, what is meant by 'works'? Some people mean rehabilitation. However, prison is no better than other sentences as a method of rehabilitating offenders. According to the Home Office:

> 58 per cent of all sentenced prisoners discharged in 1995 were reconvicted of a standard list offence within two years; the analogous rate of offenders commencing community penalties in 1995 was 56 per cent.

The report continues:

> After taking into account all possible relevant factors there was no discernible difference between reconviction rates for custody and community penalties.[10]

What can we reasonably expect of our prison service?

On both the historic and international measures England and Wales suffer from a high rate of crime, but some academics claim that our problem is not too much crime, but too many people in prison. These critics are aware of public concern about the objectively high rate of crime and purport to share their concern by claiming that prison fails to reduce reoffending on release. They play down the indisputable fact that prison protects the public while offenders are inside and hold prison responsible for the behaviour of inmates after they have left. The prison authorities partly have themselves to blame for adopting utopian objectives which radically under-estimate the difficulty of changing individuals who have adopted a life of crime. Prisons are places of confinement that can be expected to ensure that offenders do not escape and are kept in clean, humane conditions. They can be expected to provide services for prisoners, including education, vocational training and rehabilitation for drug takers. But they cannot realistically be held responsible for what free people do when they are discharged from prison. Former prisoners are free to do as they wish and must take responsibility for their own actions.

Here we are concerned with the incapacitation and deterrent effects of prison. Prison incapacitates offenders in the sense that, while in prison, an offender cannot commit offences against the general public.

The debate

Zimring and Hawkins are often quoted as having proved that incapacitation does not work. MacKenzie, for example, cites them in support of her conclusion that 'correlational studies examining the association between incarceration rates and arrest rates within jurisdictions have not found any consistent relationship between the two'.[11] However, Zimring and Hawkins actually say that to discuss imprisonment while excluding incapacitation as one of its purposes 'would be absurd'. 'If prisons are good for anything' they say, 'it is as institutions of restraint'.[12]

They sum up their main finding like this: 'Most of our statistical measures suggest a reduction in reported index felony crime of about 3.5 per additional year of confinement with 90 per cent of that reduction clustered in burglary and larceny'. They then contrast arrest rates by age in their two comparison years, 1980 and 1990. Arrest rates for burglary and larceny went down for juvenile offenders, while they went up for older offenders. They assume that arrest rates are a good proxy for the amount of crime and infer that, because additional incapacitation was concentrated on older offenders, the reduction in offending could not have been due to additional imprisonment. However, arrest rates are not good proxies for criminal activity and reflect police efficiency among other factors.[13] Zimring and Hawkins also acknowledge that their measure of crime relies on police records, which are not thought to measure some crimes as well as the victim survey.[14] They regard their comparison of crime rates and incarceration rates in 17 states as a 'rough beginning', and in the same paragraph they say: 'We should emphasise the limits and crudity' of the 17-state comparison. It only compares two points in time and uses police records, which are not regarded as 'precise measures of crime trends over time or of crime levels at any particular period'.[15]

Their final conclusion is that intelligent policy making is most likely in an atmosphere 'in which incapacitation is recognised as an important, but by no means exclusive, means of social defence against serious crime'.[16] They conclude that their findings are 'equivocal' and call for more research using more refined methods.[17]

The evidence

What evidence is available? We can ask whether an increase in the rate at which criminals are caught, convicted and imprisoned leads to a fall in crime. But this measure would not distinguish between the incapacitation effect and the deterrent effect. We will ask later whether the incapacitation effect can be separated from the deterrent effect.

Two kinds of experiment would allow us to test the theory that increasing the risk of imprisonment reduces crime. First, two countries would need to pursue opposite policies: one would need to reduce the risk of punishment and another to increase it. If it is true that crime falls when the risk of punishment increases (and vice versa) then crime will rise in the country that reduces the risk of being caught, convicted and imprisoned. A second test would involve a single country reversing its policy, either by increasing or decreasing the risk of punishment, to allow an historical comparison of the impact on crime to be made.

In the social sciences opportunities for such experiments are rare, but we are lucky and both an international comparison and a single-country historical comparison are possible. We can compare the USA with England and Wales from 1981-1996 and we can contrast the impact of the anti-prison policy pursued in England and Wales from 1981-1993 with the consequences of the increased use of prison from 1993-2002.

Two-country comparison: USA and England and Wales, 1981-1996

A study carried out by Professor David Farrington of the University of Cambridge, in conjunction with Patrick Langan of the US Department of Justice, compared the USA and England and Wales between 1981 and 1996. Crime rates based on crime surveys were available in both countries up to 1995, and crime figures based on police records to 1996. The study investigated the possibility that increasing the risk of punishment would lead to falling crime. Two measures of the risk of punishment were used: the conviction rate per 1,000 alleged offenders; and the incarceration rate per 1,000 alleged offenders. The method of calculation is explained in Appendix 1.

The original study by Langan and Farrington was published in 1998 and gives imprisonment rates and crime rates in England and Wales based on the British Crime Survey (BCS) up to 1995. The original 1998 comparison showed that the USA and England and Wales pursued very different policies and produced very different results. The study found that the chances of being imprisoned increased in the USA between 1981 and 1995 and fell in England and Wales. During the same period, crime fell in the USA and increased in England and Wales.

The imprisonment rate 1981-1995

From 1981 to 1995 (1994 for the USA), an offender's risk of being caught, convicted, and sentenced to custody increased in the United States for all six crimes in the study (murder, rape, robbery, assault, burglary, and motor vehicle theft) but fell in England and Wales for all except murder. For example, in the US in 1981 there were 13 imprisoned robbers for every 1,000 alleged robbers. By 1994 there were 17. In England and Wales, there were seven imprisoned robbers for every 1,000 alleged robbers in 1981, and only four in 1995. There were 5.5 imprisoned burglars for every 1,000 alleged burglars in the US, increasing to 8.4 in 1994. In England and Wales there were 7.8 in 1981 and only 2.2 in 1995.

The graphs in Appendix 2 show the situation from 1981 until 1995, based on the Langan and Farrington study.

The crime rate 1981-1995

What happened to the crime rate during this period? According to the 1995 victim surveys, rates of robbery, assault, burglary, and motor vehicle theft were all higher in England and Wales than in the United States. According to 1996 police statistics, crime rates were higher in England and Wales for three crimes: assault, burglary, and motor vehicle theft. In the US in 1996 there were 9.4 burglaries for every 1,000 population, compared with 22.4 in England and Wales; and there were

5.3 car thefts per 1,000 population in the US compared with 9.5 in England and Wales. The 1996 recorded crime rate for robbery would have been higher in England and Wales than the United States had the police in England and Wales recorded the same proportion of robberies reported to them by the public as did the American police. In 1996 the US police recorded 78 per cent of robberies reported to them, whereas the English and Welsh police recorded only 35 per cent.

Appendix 3 shows the rates for robbery, assault, burglary and motor vehicle theft.

The major exception to the trend is the murder rate. The 1996 US murder rate was nearly six times higher than the rate in England and Wales, although the difference between the two countries narrowed from 1981 to 1996. Moreover, guns were more frequently used in violent crimes in the United States than in England and Wales. According to 1996 police statistics, firearms were used in 68 per cent of US murders and in seven per cent of English and Welsh murders, and in 41 per cent of US robberies but only five per cent of English and Welsh robberies.

The overall US crime rate—whether measured by surveys of crime victims (1995) or by police statistics (1996)—was lower than in 1981. In the US, the figures for assault, burglary, and motor vehicle theft (according to the 1995 victim survey) were the lowest recorded in the period from 1981 to 1995. The rates for murder, robbery, and burglary (according to police records) were also the lowest recorded during the period 1981-1996. By comparison, English and Welsh crime rates in 1995 (as measured by the BCS) and 1996 (based on police statistics) were higher than they had been in 1981.

How large were the differences between 1981 and 1996? And how did they change during the period studied?

- The US robbery rate as measured in the victim survey was nearly double that in England and Wales in 1981, but in 1995 the England and Wales robbery rate was 1.4 times America's.

- The England and Wales assault rate as measured by the victim survey was slightly higher than America's in 1981, but in 1995 the England and Wales assault rate was more than double America's.

- The US burglary rate as measured by the victim survey was more than double that in England and Wales in 1981, but in 1995 the England and Wales burglary rate was nearly double America's.

- The England and Wales motor vehicle theft rate as measured in the victim survey was 1.5 times America's in 1981, but in 1995 the

England and Wales rate for vehicle theft was more than double America's.

• The US murder rate as measured in police statistics was 8.7 times that in England and Wales in 1981 but 5.7 times higher in 1996.

• The US rape rate as measured in police statistics was 17 times that in England and Wales in 1981 but 3 times greater in 1996.

Public policy changes in the two countries

Langan and Farrington found that in England and Wales in the early-1990s, criminals faced a lower risk of punishment compared with the USA. Moreover, the risk had fallen between 1981 and 1995. Why did the risk of punishment fall in England and Wales and increase in the US? The study suggests three causes of diminishing conviction rates in England and Wales. First, there was an increased use of cautions and unrecorded warnings.[18] (This policy has subsequently been changed for young offenders.) Second, the Police and Criminal Evidence Act of 1984 increased the procedural safeguards for the accused. And third, the Crown Prosecution Service was established in 1986, leading to an increased tendency to drop cases.[19]

Two special factors caused the decreasing risk of prison from 1987-1991. First, official Home Office advice encouraged judges to make less use of prison and second, taking a motor vehicle without the owner's consent was downgraded in 1988 to a non-indictable offence, encouraging the use of non-custodial sentences.

From 1993, however, government policy changed and the use of prison was encouraged, especially for repeat offenders, although the rate of imprisonment remained low compared with the US. In the US, however, during the same period, the police arrested a higher proportion of total alleged offenders and prosecutors obtained more convictions. And, after 1986, US prisoners served a longer proportion of their sentences.

The risk of punishment or the severity of punishment

In addition to examining the impact of changes in the risk of punishment on the crime rate, Langan and Farrington also looked at the impact of changes in the severity of punishment. Four measures of severity were used: the proportion of those convicted who were sent to prison; length of the sentence; actual time served; and the percentage of the sentence served. They also used a measure called 'days of incarceration at risk of serving', which combines elements of both risk and severity.[20]

A negative correlation between the risk of punishment and the rate of crime was taken as support for the theory that an increased risk of punishment leads to a fall in crime. In England and Wales they found strong support for the theory that 'links falling risk of punishment to rising crime'.[21] After 1981 the conviction rate in England and Wales fell and the crime rate (whether based on victim surveys or police records) rose. Similarly, the incarceration rate fell and the crime rate rose. However, the correlations between the severity of punishment and the crime rate were mixed. There was, however, a strong link between the severity of punishment of car thieves and the rate of vehicle theft. After 1981, in England and Wales the proportion of car thieves sentenced to prison, their average sentence, the time served and the percentage of sentence served, as well as the number of days of actual incarceration, all fell. During this time, vehicle theft rose, according to both the British Crime Survey and police records.

Was it the change in risk of punishment that explains the difference in crime rates in England and Wales? Or was it the severity of sentencing? Sentences were likely to be longer in the US. For all offences (murder, rape, robbery, assault, burglary, and motor vehicle theft), courts in the United States sentenced convicted offenders to longer periods of incarceration than courts in England and Wales, and the length of time actually served before being released was also longer in the United States. However, over the period, sentences for serious crimes generally did not increase in length in the United States, while in England and Wales sentences generally did get somewhat longer for the three violent crimes, murder, rape and robbery. Overall, this evidence is consistent with the theory that the most important factor in reducing crime is the risk of imprisonment rather than the severity of the sentence as such.

Causal effect

As with all statistical correlations it is not always clear which variable is causing changes in the other one. Is it 'A' causing 'B', or 'B' causing 'A', or is a third factor responsible for both? Some researchers have argued that changes in the size of the prison population cannot be assumed to cause falls in crime because a 'counterfactual' is involved. Calculating the incapacitation effect involves making assumptions about what would have happened in the absence of prison and this state of affairs is unknown. Others argue that the causal direction is reversed: the prison population is caused by the amount of crime, so that more crime, other things being equal, leads to more prisoners.

Steven Levitt, of the University of Chicago, has tried to identify the causal direction by studying US states in which the prison population was reduced by court decisions unrelated to the amount of crime, namely those subject to court orders that prisoners must be released to reduce overcrowding.

He found that in such states reductions in the prison population led to increases in crime, demonstrating that incarceration was the independent variable. On average, a reduction of one prisoner led to 15 Index (serious) crimes.[22] In 12 states the prison régime had been subject to court orders reducing overcrowding. In these 12 states in the three years before filing of litigation, the prison population outpaced the national average by 2.3 per cent per year. In the three years after filing it lagged behind the national average by 2.5 per cent per annum. And three years after the final court order the growth rate was 4.8 per cent below the national average.[23]

Professor Nagin accepts Levitt's analysis and agrees that 'incapacitation effects make a substantial contribution' to crime reduction.[24]

Other estimates of the size of the impact have been made. William Spelman looked at the impact of imprisonment on the violent crime rate from 1971 to 1997. He concluded that it would have dropped anyway but that the crime drop would have been 27 per cent smaller if the prison population had not increased.[25] His estimate controls for economic indicators and demographic characteristics, including the age structure of the population, and it separates the effect of prison on crime from the impact of crime on the prison population.[26] America, he says, would have been a much more violent place without the increase in the prison population.[27]

Another method of estimating the amount of crime prevented by incapacitation is to ask prisoners about their crimes during the year before they were incarcerated. Nagin's survey found that self-reports of prison inmates discovered rates of offending that varied from 5-75 robberies per year and from 14-50 burglaries per year.[28] A full year in prison would prevent these crimes. However, whilst incarcerating high-rate offenders is effective, if the offenders would have stopped anyway, prison is a waste of resources. Prior record is the best indicator of future behaviour but it takes time to accumulate a record and, as they age, offenders may commit fewer crimes. For this reason, it is important to determine sentence length so that pointless incarceration is avoided.

Some claim that the prevalence of offending in groups means that incarcerated offenders are simply replaced with new offenders. Nagin concludes that it is 'unclear whether the incarceration of one member of a group will avert any crimes'. Perhaps the group will continue with one fewer member or a new member may be recruited.[29] However, for imprisonment to have zero impact on crime, a 100 per cent recruitment rate of equally prolific offenders is implied. This seems unlikely, even in drug-dealing gangs and car-theft rings.

With these caveats, Nagin's ultimate conclusion is that 'the combined deterrent and incapacitation effect generated by the collective actions of the police, courts, and prison system is very large'.[30]

Historical comparison: England and Wales before and after 1993

The graphs draw on data from Langan and Farrington's original 1998 study until 1995. In addition, we have updated the survey crime rates for three crimes subject to British Government targets: robbery, burglary and motor vehicle theft. We are very grateful to Patrick Langan and David Farrington for supplying updated figures that permit comparison with their earlier study. The data for England and Wales are from the chapter 'England and Wales' in *Cross-National Studies in Crime and Justice* by David. P. Farrington and Darrick Jolliffe (to be published by the US Bureau of Justice Statistics).

The charts in Appendix 4 update the crime survey trends and Appendix 5 shows the imprisonment rate per 1,000 alleged offenders for the three offences for which the British Government has set targets. US figures are only strictly comparable up to 1995 and are not included beyond that date.

By 1993 the rising crime rate had become a major public concern and towards the end of that year the earlier anti-prison policy was reversed. Between 1993 and 2001 the average number of people in prison rose from 45,633 to 65,771, an increase of over 44 per cent.

The average prison population in 1993 had actually gone down from 46,350 in 1992 to 45,633, but by 1996 it was up to 55,537 and by 1997, it had reached 61,940. Even if no deterrent effect is assumed, the incapacitation effect of imprisoning (on average) another 20,000 criminals was substantial.

Crime measured by the BCS fell from over 19m offences in 1995 to just over 13m in 2001. A significant part of this fall is likely to have been due to the incapacitation effect of increasing the prison population. Other explanations, apart from the deterrent effect of increasing the risk of imprisonment, are available. Many people, for example, have taken additional security precautions (burglar alarms and better window and door locks) and avoid leaving their home empty. Car theft has been made more difficult by increasing expenditure on security devices, from steering locks to GPS tracking equipment. But these changes are unlikely to account for the whole fall.

Appendix 6 shows how the fall in crime after 1993 coincided with the increase in the prison population.

Conclusions

What do these findings tell us about the effectiveness of prison as a method of crime reduction? The comparison between the US and England and Wales showed that, for crimes such as robbery, burglary, car theft and assault, increasing the risk of imprisonment produced a fall in crime in the USA. It appears to be less effective for murder and rape, and we may conjecture that this is because the motives or emotional drives leading to these offences are less subject to rational calculation. When crimes are calculated to acquire material possessions, potential offenders appear to be more likely to weigh up the risk of being punished. People addicted to drugs may also be less likely to be deterred by increasing the risk of punishment—but it is a truism to say that they are not likely to be thinking clearly, precisely because they have fallen under the sway of a narcotic substance. But in such cases the incapacitation effect works equally well.

The historical comparison of policies in England and Wales showed that the higher rate of imprisonment from 1993 onwards was followed by a fall in crime. More than one factor was at work but it is impossible to argue that incapacitating an additional 20,000 offenders on average per year had no effect at all on crime.

Two effects led to the fall in crime in America. First, there was a deterrent effect and second, an incapacitation effect. Prison works as a method of protecting the public and deterring criminals, but some commentators are reluctant to accept the truth of this conclusion because they feel that punishment and the rehabilitation of offenders are mutually exclusive alternatives. Prison is certainly a punishment, but it is not only a punishment. As we have seen, it is also a means of protecting the public from known offenders and of deterring others. But no less important, prison also offers an opportunity to reform criminals in the hope of encouraging a law-abiding lifestyle on release. And, as the Prison Service freely admits, efforts to reform prisoners are much in need of improvement.

4

Rehabilitation

Whereas incapacitation aims to restrain offenders so that they are physically incapable of committing a crime, rehabilitation aims to change offenders so that they choose not to offend.

The background

The hope that offenders could become 'new people' has dominated crime policy for over 100 years. Hopes have usually been dashed, only to be revived again. To look back at the debates that took place in the 1920s and subsequently is salutary.

Rehabilitation is often contrasted with punishment but it has been inspired by a number of different assumptions. Two stand out.

First is the idea that offending is like an illness. Criminals suffer from a condition that can be treated using a medical model of dosage and set courses of treatment. This model is favoured by psychologists, including today's champions of cognitive-behavioural therapy.

A second tradition aims at moral reform, especially through religion. Its proponents accept that crime is a wrongful act (unlike many who champion the medical model) and believe that offenders can be persuaded to change by encouraging them to see the harm they have done or to put themselves in other people's shoes. Prisons continue to have chaplains because of the belief that they can make a moral difference and religious groups visit offenders in jail in the hope of converting them to a better way of life.

In addition, there is a third tradition that is often linked to rehabilitation. It calls for reform of prison régimes to eliminate harmful influences. They should not be brutal, bullying by inmates should be eradicated, gangs should be broken up, and activity should be constructive and designed to provide basic educational skills or a vocational qualification to help inmates earn an honest living on release. At the very least, prison should not make people worse. Despite the frequent links with the rehabilitation movement, adherents of humane reform do not necessarily advocate treatment programmes for prisoners. Sometimes it is associated with the 'back to justice' movement which advocates 'humane punishment'. Prison reform is also advocated by champions of 'good prison management' who argue that inmates should be busy to keep them out of mischief.

A Home Office report of 1895 officially acknowledged rehabilitation as an aim of the prison service:

> ... prison discipline and treatment should be more effectually designed to maintain, stimulate or awaken the higher susceptibilities of prisoners, to develop their moral instincts, to train them in orderly and industrial habits, and whenever possible to turn them out of prison better men and women, both physically and morally, than when they came in.[1]

In keeping with this approach, the probation service was officially founded in 1907 (though its role had been identified much earlier), Borstal training for young offenders was introduced in 1908, and in 1919 prison warders were renamed officers.

By the 1920s and 30s, the rehabilitation movement was dominant. The prevailing attitude was summed up by the evidence of Alexander Paterson, one of the leading champions of rehabilitation, to the 1931 Persistent Offenders Committee:

> The English Courts today, facing a young offender under 21 in the dock, are not concerned like their predecessors to weigh out a dose of punishment appropriate to the proved offence, but exercised rather to diagnose his condition and to prescribe the right form of training or treatment for the condition.[2]

This approach led to criticism of short sentences. The 1925/26 report of the commissioners of prisons said:

> ...the short sentence remains an outstanding defect in our penal system... It can also be readily understood that an impediment to the development of a sound system of prison training is the presence of a number of men who only come in for a few days, and cannot therefore be taught any work other than the simplest.[3]

Today, the ineffectiveness of short sentences is used as a rationale for community punishments but from the 1920s sentences were increased to give the prison authorities sufficient time to reform individuals. Professor Malcolm Davies and his colleagues have measured the impact of this change of ethos. In 1913, 59 per cent of sentences had been for up to two weeks. The proportion had fallen to ten per cent in 1948 and six per cent in 1975. Sentences of 12 months or more had been 1.5 per cent of the total in 1913, 16 per cent in 1948 and 28 per cent in 1975.[4]

However, by the 1970s confidence in the treatment model had waned. In 1974 a landmark article by Martinson was interpreted as arguing that 'nothing works'. The treatment model was also criticised by the 'back to justice' movement in America because it led to indeterminate sentences, such as 'ten years to life', depending on the decision of the local parole board. For example, in New York State in the 1970s, the parole board of twelve had jurisdiction over anyone serving more than 90 days. If it decided a person was 'ready', he could be released after serving one-third of his sentence or three years, whichever was less. But in 1974 a study of the New York parole board found that it had not been able to differentiate between prisoners who were a threat to the public and those who were not. Over a four-year period the proportion of prisoners returned to jail after release on parole was compared with the proportion sent back after serving their full sentence (because they had been refused parole). The results were very similar: about 10-11 per cent were sent back to jail within 12 months.[5] As a result, critics argued for 'truth in sentencing', believing that fixed sentences were more just and better able to protect the public.

An important contribution to the American debate was the 1976 report of the Committee for the Study of Incarceration, written by Andrew von Hirsch, the executive director of the project. The prevailing orthodoxy was that sentences should be fashioned in order to rehabilitate offenders or, when there seemed to be no prospect of a prisoner abstaining from crime, to protect society. The Foreword by committee chairman, Charles Goodell, described the system as 'unworkable and unjust'.[6] Sentences should depend only on what an offender had done, not on the expectations of a parole board.

It was possible for sentences to be from one day to life. In Connecticut, for instance, the sentence for armed robbery ranged from unsupervised release to 20 years in prison. Many felt it unjust that parole boards did not have to give reasons for their decisions and believed that the rehabilitation model had produced numerous side effects that were less humane than an approach based on pure justice. The committee defended deterrence as a method of reducing crime, but found it an insufficient rationale for punishment. Deterrence explained why punishment was socially useful, but punishment was also 'a merited response to the actor's deed, "rectifying the balance" in the Kantian sense and expressing moral reprobation of the actor for the wrong'.[7]

Others argued that prison was an effective method of protecting the public and that, while it might be regrettable, we did not have any better methods available. In *Thinking About Crime*, published in 1975, James Q. Wilson urged the continuation of experiments to discover how to rehabilitate criminals but in the meantime, he thought, we should view the correctional system as having a different role: 'to isolate and punish'.[8] The purpose of isolating or closely supervising offenders was obvious: 'Whatever they may do when they are released, they cannot harm society while confined or closely supervised.' He knew that some people would find this cruel, but society, he argued, must be able to protect itself against dangerous offenders. It was also 'a frank admission that society really does not know how to do much else'.[9]

Rehabilitation revival

During the 1980s, however, faith in rehabilitation was revived and often it was associated with animosity to prison. Indeed, the acknowledged failure to rehabilitate prison inmates led some critics to oppose the use of prison altogether. They criticised overcrowding and argued that prison made matters worse—mixing with other criminals meant it was a 'school of crime', and the stigma made it harder to find a job on release.

This mood influenced the British government, as reflected in the consultation document, *Punishment, Custody and the Community*.[10] It was followed in 1990 by the white paper, *Crime, Justice and Protecting the Public*,[11] which led to the 1991 Criminal Justice Act. During this period the prison population was deliberately reduced. It had increased from 43,900 in 1980 to 50,100 in 1988, and was then reduced to 45,600 in 1993. Towards the end of that year, however, the policy on prison was reversed, although not at the expense of rehabilitation. Offending behaviour programmes were stepped up at the same time.

During the 1980s and early 1990s, the chief intellectual defenders of rehabilitation were Canadians, although they had significant backing from some American academics. They had a big influence on the Home Office. In the 1990s, particularly following the emergence of the meta-analytic surveys of previous research (such as Andrews 1990, and Lipsey 1992), support grew in the Home Office for new offending behaviour programmes. The term 'what works'—a riposte to the earlier 'nothing works' scepticism—began to be adopted as the umbrella title for the new movement.

Typically 'what works' programmes employ cognitive-behavioural approaches, which seek to modify negative thought processes which behaviourists hold to be at the root of crime. These programmes are taught in a fixed number of sessions, usually over a number of weeks. Examples of 'what works' programmes include Reasoning and Rehabilitation (R&R), the Enhanced Thinking Skills (ETS) course and 'anger management' courses.

James McGuire—a forensic psychologist at Ashworth High Security Hospital on Merseyside and now a professor at Liverpool University

—edited an important study in 1995.[12] The writer of the preface, Clive Hollin, then at the University of Birmingham, revealed the semi-religious nature of belief in rehabilitation when he remarked how a small group of academics and practitioners 'kept faith with the rehabilitation ideal'. Writers like Paul Gendreau and Robert Ross, he said, had begun to 'look for new ways to argue the case for rehabilitation'.

The 1996 report of the Audit Commission, *Misspent Youth*, was also a major turning point in raising the profile and increasing the credibility of the cognitive-behavioural approach.[13] However, when the Home Affairs Select Committee investigated community rehabilitation programmes in 1998, it concluded that: 'The absence of rigorous assessment of the effectiveness of community sentences is astonishing. Without it confidence in them must be limited and sentencing policy a matter of guess-work and optimism'.[14]

Yet at about that time enthusiasm in the Home Office was at its peak. In 1998, in the preface to a major review of programme evaluations the then Chief Inspector of Probation, Sir Graham Smith, noted:

> This is the most important foreword that I have ever written. The evidence drawn on in this report, states at its simplest that 'certain community programmes involving the same population significantly out-perform custodial sentences in reducing offending. Further, we now know or at least have a beginning understanding of what makes those programmes so successful'.

He continued:

> The report offers the probation service and its many valued partners an opportunity to renew and revitalise community penalties and in increasing their effectiveness, enhance public protection and reduce offending. The principles that underpin these strategies are presented in this report. They will not be easy to achieve and the implementation phase will require long-term commitment, endurance and dedication. But the rewards will be immense in terms of increased confidence and public belief in and support for community sanctions.[15]

Given the US and Canadian evidence available at the time, such confidence did not initially seem ill-founded. 'What works' programmes did, at least in theory, have a number of clear advantages over other community or prison-based rehabilitation sentences. The weekly cost seemed low compared to many other interventions. (In 2002 the Social Exclusion Unit estimated the cost of an ETS course of 40 hours to be £2,000 per prisoner and a course for a high risk, violent offender to be £6,000. At the time the average cost of a prison place for 12 months was £37,500.) Programmes lasted for a fixed period of time, and operated on a clear medical treatment model, involving a fixed 'dose' of treatment leading to a 'cure' in a certain percentage of cases.

However, the Audit Commission report, *Misspent Youth* (1996), while accepting that the weekly costs of 'intermediate treatment' (as it was then called) were lower than those for custody, pointed out that the greater length of time involved in community treatments brought the total cost to the same level. The Audit Commission concluded: 'Community interventions are not, in fact, a cheap alternative to custody.'[16]

A major programme was introduced and in 2000-01 6,000 offenders were put through accredited courses. In 2003-04 the Prison Service target was 8,900 and the Probation Service 30,000 in the community.

Initially, the standard of evaluation in England and Wales was very low. In the report prefaced by Sir Graham Smith above, Andrew Underdown noted that out of 210 programme evaluations only 11 met the strict evaluation criteria laid down in 'best practice' guidelines. Only around half included, or claimed to include, reconviction data. In response to this report, the eminent criminologist Ken Pease, Home Office adviser, Professor at the University of Huddersfield, and Visiting Professor at the Jill Dando Institute, University of London, pointed out to the Home Affairs Select Committee that the real situation was even worse:

> I applaud any attempt by the Probation Service or anyone else to do what they do better. However, I think Andrew Underdown ... is admirably clear in showing how dire the level of programme evaluation is in probation.

He pointed out that:

- 22 per cent of services did not notify Mr Underdown of any evaluated schemes.
- Of the 210 schemes notified only 109 claimed to include reconviction data.
- Of the 109 programmes claiming evaluation which included reconviction, 22 had in fact done no such evaluation, and in others the results of evaluation were not yet available, leaving only 50 apparently worth further scrutiny.
- Of those, 15 were excluded because of poor data or recentness of programme start.
- Of the remainder, only three used reconviction periods recommended by the Home Office.

He concluded that 'only a handful of schemes merit serious consideration as evaluations. Of those which do, none seems, even at face value, to be remotely close to outperforming expectations to an extent which would offset the direct incapacitation effect of prison'.[17]

An example of the type of study carried out in England was the Swindon Probation Service study conducted by James McGuire. He followed 15 offenders treated under the Reasoning and Rehabilitation (R&R) programme and a control group of 14 offenders, who were offered an intensive job search service, but not given R&R. After six months, 21 per cent of the control group was reconvicted and 13 per cent of the R&R group. After 12 months, 64 per cent (9/14) of the control group and 38 per cent (5/13) of the R&R group had been reconvicted. However, as Gerald Gaes and colleagues point out, the results were based on unofficial outcome data collected by probation staff and no information is given about the comparability of the two groups.[18] Neither the scale of the study, nor the quality of the evaluation allows an objective observer to draw any firm conclusions.

The first scientifically valid evaluation of the cognitive skills approach in England and Wales was carried out by Mid-Glamorgan probation service.[19] Raynor and Vanstone compared 59 offenders sentenced to probation who completed the Straight Thinking on Probation Programme (STOP) with 100 offenders referred to other probation options who were judged to have a similar risk of reoffending. Results from the 12-month follow up indicated that the STOP completers' actual rate of reconviction was eight percentage points lower than their expected rates based on a set of known characteristics (39 per cent as opposed to 47 per cent). The actual reconviction rate of the other probationers was equivalent to their expected rate. However, the effect diminished after two years: the STOP completers' predicted rate of reconviction was 66 per cent and their actual rate was 68 per cent, similar to the actual rate of the comparison group. In addition, there are methodological doubts about the study. There was a very high attrition rate within the STOP group. Thirty-eight per cent of the original group dropped out before completion. This could have produced a biased result.[20]

The only large-scale systematic evidence about the effectiveness of offending behaviour programmes is based on courses carried out in prison. Cognitive skills courses were first introduced in England and Wales in 1992 and have been stepped up under the Blair Government. They are based on the idea that criminals carry out crimes because of mistaken beliefs. They might tell themselves that no one gets hurt (they are all insured) or interpret innocent actions as aggressive (demanding to know 'what are you looking at' if you catch their eye in the street) or they may simply be unable to put themselves in other people's shoes. Psychologists claim to know how to alter these attitudes and the Home Office has been increasing the number of offending behaviour programmes inspired by their theories.

Three evaluations have been published by the Home Office. The first claimed that the courses were effective.[21] However, a closer look reveals that cognitive-behavioural treatment made no real difference. The first bullet point says: 'Reconviction fell considerably after cognitive skills treatment. For example, two-year reconviction rates for treatment groups were up to 14 percentage points lower than matched comparison groups.' The report claims that this represents 21,000 crimes prevented.

However, if you read on, it turns out that the 14 percentage-point reduction was for those classified as 'medium-low' risk. There were four groups: low risk of conviction, medium-low, medium-high and high. But if you add up the reconvictions for all four groups, the rate is 44 per cent, not the 18 per cent for the medium-low group. And if you compare this proportion with the control group, the overall reconviction rate of the treatment group was *worse* than that of the control group (44 per cent compared with 40 per cent). The Home Office has pointed out in private correspondence with Civitas that the treatment group had a higher risk of offending because, inexplicably, the samples were not matched. After allowing for differences in the predicted risk of reoffending the results of the scheme were neutral. That is, overall, the treatment made no difference.

But perhaps the treatment works well with medium-low risk offenders and not with high-risk offenders, in which case it would be legitimate to break the treatment group into such categories. However, in a journal article (in *Legal and Criminological Psychology*[22]) the same Home Office researchers reported that they tested the possibility that the treatment might be more effective for medium-risk offenders. They found that there was no 'statistically significant interaction' and concluded that 'this suggested that treatment impacts on reconviction rates despite the offenders' prior level of risk of reconviction'. In other words, there was no apparent justification for breaking the sample down into groups. In any event, previous studies in Canada suggested that the schemes worked best on high-risk offenders. Andrews and his colleagues argued that the effects of treatment were greater in high-risk cases.[23] As a result, Andrews has argued that treatment should be matched to risk—a higher 'dose' for higher-risk cases.[24]

It came as no surprise that two subsequent Home Office publications in 2003 acknowledge that the schemes failed.[25] The summary of the July 2003 report states:

> This evaluation found no differences in the two-year reconviction rates for prisoners who had participated in a cognitive skills programme between 1996-1998 and a matched comparison group. This contrasts with the reduction in reconviction shown in the previous evaluation of cognitive skills programmes for prisoners, delivered between 1992-1996.[26]

The UK evidence is by no means as comprehensive as the North American evidence, as attested to by the findings of the Underdown report. Performance indicators vary widely, as do the methodologies and guiding principles of researchers. As a result, Home Office interest has continued to focus largely on US and Canadian 'what works' evidence. Consequently, many of the programmes currently accredited by the Joint Prison/Probation Accreditation Panel (now the Correctional Services Accreditation Panel) are those imported from North America. (There are a few notable exceptions, such as the Prison Service's internally-devised Sex Offender's Treatment Programme or SOTP.)

The UK evidence so far is that rehabilitation based on cognitive skills has not worked. How can the failure of the schemes in England and Wales be explained?

The meta-analyses of rehabilitation had a big influence on opinion. The Sherman study accepted their authenticity, even though the technique involved adding up the results of programmes that might not individually have qualified under their scientific methods scale. However, the meta-analyses have been challenged and a fuller understanding of these criticisms goes a long way towards explaining the poor results of schemes in England and Wales.

Meta-analysis—flawed evidence?

Despite the vast quantity of literature available, US and Canadian evaluators have for a long time had problems explaining the apparent success of rehabilitation programmes. Much of the new evidence came from meta-analysis, a set of statistical procedures which allow researchers to accumulate experimental and correlational results from a large number of independent studies. (It is commonly used in medical experiments.) Essentially, adjustments are made to allow a large number of small studies to be put into a single database where various statistical tests can be run.

The first meta-analysis was carried out by C.J. Garrett and published in 1985. It found positive effects in 111 studies of juveniles. Gottschalk and colleagues (1987) also found positive effects, although Whitehead and Lab (1989) found negative results, with some exceptions.

Andrews and colleagues (1990) looked at 150 previous schemes, and Lipsey (1992) examined 397 studies, mainly involving young offenders aged 12-21. McGuire and Priestley in summarising the findings claim that the average reduction in recidivism in these meta-analyses is 10-12 per cent.[27]

However, as James McGuire, one of the chief enthusiasts for this approach acknowledges, researchers add together the results of studies of different types which vary in the 'rigour of their experimental design'.[28] The size of a programme's effect is usually expressed as an 'effect size', a concept that is not easy for the non-specialist to understand. It is a measure of the difference between the programme and control groups relative to the standard deviation. This 'standardised mean difference effect size' allows studies to be compared. The usual range is from 'negative 1' to 'positive 1', though larger values are found. If the effect size is +1.0, the treatment group performed one standard deviation higher than the control group.[29]

Another way of representing the impact of an intervention is to convert the 'effect size' to a 'binomial effect size display', or BESD, representing the change in success (or failure) rate attributable to a treatment.[30]

An experiment with a BESD of .10 implies a difference of ten percentage points between the treatment and control groups. Assuming an overall reoffending rate of 50 per cent, the treatment would reduce offending from 55 to 45 per cent. A BESD of .05 would suggest a reoffending rate of 47.5 per cent for the treatment group and 52.5 per cent for the control, and a BESD of .20 represents scores of 40 per cent and 60 per cent.[31]

Based on Mark Lipsey's study, the average effect size for juvenile interventions (on all measures and not only reoffending) is .10 (ten percentage points between the treatment and control groups). Losel (1995) has drawn similar conclusions, implying a reduction in recidivism from 55 to 45 per cent. The effect sizes observed in the initial CDATE adult interventions would represent an average reduction in recidivism from about 52.5 per cent to 47.5 per cent.[32]

But how can policy makers decide what policies may help to reduce offending? What is actually working? One of the most respected meta-analyses is that of Mark Lipsey, and when summarising his findings, he concedes that it is not easy to establish a causal link between a given treatment and a behavioural outcome. His meta-analysis of nearly 400 programmes found that, over a period averaging about six months after treatment, untreated (treatment as usual) control groups averaged about 50 per cent recidivism (measured by police contact or arrest), whereas the average for treated juveniles was 45 per cent.[33]

The results showed great variability, explained by two groups of factors: the characteristics of offenders and the treatment circumstances. Those at higher risk showed more effects, but he warns that 'it is most important to recognise' that this relationship is 'very modest'. In general, treatment 'seems to have' much the same overall average effects whatever the characteristics of offenders.[34]

By contrast, he found that the circumstances and nature of treatment had very strong relationships to effects. There were three main factors: type of treatment, degree of researcher involvement in design and implementation, and amount of treatment delivered. However, he warns that the details of studies are often not known and that coders often end up with 'rather broad, fuzzy categories'.[35] Effective types of treatment are not easy to identify, but he was able to conclude that treatments worked better when dealing with overt behaviour and when they were employment and skill related, though in the latter case, not when implemented outside the criminal justice system.[36]

After treatment type, the second strongest factor was researcher involvement. Lipsey thought this was most likely to be because the programme was carried out as intended—it ensured 'treatment integrity'. At the same time, it was also closely connected with smaller studies which yield larger effects, perhaps because more intensive treatment was possible with smaller groups.[37] The most effective schemes—with researcher involvement, of high 'dosage' and focusing on skills, employment and behavioural principles—secured reductions of 25 per cent compared with controls.[38] Lipsey argues that the most effective treatments last at least six months and involve at least 100 hours of programmed interventions, with at least two contacts each week.[39]

Two of the most influential advocates of 'what works' in North America, Don Andrews and James Bonta, have argued that 'implementation factors' determined the level of success of particular programmes. These factors include the ability of staff to follow the course according to its strict pattern, the selection of appropriate candidates for different interventions, and matching the 'dosage' of the intervention to the level of offending being challenged. This emphasis on situational and implementation factors creates difficulties for the evaluator. If these factors are of such great importance, how is it possible to separate the effects of the content of a programme from the form of its implementation or (given the importance of researcher involvement) the particular people involved? One of the regular problems of transferring pilot schemes to large-scale implementation is that the enthusiasm and commitment of the initial investigators may be very difficult to replicate.

When trying to pinpoint the reason for effective correctional treatment Don Andrews identifies three questions and answers relating to the risk of reoffending, the needs of offenders and their responsiveness.[40]

- To whom do we offer treatment?: High-risk offenders should be offered intensive treatment.

- What do we target?: Criminogenic needs—the dynamic (changeable) characteristics of individuals.

- What methods and styles should be used?: Teaching approaches should be matched to the learning styles of individuals. Structured behavioural approaches, for example, work best for those with fewer interpersonal skills and a low IQ. Verbal approaches work better for those with verbal skills, and non-confrontational approaches for the anxious.

Despite these efforts, meta-analyses have come under strong criticism. Charles Logan of the University of Connecticut and Gerald Gaes, Director of Research at the US Federal Bureau of Prisons, argue that 'the claim that meta-analysis now demonstrates that rehabilitative treatment "works" (in the sense of being significantly and reliably effective) as long as it is of the "appropriate" type and is applied "appropriately", is seriously flawed, unsubstantiated and largely circular':

> It is often said of psychotherapy that it 'can be effective, but only if the patient wants to change'. Likewise, treatment of criminals can be effective; but only if they need to change, want to change, are amenable to change, and receive treatment that is matched to their need, desire, and amenability to change. If this is what meta-analysts mean when they say that we are now beginning to know that 'some things work sometimes,' then in fact we are not far removed from the stage of 'nothing works' or 'we don't know what works'.[41]

Logan and Gaes suspect meta-analysis as a kind of alchemy. They point out that it does not yield new findings, but re-studies old studies, deploying complex statistical procedures.

Logan and Gaes are not alone. One of the most effective critiques has been made by Ray Pawson and Nick Tilley in their widely-read book, *Realistic Evaluation*.[42] It is not only a critique of meta-analysis but also of the tradition of evaluation that relies heavily on statistical associations.

Such explanations do not allow the identification of the exact mechanisms that work, or indeed the contexts in which they are effective. Drawing on earlier theoretical traditions, Pawson and Tilley distinguish between two scientific theories of causation: the 'successionist' and the 'generative'. Successionist theories of causation are concerned to establish links between A and B which arise for reasons other than chance. The favoured method is to divide a group of people into a treatment group and a control group and to attempt to ensure that the only difference between the two is that one has the treatment and the other does not. Any outcome can then be understood as caused by the treatment. The cause, on this interpretation, is external to the people in the experiment.[43]

Generative theories try to get closer to understanding the exact mechanism at work. Pawson and Tilley give the example of gunpowder. When a spark is applied it explodes (unless it is wet, for example). A generative theory, however, would not be content to observe regularities as if the cause were external. It would also seek to understand the internal conditions that explain the explosion or lack of it. Let's take an even more mundane example from the natural sciences: the boiling point of water.

If the hypothesis being tested were that 'water boils at 100°C', then many experiments would find that it does just that. However, when several thousand feet up a mountain, water boils at a much lower temperature. Moreover, water boils at a much higher temperature in a closed vessel (such as a pressure cooker). Similarly, if salt is added, the boiling point increases (and the freezing point reduces).

We could content ourselves with these observations, but the real challenge is to understand why the boiling point varies. Natural scientists have tried to explain the exact 'internal' mechanism and came up with something like this: water is made up of molecules which, at a particular temperature, escape at the surface of the liquid to become gas. If the air pressure is high then it stops the molecules escaping; if the air pressure is low (at the top of a mountain), then the molecules escape more easily. This 'internal' theory of causation allows a fuller understanding of why water boils (turns to gas) at different temperatures.

Observation of the effectiveness of prison programmes by contrasting treatment and control groups offers the prospect only of 'external' explanations according to which something is done to agents by outside forces. Pawson and Tilley show the importance of moving towards generative causal propositions that explain the context, mechanism and outcome. In understanding the behaviour of people as distinct from physical objects it is even more important to seek 'internal' explanations, because people have minds of their own. Individuals make 'constrained choices' and do not behave in certain ways merely because of external influences.[44]

Back to the primary studies

To get behind the potential flaws in meta-analysis, Gerald Gaes, Lawrence Motiuk (Director General of Research for the Canadian

Correctional Service), and colleagues have looked at the conclusions of the leading primary studies of cognitive skills training.

Because meta-analysis does not add new findings to the existing stock of knowledge, but merely looks again at old studies, Gaes and colleagues went back to the leading primary investigations. The most widely adopted approach is the cognitive thinking skills course developed by Robert Ross and Elizabeth Fabiano in Canada (to become the R&R programme). It has been implemented in the US, Australia and England and Wales.

Ross and Fabiano identified attitudes and beliefs that were associated with crime including impulsivity, weak means-end reasoning, a thinking style that failed to appreciate the feelings of others, an inclination to repeat self-defeating behaviour, poor inter-personal problem-solving skills, poor critical reasoning, and a selfish perspective that led offenders to ignore the effects of their actions on others.

They found that therapists could reduce impulsiveness by teaching consequential thinking. Fatalistic thinking could be reduced by teaching offenders that their thoughts influenced their actions. Rigid thinking could be minimised by teaching offenders creative thinking skills. Illogical thinking could be modified by critical reasoning skills. Egocentrism could be overcome by teaching offenders how to consider other people and how to control their own feelings.

In Canada, the R&R programme was made up of 35 two-hour sessions. Offenders were taught in groups of four to ten from two to four times a week. Didactic methods were discouraged, not least because many offenders were school dropouts, and trainers used role playing, group discussion, games and practical exercises. Much effort was expended on training teachers and urging them to stick to a highly prescriptive manual.

The first large-scale evaluation was conducted by David Robinson in Canada involving 2,125 offenders: 1,444 programme completers, 302 programme drop-outs, and 379 waiting list controls. Offenders were randomly assigned to the treatment or waiting list group. Recidivism data were collected after inmates had been released for a minimum of one year. Overall, the results indicated a small significant difference favouring the treatment group: 44.5 per cent of the programme completers were readmitted to custody during the first year in the community compared to 50.1 per cent of the waiting list controls.

When the outcome criterion was reconviction, there was also a small, significant difference between the groups: 19.7 per cent of the treatment group were reconvicted, compared with 24.8 per cent of the control group. In both cases, the worst outcomes were for the dropouts, whose readmission and reconviction rates were 58.2 per cent and 28.8 per cent respectively.[45]

Some researchers have claimed that cognitive skills courses work better in the community than in prison.[46] What did the Canadian study find? Robinson found the largest treatment effect for those offenders who received the programme in the community, 131 offenders. However, there was no community-based control group, and Robinson compared the community treatment group to the control group used for the custodial sample and found a significant treatment effect. He found that 8.4 per cent of the community treatment group were reconvicted during the follow-up period, compared to 24.8 per cent of the custody control group.[47] However, the dropout rate in the community treatment sample was much higher than that of the prison group (30.6 per cent of the community sample compared to 14.2 per cent). According to Gaes et al., this high drop out rate was 'likely to have distilled the most motivated and stable offenders who remained in the treatment group', strongly biasing the result.[48] It would, therefore, be unwise to rely on it without further study.

Conclusions

In summary then, the first large scale outcome study of the Cognitive Skills program provided evidence of a modest effect in reducing recidivism of about five percentage points compared with the control group.

Gaes and colleagues concluded that the position has not altered much since the National Academy of Sciences Panel on Rehabilitative Techniques looked at the state of knowledge in 1979 and when Lipton, Martinson and Wilks (1975) conducted their review. Although their conclusions were represented as 'nothing works', a closer reading of these publications shows that the authors thought that some programmes were promising, as many others have pointed out. Gaes and his colleagues thought in 1998 that we were 'in a position to make a stronger statement, namely that correctional treatment for adults has modest but substantively meaningful effects'.[49]

However, the state of evaluation still falls a long way short of what is expected in social science at its best and there is still a very long way to go before these interventions can be relied on for public protection. The evidence so far justifies further investigation of what works and why, but not the large-scale substitution of these programmes for prison. If such a policy were pursued across the board, there would be many more victims of crime.

Investigators should aim at what Gaes calls 'strong inference' research designs. For example, the investigator should state in advance a hypothesis declaring that an input is likely to lead to a particular outcome (and the reasons why). If it is true that offenders at high-risk of reoffending are more likely to benefit from cognitive skills courses, then one hypothesis might be: 'After undergoing a 35-session cognitive skills course, male offenders aged 15-17 with more than ten previous convictions will offend less frequently than a matched group of offenders who do not receive the treatment'.

If reoffending is not reduced on every occasion then other factors, not as yet identified or at least not included in the hypothesis, are at work. There may, for example, be a 'Hawthorne effect', a phenomenon named after a 1930s study of the Western Electric Company, where researchers found that almost any intervention made a difference to behaviour because all such interventions were taken by beneficiaries as signs of concern. In medicine, the 'placebo effect' is similar.

The Paint Creek Youth Centre

It is worth looking at another primary study, this time for juveniles. Greenwood and Turner (1993) examined the Paint Creek Youth Centre (PCYC) in Ohio. Their study was awarded a three on the Maryland scientific methods scale. It is an important indicator of the effectiveness of the cognitive-behavioural approach because it follows the principles enunciated by Andrews *et al.* (1990). High-risk youths were selected and cognitive-behavioural methods were a prominent part of the scheme.

PCYC is located in southern Ohio and was established to provide a comprehensive range of services for youths convicted of serious felonies. The evaluation was designed to determine whether the enhanced services provided at PCYC improved post-release behaviour compared to the other régimes operating in young offenders' institutions in southern Ohio.

Eligible youths (defined as males over fifteen who were committed to the Ohio Department of Youth services for first or second degree felonies) were randomly assigned to either the experimental group (PCYC) or to control conditions (standard young offenders' institutions). Both the experimental and the control groups numbered 75. Most of the participants remained on the programme for at least one year, unless they were removed for disciplinary reasons.

The Paint Creek programme was divided into distinct phases, beginning with a three-day orientation period and culminating in a closely supervised transition phase, as the offender was prepared for reintegration into the community. Progression was dependent on successful completion of the previous phase. Key components of the programme were as follows:

- The centre was smaller than the control centres, with beds for 30-35 rather than several hundred.

- Security was founded on close staff supervision and attempts to enforce peer supervision; there were no methods of physical restraint, such as locks, fences or gates.

- A highly formalised system for assessing and tracking behavioural deficits (failure to attend classes, demonstrations of anger etc.) and assets (promptness, politeness etc.).

- A clear structure of incentives and sanctions for behaviour.

- Cognitive behavioural training.

- Daily group sessions of instruction, counselling etc.

- Family group therapy.

- Intensive community reintegration and aftercare.

Those offenders assigned to the control group were sent either to the Training Institute for Central Ohio (TICO), a maximum-security institution housing around 190 older youths, or to Riverview, housing younger offenders. In both institutions offenders also received remedial education and vocational training. Supervision facilities were stricter, with boys being locked in their rooms at night. Outside volunteers were relied upon heavily to provide much of the therapy, and group and individual counselling sessions were offered at the discretion of the staff.

The evaluators collected background data on offender characteristics. They found only minor variations between the experimental and the control group. A higher percentage of the experimental group were on probation at the time of arrest (43 per cent compared to 31 per cent), and they averaged more prior convictions (3.1 compared to 2.6). However, the characteristics of the two groups were very similar, suggesting that the random assignment process had been broadly successful.

The results measured the recidivism rate (percentage with at least one post-release conviction) and survival rate (time to first arrest). The results showed that the youths in the experimental group had a lower rate of re-arrest (51 per cent) than those in the control (61 per cent). However, the result was not statistically significant.[50] The only statistically significant variation in reoffending rates was for those offenders who were removed from the programme for disciplinary reasons measured as a separate group. Here, 87.5 per cent of the offenders were re-arrested.

Self-reported rates of recidivism also show no statistically significant difference. Seventy-five per cent of the experimental group reported committing at least one offence during the follow-up period, compared to 62 per cent of the control group, although there were some variations in the types of offence reported.

The failure of the programme to demonstrate a marked reduction in reoffending rates cannot be attributed to experimental design flaws common to many other programmes. It is not likely that the characteristics of the offenders played any significant part in the results. The authors performed statistical tests to adjust for any variations in background characteristics that might have emerged in spite of the random assignment process. The inclusion of these covariates made no difference to the pattern of outcomes. The authors also ensured that the Paint Creek intervention did in fact offer more services to the experimental group than to the control. Participants at Paint Creek were much more likely to have a job while in custody, have family counselling, receive drug and alcohol counselling and receive home stays. The Paint Creek staff were also found to be more positive towards their programme director and the programme itself, and happier with their jobs.

The sample size was fairly small, with only 75 candidates per programme. To detect the modest ten per cent to 20 per cent impacts that even the best interventions are expected to achieve, a much larger sample would be needed. Moreover, there was a very high rate of attrition, with 23 per cent (17 out of 75) of the youths being removed from the programme for disciplinary reasons and being sent to normal training schools.

Overall, the Paint Creek study offers no support for rehabilitation schemes with multiple components, including cognitive skills.

Dietary supplements

One of the most rigorous studies of a crime reduction programme has recently been completed. It looked at the impact of dietary supplements on offending behaviour. Drawing on theories that reach as far back as the 1942 government policy of supplementing all British children's diets with orange juice and cod-liver oil to help curb anti-social behaviour, and in the light of evidence from numerous studies conducted in the 1970s, 1980s and 1990s, Gesch *et al.* decided to look for a causal link between 'micronutrient deficiencies and antisocial behaviour'.[51]

The study, which began in September 1996, considered 231 volunteers, young adult prisoners (above the age of 18), who were divided by a random number generator into either the placebo-taking control group or the vitamin-taking experimental group. One hundred and seventy-two prisoners took supplements, while 59 took placebos, both groups taking pills for a minimum of two weeks up to a maximum of nine months. The experimental group and the control group both spent an average of about 142 days on the treatment. The vitamin/mineral supplement called 'Forceval' as well as omega-6 and omega-3 essential fatty acids were provided daily to the experimental group in the form of five separate capsules while five vegetable oil-based placebos of physical appearances identical to the real pills were given to the control group daily.

Antisocial behaviours were 'adjudicated' through Governor reports or 'minor reports' and were, therefore, subject to a standard of proof considered beyond 'reasonable doubt' before they were recorded as offences committed by participants in the study.[52] The method of analysis employed by the researchers assumed that each offence was an act independent of any previous or future offences committed.

Gesch first tested the hypothesis that 'there was no difference between the change of rates of disciplinary incidents during active and placebo supplement'. A total of 532 Governor reports and 601 minor reports were recorded over the period of study, indicating that members of the experimental group committed 11.8 infringements per 1000 person-days on average, a 26 per cent drop compared to the control group.

However, the analysis included 13 participants who failed to take their medication, six who were also taking psychotropic medication and 40 who did not complete the two-week minimum participation period. Thus, the actual sample size was adjusted to 172, reflecting the 82 remaining members of the experimental group and the 90 of the placebo group.

In order to compile more exacting results, Gesch imposed two minimum treatment periods for comparison. The original two-week minimum period was increased to 21 days, and the second was set at 28 days. Relying on 338 Governor and 416 minor reports, Gesch *et al.* found that the average number of infringements among the experimental group fell to 10.4 incidents per 1,000 person-days, indicating a 35 per cent drop, while the average among the placebo group only decreased by seven per cent.[53] In further dividing their analysis, Gesch *et al.* determined that the greatest impact among vitamin supplement users was in reducing the number of the most serious incidents (those recorded by Governor reports), as the experimental group had an average reduction of 37 per cent while the control group had only an average reduction of ten per cent when compared to baseline figures. The results for less serious incidents indicated an average reduction of 33 per cent among the experimental group and 6.5 per cent among the placebo group.

To sum up: known offenders who underwent the vitamin treatment did offend less than those who had not been subject to it. Gesch concluded, 'supplementing prisoners' diets with physiological dosages of vitamins, minerals and essential fatty acids caused a reduction in antisocial behaviour to a remarkable degree'.[54] Furthermore, Gesch argued that vitamin supplementation should be considered on health grounds alone, irrelevant of effects on re-offending rates.[55] Some critics have said that the findings are valid only for a controlled setting like prison but, in response, Gesch has pointed out that serious young offenders living independently are likely to have even lower nutritional intakes from their diets than those eating in a controlled environment. As a result, the benefits of vitamin treatment would be even greater in such cases.

Implications for policy

It is difficult to find a study of rehabilitation that does not begin with a mention of Martinson's 1974 article which is reputed to show that 'nothing works'. However, the article itself did not claim literally that 'nothing works', although it came close. Martinson's summary had been that 'with few and isolated exceptions, the rehabilitative efforts that have been reported so far have no appreciable effect on recidivism'.[56] But more significantly Martinson had dissociated himself from the 'nothing works' conclusion in 1979, writing that 'some treatment programs do have an appreciable effect on recidivism'.[57] Moreover, the co-author of the survey (the most comprehensive at the time) on which Martinson based his article has said that Martinson 'inaccurately summarised' its findings.[58] According to Douglas Lipton, the conclusion of the study was more guarded: 'the field of corrections has not as yet found satisfactory ways to reduce recidivism by significant amounts.'[59]

This conclusion remains valid nearly 30 years later. But are cognitive skills courses worth continuing? The largest-scale experiment was conducted in Canada and found only a small effect. Even this small impact has not been replicated in the UK. On this evidence, cognitive skills courses should be scaled down and the funding transferred to more worthwhile services, particularly basic education.

The overall assessment of the Sherman study about rehabilitation can be accepted as a reasonable statement of what is known so far. There is 'a body of research supporting the conclusion that some treatment programs work with at least some offenders in some situations'.[60] The rehabilitation schemes that have worked best focused on changing criminogenic attitudes or beliefs—such as antisocial attitudes and behaviour, drug use, and quickness to anger—or provided employment-related skills. The most effective schemes were highly directive, for example, by offering clear rewards for compliance with supervisors.

However, effective schemes were labour intensive and demanding of the staff, and hence difficult to replicate. Many such schemes studied by independent researchers have been found to lack 'treatment integrity', that is they were not consistently implemented as intended. In order to be effective, programmes need to address the characteristics of the offenders that can be changed and that are associated with the individual's criminal activities. For instance, raising self-esteem might be desirable, but a lack of self-esteem may not be the cause of offending behaviour.[61]

Measuring reconvictions: the key indicator

So far we have focused on the flaws in meta-analysis and, during the course of discussion, we have taken Home Office and other reconviction figures at face value. The chief disadvantage of counting convictions as a measure of offending is that most criminals do not get caught. In 2002 only 24 per cent of offences recorded by the police led to detections and only about six per cent of recorded offences resulted in convictions.[62]

However, when comparing prison with alternatives, weaknesses in the Home Office statistics must be acknowledged, a conclusion accepted within government circles. In May 2001 a review of the methods used to compare the effectiveness of different sentences was carried out for the Home Office by Denis Allnutt of the Office for National Statistics (ONS).[63] It recommended substantial changes in the method of collecting information.

In particular, it criticised the way in which information about reconvictions was collected. When comparing reconviction rates for custodial and non-custodial sentences the Home Office 'starts the clock' at different times. For custodial sentences the two years begins at the end of the sentence, whereas for non-custodial sentences it begins on the date of conviction. This fails to count the incapacitation effect of prison.[64]

The ONS review not only recommended that the start date should be the same for all sentences, but also that the analysis should be based on the date of the offence, rather than the date of conviction, to remove the need for what it called, the 'crude "pseudo-reconviction" adjustment'. Many criminals are repeat offenders and there is often a long gap between the date of the offence and the date of conviction, during which they may reoffend. When counting reconvictions by already-convicted offenders the Home Office ignores those that occur after the date of conviction for the offence currently being monitored. (The Home Office calls such convictions 'pseudo-reconvictions', implying that they are not real, when the victims might well disagree rather strongly.) The ONS argued that, if the date of the offence were the point from which monitoring began, there would be no need for adjustments. The ONS also argued that analyses should use a range of reconviction periods, rather than focusing primarily on reconviction within two years. In addition, it thought that measurement should reflect the interaction between (a) the efficacy of different sentences (as measured by reconviction) (b) the type of offence and (c) the conviction and sentencing history of the individual. The review thought that this would avoid 'over simplified conclusions' such as 'there was no discernible difference between the reconviction rates for custody and community penalties'.[65]

The review found the available data on convictions (because of the very different nature of the opportunities for reoffending experienced by prisoners and individuals being supervised by the probation service) to be a 'particularly poor proxy for offending patterns in the context of assessing the relative incapacitation effects of different sentences'.[66] It recommended that efforts should be made to devise a measure based on 'offences saved per offender month'.[67]

The ONS also recommended that offences committed in prison should be taken into account, where they were also offences in the outside world (and not merely disciplinary offences).[68] Offending ought to be measured during the sentence, after the sentence, with throughcare and without it. The incapacitation or 'public protection' effect ought to be distinguished for each sentence type.

We noted the earlier 1998 conclusion of the Home Affairs Select Committee that the absence of rigorous assessment of the effectiveness of community sentences was 'astonishing'. If it conducted a similar review today, it would find some improvement, but the evidence base still falls a long way short of the ideal.

5

Prison-Based Therapeutic Communities

Therapeutic communities for drug users—with (and without) community-based follow-up

The most difficult offenders to reform are those on drugs. One Home Office study estimates that 60-70 per cent of prisoners used drugs in the 12 months before incarceration. The Sherman study found that prison-based therapeutic community (TC) treatment for drug offenders was effective in reducing drug use and reoffending. There is also considerable evidence that the impact on behaviour weakens with the passage of time, but that the improvement can be maintained if offenders are provided with support after their release from jail.

The first TC programme for drug addiction was California's Synanon, which based some of its concepts on psychiatric therapeutic communities and on the blend of mutual support and self-help characteristic of Alcoholics Anonymous. Participation usually lasts at least a couple of months and sometimes more than a year. There are now several such schemes, including Stay'n Out in New York State, Cornerstone in Oregon, Key-Crest in Delaware, New Vision at the Kyle Unit in Texas, and the Amity Project in California.

Therapeutic communities isolate the drug-dependent offender from the rest of the prison population. This increases social pressure from other group members to commit to the programme and decreases peer pressure from outside the group. TCs often use ex-offenders and ex-addicts as staff, and work through confrontation and support groups. A set of rules governs behaviour, and group members are expected to enforce the rules against one another, often in meetings of the whole group where feelings can run high. The isolation and comprehensive pressure to which participants are subject go a long way to explaining the impact of TCs.

Stay'n Out, New York State

The Stay'n Out prison-based TC programme was begun in New York in 1977 by recovered addicts who were ex-offenders. It was

79

rather loosely evaluated in 1984, and found to reduce re-arrests for both men and women. Participants had a significantly lower arrest rate than those receiving no treatment or other types of treatment. The figures were:

	Arrests (%)
• Males on TC	27
• Milieu Therapy	35
• Counselling	40
• No Treatment	41

Drug abusers who remained in the prison-based TC for 9-12 months were also much more likely to succeed than those who left earlier.[1] The promising results in New York State encouraged other similar schemes to be established. These have now been subject to more rigorous evaluation.

Amity Project, San Diego, California

The Amity Prison TC programme was established in 1989. It serves a 200-bed unit housing men with a history of drug abuse. Modelled on Stay'n Out, it consists of three phases, lasting 12 months altogether: observation, assessment, and orientation; involvement through encounter groups and counselling; and community re-entry. When released, participants are offered aftercare in a community-based TC.

The biggest problem faced by evaluators is to avoid selection bias. Some drug addicts would have given up anyway and a scheme based on volunteers could give a false impression. One technique used to control for selection bias is to divide the volunteers into a treatment and a control group. To avoid resentment by offenders who volunteered only to find themselves being denied help, the treatment group is selected from those who have sufficient time in jail to complete the programme. Control groups are selected from inmates who also volunteer but do not have enough time to complete the programme. This 'intent-to-treat' design was used to evaluate the Amity Project, as follows.

An eligible pool was created from a waiting list of volunteers who were between nine and 14 months from parole. The volunteers were randomly assigned to the treatment group, as bed space became available. Inmates who were not randomly selected remained in the pool until they had less than nine months to serve, at which time they became members of the no-treatment control group.[2] Results were checked 12, 24 and 36 months after release from jail.

The treatment group consisted of three subgroups, each with different lengths of total time in treatment: 73 inmates who dropped out of the in-prison TC (191 days in treatment on average), 154 who completed the in-prison TC, but either decided not to participate in aftercare, or who volunteered for aftercare and then withdrew within the first 90 days (an average of 380 days in treatment), and 62 who completed aftercare (640 days of treatment, on average).[3] About five per cent of the sample who were beginning to show signs of relapse, known as 'dry outs', were returned to prison for 30 days or less. They were not counted as recidivists because the brief return to prison was considered a treatment intervention.

The original Amity sample of 715 was followed up 12 months after release from prison. After 12 months, the re-incarceration rate of those who completed both programmes—aftercare and the prison-based TC—was lower than for those in the prison-based TC alone. While 63 percent of the control group was reincarcerated within a year after release, this was true for only 26 per cent of those who completed the programme plus the aftercare. However, the moderate improvements shown at 12 and 24 months by the inmates who completed the prison TC but not the aftercare phase disappeared at 36 months.[4]

After three years there were 478 participants remaining, consisting of 189 control and 289 in the treatment group. The control group did not receive any formal substance abuse treatment during their prison stay, although limited drug education and the 12-step programme (like RAPt in the UK, below) were available.

After three years, there was a strong association between completing both the in-prison and community aftercare treatment programmes and the return-to-custody outcome. About three-quarters of the control group, the programme dropouts and the 'prison only' treatment completers were returned to custody, whereas only 27 per cent of those who completed the prison and community programmes were returned.[5] The 36-month results, based on re-incarceration after release were:

	Re-incarceration (%)
• No treatment	75
• All treatment groups	69
• prison dropouts	82
• prison completers	79
• prison TC plus aftercare	27

Key-Crest, Delaware

One of the more effective US schemes has been carried out in Delaware. It takes criminals with a drug problem, and puts them through a programme lasting 12 months just prior to release from jail. The Key programme began in 1987 as a total treatment environment isolated from the rest of the prison. Many of the staff were reformed drug addicts who had themselves been rehabilitated in a prison-based therapeutic community. According to James Inciardi, who has studied the scheme for several years, Key assumes that drug abuse is a disorder of the whole person. The person is the problem and addiction the symptom, and the programme aims to change negative habits of thinking, feeling and behaving.

In 1991 it was followed by the Crest programme, a six-month transitional residential scheme (halfway house) designed to ease individuals back into the community by means of a work-release scheme, allowing them out to work in the day and expecting them to return for evenings and weekends. When they were released straight from jail, without support, it was found that many drug users relapsed very quickly.[6]

The initial period at the Crest centre offered training focused on job-readiness, interview technique and preparing job applications. When ready, individuals were allowed out to work.

After leaving Crest, offenders were offered a place on an aftercare programme, also lasting six months, which required offenders to return once a week to the Crest centre for group support sessions, not unlike Alcoholics Anonymous programmes. During this period they were supervised by probation officers and were expected to live in 'host houses' with authorised families who had to submit reports on their activities, including phone calls.

Of those offenders who had undergone the in-prison programme of 12 months and the follow-up régime of six months in Crest and six months aftercare, 72 per cent were free of drugs after 18 months, compared with 35 per cent for the control group. The study suggests that the combined effect of completing all three stages: prison TC, work-release TC, and aftercare was substantial. Fifty-three per cent of those who completed prison TC only were drug-free after 18 months and 51 per cent of those who completed the work-release and aftercare only were drug-free.

However, after three years there had been significant attrition, with more offenders back on drugs. The results after three years were:[7]

		Drug-free (%)
•	No treatment	6
•	Key only	22
•	Crest only	23
•	Key-Crest	23

The three-year findings appear to show no significant cumulative effect resulting from the aftercare, and so the authors looked more closely at the impact of Crest's day-release programme with and without the additional six months aftercare. After three years the results were:[8]

		Drug-free (%)
•	No treatment	5
•	Crest dropouts	17
•	Crest completers	27
•	Crest completers plus aftercare	35

Of the 279 in the sample, only 21 per cent had been in the prison TC and so the authors were unable to test the theory that treatment effects accumulate over the three stages. However, they did conclude that coming from an in-prison TC did 'seem predictive of retention in the TC continuum'. They found that 14 per cent of Crest dropouts, 21 per cent of Crest completers and 32 per cent of Crest and aftercare completers came from the in-prison TC.[9] The flawed research design does not allow full confidence to be placed in this finding, but it does suggest that aftercare was sufficiently promising to be more rigorously tested.

The researchers also looked at the impact on reoffending. When the measure of reoffending was based on arrests, the results also suggest limited benefits from the combined effect of completing all three stages: prison TC, work-release, and aftercare. After three years the results were:[10]

		Arrest-free (%)
•	Control group	29
•	Crest dropouts	28
•	Crest completers	55
•	Crest completers plus aftercare	69

The Jail Addiction Services Project: Montgomery County, Maryland

Taxman and Spinner conducted a 24-month follow-up study of the Montgomery County Jail Addiction Services (JAS) Project. The project was designed to provide primary treatment services for incarcerated offenders who were likely to be released soon. The JAS programme incorporated two elements: an intensive eight week jail-based programme of treatment and case management services provided by Treatment Alternatives to Street Crime (TASC) to facilitate continued treatment within the community.

The JAS programme operates within a therapeutic community, and JAS participants were housed in separate units within the jail. Treatment consists of a minimum of 40 hours per week and includes community meetings, group therapeutic activities, self-help group meetings, individual counselling, cognitive behavioural skills building sessions and aftercare activities. In addition, the TASC case managers work with JAS participants to prepare offenders for community services.

Four hundred and one offenders on the JAS programme and 324 in a comparison group were tracked for a minimum of 24 months after release from jail from November 1991 to May 1993. Data were collected on 296 of the control group (73 per cent) and 232 of the comparison group (71 per cent).[11]

The participants were not randomly selected. The experimental group represented all offenders participating in the JAS project as part of their jail term; the comparison group was selected from a census of all offenders entering the Montgomery County Detention Centre from 1991 until May 1993. The comparison group were selected according to certain characteristics in order to ensure similarity to the experimental group. These included: residence in the same area; a criminal history similar to those of the JAS offenders; and a problem with alcohol and/or drugs coupled with desire for substance abuse treatment upon entry into jail. The characteristics were broadly similar, but, in spite of the matching process some statistically significant differences did emerge in three areas: ethnicity, legal status, and drug history. A significantly larger proportion of the experimental group were of African-American origin. Self-reported drug use and drug behaviours also differed between the groups, with a greater proportion of the comparison group reporting drug use and a desire for treatment.[12] Both groups consisted of persistent chronic offenders, although more of the comparison group had been arrested for minor charges, such as traffic offences, probation violations or failures to appear in court,

(44 per cent) compared to the treatment group (34 per cent). A higher proportion of the comparison group were on remand than had been sentenced, whereas a higher proportion of the JAS group had been sentenced than were on remand.

The JAS group had lower re-arrest rates than the comparison group, 55 per cent compared to 68 per cent. This was found to be statistically significant.[13] Re-arrest rates for new offences among the JAS group were also significantly lower than those for the comparison group, 39 per cent compared to 49 per cent. Taxman and Spinner also performed statistical tests in order to allow for the differences in offender characteristics between the sample groups. This also found that, regardless of other offender characteristics, offenders participating in the JAS programme were less likely to reoffend than those who did not participate in the programme.[14] The researchers also measured the length of time until the participants reoffended. They found that on average, the JAS group lasted 255 days until they reoffended, compared to 212 days for the comparison group.

The results also reveal evidence of the impact of post-release treatment on reoffending. Part of the JAS programme involved case management of offenders in community treatment programmes. This did not mean that all JAS participants automatically went into some form of aftercare or community treatment. Only 52 per cent of the JAS offenders took part in a community treatment programme whereas 12 per cent of the comparison group participated in such programmes. The results showed that both for the JAS group and for the control group, community treatment had a significant independent impact on reoffending. The researchers estimated that community treatment reduced the likelihood of reoffending by 34 per cent, but that JAS participation reduced the likelihood of reoffending by 43 per cent, suggesting that the main factor in reducing reoffending remained JAS participation. For both groups the researchers found that offenders who received community treatment, either following JAS, or without jail-based treatment, performed better than those who did not.

Overall these results suggest that jail-based drug treatment reduces reoffending. The study was robustly designed and was awarded a 5 on the Maryland scientific methods scale. The sample sizes were sufficiently large for the results to be considered reliable. The comparison and the experimental samples were also matched.

Some caveats remain however. Most importantly the samples were not randomly assigned. Also, only 12 per cent of the comparison group participated in the community treatment, so while the original sample was fairly large, drawing meaningful conclusions about the relative effects of aftercare treatment and jail-based treatment is more difficult.

RAPt

The nearest things to in-prison therapeutic communities for addicts in Britain are schemes run by the Rehabilitation of Addicted Prisoners Trust (RAPt). One programme was subject to an independent evaluation between August 1997 and August 1999.[15] There were 200 in the sample, 95 completers, 35 drop-outs and 70 non-starters. However, only 75 were traced for the follow-up after release, 42 completers, 13 drop-outs and 20 non-starters.

The work of RAPt is based on a 12-step programme with a strong religious focus, originally developed in Minnesota. Step 1 involves admitting the problem. Step 2 is: 'We came to believe that a Power greater than ourselves could restore us to sanity'. And Step 3: 'We made a decision to turn our will and our lives over to the care of God as we understand Him.' The underlying philosophy is that addiction can never be fully overcome and must be managed, and that the best way to recovery is to abstain from all mood-altering substances, including alcohol.[16] After a pre-admission phase for assessment of the problem, the treatment period normally lasts for 12 weeks when the 12-steps are followed and participants function as a therapeutic community. However, a TC should ideally be entirely separate from the rest of the prison and this was not possible for all the schemes. To join the therapeutic community individuals must sign a contract accepting rules, which are enforced by a meeting of the community. The rules include total abstention and participation in community meetings, during which common concerns are discussed and individual behaviour remarked upon.

The 12-step tradition was inspired by Alcoholics Anonymous, which first emerged in the 1930s. Avowedly religious, the programme is open to non-believers and all are able to interpret the 'higher power' and 'God' as they see fit. The main aim is to encourage self-denial and to provide a network of mutual self-help.

The US studies of Key-Crest and Amity show the importance of community follow-up, but for RAPt aftercare was not well developed at the time of the study. However, course completers were expected to attend sessions twice a week, to attend Alcoholics Anonymous or Narcotics Anonymous and to submit to regular drug tests.

Of the 75 followed up, 77 per cent had used drugs after release from prison. Of the completers, 62 per cent had relapsed, compared with 100 per cent of the non-starters.[17] However, many recovered from a relapse. Of those who had been released for 12 months or longer, reconviction for any offence stood at 28 per cent for completers and 52 per cent for non-completers.[18]

Conclusion

As the RAPt programme recognises, and evidence suggests, once individuals have become addicted, it is very difficult for them to become drug-free. Relapses are common. The evidence from America is that, while treatment in a prison-based TC is effective for a year or so after release, its impact weakens with time and continuous follow-up and support appear to be necessary. Much remains to be learnt, but in-prison TCs with aftercare are effective methods of reducing drug dependency and reducing reoffending.

Sex offenders

A second group thought to be resistant to reform is sex offenders.

Hanson, Steffy and Gauthier conducted a study on long-term reoffending rates of child molesters. Their sample consisted of 197 male child molesters,[19] sentenced to between two and 24 months incarceration, released from a maximum-security provincial correctional institution in southern Ontario between the years of 1958 and 1974. Thereafter, data were compiled on their reconviction rates based on the following ten to 31 years.

Hanson *et al.* used three groups to conduct their experiment: a treatment group, control group 1 and control group 2. The treatment group consisted of 125 male child molesters who had been imprisoned in the same institution from 1965 to 1973. However, follow-up data were available for only 106 of the 125. The actual treatment programme attended by members of this group varied, because the number of weeks in treatment, mode of release (parole, discharge or transfer to another institution) and the number of follow-up sessions attended differed for each participant.

Control group 1 was made up of 45 offenders who had been incarcerated in the same prison as the treatment group but in earlier years, before the treatment programme was an option. As the offenders in control group 1 were eventually transferred from the maximum-security facility to a minimum-security facility with rehabilitative programmes, they were controlled for the influences of the prison experience. The profile of control group 1 matched that of the treatment group with regard to age and type of current offence, but the control group had had fewer prior sexual convictions than the treatment group. Reoffending records were available for only 31 of the 45 members of control group 1.

Control group 2 was composed of 60 offenders from the same institution and incarcerated at the same time as the treatment group. Inmates in control group 2 remained in the maximum security setting for the duration of their sentences. The following characteristics matched those of the treatment group: age, education, previous non-sexual offences, marital status and victim type. However, control group 2 had fewer previous sexual offences.

'Reoffending' for the purposes of this study constituted 'reconviction for a sexual offence, a violent offence, or both.'[20] Hanson *et al.* explained that assault convictions were included along with explicitly sexual offences as sexual assault charges are often reduced to common assaults as a result of plea bargaining.[21]

Eighty-two of the 197 sexual offenders were reconvicted, a 42 per cent rate. The reconviction rate was highest in the first six years after release—averaging 5.8 per cent—and then fell to 1.8 per cent in the following 20 years. The reoffending rates for the three groups did not differ significantly: 44 per cent for the treatment group (47 of 106), 48 per cent for control group 1 (15 of 31), and 33 per cent for control group 2 (20 of 60).[22]

Members of all three groups were also divided into four categories, according to victim profiles: extrafamilial boys; extrafamilial girls; heterosexual incest (female children only); and children of both sexes,[23] in order to further assess the influences on reoffending rates of other factors besides the treatment programme. Hanson *et al.* found a correlation between victim type and reoffending rates, as offenders against boys were most likely to be reconvicted, followed by offenders against girls, whereas incest offenders were the least likely.[24]

Hanson *et al.* tested other variables for their effects on reoffending rates, including: victim age, history of exhibitionism, history of own sexual victimisation, poor relationship with mother, poor relationship with father, alcohol or drug use, prior non-sexual convictions, education and IQ. None of those were found to be statistically significant influences on reoffending levels. Within the treatment group, the number of weeks spent in treatment, type of release and follow-up visits post-release did not affect reoffending rates. Hanson *et al.* concluded that 'any short-term treatment, no matter how well conceived and well delivered, is unlikely to effectively control many child molesters'.[25]

Sherman *et al.* rated the study a 4 on the Maryland SMS, but stated that the findings were inconclusive. However, another study, by Nicholaichuk, quoted by Sherman, focused on cognitive behavioural treatments based in prison and found a greater variance between participants and non-participants among sexual offenders. Based on Nicholaichuk *et al.*'s work, Sherman put prison-based sex offender treatment in the 'what's promising' category of solutions, but considerable uncertainty remains.

HMP Grendon

HMP Grendon, near Aylesbury, is a specialist prison for males, run on the lines of a therapeutic community for those with a personality disorder. No one is sent there against his will. Motivation to change and willingness to participate in group work are important selection criteria. Inmates can return to the general prison system if they wish or can be sent back without consent.

Grendon operates like other prisons on a wing basis. However, each wing has a degree of autonomy and elects a representative council, which is responsible for overseeing the prison's strict 'no violence, no sex, no drugs' policy.

The régime emphasises group therapy and a communal approach. Offenders spend long periods of time discussing, facing up to and accepting responsibility for, the offence that led to conviction. They are also forced to examine and challenge the patterns of behavioural development that have led them to offend. The structure of the prison is deliberately non-hierarchical and 'progressive'. Prison officers refer to inmates by first names and take an active role in leading the therapy.

Two studies of the impact of the Grendon régime upon recidivism have been carried out recently by the Home Office. In the first, Marshall examined reconviction rates over a four-year period following release. Marshall examined a group of just over 700 prisoners who had been admitted to Grendon between 1984 and 1989. Life-sentence prisoners and some other long-term prisoners were excluded, either because they had not yet been released from prison, or had not been released for long enough to be included in a reconviction study.[26]

Two comparison groups were used: a waiting list control group of 142 prisoners selected for Grendon who did not actually go there (either because no place became available soon enough, or because they were released on parole earlier than expected); and a general prison group, made up of prisoners with similar characteristics, in terms of age, offence type and sentence length.

Marshall's main findings were:

- Prisoners selected for Grendon tended to be high-risk offenders, when compared with other prisoners of similar age, and serving similar sentence lengths for similar offences.

- Lower rates of reconviction were found for prisoners who went to Grendon than for prisoners selected for Grendon but who did not go.

- Time spent at Grendon was strongly related to reconviction—that is reconviction rates were lower for prisoners who stayed for longer periods. Prisoners who stayed for 18 months at Grendon were reconvicted 20-25 per cent less frequently than the general prison control group.

- Both mode of release from Grendon (i.e. transfer back to the prison system or release into the community) and length of stay at Grendon had an impact on reconviction rates, but of the two, length of stay seemed considerably more important.

- Treatment effects for sexual and violent offenders were less clear but, for those who stayed at Grendon for longer periods, there appeared to be some reduction in reconviction rates for sexual and violent offences—particularly among sexual offenders.

It should be noted that Marshall's findings suggested that Grendon's effects were complex. For instance, Marshall noted that Grendon seemed to have a negative impact upon offenders under 30 who had been convicted of only one previous violent offence. However, for all other offence types and age groups positive effects were recorded.[27]

The second study, using the same sample and control groups but following up over a period of seven years, was carried out by Ricky Taylor.[28] This survey had the benefit of a longer examination period (many sex offenders—who form a large proportion of Grendon's population—did not reoffend until several years after they had been released).

Overall findings from this study were broadly similar to Marshall's, although Taylor's findings were slightly more positive. While these results are not conclusive, these two surveys do suggest that Grendon has an impact on offending behaviour. In some cases this impact may be negative. The results of these surveys suggest that Grendon is not a suitable régime for younger, first-time violent offenders. However, it does seem to have an impact on the offending of groups often thought to be particularly troublesome, dangerous or beyond help, such as older repeat sexual and violent offenders.

Conclusions

In-prison TCs, especially for drug users, help to reduce offending. However, without long-term support and supervision the effects wear off quickly.

6

Prison Education and Work

Efforts to educate prisoners, along with prison work for inmates, began in the nineteenth century. Education may reduce offending in several ways:

- Offenders often lack basic skills and providing them may increase prospects for legal employment.

- If offenders are encouraged to take part in education, it may bring out better qualities, such as perseverance, willingness to work, and consideration for other people.

- Through exposure to literature and science they may come into contact with better role models or acquire greater self-under-standing.

- The discipline inevitably involved in learning may help an individual to lead a law-abiding life.

In-prison education in England and Wales

In England and Wales the scale of activity is limited, not least because of prison overcrowding. In 2001 the annual average number of prisoners was 66,301. Since then the number has increased to over 74,000. Considerably more offenders spend part of the year in jail. During the course of 2001, 141,400 prisoners were received into custody, 82,700 of them on remand.

In 2001-02 the Prison Service had key performance indicators (KPI) for education, including the number of hours spent on purposeful activity, and the number of prisoners completing accredited offending behaviour programmes.

The KPI for purposeful activity was 24 hours per week (it achieved 23.4). Purposeful activity includes education and training courses, employment in workshops, farms, kitchens, gardens and laundries, induction, resettlement and rehabilitation activities, sports, religious activities and visits.

Educational activity included basic skills, IT, social and life skills and English for speakers of other languages (ESOL). GCSEs were taught and vocational qualifications and Open University degree programmes were offered. In 2001, 6.59 hours per prisoner per week were spent on education and vocational skills training.[1]

There are no UK studies that allow us to judge one way or the other whether these activities reduce offending. Their value is that they are intrinsically desirable and few dispute that it is of the utmost importance that prison régimes should be humane and offer any willing prisoner the chance to be a better person. However, there are some overseas studies.

The evidence from overseas

It is very difficult to link education programmes with subsequent offending behaviour. Moreover, when carrying out studies it is very difficult to avoid selection bias. Prisons in most countries invariably have targets set by the government requiring them to put a certain number of people through education courses and this makes random assignment to treatment and non-treatment groups virtually impossible. Programmes vary and may include life skills, academic training at any stage from basic skills to college degrees, as well as vocational training.

Life skills

The content of these programmes varies widely. Some focus on skills needed for daily living, such as hygiene, interacting with others, and basic financial management. Others focus on skills such as conflict avoidance and verbal communication skills. No final conclusions can be drawn about their impact on reoffending.

Education in US Federal prisons

Sherman looked at two studies of adult education completed by Harer[2] that merited 4 ratings on the Maryland SMS. Harer hypothesised that offenders who participated in prison education programmes would reoffend less than those who did not take part in these programmes and that the lower rates of recidivism would be a result of the overall process of 'normalisation' (defined below), and not only of education measures. Harer selected a random group of 1,205 inmates released to American communities either directly from Federal prisons or via halfway houses between 1 January and 30 June 1987, who had been sentenced to more than three months imprisonment. He then selected the 619 who had remained in prison for over a year, to allow for sufficient time to have been spent in education programmes.

Harer divided all the inmates in the study into five groups, according to the level of education they had attained on admission to prison: '8th grade or less', 'some high school', 'high school graduate', 'some college' and 'college graduate'. He then measured the rates of reoffending for the groups, according to three categories reflecting the amount of time spent undergoing education: '0 courses per six months served', '0 to less than 0.5 courses per six months served', and 'equal or greater than 0.5 courses per six months served'. However, Harer counted all 'courses' equally for his measurements; thereby including adult basic education (ABE), adult continuing education (ACE), post secondary education (PSE: college courses and vocational training), and social skills courses (e.g. parenting), making it impossible to distinguish the outcomes according to education type.

Harer measured the following results within three years of release from prison: of those with '8th grade or less', 53 per cent of those who took part in fewer than 0.5 courses reoffended compared with 45 per cent of those who attended at least 0.5 courses; of those with 'some high school', 63 per cent reoffended versus 47 per cent with at least 0.5 courses; of 'high school graduates', 39 per cent reoffended versus 24 per cent with at least 0.5 courses; and of those with 'some college', 27 per cent versus 18 per cent with at least 0.5 courses.[3]

As participants in education programmes in Federal prisons were drawn from volunteers, Harer needed to control for selection bias. To do so, he estimated 'propensity scores' to predict the participation rate in education programmes, based on sex, history of heroin use, number of school years completed upon admission to prison, halfway house residency after prison, and age at release. He plotted the propensity scores against the probability of reoffending, and found that the most telling factor in determining reoffending was participation in education programmes. Thus, he predicted that even inmates who were the least likely to participate in education programmes would reoffend less as result of prison education.[4]

In order to isolate the effects of prison education programmes, Harer used a multivariate method. He measured the influence of several key variables on reoffending, including number of prior convictions, heroin abuse, alcohol abuse, being under criminal justice supervision when the previous offence was committed, stable employment prior to the prison-term, employment at the time of release, age, living with a spouse after release, and prison education participation. By controlling for these additional factors, Harer set out to isolate the influence of education on reoffending rates.

Harer's study indicated that any level or type of education experienced at a rate of at least half a course per six month period would decrease reoffending. However, as it considered education of any kind equally, Harer's study does not tell us about the relative effectiveness of education type, including vocational training, basic skills or academic courses.

Harer claimed that his study found that participation in education programmes lowered reoffending rates 'possibly through normalisation'.[5] Examples of normalising practices pursued regularly are: employing female officers in men's prisons; promoting humane treatment of inmates by prison staff; due process in penalising prisoners' misconduct; and providing education, prison industries and work programmes. As the advantages of normalisation for inmates include an easier transition to life beyond prison, they have the effect of reducing recidivism.

A particular weakness of Harer's study is that it did not use very refined measures of time spent undergoing education. A Texas study allows greater insight.

Texas

In a study of recidivism among more than 14,000 inmates released from Texas prisons in 1991 and 1992, Adams et al. investigated several behavioural outcomes associated with educational programmes.[6] Among other findings, this study demonstrated the importance of studying the length of time offenders participated in education. When a simple dichotomy was used—participation or non-participation—there was no relationship with recidivism (defined as reincarceration). But when the hours of participation were measured, both vocational and academic education programmes showed reduced recidivism among inmates whose exposure to the programmes was greatest. For example, inmates with fewer than 100 hours in academic programmes at the time of release had a reincarceration rate of 25 per cent compared to 17 per cent for inmates with more than 300 hours in academic programmes and 24 per cent for inmates who did not participate. Inmates with fewer than 100 hours in vocational programmes had a recidivism rate of 23 per cent; inmates with more than 300 hours in vocational programmes had a rate of 18 per cent; and inmates who did not participate had a rate of 22 per cent.[7]

Adult basic education

Sherman examined the impact on reoffending of Adult Basic Education (ABE) and training for the General Equivalency Diploma (GED), the equivalent of a US high school diploma. They considered thirteen studies, including five that were rated 3 or 4 on their scientific methods scale. Nonetheless, of the five, only one of the studies produced significant results.[8] The other four either failed to use statistical significance tests or had mixed or quite moderate results for ABE/GED training. Consequently, Sherman placed ABE/GED in the 'what looks promising' category.

Anthony Walsh considered rates of reoffending by probationers pursuing a GED (Graduate Equivalency Diploma) as compared to probationers who were not doing so. For his study, Walsh chose 50 male[9] probationers participating in the GED programme maintained by the Lucas County Adult Probation Department in Toledo, Ohio from 1979 to 1981. For the control group, Walsh selected 50 male probationers not enrolled in the GED programme, meeting the criteria that they did not have a high school diploma and that their period of probation coincided with that of the programme group. Walsh made the two groups as random as possible, although he conceded that there was a degree of self-selection within the test group, because counsellors assigned promising candidates to the GED programme. Before pursuing his analyses of reoffending records between the two groups, Walsh controlled for offenders' ages at the start of their probationary period as well as their prior records.[10]

Walsh reviewed the felony and first-degree misdemeanour records of all 100 probationers for a three and a half year period, following release from probation, including completion of the GED programme. Since some probationers had pending cases at the time that Walsh was compiling the data, he chose to compare the re-arrest rates of the groups, instead of re-conviction rates. He not only considered whether probationers were arrested, but also the number of arrests and the severity of the offences (rating them on a numeric scale). Walsh found that ten more members of the non-participant group had been arrested at least once, constituting a re-arrest rate 20 per cent greater than that of the GED programme participants.[11]

The structure of the Lucas County GED programme ensured that each student received individual attention to proceed at his own pace without embarrassment. Attendance was often compulsory as a condition of probation, but nevertheless, half (25) of the participant group failed to complete the programme.

Thirty-two per cent of the probationers who began the scheme and then dropped out were re-arrested as compared to only 16 per cent of those who had completed the programme. Walsh suggested that this was partly owing to the slightly more serious criminal histories of the non-completers. Walsh also observed a 17 per cent rise in the seriousness of the non-participants' post-probation offences, when compared to the totals of the completers and non-completers combined.[12]

He concluded that adult basic education reduced the probability of re-arrest among probationers, while offering them:

> the sense of personal accomplishment, the sense of participating in a socially valued endeavor, the anticipation of legitimate employment, and the idea that 'the system' finds one worthy enough to make an investment in time and resources to provide one with a second chance.[13]

Sherman rated Walsh's study a 3 on the Maryland SMS. Moreover, Sherman concluded that the 16 per cent re-arrest rate for GED completers compared to the 44 per cent rate by non-participants qualified ABE for the 'what's promising' category of rehabilitative programmes.[14]

Simon Fraser University Programme

Ray Pawson and Nick Tilley describe the Simon Fraser Prison Education Programme, which set out to establish a university campus in a prison. For about 20 years, over 1,000 men studied for degrees.

Pawson and Tilley urge evaluators to take a more realistic approach. In particular, they argue that social scientists should stop thinking of a programme as a 'unitary happening' which works or doesn't work.[15] The evaluators began with what they considered to be a realistic assumption: that a non-therapeutic objective like education can 'in some cases' have therapeutic outcomes, that is, reduce offending.

Such a modest aim, they believe, is more compatible with the real situation. Individual prisoners may be aged from 18 to 30. Their many years of life before entering prison will have left their mark. Some may be unwilling to allow any prison education programme to influence them. Moreover, their time inside may be a relatively brief interlude in their lives. When they leave they may revert to old attitudes and long-established friendships. The prison teachers typically have no contact with them after release, let alone any control. Any in-prison programme can therefore only realistically hope to implant some ideas, beliefs or skills that will assist a willing person to lead a law-abiding life. Whether the programme 'works' depends on much more than the programme itself.

Profiles were produced for nearly 700 men who had taken part in education for at least two semesters. Researchers deployed a predictor variable known as statistical information on recidivism (SIR) which uses demographic information and criminal history to predict the likelihood of reoffending. It allows evaluators to ask 'did they beat history or repeat history?'.[16]

The SIR prediction was that 58 per cent of participants would remain out of prison for three years after release. The actual result was 75 per cent. Two hypotheses were tested. The 'high engagement' hypothesis was that the longer and more extensive the engagement the greater the chance of success.

The second hypothesis was called the 'mediocrity hypothesis' and held that prisoners of modest ability who were offered a modest education would be most likely to succeed.

The group 1 subjects were those with three or more convictions who entered prison with a school education of grade 10 or below. Group 2 members had served all or most of their sentence in maximum security.

The offenders in group 2, who achieved above-average grades, were more likely to stay out of jail than similar offenders whose achievements were lower. The SIR prediction for above-average achievers was that 51 per cent would remain out of jail, and the actual rate was 74 per cent. If their grade achievements were below average, there was little difference in reoffending. Their SIR prediction was that 49 per cent would remain out of prison and the actual rate was 50 per cent.[17]

For the group 1 offenders with low attainments prior to jail, any involvement with the education programme seemed beneficial. Those who achieved below-average grades had a SIR prediction that 47 per cent would remain out of jail, and the actual proportion was 63 per cent. Those who achieved above-average grades had a similar SIR prediction of 46 per cent jail-free and an actual rate of 68 per cent.

Pawson and Tilley concluded that any sustained educational programme was beneficial for less able prisoners, but that for hardened offenders only highly intensive efforts were worthwhile.

Higher education

Gerber and Fritsch examined 14 studies of the effect of college programmes in prisons. Again, measurement of programme participation varied across studies, from simple measures of 'participation', to completion of 12 college credit hours, to completion of a college degree. Overall, they found that in 10 out of 14 studies, as participation in college programmes increased, recidivism rates decreased.[18]

Vocational education

Sherman analysed the effects that 12 vocational education programmes had on recidivism by adult offenders. Vocational education programmes vary in structure (some are conducted in prisons and others are undertaken once inmates are out); purpose (some hope to put offenders into stable employment and others focus on increasing inmates' education levels); and scope (some teach skills relevant to a specific industry and others provide job search assistance after release). Sherman concluded that two studies, Lattimore *et al.* with a 4 SMS rating and Saylor and Gaes with a 3 SMS rating, showed that vocational education reduced reoffending.

Sandhills

Lattimore *et al.* examined the Sandhills Vocational Delivery System (VDS), as implemented at two North Carolina prisons from June 1983 to July 1986, testing the thesis that 'improved potential to earn legal wages will reduce participation in crime'.[19]

The total sample included 591 male inmates of 18 to 22 years old, randomly divided into 295 experimental and 296 control group members. The two groups were similar in their socio-demographics, employment history and other measures related to criminality. All members of both groups had committed income-producing offences; had an IQ equal to or greater than 70; were in good health; anticipated an in-state release; and were sentenced to remain at the youth centres between eight months and three years.[20]

The VDS programme included an external evaluation of each participant's vocational interests and aptitudes, integrated academic, self-improvement and life enrichment opportunities, as well as a collaborative effort made by the case manager, course instructors and others involved with implementation of the programme. Control group members were offered some training, though at a rate routine to the prison. This meant that 55 per cent of the control group, in contrast to 65 per cent of the experimental group, were assigned to at least one vocational programme. However, the experimental group had preferential access to facilities, resulting in almost 66 per cent of the experimental group starting a vocational programme, while only 46 per cent of controls did so.[21] Therefore, while the study admitted that 20 to 25 per cent of offenders were participating in no activities (including 21 per cent of the experimental group), the experimental group did receive more services, notably completing more vocational training courses than the control group.

Two years after the subjects' release from prison, data were collected on 247 of the subjects (138 experimental and 109 control group members). Overall 40 per cent had been arrested, including 46 per cent of the control group and 36 per cent of the experimental group. According to these statistics, Lattimore *et al.* concluded that 'a stronger (better implemented) version of the VDS program could prove effective in reducing the post-release criminal behaviour of young property offenders.'[22] However, the study does not explain why data were collected on only 247 subjects, out of the original sample of 591 males. It appears that the remaining 344 subjects were unable to complete the programme. Thus, while the ten per cent difference in arrests between the experimental and control groups seems significant, the inability of more than half of the subjects to complete the study suggests that the results should be treated with caution.

Prison work programmes and vocational education

The most comprehensive study is the Post-Release Employment Project (PREP) carried out for the US Federal Bureau of Prisons by Saylor and Gaes (1992). They also carried out a follow-up in 1997.

Saylor and Gaes devised the Post-Release Employment Project (PREP) to measure the changes in prisoner behaviour after release, both professionally and criminally, as a result of prison work experience, vocational and apprenticeship training. The evaluation of 7,000 prisoners occurred between 1983 and October 1987. Offenders chosen for the study had contributed to industrial work within prison for at least six months prior to release, or had received vocational and/or apprenticeship training. Fifty-seven per cent of subjects had worked in prison industries solely, 19 per cent had prison industry experience complemented by vocational training, and 24 per cent had vocational and/or apprenticeship training.

Random assignment was not possible and a quasi-experimental design was used in which the comparison group was chosen from those prisoners released in the same calendar quarter. In order to prevent a 'selection bias' between the programme and comparison groups, Saylor and Gaes gave each offender a 'propensity score' measuring the likelihood that they would be selected for education or work. Individuals with a high propensity score were equally divided between programme and comparison groups, so that as far as possible the two groups were matched except for their participation in work or vocational training. Moreover, to further validate the findings of the experiment, Saylor and Gaes developed a 'strong inference design', based on supervisors' estimates of expected outcomes for released offenders. Their hypothesis was that an offender's performance in his prison programme should coincide with his performance once released. Thus, should the study indicate marked differences in performance between treated and untreated offenders, corresponding with expectations, Saylor and Gaes could state with conviction that these improvements were not a result of selection bias or other fault in the methodology of the experiment.

Twelve months after inmates' release, Saylor and Gaes found that members of both the experimental and control groups held similar jobs: clerical/sales, structural (welding, painting, plastering, cementing, construction) and miscellaneous (transportation, amusement, recreation). Nonetheless, in prison, the training for the experimental group had focused on bench work (fabrication, assembly, repair of metal products, electrical products) because this was considered to be learning a skill.

Of the inmates who left prison and moved on to halfway houses, 87 per cent of the experimental group had full-time jobs and nine per cent had day-labour jobs, while only 62 per cent of the control group were employed full-time and one per cent were day labourers. Employment levels for the study overall indicated that 71 per cent of the experimental group were likely to be working while only 63 per cent of the control group were; thus, inmates who had experienced prison work and vocational and/or apprenticeship training were 13 per cent more likely to be employed at 12 months after their release. Moreover, members of the experimental group reoffended 35 per cent less frequently than members of the control group.

In 1995, Saylor and Gaes consulted the Bureau of Prisons records, looking at the same inmates who had been released for eight to 12 years since the initial phase of the study, to see how many of them had been recommitted to federal prisons for new offences or had violated the terms of their release.[23]

In 1995, when these records were searched, if an offender had not been returned to prison, he or she would have been released a minimum of eight years without a federal reconviction. Many of these former PREP study participants had been released for 12 years. Although there were no significant programme effects among women, there were significant differences among the men.[24]

The results were the following: inmates who had worked in prison industries were 24 per cent less likely than the control group to have reoffended; those who had undergone vocational or apprenticeship training were 33 per cent less likely to have reoffended; and those who had participated in all three programmes were 23 per cent less likely to have reoffended. Thus, Saylor and Gaes concluded that there are measurable impacts on recidivism rates as a result of prison industry work, vocational and/or apprenticeship training. These effects are strongest for vocational education.

Saylor and Gaes also investigated the impact of vocational-technical training in the Federal Bureau of Prisons on internal discipline. They found that 'inmates who received vocational training while in prison showed better "institutional adjustment" (fewer rule violations) than those who did not receive such training, were more likely to complete stays in a halfway house, were less likely to have their paroles revoked, and were more likely to be employed' after release.[25]

Conclusions

It is always difficult to evaluate the impact of prison work and education on reoffending. As Pawson and Tilley have remarked, education is only part of the prison experience and it is not easy to determine what elements had the most impact on subsequent behaviour. Moreover, once released, the prison experience itself may be only a small influence on the life of a former inmate. The ultimate test of success is whether offending has been reduced, but there are other worthwhile output measures, including teaching prisoners both basic and work-oriented skills, so that they are equipped to earn an honest living if they choose to reject crime. We cannot say that both prison and community punishments have failed merely because offenders make a free choice not to take advantage of the skills provided during their sentence.

However, the largest-scale study by Saylor and Gaes shows that participation in prison industries and vocational education had beneficial effects and helped to reduce reoffending.

7

Intensive Supervision in the Community

Government policy reflects two potentially contradictory lines of thought. Many in the Home Office are hostile to prison and want to reduce its use, but their influence has been tempered by the acknowledgement that community sentences do not adequately protect the public. This realism has led the Government to the search for 'tough community sentences' that are a 'credible alternative to custody', including community sentences with multiple conditions like tagging, reparation and drug treatment and testing. It is imperative, according to the Government, that 'we have a correctional system which punishes but also reduces reoffending through the rehabilitation of the offender'.[1] Consequently, it says, a genuine third option is needed in addition to custody and community punishment.

Intensive Supervision and Surveillance Programme

The most important of these third options to be implemented so far is the Intensive Supervision and Surveillance Programme (ISSP) which began in April 2001 with an investment of £45m over three years.

According to the white paper, *Justice for All*, ISSP is the most rigorous non-custodial intervention available for young offenders. It initially targeted 2,500 of the most serious and prolific young offenders (aged 10 to 17) per year. They were thought to be responsible for a quarter of all youth crime. ISSP is available for convicted young offenders and for persistent young offenders on bail to prevent them from committing more crimes while awaiting trial. According to the Youth Justice Board (YJB), the most serious offenders are defined as those who have been charged or convicted of an offence and have either been charged or warned for an imprisonable offence on four or more separate occasions within the past 12 months, or previously received at least one community or custodial penalty.

Most participants will spend six months on ISSP. The most intensive supervision (25 hours per week) lasts for the first three months of the programme, after which the supervision continues at a reduced intensity (a minimum of five hours per week) for a further three months.

Young offenders on ISSP can be subject to intensive monitoring for up to 24 hours a day, seven days a week if necessary (although usually it is for a far shorter period). Electronic tagging and voice verification (telephone checking of an offender's 'voice print') can be used to monitor offenders, as well as intelligence-led policing and 'tracking' of their movements by case workers from the Youth Offending Team. The minimum requirement is for two surveillance checks per day.

The structured programme of activities for 25 hours a week for three months can include education and training, interventions to tackle offending behaviour and reparation to victims.

The YJB claims that ISSP is based on the best evidence of what will reduce the frequency and seriousness of offending. It promises to bring structure to offenders' lifestyles, and to tackle the factors contributing to their offending behaviour, lack of educational qualifications, weaknesses in thinking skills, or drug misuse. But what is the evidence suggesting that ISSP is likely to be successful?

The Sherman study looked at similar schemes in the US, variously called intensive community supervision or Intensive Supervised Probation (or Parole) (ISP). It found that ISP, including schemes under which offenders were tagged, did not reduce offending. However, the Sherman study thought that combining restraint with rehabilitation might improve the record of these schemes.

Evidence from England and Wales

First, what is the evidence so far in England and Wales? Until September 2004 the main evidence drawn from England and Wales was based on a pilot scheme in Rotherham, conducted from August 2000 to June 2001. The government web site[2] was claiming in September 2004 that 27 young offenders in Rotherham had been convicted for 160 offences in the nine months before the scheme, but during the programme they committed only 47 offences.

The final evaluation of the Rotherham Intensive Supervision, Support and Advocacy Programme (RISSAP) does conclude that the scheme was successful but a careful reading suggests why the report was never published in full. It found that seven per cent more of the programme group did not offend by comparison with the control group. However, the programme group was 35 strong and the control group 18. Seven out of 18 members of the control group (39 per cent) and 16 out of 35 members of the programme group (46 per cent) did not offend. Therefore, if one person had changed sides in each group, so that eight out of 18 (44 per cent) control-group members and 15 out of 35 (43 per cent) programme-group members had not reoffended, the result would have been reversed. This is hardly a scientifically valid study on which a multi-million prog-ramme ought to be based. Yet a large number of schemes were established in April 2001 and more in July 2001 on this evidence. In April 2003 another variation was introduced, the Intensive Control and Change Programme for 18-20 year-olds. It was similar to ISSP with a sharper focus on a scheme for compensating victims.

Tagging improves compliance with rehabilitation programmes

A Youth Justice Board 'briefing' about ISSP was available on its web site until mid-2004. This online briefing was said to based on 'research collated by Oxford University and PA Consulting'. Among its claims was this: 'Research from Canada has shown that electronic monitoring can aid effective rehabilitation by improving compliance with more rehabilitative community interventions.' The source for this claim is given as 'Bonta, Rooney and Wallace-Copreta, *Electronic Monitoring in Canada*, 1999.'[3] This sentence from the Youth Justice Board briefing, however, reports only part of the Canadian findings, and the least significant at that. Moreover, closer examination reveals it to be a carefully worded sentence that manages to be highly misleading without being completely untrue.

The main finding of the study, *Electronic Monitoring in Canada*, was that recidivism rates of offenders did *not* change significantly as a result of electronic monitoring (EM). The study considered three methods of punishment and control: EM, probation and prison. The crude scores initially suggest a benefit from EM. Reconviction rates were 27 per cent for EM participants, 33 per cent for probationers and 38 per cent for offenders who had been imprisoned.[4] However, the three groups were not equal. They had all been assessed on a 'risk-needs' scale previously found to be a reliable indicator of future offending. The report concluded that the 'lower recidivism rates found with EM participants could be explained by the differences in risk-needs levels'. Consequently, the reduced reoffending was not the result of the type of sanction. The researchers concluded that adding electronic monitoring to the supervision of offenders had 'little effect on recidivism'.[5] Moreover, they found no lasting post-programme effect on criminal behaviour.[6]

Offenders also took part in an intensive treatment programme, based on cognitive-behavioural psychology, consisting of 2.5 hours of treatment per day for four days a week. Those on EM and probation were combined to form a treatment group and compared with a control group of offenders who had been sentenced to prison. The overall result showed slightly worse results for the treatment group (32 per cent reoffended compared with 31 per cent of the control). However, when the groups were divided according to their risk-needs score it was found that recidivism for high-risk offenders in the treatment group was lower than for those in the control group (32 per cent compared with 51 per cent). The researchers conjectured that the educational scheme was more effective for high-risk offenders, although they were unable to explain why. Treatment resources, they said, were 'wasted' on low-risk offenders.[7]

The only benefit of EM was the one mentioned by the YJB, namely that tagged offenders who attended the educational programme were more likely to complete it than the probationers (87.5 per cent for those on EM and 53 per cent for those on probation). However, the probation sample was small (17 people) and the researchers thought that the additional requirements of EM, including 'the threat of a return to prison for non-cooperation' might explain the difference.[8]

Thus, the YJB claimed that this scheme was evidence of the efficacy of tagging under a community sentence, when it is really evidence of the deterrent effect of prison. A more impartial summary of the Canadian findings would have been that electronic monitoring made no difference to reoffending, that the rehabilitation programme also made no overall difference (when all risk groups were combined), but that the threat of a return to prison encouraged those on electronic monitoring to complete the rehabilitation course. Altogether, these findings do not add up to a very powerful case for an ISSP scheme which combines tagging and rehabilitation in the community. It is, therefore, not surprising that ISSP failed to reduce offending (see below).

Home detention curfew

The Government not only believes that tagging increases attendance of rehabilitation courses, it also relies heavily on tagging to protect the public from offenders serving community sentences. However, the only study of tagging to look at the impact on reconviction rates found that it made no lasting difference.

The best evidence we have so far is from the home detention curfew (HDC) scheme. The scheme was introduced throughout England and Wales in January 1999. The Home Office has reported on the results after the first 16 months of the scheme.[9] Prisoners could be released for up to 60 days (increased to 90 days from December 2002 and to four months from July 2003) before the normal end of their sentence. The original maximum period of tagging was 60 days and the minimum 14. The curfew applied for a minimum of nine hours and a maximum of 12.

Mr Blunkett claimed that tagging was an important part of his strategy for cutting reconviction rates. In a press release (21 March 2002) about the home detention curfew he said:

> Reconviction rates are dramatically lower for those who have been released under HDC than those who have served the final weeks of their sentence in prison. It is an important part of our crime reduction package and our drive to cut reconviction rates.

This statement implies that tagging will lead to a reduction in reoffending, but a closer look reveals that the lower reconviction rate reflects the selection process. Prisoners chosen for early release under HDC were considered by prison governors to be less likely to reoffend, and were released for that reason. A Home Office study of reoffending by prisoners released under HDC did find a lower rate of offending, but effectively only confirmed that prison governors made reasonably reliable assessments of the risk of reoffending. There was no lasting effect on reoffending once the tag had been removed.

The Home Office study looked at the first 16 months of HDC, during which 21,400 prisoners had been released under the scheme, of which 1,100 (five per cent) were recalled to prison because they failed to comply with the conditions. The re-conviction rate during HDC was 2.1 per cent.[10] The reconviction rate for those subject to HDC during the six month period after their automatic release date was 9.3 per cent, compared with a rate of 40.5 per cent of those who were refused HDC.[11] The Home Office researchers accepted that this is evidence that prison governors made accurate assessments of the risk posed by offenders. But what is the evidence that tagging has a more lasting effect on reoffending? Moreover, under ISSP, tagging is applied to serious offenders, not those hand-picked by prison governors because they are believed to present a low risk to society.

Reasonable people could disagree about whether or not early release under tag has been justified. Tagging is cheaper than prison and releases prison space. These benefits have to be set against the cost in human suffering and money of the crimes that were committed but which would have been prevented by imprisonment.

To gain more insight into the enduring effect of tagging, a short-term reconviction analysis was carried out on a sample of prisoners who were eligible for discharge under HDC in May and June 1999, some of whom were released on HDC and some of whom were not. This programme group was compared with a control group of similar prisoners discharged in October and November 1998 who would have been eligible for consideration for HDC had.it been in force at the time.

In the six months after the normal discharge date, offenders eligible for HDC in 1999 had very similar reconviction rates to the 1998 control group (30.5 per cent and 30 per cent respectively, or 30.8 per cent and 30 per cent if offences during the curfew period were included). The rates of reconviction were much higher for some groups, defined by their original offence. Of those serving a sentence for violence against the person, six per cent were reconvicted within only four months; of those sentenced for theft, 11 per cent had been reconvicted within four months; and of those sentenced for burglary, 22 per cent had been reconvicted within four months.[12] The researchers concluded that the impact of HDC on reoffending was 'broadly neutral' when compared with the results for the control group.[13]

To sum up: HDC is neutral in its impact on reoffending. While they were tagged for up to 60 days, it had a restraining effect on offenders, though not as powerful as prison, which prevented any offences being committed against members of the public. But it had no lasting effect on offending behaviour.

Conclusions

There are two main elements of the new community sentences, summed up by the name of the latest variant, the Intensive Control and Change Programme (ICCP). This scheme is for 18-20 year-olds but similar principles are applied to other age groups, under the name Intensive Supervision and Surveillance Programme (ISSP).

The 'change' element includes teaching educational skills, both general and vocational, and providing 'offending behaviour prog-rammes' inspired by cognitive behavioural therapy. What we know about the effectiveness of these programmes suggests they are highly imperfect substitutes for prison. The 'control' element includes curfew or home detention and monitoring by probation officers.

The UK evidence so far suggests they have little long-term effect. But how effective have such schemes been overseas?

Overseas Evidence

By the early 1990s most US states had developed some type of intensive supervision programme. Expectations had been raised by studies of New Jersey and Georgia which suggested that ISP led to a significant decrease in re-incarceration (Erwin 1986) and re-arrests (Pearson 1987). However, the National Institute of Justice (NIJ) funded RAND to evaluate fourteen ISP programmes in nine states using an experimental design with random assignment of offenders to ISP and control groups.[14] Recidivism was measured using arrests and technical violations.

When ISP participants were compared to the control group, there were no significant differences in arrests. At the end of the one-year study period, about 37 per cent of the ISP participants and 33 per cent of the control group had been arrested. Moreover, technical violations were found to be 65 per cent for ISP participants compared with 38 per cent for the controls. In other words, while there was no evidence that the increased surveillance in the community deterred offenders from committing crimes, it did seem to increase the probability that both criminal and technical violations would be detected.

In a study of Minnesota, also commissioned by the NIJ, Deschenes, Turner and Petersilia (1995) drew similar conclusions. One group was sentenced to ISP instead of prison and the other was sentenced to ISP after release from prison. As Petersilia and Turner's earlier study found, there was no significant difference between groups.

There is a tendency to describe the schemes as both 'aftercare' and 'intensive supervision in the community' and it is in practice very difficult to distinguish between the two elements. In general 'aftercare' implies the provision of services for offenders with the intention of encouraging behavioural change or overcoming personal problems thought to be the cause of their offending. Intensive supervision, however, implies a measure of incapacitation due to increased surveillance. Here we are focusing on intensive supervision; aftercare is discussed in a separate chapter. The remainder of this chapter describes three schemes, all independently evaluated according to the highest methodological standards.

North Carolina Court Counsellors' Intensive Protective Supervision Project

The Intensive Protective Supervision Project (IPSP) was evaluated by Land and his colleagues between 1987 and 1989. The study was awarded a five on the Maryland scientific methods scale. This was a randomised study that followed so-called 'status offenders' (total sample number not reported). A status offender is defined as a juvenile under sixteen who either (a) has run away from home, (b) is unlawfully absent from school, (c) is regularly disobedient to parents or guardians to an extent beyond their disciplinary control, or (d) is regularly found in places where it is unlawful for a juvenile to be. The juveniles varied widely in their status and offending behaviour: some had already been referred for delinquent behaviour and others had not previously come to the attention of the authorities.

The offenders in the experimental programme were all assigned counsellors, who had a far lower caseload than normal and so could spend more time with the offender, and who had a budget with which they could commission external services, such as child therapy. The programme started with an initial appraisal to establish the programme objectives for the subject, followed by frequent home visits and organisation of a programme of therapeutic interventions. Those in the control sample were offered 'standard protective supervision'. They too had a counsellor, but this individual had a far higher caseload (35 to 50 concurrent cases compared to no more than ten for counsellors on the IPSP experiment). They had a requirement to contact the participant only once every 90 days.

Land used three measures: whether juveniles were charged with one or more delinquent offences during their period of supervision, whether they were charged with one or more status offences,[15] or whether offenders were deemed to have succeeded on the programme.[16]

It was found that, for youths with no prior delinquent offence records, those in the treatment group were referred less frequently than the control group for delinquency offences (12 per cent compared to 27 per cent). However, the rate of reoffending for status offences was almost identical (21.4 per cent compared to 21.6 per cent). The percentage deemed to have completed the course successfully was higher for the treatment group (71 per cent compared to 49 per cent). This was statistically significant. However, the definition of success included a number of subjective factors, determined by the aftercare worker. Indeed, evaluators noted that some counsellors' definitions of 'success' included 'any significant progress whatsoever'.

For youths *with* prior delinquent offences, Land found different results. He reported a higher rate of reoffending for the experimental group for delinquent offences (57 per cent), than for the control group (33 per cent). However, the status offence rate was much lower among the experimental group (zero per cent compared to seven per cent).

These mixed results may have something to do with the fact that the sample size for the youths with prior delinquent convictions was fairly small. The experimental group had 13 members with one or more prior delinquent referrals (14 per cent) and the control group had only seven (eight per cent).

Apart from this distortion, the study design is fairly rigorous. It employed a random assignment design and allowed for a prolonged follow-up period. Statistical tests were performed to control for offender demographic characteristics—race, age, gender and offending history—and these showed that the treatment effect remained substantial and statistically significant for all participants. There was no statistically significant variation in the rate of attrition over the course of the experiment.

However, what is not clear from the experimental design is whether the perceived positive impact of the programme comes from the increased supervision or from the IPSP treatment programme, i.e. whether youths had less opportunities to offend and faced a greater likelihood of sanction, or whether youths were less inclined to offend thanks to professional counselling, team meetings and service plans, etc. This study does not make it possible to disentangle the two effects.

Intensive aftercare probation

Sontheimer and Goodstein designed a study to measure the 'aftercare' versus the 'system response' effects of a juvenile intensive aftercare probation (IAP) programme in Philadelphia.[17] Their evaluation was awarded a 5 on the Maryland scientific methods scale. The researchers sought to examine whether the IAP reduced offending, and if so, whether this was a result of the aftercare provided; that is, whether the offender's behaviour had been materially altered by the services received, or whether this was a result of increased supervision and speedier interventions on the part of probation officers, which would reduce the opportunities for committing crime. The programme was established in 1988 and the evaluation was funded as part of its implementation.

The sample participants were male delinquents committed to the Bensalem Youth Development Centre (YDC). Eligible youths had one prior adjudication for aggravated assault, rape, involuntary deviate sexual intercourse, arson, robbery or a felony-level drugs offence, or at least two prior adjudications for burglary. One hundred and six eligible youths were randomly assigned either to a control group or to the experimental group. An additional 52 cases were also considered for inclusion in the programme, either as replacements for participants in the programme or to supplement the data. Forty-two of the original subjects had to be replaced, for various reasons, including absconding or early release. Allowing for sample attrition for all reasons, the final study was based on the results of 44 experimental and 46 control cases. All of the cases were released from the YDC between December 1988 and January 1990. The participants were tracked for a period of three to sixteen months.

According to IAP guidelines, participants assigned to the experimental programme were meant to receive three face-to-face contacts per week with their IAP officer for the first six weeks. This would be reduced after six weeks, on the basis of satisfactory progress, to two contacts a week, and after twelve weeks, to one. In addition, the IAP officers were to maintain at least weekly contact with the offender's parents or guardians, and one fortnightly contact at least with school authorities or employers. At least 30 per cent of their contacts with the offender were to be made outside normal hours, during evenings and at weekends. No particular treatment philosophy was emphasised; the services offered or brokered by IAP officers and the emphasis of the individual programmes were left to the discretion of staff. There was no electronic monitoring or drug testing. The caseload for IAP officers was no more than 12 offenders at any one time, compared to a caseload of 70 to 100 offenders for the standard probation service.

The control group was offered a standard probation service. Probation officers were required to see clients twice a month following release. Services were offered to participants at the officers' discretion.

The sample groups were analysed, to check that they had comparable characteristics, and that the IAP did in fact offer a greater level of supervision and service than standard probation. There were slight, statistically insignificant differences in the most serious offence for which offenders had been incarcerated. There was a statistically significant difference in the number of problems at school, with the experimental group displaying more behavioural problems. However, apart from these two differences, the two sample groups were found to be comparable.

The data collected on the implementation of the programme showed that the IAP officers made about ten times as many contacts with the participants after release than the control group officers. For the first six months after release the experimental group had an average of 16.7 contacts, compared to 1.3 contacts for the control group. The experimental group had more preparatory contacts with their IAP officers while still incarcerated (10.1 compared to 5.1). IAP officers had about ten times the number of contacts with parents, schools and other service providers as the standard probation officers. For each of the first six months after release, the IAP officers made approximately ten per cent of their visits on weekends, 20 per cent fewer than guidelines required, but considerably more than standard probation (almost zero). In general, while the implementation of the IAP programme did not quite fulfil expectations, for the purposes of the evaluation, the experimental group did receive far more attention than the control group.

Two potential effects were measured by the study of re-arrest and reconviction rates—the 'aftercare' effect and the 'system response' effect. The first presupposes that the individual's propensity to commit crime is altered by the process of aftercare. Increased contact, greater opportunity to arrange employment and education, and advice from the probation officer may all help offenders to change their patterns of behaviour. The system response effect does not presuppose any change in the propensity to commit crime by the individual. Rather it relies on probation officers being able to detect violations or potential violations much faster than would otherwise be the case, allowing them to incapacitate offenders, thus reducing their opportunity to offend. Disentangling the two effects is very difficult, and isolating any causal links from the statistics even more so.

When looking at rates of reoffending a number of factors might be operating. If the 'system response' effect is at work, we might expect that the proportion of reoffenders remains the same (as their criminal behaviour is not fundamentally changed), but the total number of offences committed might be reduced because offenders are incapacitated faster after a transgression and have less opportunity to reoffend. If the 'aftercare' effect is at work, then we might expect the proportion of reoffenders to go down. The rate of reoffending might be reduced due to any one of these effects, but intensive supervision might also result in a *higher* reoffending rate. Increased supervision and surveillance might mean that probation officers have their clients taken back into custody for more minor offences, or indeed higher re-arrest rates might simply reflect the actual number of offences taking place—those that are otherwise missed by normal probation officers. Looking at straight reconviction rates is problematic, therefore.

The usefulness of the data can be improved in a number of ways. The actual numbers of crimes being committed rather than those being simply identified by re-arrest can be corroborated using self-reported crime figures. The effect of IAP officers being 'alert to more crimes' is modified in this way. Breaking down the arrests by offence can also help to identify those offences related to closer supervision, such as violations of probation, in comparison to those that the participant would commit regardless of supervision. Measuring the re-arrest rate by 'time at risk' rather than the total time following release also allows researchers to control for the greater likelihood that the programme group will be taken off the streets due to closer supervision. Moreover, researchers calculated a re-arrest rate for each subject; that is, the number of times the offender reoffends during the 'at risk' period.

Measuring the percentage of subjects re-arrested over the whole period, fewer IAP participants were re-arrested compared with the control group (50 per cent compared to 74 per cent), a statistically significant difference. Looking at felony (more serious) arrests alone 25 per cent of the experimental group were re-arrested, compared to 41 per cent. However this difference is not statistically significant, due to the small number of total felony arrests (30).

The researchers also measured the frequency of re-arrests: the number of arrests per offender during the time at risk. The experimental group showed a significantly lower level of re-offending than controls for all types of offence (1.65 mean annualised re-arrests compared to 2.79 mean annualised re-arrests), and for felony arrests alone (0.41 felony re-arrests compared to 0.76 re-arrests).

As to the relative effects of the aftercare component and increased surveillance, the authors concluded that the two types of effect cannot be satisfactorily separated. Interviews with probation officers did indicate that IAP officers tended to pick up transgressions faster than their 'normal probation' counterparts; however, the design of the study meant that the reasons behind the results remained difficult to isolate.

Wayne County in-home ISPs

Barton and Butts evaluated three in-home intensive supervision programmes as alternatives to commitment to residential programmes. Their evaluation was awarded a 5 on the Maryland SMS.[18]

The most severe course of action available to Michigan juvenile courts, short of transferring offenders to an adult court, was to commit young offenders to the state Department of Social Services (DSS) for supervision and placement. The majority of young offenders were then sent to residential training schools. As a response to growing numbers of commitments, the state limited the number of offenders it would accept from 1983 onwards to 500 per year. Wayne County, in turn, implemented three experimental programmes to provide alternative services to youths who would otherwise be committed. While the three differed slightly in structure and treatment focus, all had in common intensive probation services, provided in the community, using small caseloads and frequent contact.

The authors conducted a randomised study comparing in-home ISPs to conventional interventions with youth offenders. This was not an evaluation of ISPs as an alternative to incarceration *per se* but rather as an alternative to commitment to the DSS. However, about 80 per cent of youths committed to the DSS were placed out of the home, and of these 90 per cent were placed in institutions, i.e. 72 per cent of the control group were incarcerated in some form.

Between February 1983 and March 1985 every youth recommended by the juvenile court for commitment to the DSS was screened for eligibility. Very violent offenders, those with a history of psychiatric disturbance, and those with no potential home to go to were excluded. Five hundred and eleven eligible participants were randomly assigned to one of the three experimental programmes (326 youths) or the control group (185 youths). Each youth was followed for two years and reoffending rates were measured.

All three experimental programmes restricted caseloads to between six and ten youths per worker. The programmes were expected to last for approximately one year. The amount of contact varied between the programmes. The Michigan Human Services (MHS) programme had an average of 14 contacts with the young offenders each month, and the other two programmes, the Intensive Probation Unit (IPU) and the Comprehensive Youth Training and Community Involvement Programme (CYTCIP), averaged between 10 and 11 contacts per month. The pattern of home contacts and site contacts reflected the content of the particular programmes. MHS, the most family-focused programme, had more than six home contacts per month, compared to four for IPU and two for CYTCIP. CYTCIP, with an on-site educational and recreational emphasis had more than five programme-site contacts per month, compared to the other two (less than two). IPU placed emphasis on behavioural supervision, and resembled probation but at a more intensive level, with increased levels of contacts of all forms. All of the programmes employed behavioural supervision and individual counselling with nearly every youth. School placement and social skills training were also used frequently. Again the service delivery in each programme reflected differing emphases, CYTCIP having a high participation rate in youth groups and recreational activities, MHS making use of parent counselling and parent groups.

In spite of the differences between the programmes, the outcomes for all three were fairly similar. The proportion of offenders who completed their programmes was similar for all three programmes, on average, 46 per cent. Those who did not, in most cases, had their programmes terminated because they reoffended or failed to comply with programme requirements.

During the follow-up period, 78 per cent of the in-home programme youths reappeared in an adult or juvenile court, compared to 53 per cent of the control group. However, this does not take into account the relative amounts of time that the offenders were actually in the community and therefore at risk of offending (the control group having spent more time incarcerated). The authors, therefore, estimated the level of offending had all offenders been at large for the entirety of the 24-month period. They did so by dividing the number of charges filed against the offenders by the number of months 'at risk' and then multiplying by 24 to give a two-year offending estimate. After adjusting for time at risk, the official recidivism of the experimental and control groups was found to be fairly similar. Thus, while the experimental group had significantly more charges (2.63 per case) than the control group (1.31), the differences when time at large is taken into account are not statistically significant, 5.41 charges per case compared to 4.05. Looking at criminal charges only, the rates are almost identical.

The researchers also looked at the most serious offence for which the youths were charged. Control youths tended to be charged for more serious offences than the experimentals. 25 per cent of the experimental group committed less serious 'status offences', compared to ten per cent of the control group. Offending rates for vehicle theft (13 per cent versus 15 per cent) and breaking and entering (ten per cent versus 12 per cent) were similar, but the percentage of serious crimes was higher for the control group (4.4 per cent of the experimental group for armed robbery versus 6.6 per cent for the control; and three per cent of the experimental group committed rape, attempted murder or murder versus 7.5 per cent for the control).

These results indicate that in-home ISPs are no less effective at reducing subsequent recidivism than commitment to institutions. The proclivity of offenders to reoffend seems to remain the same for both types of intervention. However, the total number of offences was higher for the experimental group, because they were not incapacitated. On the other hand, the average seriousness of the offences for which they were re-arrested was higher for the control group.

Another caveat should be added. Only half of the experimental group actually completed their programme, and yet results were collected on all 185 participants. After the follow-up, 78.1 per cent of the successful programme graduates were free of new charges, suggesting that the programme, when followed, was fairly successful. However, those who completed the programme were perhaps less likely to reoffend anyway.

Bearing in mind the lack of clear distinction between intensive supervision and aftercare programmes, direct UK equivalents of US-style 'juvenile aftercare' are difficult to identify. There are elements of the programmes outlined above in both juvenile Intensive Supervision and Surveillance Programmes (ISSP) and the work of Youth Offending Teams (YOT).

Electronic monitoring

Electronic monitoring has been enthusiastically taken up as a means of diverting offenders from prison while restricting them to specified environments (usually the offender's home and surrounding area). The argument in favour of electronic monitoring is that, in theory, it provides constant computer surveillance of medium-to-low-risk offenders in place of intermittent manual surveillance that would need to be carried out by probation officers, thus reducing the workload of supervision involved in community restraint at the same time as increasing the level of supervision that offenders are subjected to. Sherman reviewed several studies comparing the effectiveness of electronic monitoring with that of manual monitoring, noting that much of the early research was undermined by poor research designs, lack of programme integrity and the low-risk offenders placed in the programmes. But Sherman gave two studies ratings of SMS 5. One of these was by Baumer and Mendelsohn, and showed that electronic monitoring offers no benefits over manual monitoring in terms of recidivism rates.

Baumer and Mendelsohn were reported in Sherman to have found that offenders monitored electronically received more revocations (21 per cent) than those monitored manually (18 per cent).[19] This suggests that electronically monitored offenders are more likely to reoffend than manually monitored offenders, but 'revocations' would encompass recalls to prison for technical violations of their parole as well as new convictions. Technical violations are more likely to be picked up under 24-hour electronic surveillance than under manual supervision and may distort the data.

A later, discursive overview of the effectiveness of electrically monitored home confinement, by Baumer and Mendelsohn,[20] described many of the problems involved with implementing an electronic monitoring programme, ranging from technical problems, such as interferences with radio frequency signals from FM radio stations and even cast-iron bathtubs, to equipment and operational issues. The researchers' view was that findings of studies into electronic monitoring may not be representative of the effectiveness of electronic monitoring *per se*. They claimed that as the industry matured (electronic monitoring had only been available for six years in 1992), and problems were dealt with more effectively, electronic monitoring programmes might become more efficient.

In addition to problems with implementation, Baumer and Mendelsohn[21] argued that certain offender types were more likely to benefit from monitoring than others. A previous study, also conducted by Baumer and Mendelsohn,[22] showed that offenders charged with driving whilst intoxicated (DWI) 'performed significantly better'[23] than those charged with other offences. In particular, home confinement and controlled alcohol in-take prevented them from leaving their homes in their cars. The researchers were also convinced that DWI offenders were less committed to a criminal lifestyle, eager to avoid custodial sentences, and had histories of fairly low offending rates.

Baumer and Mendelsohn were conscious of the limitations of electronic monitoring in providing an alternative to custody, because the terms of a home confinement order were easily violated, whether discovered by the authority responsible or not. They reported that 'very few offenders finish their sentences with more than 90 per cent successful contacts',[24] and according to another study conducted by Baumer (Maxfield and Baumer, 1990), it was likely that most offenders violated the terms of their sentence. The study carried out by Baumer and Mendelsohn[25] referred to by Sherman found that 40 per cent of 78 electronically monitored offenders admitted through self-reports that they had gone out at least once without authorisation, lending support to official (electronically-monitored) estimates of the proportion of offenders who had violated the programme terms (41 per cent). The authors were positive, however, about the potential for electronic monitoring to be used as a rehabilitative intervention, stating that although technical violations tended to be high, 'most studies have reported very low levels of arrest'.[26] Self-reports indicated that offenders feel that home confinement allows them time to assess their situations and make necessary changes to their lives, and that it encourages stability.

Global Positioning System

The Global Positioning System (GPS) uses the most advanced worldwide radio-navigation technology to produce up to the minute information on the precise whereabouts of a specific object. For the past decade, criminal justice agencies have been exploring the use of GPS as a more sophisticated means of electronically monitoring offenders on home detention than the older and cheaper method of radio frequency (RF) control. An offender wears a signal box strapped to his ankle, and a series of satellites pick up the signal at frequent intervals, using their combined information to build a series of codes that indicate the offender's location to within just a few metres. The most advanced forms of GPS can make measurements to within a centimetre.[27]

Offenders monitored by RF technology know that technical violations can go undetected with little orchestration. GPS proposes to vastly improve the prevention of misdemeanours and detection of technical violations by:

• monitoring offenders' movements constantly, 24 hours a day, over a specified period of time, rather than intermittently at random intervals as does RF;

• alerting the offender if he oversteps designated boundaries set according to the terms of his sentence (the alert is continuous until remedied);

• setting off an alarm immediately at a receiving station manned by the supervising agency whenever the offender oversteps designated boundaries;

• alerting vulnerable past or potential victims of his imminent presence should he overstep designated boundaries.

• setting off an alarm immediately at a receiving station whenever the offender is not where he should be at a specific time (e.g., if he is meant to be at work at 9 a.m., receptors seek a signal at or around his place of work at 9 a.m.)

• providing police and probation officers with a detailed retrospective account of offenders' precise movements over a specified period.

The Home Office is conducting a scheme among a small number of offenders (around 100-150) to test reliability in locating people and how offenders react to the increased levels of surveillance. They hope to have some findings by April 2005. James Toon, who is overseeing the evaluation, stresses that at this stage the government is more interested in testing how offenders work with the technology and this method of supervision rather than specifically testing for reductions in reoffending.

Florida Department of Corrections has been using the system to monitor offenders since 1999.[28] A statistical report displaying the demographics and outcomes (including re-arrest status) of all offenders placed on GPS in Florida is available on their website.[29] The website also reports on the statistics relating to the demographics and outcomes of offenders placed on two other types of community sentences: 'community control' (CC)—regular, manually monitored probation, and 'radio frequency' (RF)—conventional electronic monitoring.

'Outcome' information is available for all offenders placed on the GPS and CC schemes during 1999-2000 (this shows outcomes over a three-year period), 2000-2001 (two-year outcomes) and 2001-2002 (one-year outcomes).

From the information provided on the website, we can see that a total of 973 offenders were sentenced to GPS monitoring. The number of offenders sentenced to CC in 2000-2001 was much higher at 14,903.

Offence types are collapsed into four categories of violent, property, drugs and 'other' offences. The majority of those monitored by GPS (62 per cent) fall into the violent offence category, whereas only 23 per cent of CC offenders do so. CC offences are more likely to be drug-related (34 per cent). Only 15 per cent of those placed on GPS were drug offenders. Most others on CC (31 per cent) were sentenced for property offences and 13 per cent were sentenced for 'other' offences. Of those on GPS, 18 per cent were property offenders and five per cent were 'other' offenders. The two groups are not well matched, but examining GPS outcomes against CC outcomes does have some use as an indication of restraint efficiency.

The high use of GPS for violent offenders is questionable, since GPS does not actively prevent offenders from perpetrating violence. However, this category includes men accused of domestic violence and other, more personally-motivated crimes. A message included in the Annual Report of the Florida Department of Corrections stresses that GPS 'is not an alternative to prison'.[30] GPS is considered to be particularly appropriate for the perpetrators of domestic violence and sex offenders since these are offenders who target identifiable victims in reasonably specific locations. Although the offenders are still capable in theory of going after potential victims, the accuracy of GPS tracking means that there is less chance that they will either reach victims or go undetected.

Orders were revoked for new felonies and misdemeanours as well as technical violations. Outcome data were available for 15,083 offenders on CC in 2000-2001, and 1,003 offenders on GPS tracking. Forty-two per cent of CC placements ended in a revocation (a call back to court) of some kind, compared to 26 per cent of GPS placements.

One would expect GPS offenders to be revoked more frequently for technical violations than CC offenders, because of the enhanced surveillance. Roughly 16.5 per cent of both CC revocations and GPS revocations were the result of new felonies, about 6.5 per cent of both groups for new misdemeanours, and around 77 per cent for technical violations.[31] Just 5.3 per cent of CC placements were successfully completed, compared to 13.2 per cent of GPS placements. This suggests that either GPS is more successful at dissuading offenders from breaking their parole conditions, including by reoffending, or that GPS makes it more difficult for offenders to break conditions than CC does.

The GPS device is able to sound a continuous alarm on the offender's person whenever a condition is broken, drawing conspicuous attention to the offender. Based on the limited information available at present, it would be inappropriate to place too much faith in GPS. But, it does appear to provide higher levels of restraint than regular probation and the unique system of retrospective tracking gives GPS added value over CC and other forms of EM.

Conclusion

Intensive supervision has been extensively and carefully evaluated. Overall, the evidence suggests that such schemes make very little difference to the behaviour of offenders, but do increase the chances that wrongdoing will be detected. But, for all but the least serious offenders, ISP is not an adequate substitute for custody.

8

Community-Based Drug Treatment

Some types of drug treatment for offenders with drug-use problems have been shown to reduce reoffending.

Drug treatment combined with urine testing

Drug treatment and urine testing combine measures intended to rehabilitate with a greater element of surveillance, as well as demanding greater personal accountability. We focus on four studies of drug treatment: Nurco *et al.*,[1] Hepburn and Albonetti,[2] Anglin *et al.*[3] and Taxman and Spinner.[4] Taxman and Spinner studied a jail-based programme (as described in Chapter 5), while the other three examined community-based programmes. Two of the community-based studies found no significant behavioural difference between those with treatment and urine monitoring and comparison groups. One community-based study (Nurco *et al.*)[5] found after 12 months (but not after six months) a difference in offending behaviour between those who were tested and those who were not.

Baltimore City

The study by Nurco *et al.* was awarded a 3 on the Maryland scientific methods scale. The study considered by Sherman uses only the interim results, published in 1995. These were updated in 1999. Nurco *et al.* evaluated the effectiveness of a programme of social support offered to newly released parolees from Baltimore City.[6] Those eligible were offenders who were identified as heavy drugs users and who were required to participate in some type of drug abuse programme as a condition of parole. The study was designed to examine in particular the effectiveness of 'social support' for parolees. The subjects were randomly assigned to an experimental group and two control groups. The experimental group was given counselling, client advocacy and case management, in addition to weekly urine monitoring. The first control group was assigned to routine parole supervision with weekly urine testing and the second control group was assigned to routine parole supervision with infrequent, random urine testing. Five hundred and four parolees entered the study, approximately half (270) were assigned to the experimental group, and one quarter each to the control groups (99 to urine monitoring and 135 to routine parole). At the time of the interim results, 188 had been in the programme for at least six months.

The measure of outcome was whether there had been a negative change in parole status, i.e. parole violation, issue of a warrant for arrest or actual arrest, parole revocation or incarceration. In the experimental group 48 per cent reoffended (43/90) compared to 50 per cent (25/50) in the weekly urine testing group and 56 per cent (27/48) in the routine parole group with infrequent testing. There was therefore a small reduction in the reoffending rates for offenders who received social support and urine testing, but it was not statistically significant.

The full results were collected after one year. They suggest more favourable outcomes for arrest, parole revocation, conviction for a new crime and incarceration among the experimental group receiving both social support and urine testing. The arrest rate for the experimental group was 34 per cent, compared to 44 per cent for the group receiving urine testing alone and 42 per cent for the routine parole group. The conviction rate was 14 per cent for the experimental group compared to 21 per cent for both control groups.

The results suggest that drug testing combined with social support is more effective than drug testing alone, or routine parole in reducing offending. However, measuring reoffending by official figures is problematic. The results from the urine-testing control group and the routine parole group suggest that the urine-testing group performed worse for parole violations. This is not necessarily evidence that this group actually committed more violations, but is more probably a reflection of the greater likelihood of being discovered. This is particularly likely to be the case as the rules set down by the Division of Parole and Probation stated that four positive urine specimens would lead to parole revocation or re-arrest.

As with so many of these programmes, attrition was high. Of the experimental sample, 60 per cent remained in their programme for at least six months, whereas only 34 per cent of those with urine testing remained at least six months. This is a particularly high attrition rate for the urine-testing control group. In part this reflects the stringency of the two testing programmes, whereby four positive tests would result in exclusion from the programme. It may also reflect, as the authors note, the fact that many of the participants requested transfers to routine parole where it was less likely they would be charged with parole violation. This has a number of implications for the findings. Earlier studies have found that successful outcomes are related to the duration of treatment (e.g. McLellan 1983, DeLeon 1985), but because of the drop-out rate the number of offenders who underwent treatment long enough for it to have had a marked effect was much smaller than the initial sample size suggests. Moreover, the possibility of moving between programmes diminished the effectiveness of the random assignment process. The groups became increasingly self-selecting, as subjects who worried that they might fail and have their parole revoked, removed themselves from the programme, and subjects who were more convinced of their eventual success remained in the treatment régime.

The experiment was designed to isolate 'social support including drug treatment', 'urine testing' and 'no treatment' as separate variables. However, a substantial portion of the control group was also offered drug treatment as part of their routine parole. Forty-one per cent of the urine-testing control group received substance abuse treatment following their discharge from the weekly urine monitoring programme. Furthermore, for the many who failed to complete the experimental programme, the authors could not deny them alternative treatment for the rest of the year. Twenty-eight per cent of unsuccessful candidates on the experimental programme were referred to other treatment programmes. These changes make disentangling the effects of the various treatments highly problematic. However, the authors did monitor the results for routine parolees receiving treatment and those not receiving treatment, and 44 per cent of the treated parolees reoffended in some way over the course of a year, compared to 78 per cent of untreated parolees, in line with the overall findings.

The study design also makes it impossible to evaluate the impact of the combined programme of treatment and urine testing as against 'treatment alone' or 'testing alone'. Urine ptesting and drug treatment work on different assumptions: the latter is designed to alter the subject's behaviour; and the former to increase accountability and supervision. No control group was subject to drug treatment on its own, nor offered routine parole with no testing at all. It is not possible, on the basis of the control groups selected, to evaluate, for example, the *additional* impact urine testing has on the effectiveness of standard treatment programmes.

Intensive supervision programmes for drug offenders

Intensive supervision programmes (ISPs) usually have three basic goals: to reduce prison overcrowding at lower cost than building more prisons, to ensure community safety by close surveillance and monitoring of offenders' behaviour, and to offer an immediate sanction that is more severe than routine probation. ISPs for drug-offenders involve a fourth element— treatment to rehabilitate offenders. The programmes are designed to combine both punishment and rehabilitation for offenders, in the community. The punitive aspect of the ISP (curfews, reporting etc.) distinguishes it from drug treatment with urine testing described above, where the emphasis is more heavily placed on treatment and support. However, this distinction is a matter of emphasis. Many aspects of the two programme types resemble each other closely: the dual approach of supervision and treatment, the nature of the services offered to the offender, the type of offender targeted, and the timing of the intervention in the criminal justice process (most often replacing a probation order).

Petersilia and Turner[7] evaluated a seven-site study of ISPs for drug offenders. Their evaluation was awarded a 5 on the Maryland SMS. Seven separate programmes were set up with the aid of the Bureau of Justice Assistance for the express purpose of evaluating highly structured non-custodial programmes that were less severe than jail but more stringent than probation or parole. Participants in the study were randomly assigned to either intensive supervision or a control programme, involving routine parole supervision. The evaluation ran from 1987 to 1990 and the subjects were followed up 12 months from the beginning of their individual programmes.

Each site was responsible for its own ISP development and so each differed slightly. The Georgia experiment, for example, was designed to test whether different forms of monitoring would provide additional benefits compared with existing ISPs and so in Georgia the only difference between the test and control groups was greater monitoring. All programmes, however, were designed to increase the supervision received by offenders on parole, as opposed to *diversion* programmes, that offered alternatives to incarceration. The basic components are set out in tables 8.1a and 8.1b.

Table 8.1a

Variable	Macon	Waycross	Winchester
Offender type	Non-violent offenders sentenced to ISPs, or prisoners judged eligible for ISP for whom prison orders were rescinded	Non-violent offenders sentenced to ISPs, or prisoners judged eligible for ISP for whom prison orders were rescinded	High-risk probationers or parolees with current drug or drug-related convictions
Duration	-	-	Min 6 months
ISP components	Structured daily supervision, rehabilitative services, frequent urinalysis. 'Active electronic monitoring' using transmitters	Structured daily supervision, rehabilitative services, frequent urinalysis. Group drug-therapy with, home curfews monitored by surveillance officers	
ISP caseload	40	40	24
Supervision/ monitoring	Three phase system. Phase one: 12 face-to-face and 10 telephone contacts per month, weekly employment verification and random drug tests	Three phase system. Phase one: 12 face-to-face and 10 telephone contacts per month, weekly employment verification and random drug tests	First 2 to 3 months: 12 face-to-face contacts, 4 telephone contacts, 4 monitoring checks per month, urine testing, use of sanctions
Control	As ISP but without electronic monitoring	As ISP but without enhanced drug therapy and curfew monitoring	Routine community supervision
Control caseload	As ISP	As ISP	80
Control Supervision/ monitoring	As ISP	As ISP	2 face-to-face contacts per month, 2 telephone contacts per month, other contacts and testing at officer's discretion

Table 8.1b

Variable	Seattle	Des Moines	Santa Fe	Atlanta
Offender type	Convicted of drug-related offence and with history of drug abuse	Probationers or parolees currently convicted of drug offence or convicted of burglary but with drug abuse histories	Offenders adjudged to be at high risk of reoffending and with high needs	Non-violent offenders either sentenced to ISPs, prisoners judged eligible for ISP for whom prison orders were rescinded
Duration	-	6-12 months	-	-
ISP components	Counselling, job referrals, monitoring	Urinalysis, unannounced visits, mandatory drug and alcohol treatment, emphasis on job training and education	Therapeutic approach, emphasising counselling and job development, group therapy, urinalysis	Structured daily supervision, rehabilitative services, frequent urinalysis. 'Passive electronic monitoring' – voice verification to confirm obedience to curfews etc.
ISP caseload	20	35	35	40
Supervision/ monitoring	Five phases of supervision. First four months 12 face-to-face contacts, 8 drug tests per month, 4 law enforcement monitoring checks	First 3 months: 16 face-to-face contacts, 4 telephone contacts, 8 drug tests per month, 42 days electronic monitoring, night-time curfews	First 3 months: 12 face-to-face contacts per month, 8 unannounced home visits, 4 urine tests, 3 group therapy sessions per week	Three phase system. Phase One: 12 face-to-face and 10 telephone contacts per month, weekly employment verification and random drug tests
Control	Routine community supervision	Routine community supervision	Routine community supervision	As ISP but without electronic monitoring
Control caseload	85	70	60	As ISP
Control Supervision/ monitoring	4 face-to-face contacts per month	2 face-to-face contacts per month, one home visit every 6 months, drug and alcohol testing at officer's discretion	2 face-to-face contacts and one office contact per month. Drug referral to drug treatment and testing at officer's discretion	As ISP

The study found that, with very few exceptions, there were no statistically significant differences in reoffending rates (including parole or probation order violations, and re-arrests) between drug ISPs and routine supervision. Nor were there any statistically significant differences in the re-arrest rates or the seriousness of the crimes for which the participants were arrested. There was, however, considerable variation across sites. The proportion of ISP offenders arrested for *new* crimes ranged from 11 per cent in Atlanta to 48 per cent in Santa Fe.

The study suggests that ISPs have little impact on reoffending for drug offenders. The research design employed is very robust. It uses a random assignment, multi-site study, with a one-year follow-up for all participants. It controls for the potential increase in the amount of time the comparison group had unsupervised and therefore the greater opportunity they had to commit crime ('time at risk').

The programmes also appeared to have the required 'treatment integrity'. A problem common to some other studies is that, during implementation, the intervention being measured (such as increased supervision) is not increased for the experimental group by comparison with the control group. For example, the mere establishment of smaller caseloads in ISPs does not guarantee closer supervision than in the control. In this study, however, the supervision levels were measured and, apart from the case of Georgia (which was measuring the relative impact of electronic supervision) all sites reported that the participants in the ISPs did in fact receive considerably more supervision.

This was a rigorous study whose method and implementation have rarely been equalled and the results suggest that increased support of drug offenders in the community brought little or no behavioural change.

Drug courts in the US

Drug courts were introduced in the USA in the 1980s, in part as a response to an increase in drug-related crime (both drugs violations and crimes committed by drug users). The first was established in Miami in 1989 and since then over 1,000 have been set up in 50 states.[8] In May 2003 there were 1,079 drug courts operating in the US, with another 419 planned. Drug courts have also been established in Ireland, Australia and Canada.

Drug courts are designed to reduce drug misuse and associated offending by dealing with the offender outside the traditional court setting. Initially established to deal with less serious offenders (often first-time offenders), by 1997 most US drug courts had established probation-based programmes for offenders with more serious criminal records and a long-term history of drug abuse. Drug courts in different jurisdictions vary in structure, scope and target population, but there are some key components common to most:

- Most obviously, the 'sentencing' aspect of drug courts involves committing an offender to a programme of community-based supervised drug treatment that will avoid incarceration.
- The judge has a more proactive role, presiding over legal and procedural issues, but also assisting in structuring the offender's treatment and supervising progress while on the treatment programme.
- There is a non-adversarial relationship between the defendant and the court. This involves judges, prosecutors, defence counsel and drug treatment specialists all consulting on the offender's progress. The central feature of a drug court in comparison to a conventional court is the collaboration between criminal justice services and drug treatment services, reflecting a 'problem-solving' approach to jurisprudence.
- Drug courts are a continuous procedure: drug use is monitored through frequent urine tests; there are regular update hearings before the judge presiding over the case, and individual accountability is emphasised through a series of sanctions and rewards.

Evaluation of drug courts

An increasing number of studies have been commissioned on the impact that drug courts have on rates of recidivism. Sherman cites three studies, Deschenes et al.,[9] Gottfredson et al.,[10] and Goldkamp.[11]

Goldkamp investigated the results of the first ever drug court, the Miami Drug court in Dade County, which was designed to deal with third-degree (less serious) felony defendants.[12] The court required one year's participation in an outpatient drug abuse treatment programme with three phases: detoxification, counselling, educational assessment and training. Drug-testing was incorporated into the programme, as were frequent referrals and assessments by the court, with the use of brief periods of incarceration ('motivational jail') when the defendant had shown a poor performance.

Goldkamp focused on a cohort of 360 defendants admitted to treatment during August and September 1990. Most of them had been sentenced for third-degree drug felonies, but there were some second-degree felonies and some defendants with prior convictions. He compared their case outcomes and criminal re-involvement over an eighteen-month period with the outcomes associated with a number of control groups:[13] (A) eligible offenders not selected for drug courts (n = 84); (B) drug felony defendants not eligible for the programme due to the seriousness of their charges, or prior records (n = 199); (C) non-drug felony defendants (n = 185); (D) drug felony defendants from 1987 dealt with prior to the establishment of the drug court (i.e. those who might have been eligible for drug courts had they existed (n = 302)); and (E) non-drug felony defendants from 1987 (n = 536).

Drug court participants showed somewhat lower rates of reoffending (32 per cent did not reoffend over the 18 month period) compared to group B (drug felony defendants not tried in a drug court) (48 per cent). When compared to felony drug defendants processed prior to the establishment of the drug court in 1987, the 1990 drug court defendants showed lower rates of re-arrest (32 per cent compared to 53 per cent), even when controls were exercised for possible differences in sample composition.

Drug court defendants also averaged two to three times longer to first re-arrest than all comparison groups (median days 235, compared to 79 for drug felonies not treated in drug court and 115 for non-drug felonies).

These results must be treated with extreme caution, however, as there were a number of design weaknesses in the evaluation. The research was rated with only a 2 on the Maryland SMS. As the court was already in operation, the study involved groups assigned by the criminal justice system to a number of judicial pathways. For many of these groups it is highly likely that the offender characteristics varied considerably. Group B, for example, consisted of drugs offenders not selected for the drug courts precisely because of the seriousness of their offences. It is possible, therefore, that this group already had a higher likelihood of reoffending on the basis of its criminal history than the experimental group who were far less serious offenders.

A number of other design elements are not clear from the report. For example, the study does not specify whether the comparison is between those who completed the course successfully and the comparison groups or between all those initially admitted to the course and the comparison groups. Fifty-five per cent of drug court attendees also failed to report to court at least once. This compares to nine per cent of non-drug court attendees (although the study does not make it clear to what authority the non-drug court defendants were reporting; one might assume that this refers to their probation officers). The authors of the study note that this may well be a result of the increased reporting requirement for drug court defendants: a greater number of mandatory court appearances increases opportunities for failure. Nevertheless, supervision levels for drug court attendees were considerably lower than they were designed to be. This may well have compromised the effectiveness of the intervention and hence the impact on offending rates.

The two further studies considered in Sherman both show, if tentatively, that fewer drug court participants were re-arrested over the same period than the groups to which they were compared. Gottfredson, Coblentz and Harmon[14] evaluated technical probation violation and 'arrest warrant issue' rates in three types of drug court referrals: district courts, circuit courts and violation of probation cases. Among men, in district courts and violation of probation cases, rates were lower than for the comparison sample, but in circuit courts the rates were higher for drug court participants. Among women, in all three types of referral, drug court participants had lower rates of re-arrest than the comparison sample. However, the treatment group was small and the follow-up period relatively short (six months).[15] This study was given a score of 3 on the Maryland SMS.

Deschenes *et al.* studied the Maricopa County (Arizona) Drug Court. This differed from the other two courts in that the Maricopa County programme is a post-adjudication programme for probationers with a first-time felony conviction for drug possession. In a random assignment study, fewer drug court participants were re-arrested than probationers, although this was not found to be statistically significant. Fewer drug court arrestees were convicted (nine per cent) compared to probationer arrestees (23 per cent), which was found to be statistically significant. This study was awarded a 4 on the Maryland scientific methods scale.

The state of the research at the time did not allow Sherman *et al.* to reach any firm conclusions about the effectiveness of drug courts. However, Belenko has undertaken a wider review of drug court evaluations.[16]

Of the six studies evaluated in 2001, four included tests for statistical significance. Two of the studies reported a lower recidivism rate that was statistically significant (Truitt et al.[17]) one found that it was not statistically significant (Bavon[18]). One study found a higher recidivism rate for drug court participants that was statistically significant (Miethe et al.[19]). Three further studies measuring reoffending rates were highlighted by Belenko as having a strong project design involving randomisation: Gottfredson,[20] Breckenridge et al.[21] and Dickie.[22]

Gottfredson and colleagues assigned 235 eligible offenders randomly either to a drug court or 'treatment as usual' between February 1997 and August 1998. Reoffending was tracked for 12 months from programme entry and included re-arrest and re-conviction. The drug court sample had a lower prevalence of re-arrest (48 per cent versus 64 per cent) compared to the non-drug court sample, and a lower average number of re-arrests (0.9 versus 1.3). The percentage of offenders re-convicted on new charges was also slightly lower (31 per cent compared to 35 per cent), but this was not statistically significant. This design had a fairly strong methodology, with random assignment.

Breckenridge et al. randomly assigned convicted first-time offenders assessed as 'alcoholic' to the drug court and a control group, over a nine month period in 1997. Seventy-nine per cent of those who agreed to participate in the study were tracked over a 15-24 month period after arrest. Re-conviction was used as a measure of recidivism. Breckenridge found no statistically significant difference in re-conviction rates for traffic offences (20 per cent drug court participants compared to 17 per cent of the control group). However, participation in the drug court did have an impact on rates for 'alcohol-related or serious' offences (15 per cent compared to 22 per cent of the control group). However, the sample sizes were small (39 in the drug court and 36 in the control).

Dickie evaluated a Summit County (Ohio) juvenile drug court using random assignment. He tracked the offenders over six months. The average re-arrest in the period for the drug court group was one, compared to 2.3 for the comparison sample. Among the drug court group, 11 per cent had three or more new charges, compared to 46 per cent of the control group. However, the samples used in this experiment were very small (40 in all) and the follow-up period was relatively short.

All the studies that used random assignment, show lower relative recidivism rates for drug court participants. However, for two of these studies, the sample group is small. Furthermore, Dickie used a very short follow-up period, and Breckenridge studied alcohol abusers, not drug users. All three studies failed adequately to distinguish between post- and in-programme recidivism.

This survey highlights some of the gaps in the current research into the overall effectiveness of drug courts. Few studies include data on offender profiles entering the court. Obviously the definition of 'eligibility' will vary from one jurisdiction to another. In analysing 'what works' the question of 'what works for whom?' needs to be addressed. Another problem is that few studies include details, such as the length of the programme, the extent of supervision, and the nature of the drug treatment. On one level, this makes it difficult to distinguish the effect of increased supervision engendered by the drug court, from the drug treatment programme itself. More generally, if drug courts are identified as efficacious, it is not clear from the literature which aspects of the drug court have the biggest effect.

US evidence: conclusions

The evidence available to Sherman's team did not allow them to reach any firm conclusions about the effectiveness of drug courts. The reviews carried out by Belenko were more positive, but the evaluation studies had weak methodologies. Overall, the mixed results mean that there is too much uncertainty to go beyond saying that drug courts are 'worth trying'.

Forthcoming research

To find out how effective drug treatment has been among offender populations, the Correctional Drug Abuse Treatment Effectiveness study (CDATE) was launched in 1994 with support from the National Institute on Drug Abuse. Under the direction of the National Development and Research Institutes, CDATE researchers are analysing 25 years of research, giving special attention to drug offenders in custody, although not limited to that group. CDATE is intended as a follow-up to the survey of studies published by Douglas Lipton and colleagues in 1975.[23] Researchers are assembling and analysing the findings of all evaluation studies conducted since 1968 in the US and overseas.

Drug courts in the UK

In the UK drug courts are embryonic. In Scotland two pilots have been introduced, one in Glasgow in 2001 and one in Fife in 2002. In

England the nearest comparable arrangement to a drug court is the pilot scheme in Wakefield and Pontefract. It is a court-based treatment initiative which has been in operation since 1998 (known as STEP—Substance misuse Treatment Enforcement Programme). Offenders considered eligible for treatment were aged 18 and over and had committed serious drug-related acquisitive crimes. The procedure of the court follows fairly closely the American model.

Both drug courts in Scotland are aimed at offenders aged 21 and over, where there is an established relationship between drug misuse and offending. All offenders are subject to urine testing and a regular review. The procedural aspects of the courts have been evaluated, but it is too early for the impact on offending rates to be judged.

Drug treatment and testing orders

Drug Treatment and Testing Orders (DTTOs) were introduced in the UK through provisions in the Crime and Disorder Act 1998. A DTTO is a community sentence targeted at those who seriously misuse drugs and persistently commit acquisitive crimes to fund their addiction. The hope is to reduce the level of crime by eliminating its cause—drug addiction. DTTOs are now available to anyone aged 16 and above whom the court considers 'dependent on drugs and assessed as being a suitable candidate for treatment'.[24]

Courts can require an offender to undergo treatment for his or her drug misuse, subject to the offender's consent. DTTOs were first introduced in the UK in three pilot schemes in Croydon, Liverpool and Gloucestershire. The first Scottish scheme was established in Glasgow in October 1999, when orders became available to the Glasgow Sheriff, the Stipendiary Magistrate and (subsequently) High Courts. The first was made in February 2000. The DTTO scheme in Glasgow was implemented by criminal justice social workers and addiction workers, with treatment services provided by the Glasgow Drug Problem Service (GDPS) and Phoenix House.

The second pilot began in Fife in July 2000 when DTTOs were made available to Cupar, Dunfermline and Kirkcaldy Sheriff Courts. The first order in Fife was made in August 2000 at Kirkcaldy Sheriff Court. The orders were available nationally from October 2000.

Before sentencing, the court must have arranged a treatment place with a treatment provider, and the offender must have agreed to comply with the order. The offender need not be tested for drugs before the court hearing, but the court can order a test.

The DTTO lasts between six months and three years, and includes three compulsory components:

• A treatment requirement.

• A testing requirement (at least once a week, but not usually more than once every three days).

• A provision specifying where the offender is to reside.

The court periodically reviews the order according to a schedule made at the first mandatory review. Reviews are held not more frequently than once a month. At each review, the court receives a written report from the probation officer supervising the offender and from the treatment provider. The court may amend the order as it sees necessary, and it may make provisions for further amendments to be made without a hearing.

Breach proceedings

Early on, the pilots found that expecting an offender on a DTTO to become rapidly drug-free was unrealistic; rather, drug rehabilitation is a process, and it takes at least three months to engage in the DTTO treatment.[25] The guidance for practitioners says that in at least 'some cases, treatment should continue despite the occasional failed test'. This makes defining breaches difficult. The guidance suggests that on the first incident of testing positive for drugs, counselling may be the appropriate response, but on the second, formal consideration of breach action is necessary. Refusal to provide a sample, unacceptable non-attendance, dangerous inappropriate behaviour, or non-compliance with the residential element of the order all count as failures to comply, which ought to lead to breach action. The guidance seems to suggest that breach action is part of the treatment, and that the threat of re-sentencing (especially custody) is an incentive to complete the treatment.

Despite the guidance for DTTOs stipulating that 'in general, the court which imposed the sentence is responsible for holding the review hearings'[26] this was not common during the pilots. In Croydon, only one-third of reviews were heard by the sentencing court and in Gloucestershire, the figure was only one-fifth. In Liverpool, where they had regular sessions for DTTO hearings, the same sentencers were involved in review hearings in four-fifths of cases, and the number of cases revoked was much lower.[27] The research suggests there is 'some value in getting the original sentencers to take part in the first and subsequent reviews'.[28]

Evaluation of DTTOs

There are two ways in which the DTTO could be seen as successful: first, in reducing drug use, and second, in reducing crime. Data from the Gloucestershire, Croydon and Liverpool pilots varies substantially, because each area implemented the orders very differently.

During the pilot, the average weekly spend on drugs reduced by 94 per cent, from £400 in the four weeks prior to arrest to £25 in the first four to six weeks of the order.[29] Out of a sample of 48, ten were drug-free by the first interview and 19 were drug-free by the second. Drug use was reduced, but by no means eliminated: 60 per cent of orders (in Gloucester), 40 per cent (in Croydon) and 28 per cent (in Liverpool) of DTTOs were revoked mainly for non-compliance.[30]

There is also evidence that those on DTTOs did not commit as many offences as they had previously. There was a 75 per cent reduction, from an average of 137 crimes per week in the month before the DTTO, to an average of 34 crimes per week, in the first few weeks of the order.[31]

Of the 31 offenders interviewed on their successful completion of the DTTO, all said they were crime-free, and 27 claimed they were drug-free (except for using cannabis).[32] However, 179 did not complete their order, suggesting that DTTOs had a modest effect in only one in eight cases.

The initial evaluation in 2000 found that DTTOs were 'promising but not yet proven'. However, the results of the two-year reconviction study were 'less encouraging'. The two-year reconviction rate was 80 per cent. The completion rate was also low: of the 161 for whom information was available, 30 per cent finished the order and 67 per cent had the order revoked, mainly for non-compliance.

The rate of offending appeared to fall in the two years from the beginning of the order compared with the five years before the order began. But 53 per cent of those who completed the order were reconvicted within two years, compared with 91 per cent of those whose orders were revoked.[33] The poor results are not surprising given the similar American experience.

More recently the National Audit Office (NAO) has evaluated Drug Treatment and Testing Orders. The report was based on visits to five probation areas with the Inspectorate of Probation in May and June 2002, and a further five visits undertaken in August and

September 2003. The report also used the findings of a study (by South Bank University) of the results of the three pilots referred to above, in Croydon, Liverpool and Gloucestershire. The report highlighted several areas of concern in the implementation of DTTOs.

The completion/drop-out rate

The number of terminated orders in 2003 was approximately 5,700. This figure includes all DTTOs that were terminated in 2003, for all reasons. Table 8.2 provides a breakdown.

A total of 28 per cent of orders that were terminated in 2003 had reached the full term of the order or had been revoked early for good progress. However, this figure includes cases in which the order expired while the offender was due for a court appearance following a breach, but the order had not yet been formally revoked by the courts. That is, had the court appearance taken place earlier, these cases would have been revoked, and marked as failures, prior to the natural expiration of the order. These cases should be excluded. (From April 2004, the National Probation Directorate requires these cases to be excluded from the 'completions' group.)[34] This brings the estimate of orders completed or revoked early for good behaviour down to 22 per cent, and conversely, the number of orders not completed for various reasons up to 78 per cent.

Table 8.2

Reason for Termination of Order	Number (Adjusted Number)	Percentage (Adjusted %)
Order had reached full term or been revoked early for good progress	1,596 (1,254)	28% (22%)
Order terminated due to the offender's failure to comply with the order	2,508 (2,604)	44% (50%)
Order terminated due to conviction for another offence, either committed before the start of the order or more likely whilst on the order	1,254	22%
Order terminated for other reasons, including ill health or death	342	6%
Total	5,700	100%

The most common reason for termination was the failure of the offender to comply with the order. This may be because of the chaotic lifestyle of a drug-misuser—it may take several attempts before they can organise themselves to attend the structured programme of the DTTO.

Completion rates shown above represent a national average, it must be remembered. There was a large variation in the proportion of orders completed between areas—from 71 per cent in Dorset to eight per cent in Kent.

Successful results from DTTOs

What was special about Dorset's programme delivery? Usually, Dorset probation area issued six-month DTTOs in community-based abstinence programmes. Offenders were required to live in probation hostels. Elsewhere the more common practice was a 12-month programme of day-care. This provides a very clear implication for policy development—supervised residential approaches lead to better outcomes.

The way in which offenders are assessed for suitability also varied. It is often very difficult to assess the motivation of drug users and their commitment to the order, as their attitudes fluctuate so much from day to day. Dorset attempted to overcome this problem of assessing motivation through the use of a three-week trial period. This was to complete detoxification and demonstrate their offenders' suitability for abstinence-based treatment. This method appears to be the most effective, judging by Dorset's completion rates. However, a similar trial-period arrangement was abandoned in Cornwall because of the high drop-out rates.

In Sussex, where completion rates were above average at just over 35 per cent, there was assessment of suitability by three different practitioners: a probation officer responsible for preparing the pre-sentence report, a DTTO team representative, and a nurse or doctor. In Lambeth, however, assessment was left up to the probation officer and a single interview with a drugs worker. The NAO report suggests that this method was not thorough enough to ensure appropriate diagnosis. No conclusive evidence could be found as to whether the number of contact hours is linked to the probability of successful completion, partly because of the lack of data on contact hours.

Pilot DTTO offenders who were interviewed felt that the intensity of the support that was offered was the key to helping them overcome their addiction.[35] In cases examined by probation areas for compliance with the national standard in the period July to October 2003, just 44 per cent showed evidence that the minimum contact hours had been arranged for the first 13 weeks and 69 per cent after the first 13 weeks. That is, over half of probation areas were failing to provide even minimum contact hours during the all-important early part of the treatment period, and about 30 per cent were failing to provide the minimum level of contact hours during the later part of the treatment period.

Some offenders spoken to stated that a major problem was returning to accommodation where other people were using drugs—this led to peer group pressure to return to the habit.[36] Future programmes, therefore, ought to be residential, as in Dorset.

Evidence suggests that the length of time in drug treatment is linked to the ultimate success. Conflict exists between the desire to maintain the credibility of the order by acting on breaches and the value of offering vulnerable offenders a fair number of attempts to reduce their drug use. This is complicated by the fact that serious drug misusers are prone to relapse. Some probation staff suggested that, contrary to the National Standard, absences should be considered acceptable during early stages provided the motivation of the offender remains high. It was seen as unrealistic to expect full compliance before an offender's chaotic drug misuse was brought under control.

Enforcement of orders

It appears that comparatively little effort goes into enforcing DTTOs. In only 13 per cent of cases were two or more drug tests undertaken in the first 13 weeks, as required by the National Standard, and only 29 per cent of cases had one drug test or more in subsequent weeks. Such limited test numbers cannot be claimed to produce reliable results.

The handling of breaches was inconsistent and weak. The National Standard requires any DTTO offender who fails to attend two appointments without reasonable excuse to return to court. Staff who were interviewed felt that this was an unrealistic demand to make of a chaotic group of offenders with a relapsing condition. It takes time for the drug users to change their lifestyles and they are prone to many relapses, so it may take many attempts before there is success. The sentencing structure should take this into account, and make provisions to prevent relapses in the first place (if necessary by the removal of the offender to secure accommodation) and to enable treatment to continue after relapse. In 2003 there were 86 breaches for every 100 starts on the order (this could include more than one breach per offender).

Impact on the reduction in drug misuse and reconviction rates

The crucial measure of the success or otherwise of DTTOs is the impact on the reduction in drug misuse and the reconviction rates of the offenders.

South Bank University, from their study of the three pilots, claimed that there were reductions in drug use at the start of the order, and of the 31 offenders who completed their orders, 27 said that they were drug-free. However, these represented only 12.5 per cent of the offenders who started the order. The report states that this is in line with findings from the National Treatment Outcome Research Study, which found that about 40 per cent of people in the initial study were still using heroin at least once a week four or five years later. Continued misuse of drugs, and frequent relapses, are common to all treatments for drug misusers.

Table 8.3

Intervention	Nature of the Programme	Impact on reoffending	Ranking
DTTO[37]	Community sentence involving intensive treatment for drug-misusing offenders	Reconviction rate two years after commencement of the order of 80%	3
Schedule 1A6 Probation Order[38]	Treatment for drug mis-using offenders on a community sentence	Reconviction rate of 91% two years after commencement of the sentence	4
The RAPt programme[39]	A programme operated in male prisons, based on the 12-steps approach to drug treatment. It aims to achieve total abstinence from drugs and alcohol	Reconviction rate for those completing the programme of 40%, two years after release from prison, compared with a 50% reconviction rate for a similar group of prisoners not attending treatment	2
National Treatment Outcome Research Study[40]	Reviewed 54 residential rehabilitation and community treatment programmes representing the main range of approaches in place	Criminal involvement reported to be between 20 and 30% of clients two years after entry to treatment	1

Overall, 80 per cent of the 174 offenders whose cases were followed from the original sample of 210 had been reconvicted in the two years after the commencement of their order. For those who completed the order (30 per cent), the two year recon-viction rate was significantly lower at 53 per cent, and for this group the average number of convictions each year reduced from a high point of around six in the year before the order to under two for the two years after starting the order.[41]

The NAO report also contains a comparison between the preliminary findings of reconviction rates for DTTOs and other alternatives. The table above is reproduced from the NAO report, and the rankings for success in reducing reconviction rates by each intervention are included for clarity. The reconviction rates for DTTOs are based on the South Bank University findings.

The ranking by reconviction rate is an attempt to identify which of the alternative measures had the greatest success rate. From this, we can see that the residential rehabilitation and community treatment programmes were the most successful. This supports our previous finding, which emphasises the value of treatment in a secure setting (Chapter 5).

The NTORS is followed (in terms of rank) by the RAPt programme used in prisons. The RAPt model aims to arrange for offenders to receive on-going support when they leave custody, which increases the chances of an offender being rehabilitated in the long term. DTTOs appear to reduce the reconviction rate more than Probation Orders, despite being targeted at a group with more serious and persistent offending behaviour. However, it should be noted that the offender groups are not matched, therefore the lower reconviction rates amongst those completing the RAPt programme and higher rates among probationers may be due to their having different offending behaviour and drug misuse histories.

Policy implications

The evidence indicates that the process of reducing drug misuse takes a long time (perhaps several attempts) and patience. The initial evidence also suggests that DTTOs can reduce the reconviction rates for the minority of offenders who complete their orders. However, this has only been established in the pilot areas and it is too early to assess this properly as larger numbers of completions and a sufficiently long follow-up period are required to draw reliable conclusions. Two points are worth noting:

- The RAPt and residential and community programmes had lower reconviction rates. This would suggest that a greater element of containment and intensive supervision would lead to greater success. Offenders need to be isolated from criminal and drug-taking peers.

- The lower reconviction rates seen in the RAPt and residential programmes imply that on-going support over a long period of time is an important factor in lowering reconviction rates.

Conclusions

Counting everyone who started a drug treatment and testing régime, the reconviction rate of 80 per cent must be considered a serious failure. However, it is apparent that drug takers who already want to change can benefit from these programmes. Moreover, the mere availability of treatment must encourage others to try to free themselves from their addiction.

However, to leave offenders who have shown no inclination to change in the community is to expose members of the public to crime and cannot be justified. This danger could be avoided by adopting a graduated approach. DTTOs and other programmes could serve as methods of selecting those who are willing to change. Those who refuse or who have to be removed because of non-compliance should be placed in custody where they should be offered participation in a prison-based therapeutic community, with follow-up in a halfway house for six months, followed by further aftercare in the community. Such schemes, described in Chapter 5, have proved to be effective.

9

Boot Camps and Shock Tactics

In 1994, in part as a response to increasing concern about crime committed by young offenders, and heavily influenced by the example of American 'boot camps', the Conservative Home Secretary commissioned the Prison Service to develop proposals for an intensive régime for young offenders. Two trials were established in the UK: the Thorn Cross High Intensity Training programme (HIT) and, later, the Colchester Military Corrective Training Centre (MCTC). The results are discussed below, but first what was the American evidence?

Adult boot camps in America

Boot-camp prisons were first introduced in the United States in 1983 in Georgia and Oklahoma. These early programmes attempted to create a military atmosphere, with an emphasis on drill, strict discipline, physical training and hard labour. Later, rehabilitative elements were added to programmes. By 1994 boot camps were in operation in 36 states.

Boot camp prisons, according to Sherman, fall into the category of 'what doesn't work'. They were introduced as a means of diverting mostly young, non-violent offenders from continuing their criminal activities. Based on military training camps, they were intended to increase offenders' self-discipline, and their amenability to benign discipline by impressing upon them the benefits of highly structured activities and routines, and forcing them to overcome challenges in order to achieve goals. They have several basic components that are central to the boot camp approach: military drill and ceremony, hard labour, physical training, and strict rules and discipline,[1] although they vary in other respects that may influence reoffending. Programmes may include some rehabilitative, educational, or aftercare services (or a combination of all three) as well as providing the core elements.

The first large-scale evaluation of their effectiveness was performed by Doris MacKenzie.[2] MacKenzie and colleagues evaluated boot camps in eight states. They found that, compared to

145

control samples in other prisons, recidivism rates were lower in three states, higher in one and the same in four. The programmes with lower recidivism rates were those that involved the greatest proportion of rehabilitative activities and those with more intensive supervision after release. MacKenzie concluded that the military aspects of boot camps did not reduce recidivism.

Because the study encompassed findings from eight different states, with very different boot-camp régimes, Mackenzie employed rigorous statistical controls in order to examine the effectiveness of programmes compared with parole or probation in reducing reoffending.

The eight states included in the study were Florida, Georgia, Illinois, Louisiana, New York, Oklahoma, South Carolina and Texas. They varied greatly in size. South Carolina had a capacity of 96, whilst New York could hold up to 1,500, although this camp was an exception to the rule—most programmes took between 100 and 230 inmates. Average programme length also varied (from 83 days in Texas to 180 in New York), amount of time spent in daily training differed (from 6.5 hours in Louisiana to 12 hours in Oklahoma) and the percentage of daily activity time spent in rehabilitative activities also varied (from four per cent of activity time in Georgia to 38 per cent in New York). Other variables included the intensity of post-release supervision (in three states the level was automatically set at high for the first six months; in others the level was determined by risk, sentence, or, as in Texas, by location; and in Florida all course completers received 'regular' levels of supervision). The attrition rates also differed, whether due to dismissal or to voluntary dropping out of the programme. The attrition rate in Georgia was only three per cent, and in Florida the highest attrition rate of 51 per cent was found.[3]

Different types of reoffending were categorised as follows: 'arrest', 'any revocation', a 'new crime' or a 'technical violation', collectively referred to as 'failure modes'.[4] Arrest rates were not collected in Georgia, Illinois or Oklahoma, and both 'new crime' and 'technical violation' data are missing for Oklahoma and Texas. The reoffending rates of boot-camp completers were compared with those of prison parolees, probationers, and camp dropouts, although the availability of information about certain groups varied. In Texas, the reoffending rates of camp completers were not compared with those of parolees, and the comparison between camp completers and camp dropouts was only feasible in five of the states (Florida, Illinois, Louisiana, New York and Oklahoma). Mackenzie pointed out that comparison samples were not randomly assigned to either boot camp or other sentences, and therefore demographic and criminal history characteristics not controlled for could have influenced rates of reoffending. For instance, those who successfully completed the boot camp programme may have been at a lower risk of reoffending in the first place. The researchers suggest that the boot camp programme may merely act as a selection process, separating those who are at a low risk of reoffending (those who complete the programme) from those who are at a high risk (those who leave it).

Mackenzie charted the common characteristics of three programmes, those of Illinois, Louisiana and New York, in which boot camp completers had lower reoffending rates than comparison groups on some measures of reoffending. All three programmes were notable for the amount of time devoted to therapeutic activities (from 21 per cent of activity time in Illinois to 38 per cent in New York). These three programmes were also the only ones to recommend intensive supervision for a minimum of six months upon release as standard, which may have increased the rate of detection of technical violations in one state (15 per cent of Illinois boot camp completers were charged with technical violations compared to only three per cent of prison parolees). However, boot-camp completers performed markedly better in terms of new crimes. Only three per cent of boot camp completers were charged with a new crime compared to 12 per cent of prison parolees and 12 per cent of camp dropouts.[5]

The researchers believed that the programmes' effectiveness might have been due to the fact that relatively high numbers of participants were dismissed or chose to leave before completing the programme (31 per cent, 41 per cent and 43 per cent in New York, Illinois and Louisiana respectively). This indicates that those who completed the course were either enthusiastic about the programme enough to persevere and learn from it, or were more inclined to behave in a disciplined manner.

In New York, camp completers performed significantly better only in comparison to the camp dropouts. Only 12 per cent of the camp completers 'failed' for any revocation compared to 27 per cent of the camp dropouts. In Louisiana, arrest rates of camp completers were significantly better (44 per cent) than those of prison parolees (72 per cent), probationers (61 per cent) and camp dropouts (63 per cent), and performed better than at least one of the comparison groups in other reoffending categories.

In Georgia, the programme failed markedly. Boot camp completers performed worse than the comparison sample in every offence category (although data were not available for arrest rates). Sixty-nine per cent of camp completers failed for 'any revocation' compared to 46 per cent of parolees and 36 per cent of probationers. The researchers claim that this difference is due to the limited time spent per day in rehabilitative treatment such as educational activities, drugs treatment or counselling. It is also notable that the Georgia programme devoted only 8 hours per day to work, drill or physical training and, considering that only a further 0.3 hours were devoted to rehabilitative activities, this would leave a large portion of the day unstructured. Mackenzie also believed that the poor performance of the Georgia boot camp may have been a result of the low attrition rate (only three per cent of participants left the course early). Voluntary dropouts were not permitted, and it is possible that participants who would have been removed from other programmes were left to become apathetic and possibly resentful towards the programme. The researchers also claimed that most participants of the Georgia programme were released to 'traditional probation',[6] suggesting that offenders may not have received a sufficient level of post-release supervision.

The remaining four programmes in Florida, Oklahoma, South Carolina and Texas could not be said to have had any impact on reoffending rates. In Oklahoma, all comparison groups achieved strikingly similar results with around 20 per cent of camp completers, parolees and camp dropouts receiving a 'revocation of any kind'.

In South Carolina, researchers again put down their findings to selection procedures. The study showed that the 'new' camp completers performed very much better than 'old' camp completers and significantly better than probationers in all respects. For the 'old' programme, participants were selected from offenders sentenced to probation, whereas for the new one, participants were selected from offenders sentenced to prison.

Only five per cent of new completers failed for 'any revocation' compared to 21 per cent of old completers, nine per cent of parolees and 26 per cent of probationers; one per cent of new completers failed for a 'new crime' compared to eight per cent of old completers, three per cent of parolees and nine per cent of probationers; three per cent of new completers failed for a technical violation compared to 12 per cent of old completers, five per cent of parolees and 17 per cent of probationers.[7]

Mackenzie concluded that the militaristic elements of boot camps, which all the investigated programmes shared, did not have any significant impact on the reoffending rates of offenders.

The most recent review of the evidence, also completed by MacKenzie, identified 44 controlled studies of the effects of boot camps on recidivism. Nine found that boot camps reduced recidivism, eight that boot camps increased recidivism and 27 found no effect on recidivism.[8] Putting the results of these studies together, MacKenzie found that overall offenders in boot camps appeared just as likely to reoffend as those in control groups.[9] The only positive result was for boot camps for adults with increased aftercare. Overall, the current literature on US programmes does not suggest that the military aspects of boot camps are effective in reducing reoffending.

Juvenile boot camps: UK evidence
High intensity training—Thorn Cross

Following Home Secretary Michael Howard's visit to the US in 1994, a pilot scheme was established at Thorn Cross Young Offenders Institution. Thorn Cross bore very little resemblance to the traditional American boot camp. The young offenders wore quasi-military style uniforms and army boots; and the scheme entailed very full days (16 hours), strict discipline and regular inspections and drill. Compared with America, greater emphasis was placed on rehabilitative interventions. The programme was designed to be challenging and to make full use of the offenders' time, to challenge offending behaviour using cognitive behavioural techniques and group therapy and to provide life skills and educational training in preparation for re-entry into the community. The High Intensity Training (HIT) consisted of a 25-week programme of five phases of equal length. Each of the phases was centred on a specific intervention designed to reduce the risk of future reoffending. Progression through the phases was not performance-related.

Phase 1 Initial assessment of educational, physical, personal and offending needs of each offender. Basic education was provided and the last week involved an Outward Bound course.

Phase 2 Basic life and social skills course; Enhanced Thinking Skills (20 two-hour group sessions).

Phase 3   Vocational training leading to nationally recognised qualifications; individual case conferences to assess progress and set new targets.

Phase 4   Pre-release. Any outstanding vocational or educational work completed; engaged in life and social skills training relevant to life in the community; interviews with prospective employers or training placements.

Phase 5   Placement in the community on weekdays; placements near home; support from personal officers and mentors in the community.

The HIT centre opened in July 1996. Eligible offenders were (a) males, aged 18-21, (b) had about six months to serve, (c) were suitable for open conditions, (d) had an IQ of 80 or more and (e) had no history of mental illness. However, conditions (b) and (c) were often mutually incompatible. In practice, most young offenders with at least six months to serve who were otherwise eligible would have a sentence of at least 18 months. No offender aged 18-21 who received such a sentence would also be suitable for open conditions. As a result, offenders serving up to four years were considered eligible for HIT. This selection criterion was relaxed further when it was found that insufficient numbers of offenders were being put forward for selection. In practice the only types of offenders who were excluded were sex offenders and serious drug dealers.

Control offenders were drawn from those who were eligible for the HIT programme but not selected. The main reason was that offenders had less than six months to serve. Participants were also rejected if they were considered to lack the motivation to take part in the HIT programme. The selection process, during which the motivation of candidates was assessed, was not random and was subject to selection bias. One hundred and eighty-four offenders started the HIT programme, but 78 did not complete it (43 failed phases 1-4, 35 failed phase 5).

To measure the effectiveness of the HIT programme Farrington and colleagues compared the actual reconviction rates with a predicted rate of reconviction.[10] The analysis was based on 176 experimental and 127 control offenders. The one-year results showed that HIT participants were less likely to be reconvicted than predicted (predicted rate 47 per cent compared to actual rate 35 per cent). Control young offenders were only very slightly more likely to be reconvicted as predicted (56 per cent compared to 55 per cent).

As the predicted scores for the controls were significantly higher, the authors also performed a logistic regression analysis and found that being an experimental or a control offender did predict actual reconviction after controlling for other factors. The authors put the improvement at Thorn Cross at ten per cent.

For the two-year results, however, neither the Thorn Cross nor the control offenders performed better than predicted. The predicted reconviction rate for the experimental group was 66 per cent, and the actual rate 65 per cent. The predicted rate for the control group was 75 per cent, and the actual rate was 76 per cent. However, the time to the first new offence was 228 days for the experimental group and 177 for the controls. HIT would be expected, therefore, to delay offending by about two months.

The researchers also separated the results into those who completed the programme and those who dropped out. In order to get a control group, they matched the characteristics of the programme completers and failures against the comparison sample. They found that for both those who completed and those who failed the course, the likelihood of being reconvicted in one year was less than predicted (this was statistically significant for the non-completer group, but not for the completer group), while for their controls the likelihood was roughly the same as predicted. After two years, however, those who completed the course were reconvicted as often as predicted. Those who did not complete the course were in fact somewhat less likely to be reconvicted than predicted. These results are somewhat complicated, but they might be explained by examining the amount of time spent in the programme. Of the 71 experimental non-completers, 19 failed phase 1, but 35 failed phase 5. The other 17 failed between weeks 6 and 20, and so a large portion of the non-completers had in fact also experienced a significant part of the régime, hence their lower than predicted reconviction rate. Breaking down the results by time spent at Thorn Cross, one can say more accurately that those who spent at least six weeks, irrespective of completion, in the HIT centre were reconvicted less than predicted.

Colchester Military Corrective Training Centre

While the HIT programme was physically challenging, a need was still perceived for a programme more closely approximating the American boot camp experience, with a régime that was more overtly disciplinarian.[11] Colchester Military Corrective Training Centre (MCTC) is a military centre, housing detainees from the

Royal Navy, Royal Marines, Royal Air Force, and the Army, known to generations of service personnel as 'the glasshouse'. A proposal was made to set up a young offender institution within the military training centre. The Commandant was made the institution governor, and staff were drawn from volunteers from both the Prison Service and military personnel.

The Colchester régime was a military régime which emphasised firmness tempered with understanding. Young offenders wore military uniforms, were required to march about the establishment at all times and had to ask permission to speak or carry out any action. Offenders had fortnightly haircuts and room and kit inspections. It was, however, also emphasised by the staff that this was not a 'boot camp'.

The régime was split into three stages. Young offenders gradually earned more freedom and better living conditions as they progressed through the stages. Progression depended on recommendations in weekly reports by staff. Marks were given for appearance, inspection, attitude to staff and peers, effort and presentation.

Stage one was austere. Almost all personal possessions were removed (as would be the case in the military), all correspondence was screened and read. Offenders had no access to television and were allowed one telephone call a week. They were locked in their rooms from 8pm until 6am and were escorted wherever they went. Those judged to have the best-kept room were allowed to listen to the radio for two hours after lights out. The course consisted of drill, physical training, basic life and social skills and drugs and anger management. This lasted approximately six weeks.

In stage two offenders could wear their own trainers, use a personal stereo and watch black-and-white television and videos. They were no longer locked in their rooms at night, although the living area was locked. They continued the drill training and exercise but also received more focused vocational education, careers guidance and more life skills training. This stage lasted about eight weeks.

In stage three the young offenders were no longer escorted everywhere, had access to a bath and were allowed to watch television. They had access to a telephone and were allowed out into the town in the company of a responsible adult as earned privileges. During this period they undertook community projects, conservation projects and resettlement education. This stage lasted 12 weeks.

The régime was not quite a military detainee programme. The conditions were spartan and the offenders were shouted at and given orders. The army uniform and kit were of a high standard, and they wore full military uniform for visits. The food was universally praised, and many offenders reported enjoying both the physical aspects of the régime, and the level of activity.

Some interesting differences emerge in the role of the two sets of staff. Military staff initially had some difficulties with offenders who did not obey orders and swore at them. However, the offenders expressed their preference for the military staff over those from the Prison Service. The offenders said that the military personnel treated them with respect and encouraged them, taking an interest in their personal development, while the prison officers were viewed with suspicion and were regarded as 'screws'.

Colchester did not have any of the thinking skills or offending behaviour programmes of Thorn Cross. Nor did it have a drugs rehabilitation programme or aftercare programme.

The eligibility criteria and selection process were largely the same at Colchester and Thorn Cross. At Colchester, as with Thorn Cross, there were difficulties in randomly assigning candidates, for similar reasons. There were problems identifying suitable candidates, the criteria were adapted for pragmatic reasons (such as distance of Colchester from the offender's home), and many offenders were put off going to Colchester, either because they were misinformed about the stringency of the régime, or prison officers did not put forward those candidates most likely to benefit. The reconviction analysis was based on 66 experimental and 103 control offenders, although there was a little swapping between the groups, which meant that the results were occasionally based on different sample numbers. Reconviction rates were eventually calculated for 66 experimentals and 97 controls.

The impact of the Colchester régime was measured in the same way as the Thorn Cross régime. The researchers generated average reconviction scores for the control and experimental groups. They found the same disparities (actual overall scores were slightly lower than predicted). The results revealed no marked change in offending, but the results were not statistically significant.

The evaluation was seriously hindered by the sample size and the programme was closed after the fifth intake of offenders as it was not felt to be cost-effective.

In conclusion, neither programme reduced offending, although Thorn Cross reduced offending after one year, but not after two years.

Both programmes suffered design problems that may have affected the results. The selections were not random and the process was hindered in particular by attitudes of the prison service and offenders themselves to the programmes. There was evidence that the type of offender being put forward to both programmes was influenced by the interests of the officers in the current institutions. Colchester MCTC in particular suffered from a lack of support from the prison service. Thorn Cross did not suffer from this because it was a full part of the Prison Service, rather than a collaboration with another provider. This is reported extensively by Farrington and his colleagues. Colchester also suffered from staff shortages from the Prison Service side. The extent to which these implementation and evaluation design issues affected the overall results is not clear.

Scared straight

Sherman and his colleagues report that shock tactics were not successful in preventing future offending. One such shock tactic was to expose young offenders to prison life, using a programme called 'Scared Straight'. The idea was to deter offenders or would-be offenders from criminal activities by showing them the grim realities of maximum security institutions and introducing them to inmates, who are intended to scare them with stories of prison life. Sherman et al. briefly comment on the results of two studies that have been carried out into 'Scared Straight' programmes, stating that, in general, studies did not reveal any difference between those who participated in the programmes and comparison groups.

One of the studies mentioned by Sherman was conducted by Lewis in 1983.[12] Lewis set out to determine whether one 'Scared Straight' programme, the 'San Quentin Squires Program' (a juvenile awareness programme in California set up in 1964) affected any change either in attitude or in the behaviour of participants. The programme involved 'confrontive rap sessions, guided tours of the prison combined with personal interaction with prisoners, and a review of pictures of prison violence'. Participating youth were required to attend the prison on three consecutive Saturday mornings, where each participant was attended personally by an inmate (or 'squire') assigned to them. The 'rap sessions' are three-hour confrontations between the participating youth and his squire. The inmate must attempt to educate the youth about prison life, with a view to 'scaring' him out of offending. The youth must spend an hour 'on the hot seat', being grilled about his offences and reasons for committing them, his family, his education, his self-perception and his perception of others. Lewis states that the language used in these confrontations was 'often rough', although the scare tactics adopted by the 'squires' varied.

Sherman *et al.* did not give the study an SMS rating. Although the sample size was small (108), there was only one non-completer of the programme, and the experimental group and control group were very close in size. The control group was also well-matched to the experimental group in terms of offender characteristics. The follow-up period at 12 months was slightly shorter than most, but allowed enough time for the participants to reoffend. Thus it is fair to assume that the study might have been awarded a score of 3 if it had been assessed.

Fifty-three males were randomly assigned to the experimental group and 55 to the control group. The youths, aged between 14 and 18 with a mean age of 16.3, were from two counties in California. They each had an average of 7.4 arrests behind them. All were assessed on characteristics such as age, type and severity of prior charges, and number of months known to the justice system. They were also assessed on nine different attitudinal measures. There were no significant characteristics or attitudes differences found between the experimental and control groups prior to participation other than their average age (the average age of participants was 16.5 and of the controls, 16).

In order to measure the effect of the programme on behaviour, Lewis recorded the number of re-arrests for both experimental and control group members after 12 months. The results were very discouraging. A very high percentage of both experimentals (81 per cent) and controls (67 per cent) were re-arrested at least once within 12 months, and 34 per cent of the experimentals, compared to 33 per cent of the controls, were re-arrested three or more times. The study also examines the results for differences between the experimentals and controls in terms of the type and severity of charges brought against them, as well as for differences between time lapsed between the end of the programme and first arrest. No differences were found except in the latter category, statistically significant at the five per cent level. The findings showed that experimentals stayed out slightly longer on parole before being arrested (an average of 4.1 months) than controls (an average of 3.3 months).

In his final discussion, Lewis states that 'seriously delinquent youth cannot be turned around by short-term programs such as

Squires...'. He does, however, suggest that such programmes might produce a partial deterrent effect for certain types of offenders, but considering the lack of positive outcomes of 'Scared Straight' studies so far, there seems little reason to place any confidence in shock tactics such as this one and little purpose in continuing to evaluate them.

10

Financial Penalties

The appeal of financial sanctions is that they avoid the costs of prison, limit the probation caseloads of already overloaded caseworkers, and might provide revenue in excess of their administrative costs, and, in the case of restitution payments, alleviate the costs incurred by the victim. The main argument against their use is the absence of any incapacitation effect and the consequent risk to public safety.

There are few studies that allow conclusions to be drawn about the effectiveness of fines in reducing offending. The American evidence relies primarily on a four-site trial evaluated by Turner and Petersilia and a Los Angeles study by Gordon and Glaser.[1] The UK has implemented 12 pilot projects in an effort to improve fine enforcement and collection procedures.

Sherman pointed out that the use of monetary penalties differs between the United States and Western Europe as a whole: while the US uses them to increase the severity of a sentence, Western European countries tend to use fines as an alternative to incarceration. However, according to Sherman, an additional difference between the two criminal justice systems that has a bearing on the use of monetary penalties is that American judges are unable to impose a fine that is both proportionate to the offence committed and takes into account the financial circumstances of the offender. In some continental European countries judges link the offence and the economic status of the offender together in setting the penalties, using 'day' or 'unit' fines. Offenders with higher earnings would be expected to pay bigger fines.

Sherman cites Hillsman[2] to provide a framework for his discussion of fines and day fines. Hillsman's article draws conclusions on fines primarily from four studies funded by the American National Institute of Justice (NIJ), including one that was evaluated by Gordon and Glaser,[3] and from Western European trends, recorded mainly by West German analysts.

Hillsman points out that fines 'do not incapacitate, and they are rarely thought to rehabilitate.' Instead, their purpose lies in 'deterrence and retribution.' The greatest difficulty is in getting the amount of the monetary penalty right, so that it is effective, especially as an alternative to prison (in Sweden, England and the former West Germany[4]) or other possible sentences. A major criticism of fines is that they have little effect on the affluent and offer no means of enforcement on the poor. According to American sentencing literature and policymakers, large fines that are imposed as a result of the severity of the crime committed are effective punitive sentences. Thus, US policymakers have often set high maximum monetary penalties for specific offences; however, they are rarely applied in practice. In setting sentences, judges most often consider the means the offender has of paying the fines rather than the nature of the offence or the maximum penalty available, following the logic that if the offender fails to comply with payment, the sentence is ineffective. Thus, judges usually set monetary penalty sentences closer to the 'lowest common denominator' amount as that ensures the highest compliance rate.

Los Angeles, California

Gordon and Glaser[5] tested the use of monetary penalties in Los Angeles County in California. They chose a random sample[6] of 824 cases from 22,000 sentences imposed between 1981 and 1984. The 824 cases comprised five offence groups in the following quantities: assault (230), burglary (151), drug crimes (165), driving with an excess of alcohol (127) and theft (151).

Gordon and Glaser did not establish a control group for their study. Instead, in order to assess the relative effectiveness of monetary penalties, probation and jail, the sentences of all 824 were divided into the following four, mutually exclusive groupings: probation only, probation plus jail, probation plus financial penalty, probation plus jail and financial penalty. Gordon and Glaser examined whether sentences were associated with the offender's basic characteristics (age at conviction, sex, race, less or more than a high school education, employment status, drug problem, prior convictions) or the offence type. They found that receiving a probation only sentence (the most lenient sentence included) was largely correlated to the type of offence committed. Jail terms also reflected offence type, and were imposed mainly on those convicted of assault, burglary and theft. The sentence of probation plus financial penalties was more closely associated with offender characteristics than the crime committed, specifically: having a drug problem, number of prior convictions, and being black or Hispanic.

The most serious sentence—that of probation plus jail and monetary penalty—was largely correlated to offence type, with those convicted of assault, burglary, drink-driving or theft most likely to receive this sanction.[7] Gordon and Glaser noted that 'for offenders receiving a financial sanction, the crime was also significantly related to the amount of that assessment',[8] suggesting that Sherman's initial claim that American judges are unable to impose monetary penalties in proportion to the offence committed may be an exaggeration.

Second, Gordon and Glaser compared outcomes for the sentences imposed, according to four measures: arrests within two years of conviction; incarcerations within two years of conviction; probation revoked; financial penalty paid in full. The mean for all groups with regard to arrests within two years of conviction was 34 per cent. The breakdown showed that the mean for probation only was 36 per cent; for probation and financial penalties, 25 per cent; for probation plus jail, 50 per cent; and for probation plus jail plus financial penalties, 37 per cent.

Incarceration within two years of conviction was 26 per cent for all groups. The breakdown showed that for probation only it was 22 per cent; for probation plus financial penalties, 17 per cent; for probation plus jail, 41 per cent; and for probation plus jail plus financial penalties, 32 per cent.

Probation was revoked for 34 per cent of offenders. The breakdown showed that for probation only it was 36 per cent, for probation plus financial penalties it was 25 per cent, for probation plus jail it was 41 per cent, and for probation plus jail plus financial penalties it was 44 per cent.

Financial penalties were paid in full in 59 per cent of cases. For probation plus financial penalties it was 67 per cent, and for probation plus jail plus financial penalties it was 47 per cent.[9]

Sherman ranked Gordon and Glaser[10] as a 3 on the Maryland SMS. While the study considered various sentencing schemes and offender characteristics, the lack of a suitable control group undermines the usefulness of their outcome measures.

Day fines in four US jurisdictions

Sherman *et al.* cited Turner and Petersilia's study, 'Day Fines in Four US Jurisdictions'[11] as evidence that fines and day fines, proportionate to incomes should be considered in the 'what's promising' category of sanctions. Turner and Petersilia's complete study, an evaluation conducted on behalf of RAND, reviews the multi-site demonstration project funded by the Bureau of Justice Assistance in 1991, including: Maricopa County, Arizona; Des Moines, Iowa; Bridgeport, Connecticut; and Marion, Malheur, Coos and Josephine Counties, Oregon.

Of the four jurisdictions, the most successful experiment and strongest research design, meriting a 5 on the Maryland SMS, were those of Maricopa County.[12] Day fines were associated with fewer technical violations (nine per cent compared with 21 per cent for controls) and fewer re-arrests (11 per cent and 17 per cent).[13] Although only the technical violations result was statistically significant, day fine recipients did not appear to pose a greater risk to society as compared to controls. None of the others allow inclusions about effectiveness on reoffending to be drawn.

The FARE Experiment in Maricopa County, Arizona

The Financial Assessment Related to Employability (FARE) programme was developed as an intermediate sanction between summary and routine probation. The FARE penalties were both to punish and to impose an economic hardship that the offender would actually be able to pay in full, leading to more effective sentence than routine probation or un-enforced monetary sanctions.

The FARE Program was implemented in Maricopa County, Arizona in 1991, targeting offenders who fitted the following three criteria:

- The defendant's conviction is for a probation-eligible offence.

- The defendant was not a chronic offender and did not pose a threat to society and thus did not require formal supervision as would be afforded under probation or incarceration.

- The defendant did not require treatment, education or training to alleviate personal or social problems.[14]

FARE programme organisers divided offences into 14 levels of severity. The organisers assigned penalty units for every offence within each of the 14 levels (the highest three offences normally carried prison terms instead of monetary penalties for the offenders) from a bottom score of ten to the top score of 360. The value of each penalty unit was decided according to the offender's 'daily net income'; sometimes the pre-sentence investigator and courts considered only the offender's disposable income for light sentencing while sometimes they drew on the total 'take-home pay' for those cases requiring more serious sentencing. However, the FARE program was to maintain overall sentencing revenue equal to that of existing practices. Once an offender was recommended a FARE penalty by a pre-sentence investigator and was sentenced to it by a FARE judge, the offender was assigned to a FARE probation officer who developed an appropriate payment schedule.

In addition to providing a more proportionate monetary penalty, the FARE programme sought to improve payment rates by centralising collection. The staff achieved higher retrieval rates through setting short, regular instalment payments based on the day fine system, providing timely reminders for payment, issuing warnings for late payments (the first three were issued in writing, the fourth in person), and sending chronic delinquents back to court for re-sentencing.

For the experiment, Turner and Greene identified 257 defendants who had received FARE sentences in 1991 and 1992. For each FARE client that was included in the experiment, Turner and Greene looked for a matching offender to be used as a control, based on the following characteristics: offence type (theft, drug, white collar, and other), felony or misdemeanour conviction, age (under 21, 21-25, 26-30, and over 30), race, sex, and date of conviction. All of the control group candidates met general FARE criteria, including being of low risk to society, not requiring formal supervision and not having sentences with a large element of restitution. Controls could be found for 191 (approximately 75 per cent) of the FARE clients; thus, the final sample size for each group was 191.

Turner and Greene recorded further information on all offenders in both groups in the study, including: history of drug use, prior criminal record, basic demographic characteristics, current arrest and conviction charges, sentence, employment status, income, and level of risk they posed. The FARE group and the control group matched with respect to sex, race, age at conviction and offence type. The two groups displayed similar employment statistics, with over half working full or part-time, with an average monthly income of $1,000. Based on the offence itself, prior record and risk scores, however, the FARE group appeared to be a slightly less serious set of offenders than the control group.[15]

As Turner and Greene had matched the FARE group with a control group by looking at the sentences imposed on controls, they could determine what sentences FARE penalties replaced. They found that more than 77 per cent of control group offenders were placed on routine probation and 16 per cent were sent to jail.[16] Thus, Turner and Greene confirmed that FARE sentences replaced routine probation in most cases, in accordance with the programme's target.

While 100 per cent of FARE offenders were sentenced to monetary sanctions, only 93 per cent of controls were.[17] Offenders sentenced to the FARE plan had the additional incentive that once payment was made in full, the offenders were released from probation. At 12 months, Turner and Greene found that while more than 50 per cent of FARE offenders had been released from probation, only ten per cent of control group probationers had been. After one year, just over 33 per cent of FARE offenders continued as probationers as compared to almost 70 per cent of controls.[18] Moreover, fewer than five per cent of FARE offenders had had warrants issued against them, and none had had their sentences retracted.[19]

Ninety-six per cent of FARE offenders made at least some payment by the end of the first 12 months after sentencing, as compared to 77 per cent of controls. The FARE payments averaged higher, at $694, than those of the controls, at $447, for the first year. Considering payments by quarters within the first year, Turner and Greene found: within the first three months of sentencing, 21 per cent of FARE offenders had paid in full versus only one per cent of controls; at six months, 32 per cent of FARE offenders versus four per cent; at nine months, 40 per cent of FARE offenders versus eight per cent.[20] In total, FARE offenders paid an average of $325 more each month for twelve months than did controls, resulting in $62,000 in increased collections.[21]

Turner and Greene measured reoffending rates to ensure that FARE offenders did not pose an additional risk to society, as FARE offenders were under looser supervision than routine probationers. Eleven per cent of FARE offenders and 17 per cent of controls were arrested during the twelve-month follow-up period, indicating at least no greater risk associated with the lighter supervision accorded under the FARE programme.[22] As FARE offenders were subject to fewer technical rules than routine probationers, the controls committed more technical violations of their sentences than did the treatment group, 21 per cent and nine per cent respectively.[23]

The FARE probation experiment was conducted primarily to compare the effectiveness of the FARE programme with that of routine probation. Turner and Greene measured reoffending rates, sentence completion (including payment of monetary sanctions in full and in part), sentence revocations and sentence violations. They found that FARE offenders did not pose an additional risk to society and had a higher incidence of compliance with monetary sanctions, making higher payments each time, than did routine probationers. Thus, Turner and Greene concluded that the day fine can 'bring a new degree of rationality and manageability to a hodgepodge of financial assessments, which had grown to unwieldy proportions and had convinced many court officials that prospects for administrative reform were nearly hopeless'.[24] As the treatment and control groups were well matched and the study pursued a variety of outcome criteria, including reoffending rates and sentence follow-through, the study should be rated a 5 on the Maryland SMS.

Day fines in Europe

The National Audit Office (NAO) publication of March 2002[25] determined that 70 per cent of UK sentences took the form of fines and/or other financial penalties. Fines can be imposed by the magistrates' courts and the Crown Court. The police can issue fixed-penalty notices, although an appeal to a court is always available. As the magistrates' courts handle most less-serious offences, the vast majority of fines are imposed by them. The magistrates' courts are also responsible for collecting fines from offenders, regardless of which court imposed the sentence. The NAO reported that in 2000-01, the 42 magistrates' courts committees collected 63 per cent of the year's financial penalties, which totalled £385 million, constituting fines, compensation and prosecutors' costs.[26] However, less than a third of penalties were paid without further enforcement proceedings. Magistrates' courts do not always keep records of how often full payments are made on the day of sentencing, but the examples the NAO offered show Durham (South) collecting two per cent, and Brent and Avon (Woodspring) collecting four per cent.[27]

Consistent with Hillsman's 1990 analysis, the British courts set a fine amount based on the seriousness of the offence as well as the financial means of the offender. However, knowledge of the offender's ability to pay is often less complete than courts presume on the day of sentencing, as the offender's debts, including other monetary penalties, have often not been disclosed during the trial.

Methods for enforcing fine payment leave much room for improvement. Though the NAO determined the payment rates for each of the magistrates' courts for 2000-01 in their March 2002 publication, individual courts do not always maintain accurate records of payments and overall enforcement performance is unknown. Moreover, the magistrates' courts do not share information with one another.

If an offender does not make complete payment of his fine on the day of sentencing, the court will normally require payment within the next 14 to 28 days. If the court has not received payment within that initial period, it will send a warning to the offender. Defaulters may receive two warning letters before someone from the courts visits them to demand payment. However, interest on the debt does not accrue during this period. Thus, as the NAO report points out, there is not much incentive to make payments immediately. However, if the offender has still not paid his fines at this stage, the court may issue a warrant. If the court sends a bailiff with a distress warrant to collect the money from the defaulter, the offender must pay not only his fine amount but also the bailiff's fee. Thus, the courts are limited to allowing offenders to pay in instalments, issuing distress warrants that allow for seizures of assets for payment and incarceration. However, in order to imprison a defaulter, the court must prove that it was the defaulter's 'wilful refusal or culpable neglect' that prevented him from paying and that the court had 'considered or tried all other methods of enforcement'.[28] Thus, an offender who *cannot* pay the fine will not be sent to prison. The NAO reports that in 2000, only 2,476 defaulters were incarcerated while in 1994, 22,469 were.[29]

Home Office evaluation of 12 pilot projects to increase fine payments

In September 2003, the Home Office published *Clearing the Debts: The Enforcement of Financial Penalties in Magistrates' Courts*. The report revealed that the use of monetary penalties for indictable offences had dropped from 51 per cent in 1989 to 31 per cent in 2000, though it has been largely compensated by an increase in the use of community sentencing. Incarceration sentences for indictable offences in the magistrates' courts fell from 7.5 per cent in 1987 to 4.5 per cent in 1990 but then rose to just under 14 per cent in 2000.[30]

The report reviewed 12 pilot projects as they were implemented over a two-year period at 18 different magistrates' courts.[31] Each pilot project was aimed at one of the following four challenges: 'imposing financial penalties effectively; organising for and administering enforcement; tracing defaulters; and dealing with persistent default'.[32] The main indicator for success in the pilots was the 'payment rate' per week, but only 54 per cent of the pilots included pre-intervention payment rates.[33]

Two pilot programmes were introduced to improve the impo-sition of financial penalties. The first included five main features: improving the financial information available on each offender at the time of sentencing; stressing to offenders the importance of timely payment; gathering the offender's contact details for future use in the case of untimely payment; encouraging magistrates to sentence offenders to 'full and forthwith' payment over 'time-to-pay' schemes; and encouraging magistrates to sentence only offenders with minimal risk of default to the 'time-to-pay' option. The pilot programme was carried out in two courts, Barrow and Bridgend, and yielded radically different results. Payment rates increased in Barrow by 79 per cent and decreased in Bridgend by 47 per cent,[34] largely because the cash office in Bridgend was closed!

The second pilot allowed credit and debit card transactions as payment for fines. Payments could be made in person or over the telephone. At the two courts tested, the results were mixed. In Blackpool, two per cent of fines were paid by credit card, and the payment rate increased by six per cent.

Four pilot programmes were implemented to organise and administer enforcement proceedings. Pilot scheme 3 shortened the intervals between stages of enforcement actions in two courts: Wrexham and Croydon. The programme varied in design between the two courts. In Wrexham, the time between default and issuing the 'final demand' letter was reduced from three weeks to two, and the 'final demand' letter was followed by a summons for non-payment after three weeks instead of six. In Croydon, the fines office staff identified previous defaulters who had responded positively to a summons from the court and issued summonses to them instead of the costlier and potentially more time consuming distress warrant. The results for payment rates for this pilot programme were a decrease of one per cent in Wrexham and a decrease of five per cent in Croydon.[35]

The pilot programme 4, tested in North Tyneside, hired police officers during unsocial hours to trace and arrest defaulters. The police did not have a high success rate in executing warrants, as in the first set of 68 warrants only 18 resulted in any action, and in the second set of 49 warrants only three were executed. Thus, the project was not successful and actually resulted in a decrease in the payment rate of 88 per cent.[36]

Pilot scheme 5, piloted in Northampton and Teesside, sought to address outstanding debts owed by previous offenders who were facing the courts for a new offence. The percentages of arrears that were dealt with positively at the court visits were 86 per cent for Northampton and 3.5 per cent for Teesside. However, the overall payment rates of the courts for the period of the pilot programme decreased by 63 per cent in Northampton and decreased by 58 per cent in Teesside.[37]

Pilot scheme 6 introduced a computerised warrant tracking system to the Beverly court. The database provided up-to-date information on outstanding warrants and could be sorted according to several variables, including geographical areas, making it easier for civilian enforcement officers to plan routes. Nevertheless, the payment rate for Beverly after the implementation of the database fell by 77 per cent. The researchers maintained that the drop was 'almost certainly a reflection of other factors than the project'.[38]

The third challenge, that of tracing defaulters, was addressed by two different pilot programmes. Pilot scheme 7 relied on the Department for Work and Pensions (DWP) computer systems to find defaulters at four pilot courts: Bridgend, Northampton, Nottingham and Blackpool. The DWP provided a trace service from January 2001 to March 2001, providing new information in 71 per cent of cases in Bridgend, 56 per cent in Northampton, 69 per cent in Nottingham, and 34 per cent in Blackpool. However, information about 10 to 15 per cent of the cases proved to be outdated.[39] While the information provided was welcomed by the courts, the enforcement proceedings often did not follow immediately, averaging four weeks in three of the courts, thereby potentially limiting the value of the new information as time went by. The resulting payment rates varied: Bridgend's worsened by 47 per cent, Northampton's worsened by 58 per cent, Nottingham's improved by 228 per cent, and Blackpool's improved by six per cent.[40] In addition to clear inconsistencies in the results across the four courts, one must note that all four of the pilot courts were subject to other pilot programmes simultaneous to this one, making the results of this study even more difficult to measure. Nevertheless, since April 2001, under the direction of the Lord Chancellor's Department, a national trace service through the DWP has been implemented in all courts.

Pilot programme 8 campaigned with local media to 'name and shame' persistent defaulters in order to help track them down. The programme was tested at two courts: Watford and Knowsley. The two courts reported the following success rates among those who were 'named and shamed': 14 per cent for Watford and nine per cent for Knowsley. However, the payment rate outcomes for the two courts were very different: decreasing by 71 per cent in Watford, while increasing by 1,197 per cent in Knowsley.[41]

The last four pilot schemes were designed to improve payment levels among persistent defaulters. Two courts, Swindon and Grimsby, established fines clinics providing one-on-one attention for defaulters. The programme launched more effectively at Swindon than at Grimsby, as the take-up rates for the service were 29 per cent and 0.1 per cent respectively.[42] The payment rate improved by eight per cent in Swindon and zero in Grimsby.[43]

The Leicester court provided additional training for the staff that was specifically for handling defaulters. A private company, the Lidbury Partnership, taught the enforcement staff skills and techniques for interviewing defaulters. The training lasted between three and eight days and was considered highly successful. Within the pilot period, the newly trained staff interviewed 16 per cent of defaulters.[44] The payment rate over the period improved by 382 per cent,[45] but other factors may also have been at work.

Providing special training for magistrates who deal with persistent defaulters was piloted by magistrates in Brighton and Nottingham. They welcomed the course that focused primarily on attitudes and skills to enable them to confront defaulters. The percentages of persistent defaulters confronted by the newly trained magistrates in Brighton and Nottingham were: seven per cent and 54 per cent, respectively. The payment rates for the two courts improved by 20 per cent in Brighton and by 228 per cent in Nottingham.[46] However, the researchers viewed the improvement in Nottingham with particular scepticism, as the 'control' group's payment rates in the same period did not differ significantly from those of the 'treated' group's, and Nottingham was also subject to a second pilot project at the same time.

It has sometimes been difficult to keep a straight face while describing these pilot schemes. Pitiful is the word that springs to mind. Above all, without control groups it was impossible for the researchers to determine the true effect of the schemes.

Merseyside

In 2000-01 Merseyside County had the lowest payment rate at 47 per cent as compared to the national average of 63 per cent.[47] In November 2001, the Merseyside Magistrates' Court hired Reliance Security Group plc. to provide warrant enforcement services to improve payment rates. A 'bail' warrant is issued once the offender has received several reminders and warnings by post and in person. At this stage, the defaulter may either pay the fine 'on the spot' to the enforcer or to the bailiff or sign a warrant, agreeing to appear in court. However, if the defaulter fails to appear in court on the date specified, a 'no bail' warrant is issued. Normally, when the defaulter is tracked down at this stage, he will pay the full amount or he will be arrested and appear before the next available court. A warrant has been 'executed' when the defaulter has paid his fine (or at least part of it), has agreed to appear in court or has been arrested, awaiting trial.

While the magistrates' court has not disclosed benchmark figures for warrant execution rates, Reliance Security surpassed the target set by the court for the first year of the contract; the target was 28 per cent of 35,000 warrants, and Reliance executed 32 per cent. Reliance Security's Contract Manager Mike Baker believes that a 60 per cent execution rate for 55,000 warrants is quite possible, but it would require additional resources, including personnel.[48]

The main contribution Reliance Security has made towards tracking down defaulters has been in creating a database of all offenders for whom warrants have been issued, that is accessible 24 hours a day to the company and all police across the country. Thus, when the police stop someone, they are able to identify if there is an outstanding warrant for that person. At this point, the police can execute a warrant and call Reliance Security, who will then take care of all the relevant paperwork for the particular case. As part of the contract with the Merseyside Magistrates' Court, Reliance Security fills out all of the paperwork related to executing warrants, substantially cutting down the administrative workload of the police. The greatest handicap for the company has been that when a 'no bail' warrant has been issued for an offender, the court has requested that Reliance Security personnel should not arrest the defaulter. Thus, the company is often forced to rely only on payment compliance on the spot or an agreement on the part of the defaulter to attend his court hearing.

While it is difficult to measure the success of the Merseyside public-private partnership, the improvement in the number of warrant executions from one year to the next in addition to the technological advances provided for the police services in keeping track of defaulters are useful. Other magistrates' courts would benefit from learning of the developments in Merseyside and considering which aspects of the project would be applicable to their own counties.

Conclusions

While there has been a drop in the use of fines since 1987 when they constituted 80 per cent of sentences, the courts still sentence the vast majority of offenders to monetary penalties. However, the Government hopes to increase the use of fines and, according to Home Secretary David Blunkett, in the Government's response to the Carter report, fines must be 'rebuilt as a credible punishment'.[49] They are an important tool for the criminal justice system, but as clearly indicated by experience in the UK, much remains to be done to ensure reasonable levels of enforcement.

11

Post-Release Support of Prisoners— Throughcare

Rehabilitation efforts begun in prison are rarely carried through on release. Yet this is a time when offenders are most vulnerable. They may need support to establish themselves as law-abiding members of society, and to avoid renewing their ties to other criminals. Could post-release support be improved?

Throughcare

Various terms have been used to refer to this aspect of release, including throughcare, aftercare, and resettlement, each carrying slightly different connotations.[1] A definition of the term 'throughcare' emphasises the continued element of resettlement:

> A range of social work and associated services carried through from the point of sentence or remand, during the period of imprisonment and following release into the community.[2]

Preparation for release

All prisons have a responsibility to prepare prisoners for release. This involves helping them to address their offending behaviour; helping them to find education, training or employment (ETE) to commence soon after release; helping them to organise benefits to commence on release; helping them to overcome any difficulties with managing finances; helping them to address substance misuse; ensuring that they have somewhere to live after release; and helping them to make contact with external agencies that can help. Fundamental to effective throughcare services are the following:

- Needs assessment, in order to establish what kinds of services the offender requires;

- Sentence or training planning[3] on induction, in order to construct a feasible action plan for each individual offender, so that resettlement work can begin in prison as soon as possible, and preparations can be made for the work to be continued after the custodial term has ended;

170

- Effective delivery of offending behaviour and substance misuse programmes, in order to ensure that offenders address their problems whilst in custody;

- Reintegration planning that takes place both within prison and outside, to help offenders find their feet on release. 'Reintegration planning' also refers to the use of release on temporary license (ROTL) to ease the transition of prisoners from custody to liberty;

- The availability of 'key workers' or personal officers responsible for ensuring that sentence/training plans are carried out and that the prisoner progresses through the system appropriately.

To make sure that prisoners receive these services where they are required, all custodial establishments are meant to assign each prisoner a prison officer to act as a personal officer, who is supposed to help offenders with the transition from prison to civilian life.

However, prison inspection reports highlight various problems with the personal officer scheme and sentence planning. Frequently, inspectors reported that personal officers' recommendations for sentence plans were lacking in detail and did not influence prisoners' experience. Only 42 per cent of prisoners in local prisons, where most short-term prisoners are likely to be held, reported that they found their personal officers helpful,[4] and in some prisons, inmates have described their personal officers as unapproachable or admitted that it is often simpler to approach any member of staff.[5] Some prisons have failed to allocate personal officers to prisoners at all.

If offered, prisoners may be able to take part in a modular course in Inmate Development and Pre-Release Training. This course covers topics such as relationships, communication, gambling, drugs, alcohol, health, accommodation, employment, benefits and rights, but tends not to be provided until the last couple of weeks in custody, by which time it is often too late to start making arrangements for hostel spaces or relationship counselling.

Most prisons have staff trained to offer advice to prisoners about housing and employment matters, but administration is haphazard and often the workload is too great to be handled by single officers. There are plans to introduce a computer-based information service into prisons, providing up to date information on housing, employment, training and education, benefits and money advice and counselling services (the EASI system: 'Easily Accessible Service Information'). The Prison Service also works with Training and Enterprise Councils (TECS)—which are responsible for employment training and youth training schemes. Some prisons also operate Jobclubs and interview training.

There are a number of open or resettlement prisons and units, including Pre-Release Employment Scheme (PRES) Hostels. These are designed to help prisoners prepare for release. Some prisoners are able to go out to training or work from the unit or prison and return when they have finished. One resettlement prison, Latchmere House, was inspected in August 2003, and was revealed as not fulfilling its responsibilities as a resettlement prison. A resettlement policy had not been made public and its main points were unclear to inspectors, despite the fact that such a strategy is fundamental to the organisation of any prison, and a resettlement prison has an obligation to place more emphasis on this than most. However, the employment strategy was not a complete failure: of 193 prisoners released in the previous year, 146 had left the prison with employment.

The Annual Prison Inspector's Report for 2002-2003 reveals that resettlement prisons were failing in many of their purposes: work placements were not being filled, partly because many inmates had been sent there as a result of overcrowding and were not suited to open conditions; the physical environment of many was unsatisfactory, some conditions being described as 'appalling';[6] and the qualifications offered by prison jobs were not varied, useful or transferable enough.

Overall, prison inspection reports show that most prisons in 2003 were failing to provide reasonable levels of service in resettlement. Statutory throughcare provision is generally discredited as patchy, over-reliant upon particular key individuals, and stopping at the prison exit-gate. The most common explanation for ineffective prison resettlement policies is that the prison has limited staff and is under-resourced.

The joint report about resettlement by the Chief Inspectors of Prisons and Probation, Anne Owers and Rod Morgan, 'Through the Prison Gate', identified key failings with current provision for resettlement, including:

• Insufficient priority was given by the prison service to resettlement work and outcomes.

• Probation areas needed to re-order priorities. They focused mainly on planning for those serving sentences wholly in the community.

- There needed to be better liaison between prisons and probation areas, and between different prisons, in order to ensure that sentence planning and management work was carried through.

- Neither Prison nor Probation services made proper use of the resources that were available within the community or in partnership with the voluntary sector.

The report also highlighted the failure of resettlement services to meet the needs of short-term prisoners (those serving sentences of 12 months or less) and noted that work done to address offending behaviour in prison is rarely followed up in the community. Where it is followed up, work relies heavily on voluntary and community sector organisations.[7]

Voluntary sector

Much of the existing throughcare in prisons is provided by local and nation-wide voluntary agencies, or at least supported by them. Often the organisation will provide a representative to work at the prison full-time, or to visit the prison once a week. Sometimes resettlement officers have been trained by voluntary organisations or use resources developed by them. Voluntary services are indispensable to the prison service: the funding is simply not available to enable prisons to provide the approved standard of throughcare without the help of the voluntary sector.

NACRO is the largest and best known of the voluntary agencies (National Association for the Care and Resettlement of Offenders). It provides a number of services to offenders and ex-offenders: Nacro Services Resettlement Plus Helpline offers information and advice to ex-offenders, serving prisoners, their families and friends and organisations working with them. Their EASI (Easily Accessible Services Information) database contains over 16,000 projects that provide a wide range of services to ex-offenders, from help with drug problems to housing and employment services. EASI is available on-line to all probation services nationwide.

NACRO houses 1,400 people in flats, shared houses and hostels for ex-offenders. It also provides housing advice and training in skills like budgeting, shopping, cooking, finding work, training and education and literacy and numeracy.

Short-term prisoners

The Social Exclusion Unit published a report in 2002, which emphasised the link between short-term prisoners (those sentenced to less than 12 months), homelessness, unemployment, substance misuse and 'the revolving prison door'.[8] Short-term prisoners make up the majority of the prison population— two-thirds of prisoners are sentenced to prison for less than a year[9] and are often the most vulnerable prisoners.[10]

Despite this, serving a short sentence is one of the most common reasons for excluding a prisoner from in-prison programmes, since most are taught over a period of several months and there is generally a lengthy waiting list. There is also no statutory post-release supervision or throughcare (in the form of probation or otherwise) for short-term prisoners. The brevity of their sentences and the frequency with which they are relocated within the prison system means that they have little access to any services that are available and, without statutory probation, they are likely to find it more difficult to access other forms of assistance after release.

In 2001, aware that many prisons were failing to provide throughcare to the required standard, the government issued an official Prison Service Order (PSO 2300) on resettlement, charging each UK prison to develop and manage effective resettlement services suitable for the prison population. The order specified the need for individual prisons to establish joint planning processes with the local probation service and to develop close links with external agencies.[11] The government has developed a number of initiatives for implementation in prisons and by the probation service. Not all have been designed for short-termers, but most have.

CARAT

One of the most widely employed initiatives is the Counselling, Assessment, Referral, Advice and Throughcare (CARAT) services provided to offenders with histories of substance misuse. This was introduced in 2002, with the following objectives: to provide emotional support (through counselling), to assess prisoners' needs; to refer them to other agencies if necessary; to give advice where necessary, and to continue all services after release to prevent relapse. Although the means to implement the programme are available in all prisons, the Prison Inspector's report of 2002-03 states that CARAT is not working as it should. In most prisons, the CARAT teams are understaffed, and although assessments are carried out effectively, actual work on the problems identified by assessment is less evident.[12]

Custody to Work Unit

The establishment of the Custody to Work (C2W) Unit, encompassing initiatives such as Dependency to Work (D2W), Welfare to Work (W2W), and Jobcentre Plus, is the hoped-for answer to the problem of unemployment among prisoners. The prison service seeks to increase the number of prisoners getting into jobs or training on release by 5,000 in 2003-04, hoisting the 2001-02 target of 28,200 (which was achieved) up to 31,500 for 2003-04.[13]

So far, £30 million has been spent on C2W. The unit takes a multi-agency approach, combining the efforts and expertise of the Department for Education and Skills (DfES), the Social Exclusion Unit (SEU) and the Offending Behaviour Programmes Unit (OBPU).

Dependency to Work

The D2W project was started in January 2000. The idea was to organise a multi-agency approach to getting people out of dependency of all sorts. It is exclusively aimed at people who have criminal histories or are at risk of offending, but targets areas such as mental illness and drug-dependency as well. Some prisons, such as HMP Wandsworth, have installed a D2W worker, responsible for identifying, assessing and referring prisoners to the agencies related to D2W. In other prisons, responsibility for referral lies with a resettlement officer within the prison. Referrals can also be made from many other parties, including Youth Offending Teams (YOTs), probation officers and social workers.

After being referred to the project, a 'needs assessment' is made. If individuals fail to remain in the programme long enough to be assessed, they are considered not to have been referred. A number of referrals are 'lost' in this way. If individuals are identified as having any needs, arrangements are made for them to be addressed.

An evaluation and reconviction study is in progress but the findings are not yet available.

The Pathfinder projects

The Pathfinder projects are currently still undergoing evaluation, but an interim study by the Home Office was published recently.[14] It examined seven resettlement programmes that were aimed specifically at short-term prisoners. The projects were set up between 1999 and 2001 in different probation areas around the UK. Of these, four were government-run, led by the probation service itself, while three were led by voluntary organisations.

One-to-one work between offenders and advisors (to help with practical resettlement issues such as accommodation or employment) formed the basis of all programmes. Two programmes also made use of volunteer mentors.

A total of 1,081 prisoners initially signed up to join the project. 160 of these dropped out or were moved to another prison before work could begin. The researchers did not include these prisoners in the evaluation. This left 921 participants who went on to complete a needs assessment.

The most frequently identified problem was that of accommodation (overall, housing was thought to pose a problem for 51 per cent of participants), closely followed by drugs (50 per cent) and thinking skills (46 per cent). The next most commonly identified problems were employment (40 per cent), education and training (35 per cent), alcohol (32 per cent) and finance management (32 per cent).

In general, work took the form of interviews or counselling sessions, from which resulted a series of recommendations or referrals. Only 56 per cent of participants were referred to an agency of some kind to help them deal with their concerns.

OASys

The OASys is a new system for assessing offenders that was designed (and can be used) by both the prison and probation service. The tool examines many factors associated with crime:

- Offending history and current offence;

- Social and economic factors, including: access to accommodation; education, training and employability; financial management and income; lifestyle and associates; relationships; drug and alcohol misuse;

- Personal factors: thinking and behaviour; attitude towards supervision; emotional factors such as anxiety or depression.

Offenders are given a rating for each factor indicating whether the individual has a long or short offending history, a stable or unstable accommodation situation, etc., and all the individual factor ratings are added up to produce a risk score. Factors on which offenders receive weak scores are highlighted as areas on which sentence plans should focus. Because it covers so many factors associated with offending, the system can be used in practically every stage of the criminal justice process, including constructing pre-sentence reports and making decisions about bail and ROTL. At present the tool has yet not been established for use in all probation areas and prisons. Introduced in Spring 2003 in both a paper version and an electronic (computerised) version, all probation areas and prisons were expected to have installed the electronic version (e-OASys) by the end of 2004.

Custody Minus and Custody Plus

Two new sentences, 'Custody Minus' and 'Custody Plus', are already being implemented. They are especially designed to ensure that offenders sentenced to short spells inside receive the services that they require. Custody Minus is a suspended prison sentence given on the proviso that the offender must fulfil certain requirements in the community, which might consist of attending counselling for alcohol use, 'drying out' and participating in an anger-management programme, for example. Custody Plus proposals 'are intended to ensure that those sentenced to less than 12 months receive probation supervision and agency-support after release'.[15]

Overseas Evidence

Longitudinal studies have often shown that residential programmes for juvenile offenders have led to improvement in educational involvement and improved behaviour. However, they have also shown that these improvements are lost when the offender returns to the community (Deschenes and Greenwood 1998). Offenders quickly fit back into former social networks, and continue to have dysfunctional families and drug-using friends. Juvenile aftercare is designed to break the cycle of reoffending by offering transitional services for juveniles after a period of incarceration or placement in residential programmes. Aftercare or throughcare are often distinguished from intensive supervision. The main difference is that aftercare emphasises treatment or help, whereas intensive supervision programmes emphasise oversight. However, the balance between supervision and treatment varies from programme to programme, and the distinction is not easy to make in practice.

Sherman considered a number of studies that evaluated what might be classified as juvenile aftercare programmes, including: Sontheimer and Goodstein,[16] Greenwood, Deschenes and Adams[17] and Minor and Elrod.[18]

The Skillman Intensive Aftercare Programme

Sherman awarded the study of the Skillman Intensive Aftercare Programme a 5 on the Maryland scientific methods scale. Two experimental programmes were set up, one in Detroit and the other in Pittsburgh. The two programmes took juvenile offenders who were returning from residential placements to their homes and assigned them randomly either to the aftercare programme or standard forms of post-release supervision.

One hundred youth offenders in Detroit and 87 in Pittsburgh were randomly assigned to treatment and control groups. In Detroit their average age was 17. Over 40 per cent had learning or mental health problems, the average age at first arrest was 14 and they averaged three prior arrests. Fewer than one-third were known gang members but over half were known drug dealers. The Pittsburgh sample consisted of youths who had often failed in other placements and were slightly more serious offenders, with an average of five prior arrests.

Eligible youths were referred to the experiment three months before their expected date of release. After agreeing to participate they were randomly assigned to either the experiment or control. The programme of aftercare lasted approximately six months. The experimental programme contained the following basic components:

- Pre-release contact and planning between the caseworker and the offender;
- Intensive supervision, including several contacts a day over the first few weeks;
- Efforts to improve family functioning through counselling and other resources;
- Efforts to improve educational or employment prospects;
- Attempts by the caseworker to act as a 'mentor' or even 'role model'.

The Detroit programme averaged more than 20 contacts per month for the treatment group compared with fewer than five for the controls. The Pittsburgh programme averaged more than 100 contacts a month compared to nine for the controls. There were more face-to-face contacts in the experimental programmes, although the level of counselling was roughly the same in Detroit, but higher for the experimental group in Pittsburgh.

The results were collected after a one-year follow-up period. After being adjusted for attrition and response bias, there was little difference between the re-arrest rates of the groups in Detroit (1.3 re-arrests for the programme group versus 1.6 for the control), and there was a small but statistically insignificant difference in favour of the programme group in Pittsburgh (2.9 re-arrests versus 2.0). Self-reported data for the two sets of groups also offered no statistically significant results. Nor were there any major differences in the reduction of exposure to risk factors that might increase the likelihood of criminal involvement: in Detroit 91 per cent of the control group were in education or employment, compared to 79 per cent of the experimental group, whereas in Pittsburgh 69 per cent of the control group were in education or employment, compared to 83 per cent of the experimental group (not statistically significant); and self-reported drug use showed no differences. There was a decrease in association with delinquent peers during the study but it applied to both the programme group and the controls and was not therefore the result of aftercare.

This study suggests that the increased supervision and services provided by the programme, including counselling and job advocacy, have little impact on rates of reoffending. However, a number of caveats must be inserted. These fall into two groups: experiment design and implementation.

Overall the experiment methodology was robust. The subjects were randomly assigned, the follow-up period was reasonably long and consistent for both sample groups, adjustment was made for attrition and response bias, and self-reported offending as well as arrest rate were used as measures of reoffending.

There are doubts concerning the 'treatment integrity' of the study. The fact that the results showed the same level of educational involvement, drug use and association with delinquent peers, is not merely a result of the ineffectiveness of the aftercare programmes. It also illustrates that in the design and implementation, the experiments failed to reduce exposure to the risk factors that might have an impact on reoffending. The authors of the report mentioned the difficulty of finding the youths lasting jobs and improving family support networks. The authors concluded that for serious youth offenders a 'prompt custodial response' would have been more effective in protecting the public than the aftercare programme.

Bearing in mind the lack of clear distinction between intensive supervision and aftercare programmes (the latter including a considerable portion of the former), direct UK equivalents of US-style 'juvenile aftercare' are difficult to identify. There are elements of the programmes outlined above in both juvenile Intensive Supervision and Surveillance Programmes (ISSP) and the work of Youth Offending Teams (YOTs), and the On-Side project discussed below is a similar effort to help young offenders to equip themselves appropriately for life on the outside, but does not include the supervision element.

Work release

Work release programmes have been proposed to ease the transition between prison and the outside world. As work release participants are monitored, they are required to abide by a strict set of rules, including maintaining drug-free lifestyles and returning to their assigned residencies or to prison during non-work hours. Moreover, participants learn to work productively and regularly, as many have held few or no prior legal jobs, and improve their living habits. They earn an income, which they must use to pay for rent and other costs incurred by the state. In addition, work release participants start to build up their savings for use once they have been fully released from prison.

Turner and Petersilia set out to test these arguments in two studies. The first studied which inmates released from custody in 1990 in the state of Washington participated in work release and how successfully they did so. The methods for entering and exiting the work release programmes were also analysed, to collect data to compare the costs of work release and prison. The second study, focusing on Seattle programmes, relied on comparing a control group with an experimental group.

The first study considered the experiences of 2,452 male inmates. Of these prisoners, 49 per cent applied for work release, and 39 per cent (965 inmates) were granted participation in a programme. Inmates could apply for work release if:

- they had minimum security status;
- they had less than two years to serve on the minimum term including anticipated good-time credits;
- they had not been convicted of rape in the first degree; and
- they were not convicted of murder in the first degree.[19]

The Division of Community Corrections (DOC) within the State Department of Corrections conducted the initial screening for eligible participants. They denied work release to those who had assaulted others while in prison, had made threats to their victims during incarceration, those whose victim(s) resided in the vicinity and those who had been unsuccessful at least twice in work release schemes under their current sentence. The Community Screening Board, assembled by work release personnel and local citizens, would next approve all candidates prior to their appointment to the community (almost all were accepted). The application process took ten months, leaving about five months for work release for the average participant.

The DOC oversaw the correctional officers responsible for work release facilities, co-ordinated living quarters, sign-in and sign-out sheets, urine analysis and job checks, although the inmates themselves found work. The DOC also provided additional support services, such as substance abuse discussions with participants, to help them succeed in work release.

Five hundred and forty-four (56 per cent) of the 965 participants were able to complete work release without rule infractions and new crimes recorded on their records, and were able to move directly into the community after their sentence. These offenders were deemed 'successful' by Turner and Petersilia. Thus, Turner and Petersilia calculated that 'almost one out of four inmates in Washington successfully transitioned to the community through work release'.[20] One hundred and thirty-one (13 per cent) of the participants were deemed 'moderately successful', meaning they had incurred an infraction that did not result in permanent removal from work release, and 290 (30 per cent) were deemed 'unsuccessful', meaning they had committed an infraction that resulted in re-incarceration.[21] Offenders were most frequently returned to prison as a result of programme rule violations, constituting 42 per cent; followed by drug possession at 35 per cent; while new crimes were equal to medical conditions as the least frequent reasons at four per cent each.[22]

Turner and Petersilia compared the three-tier outcomes— successful, moderately successful and unsuccessful—for partici- pants to specific characteristics that might influence participants' reoffending rates, including race, education level, employment prior to incarceration, marital status, employment status at arrest, previous work stability, type of offence leading to conviction, prior criminal record, substance abuse dependency, and length of current sentence.[23] They found a correlation between the outcomes and the following variables: age, race, prior record and current offence.

The second study relied on a randomised experiment. Hoping to create a sample size of at least several hundred prisoners, Turner and Petersilia chose Seattle, host to 50 per cent of Washington State's work release programmes. To create the participant group, applications for work release were conducted in the same way as in the first study; however, of every ten contenders the DOC deemed eligible, only one was assigned to a work release programme as part of the experimental group, and one remained in prison as part of the control group.[24] Turner and Petersilia further tested the comparability of the two groups, considering characteristics such as age, race, current offence, and prior criminal record. They found the groups to be the same except for number of prior arrests and number of parole violations.

The study looked at rates of reoffending for 12 months after assignments to the two groups were completed. The experiment group worked an average of ten months in work release while the controls remained in prison for an average of seven months, prior to complete release. Within 12 months, including time spent under supervision (in work release or in prison) as well as post-release, 67 per cent of the experimental group committed an infraction of some sort, while only 34 per cent of the controls committed one.[25] Twenty-two per cent of the experimental group and 30 per cent of the control group were arrested for violating the law (the one year follow-up period included an average of three months post-release).[26]

Turner and Petersilia determined that the work release programme in Washington 'works' on the basis of it not costing more than incarceration and not posing a significantly greater risk to the community where inmates are released to work, as less than five per cent of work release participants committed new crimes. Turner and Petersilia maintained that while other studies relied on reducing costs and lowering reoffending rates as the criteria for an effective correctional programme, these expectations are unfair, naïve and unrealistic. Citing the work of Charles Logan, a corrections expert for the Department of Justice, they argue that prisons should be 'held accountable for keeping prisoners safe, in line (not committing crimes), healthy and busy—and try and do it all without undue suffering and as efficiently as possible'.[27]

However, for Sherman et al. reoffending rates were primary in determining whether or not rehabilitative strategies were effective. Moreover, work release programmes can potentially cost more than incarceration, particularly if participants are returned to prison at an early stage in their work release or if intensive surveillance is employed, creating all the more reason that they should provide additional benefit to justify their expense. Nevertheless, Sherman *et al.* rated the methodology of the Seattle study in Turner and Petersilia[28] a 4 on the Maryland SMS, and put community employment programmes in the 'what works' category.

UK evidence

Few resettlement projects in England and Wales have managed to secure funding and services to enable evaluation, but a handful have managed to produce an evaluation of sorts based on reconviction rates and, in some cases, interviews with participants. The On-Side project (Solanki)[29] was a small pilot conducted among young offenders. It suggested that throughcare services significantly reduced reoffending, but had a weak design. The Short-Term Prisoner Project (Berriman)[30] was another pilot conducted among adult prisoners. The experimental design was more robust than the On-Side project's design, but the results were not statistically significant.

The On-Side Project

At HMYOI Portland, NACRO introduced an innovative multi-agency pilot project called On-Side.[31] It was intended to help the youngest and most vulnerable members of the prison population to resettle in the community and avoid committing further crimes, by ensuring that they received access to relevant information, continued support after release, and access to other support services in the community. The project ran for three years, and was evaluated by an external researcher throughout. Data were collected between 1999 and 2002, and appeared to show that project participation reduced reoffending by as much as 24 per cent. However, there were only 62 in the sample and there was no control group. The study would only score an SMS of 1.

Despite the weakness of the appraisal—no randomised control group, no matching of a quasi-experimental control and the clear presence of a selection effect—the programme is being hailed as a turning point for prison resettlement strategies.

The Short-Term Prisoner Project

The Short-Term Prisoner Project (STPP) was inspired by the findings of a study into the needs of short-term prisoners at HMP

Canterbury in Kent.[32] Undertaken in 2000, it asserted that the main problems associated with reoffending were criminal history, homelessness, unemployment and substance abuse.[33] The STPP was then developed and piloted at HMP Canterbury in 2001, in close association with Thanet Police, one of nine forces serving the Kent Probation area. The police were largely responsible for the enthusiasm and funding that drove the project. It was hailed as a success in reducing both the volume and seriousness of reoffending and won the Lord Woolf Award for excellence in resettlement work in 2002. In late Spring 2003 the project was amalgamated with a similar programme that targets longer-term (those sentenced to between 12 months and four years in custody) prolific offenders to become the Kent and Medway Resettlement Programme, now operating in all nine police forces across the county. An evaluation of the new programme is ongoing, but findings will not be available until 2005.

The STPP was a multi-agency project, involving local employment and housing agencies, volunteer mentors and Thanet Police Force Community Support Officers (CSOs). The idea was to work with prisoners prior to their release to fix problems with housing/drug abuse etc. and to provide post-release aftercare and emotional support, although its ultimate aim was to break the criminal offending cycle.

Lucy Berriman, a student at the University of Kent, evaluated the project in 2002.[34] Her study was more rigorous than the On-Side study, and would have an SMS of 3, the minimum design considered to be acceptable for drawing conclusions about what works. The researcher used both quantitative data (including the Police National Computer), and qualitative data (gathered from semi-structured interviews with thirty of the participants). Fifty-nine male prisoners were eventually selected through a process of inviting all new prisoners with a history of persistent offending and of medium-to-high risk, who were sentenced to more than three but less than 12 months, to join the programme.

All participants were aged between 21 and 56, with a mean age of 32 years and 11 months. A control group of 59 prisoners aged between 22 and 54, the mean average being 33 years and one month, was also selected. They, like the experimental group, were all from either the Thanet or Canterbury area of East Kent. The two groups were also matched on ethnic group, index offence type (the one for which they had received their custodial sentence), sentence length, number of days served in custody, number of previous convictions, number of previous offences committed and their assessed risk level. In marked contrast with the On-Side project, the evaluators took pains to select a control group with similar characteristics.

After selection, participants were asked to complete a self-assessment form (asking about their post-release needs) and a benefits form. On the basis of their needs, a strategy was devised for addressing them. The work involved providing the right levels of internal support whilst in custody, such as education classes and drugs counselling, and contacting the appropriate external agencies to address other needs, such as housing and benefits. All the involved agencies were then invited to attend a case conference for the individual immediately prior to his release, where an inter-agency action plan would be formulated for further appointments for the prisoner to attend after discharge. The individual would then be required to sign the final action plan agreed on, promising to adhere to it. The report does not indicate whether participants did stick to their action plans or not.

After release, participation, as before, was voluntary, but the STPP provided mentors—lent by independent mentoring services—and police visits—carried out by CSOs—to those who wished to continue participating. The report argued that giving the prisoner access to positive social support may help the individual to deal successfully with stressful situations and relationships, and thereby prevent relapse.[35]

To collect the post-release reconviction data, a crime analyst extracted information from the Police National Computer detailing participants' new offences, whether they were 'charged' with the new offence, the nature and gravity of the new offence, and how much time had lapsed between release and reoffending.[36] The crime analyst checked records for each participant eight weeks after their release, yielding the main reconviction data set. Another set of reconviction data was taken for reoffending between release and the evaluation cut-off date. This took place nine weeks after the release date of the final participant. Therefore some participants had been released as much as 15 months before this took place, whereas others may only have been released nine weeks before. So although the reoffending data relating to those who had been released for longer are likely to be more accurate (in that the time lapse was closer to the conventional time lapse used in reconviction studies of two years) the rates relating to those who were released later on in the project period plausibly underestimate the true volume of reoffending, since they will only have been out of custody for a short time.

The researcher laid out three hypotheses. These were:

- The experimental group will reoffend less than the control group during their first eight weeks of release as a result of their involvement with the STPP.

- Those experimental group members who do reoffend will commit the same or less serious offences than that for which they received their custodial sentence.

- The experimental group will be more successfully resettled than the control group as a result of the social support offered by the programme.

Hypothesis 1 was confirmed, but findings were not statistically significant. Ten members (17 per cent) of the experimental group and 18 members (31 per cent) of the control group reoffended within eight weeks. The later set of reoffending data, collected towards the end of the project, showed that 24 (41 per cent) of the STPP group had reoffended since release, compared to 34 (58 per cent) of the control group. This too was not statistically significant.

Hypothesis 2 was also confirmed. A total of 24 people in the STPP group reoffended. Of these, 15 (25 per cent) committed offences that were less serious than the crime for which they were incarcerated. The corresponding figure for the control group was five (5.1 per cent) out of a total of 34 who reoffended. Tests revealed this difference to be statistically significant, showing that those who reoffended from the STPP group were more likely than those who reoffended from the control group to commit an offence less serious than their original offence. Only four members (seven per cent) of the STPP group committed crimes more serious in nature than the crimes for which they were originally incarcerated, whereas 17 members (29 per cent) of the control group did so, but this was not statistically significant.

Hypothesis 3 was more complicated to prove. The results showed that those in the STPP group were resettled—i.e., stable—for a longer period (an average of 93 days) before reoffending than those in the control group (an average of 75 days), but individual 'resettlement days' totals differed wildly from the average. Some participants were resettled for very much shorter or longer periods than the average, up to 73 days on either side for the STPP group and up to 74 days on either side for the control group. The difference between periods of resettlement for each group was not found to be statistically significant.

The study has a small sample, and therefore differences between the STPP and control groups refer to small numbers of people. The singular statistically significant finding regarding the level of seriousness of new offences actually deals with a difference of ten people, between the five in the control group who committed less serious crimes, and 15 in the STPP group.

The small sample size, lack of statistically significant findings and failure to comment on which aspects of the programme appeared to be influential all make it difficult to judge whether providing resettlement aids reduces reoffending. We can say that this study appears to show that the provision of throughcare does not reduce reoffending rates, but that it does reduce the seriousness of offences committed.

However, Thanet Police department were very enthusiastic about the project. Their enthusiasm was the impetus for the countywide development of the programme and provided the funding to keep it going. Maureen Saywell, Resettlement Clerk at HMP Canterbury, explained that local police see it as being in their own interests to continue with the multi-agency and intensive support approach to address reoffending. They are confident that, even if the project does not reduce the chances of offenders returning to crime, it does significantly reduce the gravity of future offence type, and therefore reduce the workload of the police.[37]

The overall picture

The studies discussed above are not encouraging for throughcare advocates. The UK studies yield little useful information. The American studies cited provide a more reliable indicator of effectiveness: the rigorously evaluated Skillman initiative found that aftercare made little difference to offending.

With such results, and such inconsistent methodologies used to obtain them, it is almost impossible to draw any conclusion about throughcare and reoffending. Studies need to be more controlled, be evaluated over longer periods, access greater numbers of participants, be more explicit about assessment and precise achievements, and most importantly, maintain contact throughout the evaluation period with all those who are involved with the project.

What's the point?

There is no proof that throughcare is worthwhile as a method of reducing reoffending. Yet services continue to be made available, much of them provided by lay people who give up their free time to do so. Jenny Davis at Wormwood Scrubs believes it is impossible to tell if offenders will reoffend, but very frustrating when they do, since one often sees the same prisoner, for whom one has just spent three months finding a job or housing, walking right back through the prison gates.[38] One must wonder why they keep at it, when the visible rewards are so scant.

Yet throughcare providers themselves are surprisingly buoyant. They see rewards in results other than reoffending rates. The indisputable fact is that these services are needed. There is no denying that many people held in custody are ill-equipped to deal with life on the outside, and, whether helping them effects a reduction in reoffending or not, there is a clear necessity to provide these services.

Tony Shepherd, the director of New Bridge, expressed just such a sentiment whilst discussing the befriending service they provide for prisoners. He sees their service as important regardless of its influence on offending behaviour. Such friendships no doubt can lead to revolutionary changes in the prisoners' lives, but Shepherd insisted that the focus is on their primary goal of befriending, and it should not be seen as a means to an end. 'I believe our role is to try to enhance the quality of life for clients whilst in prison', he explained, emphasising the benefits of social interaction and working with the prisoners as friends who need support, rather than as 'bad people' who need to change.

The creation of NOMS will further develop the Government's efforts to make throughcare a statutory part of sentences. Whether offenders take advantage of the opportunities they are given is up to them. If all offenders were offered the chance to establish a more comfortable, profitable and law-abiding lifestyle, yet chose to continue offending, these efforts cannot be continued indefinitely, and incapacitation will remain the only guaranteed means of preventing reoffending.

12

Probation and Restorative Justice

Probation in the UK

Until March 2001 probation was a local authority service, supported by an 80 per cent central government grant. Local authorities were required to make up the 20 per cent difference. From April 2001 the National Probation Service (NPS) for England and Wales was established as part of the Home Office and probation services were provided by 42 local area probation boards which receive 100 per cent grant from the National Probation Directorate (NPD). Total public expenditure on, or in support of, the probation service in 2002-2003 was £693 million.

Workload

The probation service faces a similar problem to that of the prisons. Sheer weight of numbers makes it very difficult to devote adequate time to offenders. However, understanding that trend has become more difficult due to changes in the method of calculating the caseload. In 2002 the courts sentenced 1.42 million offenders overall; 337,000 for indictable offences and 1.08 million for summary offences. Of these, 111,600 people were sentenced to immediate custody and 186,500 to community sentences, both the highest figures on record. Community sentences were imposed in 33 per cent of indictable offence cases, compared with only 23 per cent in 1992. For summary offences, community sentences were imposed in seven per cent of cases, compared with two per cent in 1992. Community penalties are divided among three categories, community rehabilitation orders (CROs), community punishment orders (CPOs) and community punishment and rehabilitation orders (CPROs). For sentences starting in 2002, the mean length of a CRO was 16.3 months; the mean length of a CPO was 116.5 hours; and the mean length of the rehabilitation component of a CPRO was 16.2 with a mean length of 82.2 hours for the punishment component.[1]

At the end of 2002, 17,300 probation staff were in post.[2] The method used to produce figures showing the average caseload per

189

officer was reviewed in 2003, and the 'officer' figure used in calculating the average now includes Probation Services Officers (PSOs), Senior Probation Officers engaged in fieldwork duties and temporary Probation Officers, in addition to the previously included Maingrade Probation Officers and Senior Practitioners on fieldwork duties.

The method of calculating the number of cases was also modified for 2002. In particular, the types of supervision shown now include community punishment orders and drug treatment and testing orders. At the end of 2002 there were 192,856 persons under criminal supervision of all types, nearly 117,000 as a result of court orders, about 22,000 on statutory post-release supervision, and about 56,000 were under pre-release supervision.[3] The number of offenders starting new community sentences in 2002 under the supervision of the Probation Service was 127,500.[4] However, according to the Carter report,[5] the Home Office predicts that 300,000 offenders will be under the supervision of the Probation Service by 2009.

The effect of the new method has been to produce much lower average caseload figures. Under the old method, the average caseload increased from 20.7 per main grade office in 1992 to 38.2 in 2002, having peaked at 40.7 in 2001.[6] Under the new method, the average number of people supervised per officer rose each year between 1992 (16.2) and 1998 (26.0), reflecting the rising caseload over this period combined with a falling or stable number of officers in post. This average fell in 1999 and again in 2000 to reach 23.5 cases per officer, reflecting an increase in staffing levels and the fact that responsibility for supervising 16-17 year-olds on community penalties was transferred from the Probation Service to Youth Offending Teams during this period. The average has fallen again in 2002 to reach 21.0, due to a further increase in staffing levels.

Nevertheless, the time available to probation officers to have a real influence on offenders continues to be very limited, as reflected in reconviction rates.

Reconviction

Reconviction rates for 1999 indicate that, of those who were sentenced in 1995 to probation, 59 per cent were reconvicted; of those sentenced to community service orders, 52 per cent were reconvicted; and of those sentenced to combination orders, 60 per cent were reconvicted.[7] These reconviction levels suggest that probation in its present form is not effective. Can we learn from America?

Evidence from the US

The proportion of the offending population in the United States on probation constitutes almost 60 per cent of convicted adult offenders. Year-end figures for 1998 indicate that, of the 5.9 million convicted offenders in the United States, 3.4 million were probationers.[8] Between 1990 and 1996, the number of probationers increased by 28 per cent.[9] The number of juvenile offenders sentenced to probation was 613,100 in 1996.[10] There is a tremendous variety of offenders sentenced to probation, including hardened criminals who have plea-bargained their sentence down to probation. In spite of the large number of offenders sentenced to probation, few research studies have been dedicated to measuring its effectiveness, though Petersilia has pursued the issue in her 1997 study.

Petersilia: Probation in the United States

The US probation service is overstretched. What began as a commitment to the Boston Police Court by an individual man, John Augustus, to help individual offenders find employment, residence and an education, has become a significant branch of the criminal justice system whose responsibilities far outreach its current capabilities.

Petersilia states that the severe funding shortages for probation contribute to the ineffectiveness of the service. In spite of supervising two out of three offenders, probation receives one tenth of total government (local and state) corrections funding. In her comparison of prison and probation populations, Petersilia notes that for felony offences the mean incarceration sentence is for seven months, while a probation sentence is for 47 months.[11]

Caseloads are tremendous, ranging between two and 200 for juvenile probation officers and amounting to 117 per adult probation officer when measured nationally. However, Petersilia indicates that the previous figures greatly underestimate the responsibilities per officer, as they rely on dividing the number of cases among all probation staff. In reality, typically only 52 per cent of staff are line officers, while 48 per cent are clerical, support staff and management, according to a study conducted by Cunniff and Bergsmann in 1990.[12] Moreover, of the 52 per cent, only 17 per cent are responsible for adult felons.[13] Langan and Cunniff divided felony probation sentences according to the supervision levels required: ten per cent were intensive (nine contacts per month), 32 per cent were maximum (three), 37 per cent were medium (one), 12 per cent were minimum (one per three months) and nine per cent were administrative (none).[14]

Overloaded probation workers were often unable to meet with offenders, as illustrated by the 1995 Los Angeles statistic: 66 per cent of all probationers were on 'automated' caseloads —meaning no services, supervision or personal contact.[15] Moreover, in 1996 the Los Angeles County Planning Committee found that 10,000 violent offenders (convicted of rape, murder, assault, kidnap and robbery) were included in the 'automated' group.[16]

The probation service is also responsible for pre-sentence investigation (PSI) from the point of arrest, detailing the offender's criminal history, current offence, degree of risk and personal circumstances as well as stating the legal sentencing options and recommending one. PSI reports are integral to the court system, as they provide the documentation for the more than 90 per cent of felony cases in the US that are plea-bargained and dictate most decisions on incapacitation.[17]

Standard conditions for probation include reporting to the probation office, informing the office of any address changes, being employed and not leaving the area without express permission. In order to increase the severity of a probationary sentence, courts often impose additional conditions. Punitive conditions include monetary penalties, community service, victim restitution, house arrest and drug testing, while treatment conditions include substance abuse or family counselling and vocational training.[18] However, the greater the number and severity of the conditions, the greater the likelihood of the offender breaching probation.[19] Moreover, trends indicate that successful completion of probation sentences has been decreasing: 74 per cent in 1986, 67 per cent in 1992, and 60 per cent in 1994.[20] While many probationers receive suspended incarceration sentences,[21] Langan determined that only 50 per cent of known probation violators were imprisoned,[22] while Parent et al. estimated 30-50 per cent of new prison admittances were probation or parole failures.[23] Difficulties arise in locating available jail or prison space for probation violators, a problem that can increase violations as probationers are quick to discover the types of behaviour unlikely to have repercussions.

Reoffending rates have only been collected for adults convicted of felonies (constituting 42 per cent of adult probationers) and not misdemeanours, and juvenile reoffending rates have not been compiled at all.[24] Probation completion rates include both felony and misdemeanour sentences, but can be misleading as they do not reflect re-arrest rates. Petersilia explains that probationers serving sentences for misdemeanour crimes have low reoffending rates, as data indicate that nearly 75 per cent complete probation. However, Petersilia points out that previous evidence has shown that these probationers have 'few sentences and little supervision'.[25] On the other hand, reoffending rates for felon-case probationers are high. According to the 1985 RAND study of 1,672 probationers from Los Angeles and Alameda Counties that were tracked for 40 months from 1980, 65 per cent of the sample were re-arrested, 51 per cent were reconvicted and 34 per cent were imprisoned for new offences committed.[26] However, other agencies duplicated the study in additional counties and noted great variations in reoffending rates, as the severity of criminal offences, follow-up period and surveillance measures changed. Geerken and Hayes compiled 17 studies of adult felony probationers and found that reoffending rates varied between 12 and 65 per cent across different geo-graphical areas.[27]

In 1986, Petersilia and Turner conducted a three-year experiment to compare felons sentenced to probation or a split sentence and those sentenced to prison alone.[28] They identified 672 male probationers and looked for matching prisoners. The first four variables for which the two groups were matched were the year of sentencing (1980), gender (male), county of conviction (Los Angeles or Alameda) and the conviction offence type (robbery, assault, burglary, theft or drug sale/possession). The fifth variable reflected the risk-of-imprisonment of each candidate, classifying each as low, medium or high. All prisoners were to have a 24-month follow-up period, and thus must have been released before 1 July 1982. The resulting sample included a total of 1,022 offenders, composed of 511 felony probationers and 511 prisoners, all of whom were sentenced in 1980.[29]

Thereafter, Petersilia and Turner imposed additional controls in their models for the following factors that could have influenced the incarceration decision including: age of offender at conviction, number of conviction counts, adult convictions and prior prison terms, known or related to victim, caused serious injury, armed with gun, weapon used, and drug addict.[30] The authors recorded any arrests, any filings and any convictions for the first 24 months after offenders were released into the community. Comparing the reoffending rates of both groups, Turner and Petersilia found that almost 75 per cent of prisoners were re-arrested after an average of 12.5 months spent in prison, while about 66 per cent of probationers were re-arrested after an average of 3.3 months in jail, owing to split sentences.[31] In general, the authors concluded that 'the majority of both prisoners and probationers "failed" during the two-year follow-up period',[32] indicating that neither sanction was particularly effective in preventing reoffending.

Petersilia and Turner then took the incidences of re-arrest for the two groups and added the incapacitation effect by counting reoffending rates for the two groups over the entire three-year study period. They found that the prisoners committed an estimated[33] 20 per cent less crime than probationers.[34] Petersilia and Turner concluded, 'The incapacitation effect for the prisoners is nontrivial, and public safety is clearly served by incapacitating these offenders'.[35]

In order to test the correlation between imprisonment and reoffending, Petersilia and Turner used complex statistical procedures to keep all the other variables included in the study constant. They found that imprisonment was not significantly correlated to re-arrest rate probabilities for any type of offender.[36]

Next, Petersilia and Turner tested for a relationship between recidivism and the length of the prison term. Considering only the prison offenders and using the models they had developed to compare the effects of prison and probation on reoffending, they tested the effect of time served by using the number of months the prisoner served prior to first release as a continuous variable.[37] The results indicated a percentage decrease in reoffending for each month served in prison for drug, property and violent crimes, though only the correlation with drug offenders was deemed statistically significant. The estimates[38] for drug felons included a decrease of 1.8 per cent for re-arrest, 3.1 per cent for a filed charge and 2.8 per cent for conviction.[39] Thus, Petersilia and Turner concluded that reoffending rates for released prisoners were not increased as a result of a longer prison-sentence served and wrote that 'in fact, the probabilities are in the other direction'.[40]

The 1986 Petersilia and Turner study compared two groups of offenders that were matched prior to sentencing. However, as

Petersilia (1997) later admits, with identically matched offenders randomly assigned to prison or probation, one can be confident of the results, whereas for the 1986 study judges set sentences according to criteria that may or may not have been adequately controlled in the variables, since details of courtroom proceedings (such as an offender sounding repentant and thus being granted probation rather than incarceration) were not included in the data sets.[41] According to the Maryland SMS, the quasi-experimental design of this study would classify as a 3.

Reinventing probation through the broken windows model

Although a very large proportion of offenders in the USA are dealt with through probation, funding is limited. However, as the Manhattan Institute's publication, *Transforming Probation through Leadership: The Broken Windows Model*, indicates, the public does not wish to direct additional resources to a system that is widely perceived not to work. While some may advocate re-sentencing a substantial proportion of probationers to prison, the Reinventing Probation Council (authors of the Manhattan Institute report) admits that the number of offenders is simply too great to eliminate the probation service completely. Instead, probation must be 're-invented', proven to be an effective sanction and then considered for additional resources.

The two main goals of probation, according to the Manhattan Institute publication, are achieving public safety and reducing reoffending rates. Probation has the jurisdiction to protect 24 hours a day; yet the probation service has neglected to create a theory of practice to guide its employees and further colleagues. The Reinventing Probation Council believes that 'practitioners of probation must learn to work "smarter" by devising supervision strategies that are informed by a vision rooted in community values and outcomes that have clear relevance'.[42] The solution is community justice.

While community justice takes certain elements from restorative justice, the two should not be confused. Restorative justice tends to be focused primarily on the individual offender and victim, whereas the needs of the community differ from those of the individual. The community calls for retribution and punishment, but also recalls the harm endured by victims. Justice professionals, victim services providers, members of the community and professionals work with the victim through this process. Moreover, community justice depends on developing strong, new partnerships between community groups (including religious organisations and local charities) and residents. Further, the members of the court, police, probation and parole agencies must facilitate these relationships with neighbourhood groups while sanctioning offenders, preventing crime and providing safety.[43]

Part of the appeal of the community justice approach is that it goes further than offender-centred sanctions and fulfils the needs of the community and victim as well.[44] Moreover, with both the community and criminal justice system involved, sharing information and responsibility, supervision is much stricter than if just one group were responsible.

The Reinventing Probation Council lists seven key strategies for successful implementation of community justice. They are:

1) 'Place public safety first'.[45] To gain and maintain the support of the public at large, members must believe that they are safe, particularly in their own communities. Probation agencies should consider methods to improve the community and prevent the crimes from occurring within it.

2) 'Supervise probationers in the neighbourhood, not in the office'.[46] Probation relies on allowing offenders to live within a community, not within an office. In order to help an offender with necessary socialisation and to increase awareness of the probationer's current lifestyle, the probation officer must become accustomed to the offender's environment.

3) 'Rationally allocate resources'.[47] Staff must be rationed to the areas in the community where they will be most effective. Thus, the probation officer must know not only about his offender's habits and tendencies but also about the neighbourhood's potential trouble-spots.

4) 'Provide for strong enforcement of probation conditions and a quick response to violations'.[48] Probationers should not be given second chances after they have violated the rules. To do so would only teach the offender that certain breaches of probation orders are permissible.

5) 'Develop partners in the community'.[49] Probation officers should always turn to the community when developing new policies, piloting programmes and delivering services. Members of the probation agencies are also recommended to sit on neighbourhood advisory boards and other official organisations.

6) 'Establish Performance-Based Initiatives'.[50] In order for probation officers to make the best decisions regarding their offenders, they need to be well-informed of evidence-based initiatives.

7) 'Cultivate strong leadership'.[51] Real change within the probation service will require independent thinkers who will work beyond the established means of communication and organisation, and who will risk trying out new methods.

Probation in England and Wales

Since becoming a national service in 2001 a variety of new schemes have been piloted, but few evaluations are sufficiently complete to allow us to draw any conclusions.

All community sentences are subject to conditions, including keeping in contact with probation officers, turning up for community service duties and fulfilling rehabilitation orders such as attending anger management classes. A certain number of absences and non-fulfilment of sentence requirements may be acceptable, but above a certain number action is supposed to be taken. Offenders who manage to complete their probationary period without breaching their conditions tend to be in the minority. An audit conducted by the Association of Chief Officers of Probation found in 2001 that 65 per cent of community sentences were breached.[52] Increasing compliance among probationers has therefore become a key concern.

Among the recent evaluations to be completed is a joint scheme with the Department for Work and Pensions.

Withdrawal of benefits

The Department for Work and Pensions (DWP) recently piloted a project among probationers in the UK, which is loosely aimed at increasing compliance with parole conditions and reducing reoffending. The project was based on the theory that probationers on community sentences could be encouraged to comply with the terms of their sentences if threatened with the partial withdrawal of their benefits as punishment for breaching their terms. Offenders on a Community Rehabilitation Order, for instance, would be required to turn up a couple of times a week for rehabilitation sessions or classes, and offenders placed on Community Punishment Orders would be expected to attend 'work' one or more times per week.

Offenders were given a warning by the sentencer in court that breaches would be sanctioned by reducing their benefits. Once the community sentence began offenders were warned again about the policy by their probation officer. If they were suspected of breaching the conditions of their sentence, a breach hearing would be organised.[53] After the hearing, the outcome would be relayed to Jobcentre Plus only if proven. Jobcentre Plus would then be expected to impose the sanction by reducing the relevant offender's benefits by amounts ranging from 20 per cent to 100 per cent.[54]

The project began in 2001. It was conducted in four different probation areas; the results from all four have been amalgamated. It is unclear how many offenders were sentenced to community orders under the benefits-withdrawal policy, although it is reported that a total of 16,574 Community Rehabilitation Orders (CROs), Community Punishment Orders (CPOs) and Community Punishment and Rehabilitation Orders (CPROs) were issued (among the four probation areas) within the time period of the evaluation.[55]

Researchers used various methods of qualitative data collection. They conducted 31 in-depth interviews and 18 group discussions with staff from both the probation service and Jobcentre Plus; 55 in-depth interviews with offenders, 44 of whom received a sanction for breaching their conditions and 11 of whom remained sanction-free during the period of evaluation; and about 104 returned postal surveys.

Fifty-five offenders who were claiming benefits were included in the qualitative part of the study. Forty-one of them were male and 14 female. The majority (20) were aged between 20 and 24 with others evenly distributed across the age bands of under 20, 25-29, 30-34, and 35-39. Just four were over 40 years old. Most of the offenders (30) received CROs; 12 were sentenced to CPOs and 13 to combined CPROs. Thirty-four of them were claiming Job Seeker's Allowance (JSA) and 21 of them were on income support. Offenders who agreed to be interviewed for the qualitative data reported that the threat of the sanction did not influence their behaviour much.

Researchers also gathered quantitative data relating to the number of breaches they expected the offender population to commit and the estimated influence of the policy on the number of breaches. They did this by comparing a series of estimates of change in compliance levels (among both the benefit-receiving population and the non-benefit receiving population) with compliance rates from an earlier control period measured from five months immediately before the pilot began.[56] The method was cautious but complex and relied on much interpretation and estimation.

Researchers concluded that the policy had a 'small but positive' impact on compliance, reducing the rate of breach 'initiation' by 1.8 per cent. In total, they found a reduction of 2.4 per cent in breaches, but rationalised that about 0.6 per cent of this effect was due to other unrelated factors, since breach rates among non-benefits receivers dropped 0.6 per cent without the threat of sanctions.[57]

The system did not work as planned, which had some influence on the results: many probationers who received sanctions complained that they had not been clearly informed about the policy, and researchers indicate that some courts/ probation services were not always rigorous in this regard.[58] Jobcentre Plus staff complained that they received a large number of reports of breaches that were later confirmed, yet they did not receive notification of the confirmations after the hearings and therefore did not take any action in implementing sanctions.

Overall, the threat of sanctions appears to have had very little effect, if any, on compliance levels among probationers.

Since 2001 the National Probation Service (NPS) has undergone a good deal of change. In 2002 a revised 'National Standards for the Supervision of Offenders in the Community' was published setting out the probation service's responsibilities pre-sentence and post-sentence operations. Members of the probation service must prepare Bail Information Reports, Pre-Sentence Reports (PSRs) and Specific Sentence Reports as requested by the courts. For community sentences and supervision within the community, the national standard lays down contact requirements. For example, there should be weekly meetings for the first four weeks an offender is released on license, and at least 12 contacts (including one home visit) should be made within the first 12 weeks of a Community Rehabilitation Order (CRO).

Probation officers are encouraged to devote a certain amount of their time to building links in the communities of their relevant probation charges, indicating a potential for a 'community justice' approach along the lines discussed earlier. Currently, probation officers are to spend between half and one day a week on average in the community,[59] though some probation officers may devote more or less time depending on the needs of the particular probation office as well as the caseload of the officer.

The NPS has embarked on seven Crime Reduction Programme Community Service (CRP-CS) pathfinder projects, to discover what within community sentencing may reduce offending, based on several promising approaches. In Berkshire and Cambridgeshire, the principles of 'pro-social modelling' are being applied to offenders. In two different case studies, one in Norfolk and Suffolk and the other in Gloucestershire, skills accreditation is being offered to probationers. The programme applied in Northumbria and Durham combines pro-social modelling with skills accreditation. The case study in Hampshire provides pro-social modelling in conjunction with vocational skills. In Somerset, the programme combines several of the previous elements, but is testing for differences associated within a more rural setting. The Leicestershire study is testing an approach combining individualised supervision planning and skills accreditation.[60] While there have been no reoffending rates included in the published evaluations of the projects, including the final report of 2002, and rumours abound that they never will be released as they indicate unfavourable outcomes for the programmes,[61] a reconviction study, measuring outcomes at the end of 12 and 24 months, is due for completion at some point.[62]

Conclusion

The most promising approach to probation we have come across is based on 'broken windows' theory. While increased monitoring of offenders by probation officers will help, as will having enforcement devices on-hand (including prison space for violators), the community approach shows the most promise. It holds out the hope that probationers will feel greater accountability to their communities, and that members of the public will feel that improving crime-dominated neighbourhoods is worthwhile.

In addition, while the community justice model may encourage a more effective use of public funds, overall funding levels will need to increase if probation services are to supervise so many offenders effectively. However, without evidence of effectiveness few members of the public are likely to be persuaded. Nevertheless, there is a strong belief among some probation reformers, particularly in the United States, that probation can be radically improved.

Victim awareness and restorative justice

Victim awareness

Shinar and Compton's[63] study appraises restorative justice schemes that combined victim awareness with monetary penalties. The Victim Impact Panel (VIP) comprised three to five victims of

Driving While Intoxicated (DWI) who were either seriously injured or lost a loved one as a result of the offence. The victims give personal accounts of the impacts of the crime in the presence of DWI convicted offenders who were sentenced to attend the VIP programme by the courts. The hypothesis being tested was that offenders would realise how irresponsible it was to drive while drunk, be more receptive to arguments and rules against driving under the influence, and would not commit such offences in the future. Sometimes offenders were ordered to pay fees which were put towards the costs of the programme. Unfortunately, Shinar and Compton's analysis did not measure the effects of the monetary component on reoffending rates separately. Therefore, their conclusions were focused on the effectiveness of victim awareness programmes akin to UK restorative justice efforts.

Sherman *et al.* rated Shinar and Compton (1995) a 3 on the Maryland SMS. The study considered Victim Impact Panels (VIPs) in two areas: Oregon and Orange County, California. The study was designed to measure: (1) whether reoffending rates were lower among programme participants compared with matched non-participants; (2) whether the effects of VIP lessen over time; (3) whether VIP No-Shows (NS) reoffended more often than either VIP participants or controls; and (4) whether the VIP scheme had a more positive effect on older offenders. The study compared driver's licence records of those sentenced to VIPs during 1988-1989 and those of controls who were matched in age and sex for the two years that followed the VIP. As the two samples consisted of differently assembled data sets, the study must be considered in two parts, assessing the experiment in Oregon first and then that in California.

Josephine, Washington and Multnomah were the three counties included in the Oregon component of the study. The total sample included all 27,021 convicted DWI drivers in 1988-1989, divided into the following five groups:

- A programme group of 1,350 convicted drivers who were sentenced to VIP (called VIP)

- A control group of 1,350 convicted drivers who matched the VIP group in age and sex but who were not sentenced to VIP by the courts (called VIP-C)

- 295 convicted drivers who were 'No-Show' at their VIP appointments (called NS)

- A no-show control group of 295 convicted drivers who matched the VIP 'No-Show' group in age and sex but who were not sentenced to VIP by the courts (called NS-C)

- 23,545 drivers who were left over from the previous four groups.

In their analysis, however, Shinar and Compton considered only the first four groups. Further dividing the drivers into four categories according to age (16-20, 21-25, 26-35, and 36+ years old), Shinar and Compton compared reoffending rates consisting of all moving violations, crashes and DWI offences. They found that the highest rate of reoffending occurred in the 16-20 category. The VIP groups all had lower rates of reoffending than the VIP-C groups, though the difference was only statistically significant among the 36+ age group, as the observed differences in reoffending rates were so small that they were attributed to differences between the VIP sentenced and control groups. The 36+ VIP participants reoffended 39 per cent less than the VIP-C for the same age category. Shinar and Compton pointed out that the effect of the VIP programme may have been even greater as 27 per cent of VIP participants had records of previous offences while only 20 per cent of VIP-C group had them.[64]

However, in their analysis of the Oregon study by Shinar and Compton (1995), Sherman et al. reported that only 30 per cent of VIPs and 35 per cent of VIP-Cs reoffended,[65] suggesting a stronger correlation between VIP participation and reoffending rates across all age groups than indicated by Shinar and Compton in their conclusions. While the figures reported by Sherman et al. were accurate, Shinar and Compton considered them to be inconclusive because 30 per cent of the NS group reoffended; thereby undermining the argument that treatment worked.

When Shinar and Compton counted only DWI violations in determining reoffending rates in Oregon, they found statistically significant lower reoffending rates for the VIP participants, 11 per cent versus 16 per cent for VIP-C, only in the first year following treatment. By the second year, the VIP effect was not statistically significant. However, even within the first year, while 72 per cent of VIP members had one or more offence recorded, 82 per cent of NS members had offended at least once, causing Shinar and Compton to suggest that actual VIP attendance may have had a 'spurious' effect.[66]

The Orange County, California sample included only first-time offenders and this was their only court-directed penalty. The four groups consisted of 742 VIP participants, 742 VIP-C offenders, 388

NS offenders and 388 NS-C offenders. Each experimental group was matched in age, sex and number of DWI convictions. However, there were significant differences recognised according to gender and age between the groups: 36 per cent of VIP-sentenced men did not show up while only 22 per cent of VIP-sentenced women did not; 45 per cent of No-Shows were 25 years old or younger while 31 per cent of VIPs were 25 years old or younger.[67]

Shinar and Compton first measured reoffending rates by including all DWI felonies and misdemeanours, reckless driving incidents, hit-and-run crashes and any other cases of injury that led to driving convictions, all within two years. Reoffending, according to these criteria, was recorded at: 17 per cent for NS, 15 per cent for NS-C, 13 per cent for VIP and 13 per cent for VIP-C; as records did not vary much between the test and relevant control groups, Shinar and Compton concluded that there was no significant effect as measured by these standards.[68]

Second, Shinar and Compton considered DWI violations only in calculating reoffending rates. Again they found no statistically significant evidence in support of VIP programmes, as the test groups and their controls yielded very similar rates: 16 per cent for NS versus 16 per cent for NS-C and 27 per cent for VIP versus 29 per cent for VIP-C.[69]

The third method of measurement Shinar and Compton employed to determine a VIP effect was to consider the mean time to first new offence committed. They found that the mean was 11.3 months, including a mean of 11.9 months for NSs, 11.9 months for VIPs, 9.6 months for NS-Cs and 11.5 for VIP-Cs, indicating no significant deviance from the mean by any of the groups. Hypothesising that the VIP effect is more profound immediately after treatment, Shinar and Compton calculated reoffending rates for the first six months after the reference conviction; however, they found no significant variance among the reoffending rates: 3.4 per cent for the VIPs, 3.3 per cent for the VIP-Cs, 4.1 per cent for the NSs and 5.2 per cent for the NSCs.[70]

Shinar and Compton noted that reoffending rates between the VIP group and the NS group were significantly different, at six per cent and nine per cent after one year, and 11 and 16 per cent after two; yet both groups had results similar to their respective controls, suggesting a possible sampling bias between the VIP and NS groups.

Considering the evidence of both the Oregon and California components of the study, Shinar and Compton determined that

Victim Impact Panels did not produce either a consistent or lasting effect on reducing reoffending rates among known offenders. While the researchers admitted that the sample size limited their ability to measure first-time offenders in comparison to repeat offenders satisfactorily, they nevertheless concluded that VIP would probably fail to alter any behaviour among habitual drinkers. VIP treatment as applied in this study consisted of a one-time meeting with victims of a DWI offence that may or may not have been similar to that committed by the offender. Thus, offenders did not necessarily relate their behaviour to the victim's experience, negating the effect of having an offender take responsibility and admit to his/her reckless and guilty behaviour. Considering the lower reoffending rates among the 36+ age group of Oregon VIP subjects, Shinar and Compton recommended that VIP be assigned to offenders who are over the age of 35, who are not habitual drinkers (first time offenders are most likely to benefit) and who will receive sustained exposure to the treatment programme. Shinar and Compton also suggested including a role model in the panels, someone who is either a reformed offender or could be an inspiration in another capacity, who could further inspire changes in the offenders.

Re-integrative Shaming Experiments (RISE)

Sherman, Strang and Woods evaluated four Re-integrative Shaming Experiments (RISEs) in Canberra, Australia.[71] The inspiration for the project was Braithwaite's concept of re-integrative shaming: that the formal court system stigmatises offenders and their offences and adversely affects their ability to lead conscientious lives as a part of society; conversely, a restorative intervention could cause the offender to take responsibility for his/her crime while providing consolation for the victim.

Sherman, Strang and Woods' initial hypothesis was that offenders who had attended a restorative justice (RJ) conference would have lower reoffending rates than offenders only sentenced by a court.

The study consisted of 1,300 cases[72] randomly sent either to courts or to conferences that were divided among the following four offences: drink driving (blood alcohol content above 0.08) by offenders of any age, juvenile property offending (under the age of 18), juvenile shoplifting as detected by security personnel in the store, and juvenile/youth violent crime (JVC). In order to maintain comparability between the matching court and conference groups, Sherman et al. counted offenders assigned to court and those assigned to treatment at a conference, as not all of those assigned necessarily underwent treatment.

Sherman *et al.* considered the perceptions of procedural fairness by both victims and offenders, overall victim satisfaction, costs and reoffending to be important in compiling evidence of the merits and shortcomings of courts versus conferences.[73] Thus, Sherman *et al.* gathered data from offenders who attended conferences (with 85 per cent of drink drivers, 75 per cent of juvenile property offenders, 79 per cent of juvenile shoplifters and 68 per cent of youth violent crime offenders reporting) to assess their viewpoints on the fairness of the procedures, their viewpoints on the sanctions they received, their viewpoints on the repair of prior wrongs committed, and their emotive response to the treatment received.[74] In addition, the researchers collected comments from nearly all of the conferences included in the study and about 85 per cent of the offenders who appeared in court.[75]

In order to assess reoffending rates the study employed three separate measurements. They analysed the offending rates for one year before the meeting (conference or court hearing) and for one year after the meeting and recorded the differences, thereby allowing them to control for the number of prior offences across the four groups.

First, Sherman *et al.* measured the 'before and after' reoffending rates of offenders who attended standard court hearings and recorded the differences between each of the four offence groups. Second, they measured the reoffending rates of offenders who attended conferences. And third, they subtracted the differences of the four conference groups from the respective differences in the court groups. Sherman *et al.* determined that a significant change within a group in the 'before and after' measurements in one setting but not the other would indicate a treatment effect.[76]

One hundred and ten juveniles and youths had committed violent offences. The court group averaged 0.071 offences per month one year prior to the RISE experiment and averaged 0.063 offenses per month for one year after, constituting a 11 per cent drop in offending levels. On the other hand, the conference group averaged 0.081 offences prior to RISE and 0.041 afterwards, indicating a 49 per cent drop in levels. The results showed a net reduction of 38 per cent in offending levels in favour of the conference group over the control group. These findings were statistically significant.[77]

The drink driving experiment, which included 900 offenders, resulted in slight increases in one year monthly offending rates for all offences in both groups. For the court group, previous offending levels were 0.0121 and post offending levels were 0.0157, indicating an increase of 0.3 per cent. For the conference group, the levels went from 0.0106 to 0.0194, an increase of 0.8 per cent. The results suggested a one per cent increase in offending rates.[78]

The study of juvenile shoplifting detected by store security officers (135 offenders) comparisons resulted in very small differences in offending rates in both groups that were not statistically significant.[79] Similarly, the study of juvenile property crimes with personal victims (238 offenders) indicated virtually no differences in offending rates and also had low statistical significance.[80]

Thus, only the cases involving youth violence indicated a treatment effect on the conference attendees that resulted in lower offending rates while the rest of the experimental groups indicated minimal changes in offending rates. The groups were randomly chosen and the statistical controls implemented by Sherman *et al.* strengthen the reliability of the study. Based on the Maryland SMS, this study would receive a 5 for methodology.

Implications for the UK

The UK government backs restorative justice (RJ) because it helps empower victims by placing them at the centre of the criminal justice process. Moreover, the Government believes RJ 'can reduce reoffending'[81] by encouraging offenders to realise the ramifications of their actions and to take responsibility for them. In addition, RJ offers a plan to reduce future reoffending in which offenders participate, encouraging them to identify strategies to refrain from committing future crimes. However, the empirical evidence indicating that RJ programmes achieve these objectives is not strong.

While RJ has been implemented across the youth justice system since 1998, evaluations are not yet complete. Moreover, as the Government admits in its July 2002 consultation document, additional research must be conducted on the performance and outcomes of RJ for adult offenders and which elements of RJ yield the best results (such as indirect mediation, direct mediation, conferencing, or family conferencing).[82] Thus, based on the limited evidence available, we must place RJ and victim awareness programmes in the 'what we do not know' category of crime prevention measures.

Part II
Conclusions and Implications for Public Policy

13

Can We Learn from America?

We have found it useful to compare England with the United States. It has a similar legal system, a shared cultural heritage and has been conducting many of the same debates about crime, policing and prisons. As Chapter 3 showed, America has a higher rate of gun crime, more murder, and more rape, but American citizens have less chance than the English of being robbed, burgled or having their car stolen. The overall victimisation rate according to the International Crime Victim Survey is 21 per cent in America, compared with 26 per cent in England. If the rate in England had been 21 per cent, then over 2.5 million fewer people would have suffered from crime.

The US Office for Juvenile Justice and Delinquency Prevention (OJJDP) has enunciated five guiding principles for reform:

- **We must strengthen the family** in its primary responsibility to instill moral values and provide guidance and support to children. Where there is no functional family unit, we must establish a family surrogate and assist that entity to guide and nurture the child.

- **We must support core social institutions**—schools, religious institutions, and community organisations—in their roles of developing capable, mature, and responsible youth. A goal of each of these societal institutions should be to ensure that children have the opportunity and support to mature into productive law-abiding citizens.

- **We must promote delinquency prevention** as the most cost-effective approach to reducing juvenile delinquency. Families, schools, religious institutions, and community organisations, including citizen volunteers and the private sector, must be enlisted in the Nation's delinquency prevention efforts.

- **We must intervene immediately and effectively when delinquent behavior occurs** to successfully prevent delinquent offenders from becoming chronic offenders or progressively committing more serious and violent crimes. Initial intervention efforts, under an umbrella of system authorities (police, intake, and probation), should be centered in the family and other core societal institutions. Juvenile justice system authorities should ensure that an appropriate response occurs and act quickly and firmly if the need for formal system adjudication and sanctions has been demonstrated.

- **We must identify and control the small group of serious, violent, and chronic juvenile offenders** who have committed felony offenses or have failed to respond to intervention and nonsecure community-based treatment and rehabilitation services offered by the juvenile justice system. Measures to address delinquent offenders who are a threat to community safety may include placement in secure community-based facilities, training schools and other secure juvenile facilities, and, when necessary, waiver or transfer of the most violent or intractable juveniles to the criminal justice system.[1]

These guidelines suggest a society-wide approach to cutting crime, rather than one focused narrowly on what the criminal justice system can accomplish. Would such an approach make sense for England and Wales?

The social science findings and their implications

Since the 1960s, especially in America, longitudinal and cross-sectional surveys have considerably improved our understanding of offending. Two factual claims are almost universally accepted. First, a small proportion of each age group is responsible for a high proportion of crime. Second, many criminal careers begin in childhood. Moreover, the earlier a person starts committing crimes, the longer he is likely to remain a criminal.

Some of the most useful information has been gathered by the US Government since 1986 from studies in Denver, Colorado; Pittsburgh, Pennsylvania; and Rochester, New York. But America also has a long tradition of longitudinal studies. The Philadelphia birth cohort study found that chronic offenders (those with five or more police contacts) were six per cent of the cohort and responsible for 51 per cent of all offences and about two-thirds of violent crimes.[2] A later Philadelphia cohort found that seven per cent of the cohort was responsible for 61 per cent of all offences, 73 per cent of robberies and 75 per cent of forcible rapes. America's National Youth Survey (NYS) found that about five per cent of juveniles (those aged 12-17) at each age level were classified as 'serious violent offenders'. On average they committed 132 delinquent offences per year.

The English evidence also shows that a small proportion of each age group commits a high proportion of crime. Three per cent of young offenders in the early 1990s committed about 26 per cent of youth crime, and 22 per cent committed about 73 per cent.[3] According to Home Office research, under-18s committed about seven million offences in 1996. In the mid-1990s 10-17 year-olds accounted for 25 per cent of known offenders.[4] A later survey found in 1999 that 12 per cent of males were serious or persistent offenders (defined as those who had committed three or more offences or one serious offence) and that three per cent of males carried out 23 per cent of offences.[5]

American NYS data showed that 45 per cent of those who started committing crimes before age 11 continued violent careers into their 20s. But most careers only lasted one year and only four per cent lasted five years or more.[6] However, more than half of all violent offenders initiated their violent careers between ages 14 and 17.

In Rochester it was found that, of those who began violent offending at age nine or younger, 39 per cent became chronic violent offenders during adolescence. A study of Denver found that, of those who initiated violent offending at age nine or younger, 62 per cent became chronic violent offenders.[7] These US findings suggest that a blend of innate characteristics and early socialisation play a fundamental part in determining criminal behaviour.

In England 60 per cent of males born in 1953 who were first convicted of a standard list offence at age 15 were re-convicted within five years. If first convicted at age 20, the proportion was 31 per cent. If born in 1978, 70 per cent of offenders first convicted at 15 went on to be re-convicted within five years.[8]

But, like America, many criminal careers (measured by convictions) were short. An English study of those born between 1953 and 1978 found that almost 55 per cent of offenders had careers of less than a year in length and two thirds with a criminal career less than five years in length. Most offenders with a criminal career of less than one year had only one court appearance. Almost a quarter of offenders had a criminal career of at least ten years. One in ten had a criminal career of at least 20 years.[9]

Risk factors and protective factors: a basis for policy?

Surveys have also identified the personal characteristics and social circumstances (such as family breakdown) that are statistically associated with crime. These links are not necessarily causal connections but they can be viewed as 'risk factors'. The surveys also identify 'protective factors' which counteract 'risk factors'. Again, these are statistical associations and not necessarily causal connections. Does this new understanding provide a basis for improving policy?

Risk factors

From the 1998/99 Youth Lifestyles Survey, Flood-Page and colleagues identified risk factors for serious and persistent offenders. They were: being male, living in the inner city, low social class, having lone or step parents, having criminal parents, poor parental supervision, delinquent friends, bullying, truancy, exclusion from school, low achievement, and regular drinking.[10]

The survey found that, of those aged 12-17, only four per cent became serious or persistent offenders if they were associated with no risk factors. But if they were associated with four risk factors, 57 per cent became serious or persistent offenders.[11]

The 1995 *Guide for Implementing the Comprehensive Strategy for Serious, Violent, and Chronic Juvenile Offenders*, published by the US OJJDP, identifies a similar list of risk factors under four headings: community, family, school and individual/peer group. It is worth elaborating on them to highlight the importance of the wider social context.

Community risk factors

* Availability of drugs and firearms. When drugs are easily available, drug abuse is more likely. Similarly, the easy availability of firearms can escalate an 'exchange of angry words and fists into an exchange of gunfire'.

* Community laws and norms favouring drug use, firearms, and crime. The attitudes of a community towards drug use, violence, and crime are reflected in laws, informal social practices, the media, and the expectations of parents, teachers, and others. If they are favourable to a law-abiding life, young people are more likely to behave accordingly.[12]

* Media portrayals of violence. The OJJDP accepts that there is growing evidence that media violence can influence community acceptance of violence and rates of violent or aggressive behaviour.

- Mobility. When children move from one school to another, significant increases in the rates of drug use, school dropout and antisocial behaviour have been observed. Communities with high rates of mobility appear to have increased drug and crime problems.

- Low neighbourhood attachment and community disorganisation. Higher rates of juvenile drug problems, crime, and delinquency, as well as higher rates of adult crime and drug trafficking, occur in neighbourhoods where people have little attachment to the community, where the rates of vandalism are high, and where there is low surveillance of public places.[13]

- Extreme economic and social deprivation. The report refers only to 'extreme' deprivation and concedes little to determinists who present the poor as powerless victims of economic circumstance. But it acknowledges that children who live in deteriorating neighbourhoods characterised by extreme poverty and high unemployment are more likely to be delinquents, and are more likely to engage in violence toward others during adolescence and adulthood.

Family risk factors

- Family history of high-risk behaviour. Children raised in a family with a history of addiction to alcohol or other drugs are at increased risk of having alcohol or other drug problems, and children born or raised in a family with a history of criminal activity are at increased risk of delinquency. Similarly, children born to a teenage mother are more likely to be teenage parents, and children of school dropouts are more likely to drop out of school themselves.

- Family management problems. Poor family management practices are defined as not having clear expectations for behaviour, failing to supervise and monitor children, and excessively severe, harsh, or inconsistent punishment. Children exposed to these practices are at higher risk of developing health and behavioural problems.

- Family conflict. Children whose parents are divorced have higher rates of delinquency and substance abuse. However, the authors argue that it is not the divorce itself that contributes to delinquent behaviour. Rather, conflict between family members appears to be more important in predicting delinquency than family structure. They cite Rutter and Giller (1983) as the authority for this claim. This section of the report is contrary to the findings of the English Youth Lifestyles Survey which records family structure as a risk factor, especially lone parenthood and step parenthood.[14]

School risk factors

- Early and persistent antisocial behaviour. Boys who are aggressive in grades K–3 (ages 5-8) or who have trouble controlling their impulses are at higher risk for substance abuse, delinquency and violent behaviour.

- Academic failure beginning in late primary school.

- Lack of commitment to school. Children who are not committed to their school are more likely to be delinquents.

Individual and peer-group risk factors

- Rebelliousness. Young people who feel they are not part of society and not bound by its rules, who do not believe in trying to be successful or responsible, or who adopt an actively rebellious stance are at higher risk of drug abuse, delinquency, and truancy.

- Friends who engage in problem behaviours. Young people who associate with peers who engage in problem behaviours —delinquency, substance abuse, violent activity or truancy— are much more likely to engage in the same behaviours. According to the OJJDP report, this association is one of the most consistent predictors that research has identified. Even when young people come from well-managed families and are not exposed to other risk factors, simply spending time with delinquent friends greatly increases the risk of developing similar problems. However, there is much controversy about causation and it has long been debated whether delinquents seek out like-minded people ('birds of a feather flock together') or associating with delinquents itself encourages a greater degree of wrongdoing.

- Early initiation of problem behaviours. The earlier young people drop out of school, begin using drugs, and commit crimes, the greater the likelihood that they will have chronic problems with these behaviours later in life.

- Constitutional factors. Innate characteristics such as sensation seeking or impulsiveness.

Protective factors

The 'social engineering' approach to social problems is inclined to use social science to identify risk factors and then to call for public policies to reduce or eliminate them. For example, the Home Office Youth Lifestyles Survey identified exclusion from school as a risk factor for crime. For the social engineer, the logical next step is to reduce school exclusions as if they were the cause of crime, when in reality exclusion from school may reflect an underlying anti-social attitude which was the cause of both the exclusion and criminal conduct.[15] Indeed, when the Blair Government recently instructed schools to reduce school exclusions, the outcome was often an increase in disruptive behaviour in schools by youths who previously would have been expelled. Central government pressure on schools to reduce exclusions was subsequently relaxed.

The OJJDP does not over-value the social-engineering approach. It acknowledges that simple awareness of risk factors does not alone help to understand how to reduce crime. It is also necessary to understand protective factors, which they divide into three groups: those inherent in the individual; factors relating to social bonding; and social expectations, especially 'healthy beliefs and clear standards for behaviour'.[16]

Individual qualities

According to the report, individual protective factors include female gender, high intelligence, a positive social orientation, and a 'resilient temperament that helps a child bounce back in adverse circumstances'.

Social bonds

One of the most effective ways to protect young people from risk, says the report, is to strengthen their social bonds. Studies of children who avoid problem behaviour despite living in high-risk situations show that 'strong bonds with an adult' can decrease the likelihood of delinquent behaviour. Good parents are the ideal, but when they are ineffective or a bad influence, substitute adult mentors can make a difference, including other family members, teachers, sports coaches or any community member.

Social expectations

The report emphasised that social expectations are important:

When families, schools, and communities have clearly stated policies and expectations for young people's behaviour, children are less likely to become involved in crime and delinquency. Healthy beliefs and clear standards, communicated consistently by the significant individuals and social groups to whom the child is bonded, build a web of protection for young people exposed to risk.[17]

It gives the example of the 1980's 'Just Say No' campaign. Along with the War on Drugs, and Drug-Free Zones, it advocated clear rules and had an important impact on community standards. At the same time, studies reported the negative health consequences of tobacco, alcohol, and other drug use. Subsequently, there have been public health campaigns against smoking and high-fat diets.[18]

The merits of the OJJDP strategy

Can the insights gained from the social sciences help to devise an effective crime-reduction strategy? We conclude that the OJJDP guidelines point in the right direction, for four main reasons.

First, they emphasise the importance of the early socialisation of children in the family. In England 27 per cent of prisoners had been in care and 47 per cent had run away from home as a child.[19] The YLS found that lone parents and step parents were risk factors for crime. If there were less family breakdown there would be less crime. However, family breakdown is not the only family-related cause of crime: 43 per cent of prisoners had family members who had been convicted and 35 per cent a family member who had been in jail.[20] In such cases their family was a bad influence. Public policies can only achieve so much, but we urgently need a public debate to encourage a new consensus about the family, parenting and marriage.

Second, one of the most important features of the OJJDP report is its emphasis on the impact of the wider society on the expectations we have of each other and, in particular, the influence of the media and all those who contribute to opinion formation through writing and broadcasting. It reminds us that we all have a responsibility to play our part in upholding shared standards of right and wrong, and that the obligation is especially strong on people who reach wider audiences through the media of mass communication. It also reminds us that we have been going through a 'culture war' in which many of our primary institutions have been attacked, not least the family based on marriage.

Public opinion can be divided in various ways. One possibility is a division between elite opinion (those able to express their opinions through the mass media) and public opinion (those without such access). Élite opinion has been hostile to the family based on marriage for at least 30 years. A recent defence of marriage by a *Sunday Times* columnist, Ferdinand Mount, for instance, found it necessary to be apologetic about the 'M-word'.[21]

Schools also play an important role in socialising youngsters, but we have also come through a period when élite opinion among educators has been inclined to be hostile to the moral influence traditionally exerted by schools. They aimed to liberate pupils from 'conformism', which prepared them to be nothing more than the zombie employees of the powers that be. We also need a public debate about the purposes of education, in the hope of reaching a more workable consensus.

The OJJDP report admits that:

> The United States is just beginning a discussion about healthy beliefs and clear standards in response to violence in families, neighbourhoods, and communities. Responsible adults must, through words and deeds, show the Nation's youth that fighting does not solve problems and that the violent behaviour portrayed in the entertainment media does not provide a good model for real life. We need to set clear standards about acceptable, nonviolent behaviour.

A sense of community, it says, must be re-created in America:

> Each year thousands of young people in the United States begin to use tobacco, alcohol, marijuana, cocaine, and other drugs. Many of these youth do not identify with individuals or groups that communicate healthy beliefs and clear standards about drugs.[22]

Third, the report highlights the important influence on crime of local communities. Where there is strong local attachment and mutual confidence that neighbours will support one another, crime is much diminished. It allows youngsters to be guided by other adults in the locality without heavy-handed controls and in a spirit of 're-integrative shaming'. Such communities cannot easily be created, but programmes have been devised to encourage their emergence, including *Communities That Care*.[23]

Fourth, the report does not avoid tough questions about what should be done with recalcitrant offenders. Many crime reformers have a utopian or romantic view of human nature and emphasise the importance of rehabilitation and early prevention. To focus on early socialisation is fully justified, but it is necessary to face the fact that such strategies do not work in all cases. The OJJDP makes it clear that persistent offenders should be removed from the community and placed in secure facilities to prevent further harm to the public and so that a sustained effort can be made to help them reintegrate into society as law-abiding people.

Rehabilitation, punishment and prevention

Before turning to specifics, one final set of preliminary remarks is necessary. Most commentators who are against prison are usually in favour of two other approaches: the rehabilitation of existing offenders, and preventive measures to discourage young people from turning to crime in the first place.

We are strongly in favour of a renewed focus on early socialisation. However, punishment and rehabilitation are often discussed as if they are mutually exclusive, when they are not. First, it is unrealistic to expect to be able to change the personality or attitudes of an offender without maintaining clear social standards, and such standards cannot be maintained without showing that the society means what it says. Reintegration back into the community of law-abiding people is a legitimate aim of sentencing but clear moral messages must be sent. Letting criminals get away with offending gives the wrong impression and undermines efforts to rehabilitate convicted offenders. Without clear standards, the task of parents, teachers and child protection officials is inevitably much harder.

Second, punishment and rehabilitation have been successfully combined. In fact, the most successful rehabilitation schemes for seriously troubled offenders, those addicted to drugs, have combined punishment and rehabilitation in the form of prison-based therapeutic communities, with sustained follow-through programmes (Chapter 5).

Third, it must also be acknowledged that the threat of punishment often reinforces rehabilitation by encouraging offenders to be ready to change. Bonta (Chapter 4) found that the threat of a return to prison made offenders undergoing community sentences more likely to attend educational courses.

As Chapter 4 showed, despite many decades of experimentation, it has proved very difficult to rehabilitate offenders. We conclude that an effective criminal justice system must be willing to incarcerate serious offenders when rehabilitation has failed. Adult offenders should be treated as if they have exercised a choice to commit crimes and sentenced in accordance with principles of just punishment and in recognition of the need to protect the public. It is generally accepted, however, that a different approach should be adopted for juveniles, largely because (by definition) they are not fully mature and therefore more likely to change. Nevertheless, recalcitrant juveniles who persist in harming fellow citizens should be punished according to adult principles. Failure to punish a persistent offender is not only harmful in itself, but it also undermines efforts to rehabilitate other offenders by sending the message that the society is not serious about upholding its own standards.

14

Guiding Principles for Public Policy

What should we do to create a more law-abiding society? First, we should not merely ask what public policies are advisable. Much of the solution lies outside the reach of policy makers. The Western tradition of liberty separates the state and civil society and, in doing so, puts a heavy burden on institutions responsible for socialisation—above all, families, as well as schools, voluntary organisations and churches. There are four main groups of remedies.

- Social investment, both public and private, in institutions that encourage a law abiding lifestyle, especially the family.

- Reducing the net advantages of crime through 'situational' change, including reducing the opportunities for crime, or increasing the trouble and expense involved.

- Reducing the net benefits of crime by increasing the risk of detection and punishment and, in doing so, increasing the relative benefits of law-abiding behaviour.

- Personalised programmes to reduce reoffending by convicted criminals.

1. Social investment in moral education

To speak of social investment does not necessarily imply government action. It implies collective effort not necessarily undertaken by the government, or even with its involvement.

Most criminologists accept that some people in every generation are predisposed to crime. Whether they become criminals or not depends on their early socialisation as well as on the criminal justice system.

The first priority is to raise children to share in the common measure of right and wrong. If we are to uphold a just society we each need to play our part in bringing it about. This is a challenge for parents, schools, and all of us insofar as we influence other people. For some, this influence is confined to those we encounter in face-to-face dealings, and for others, with access to the means of mass communication, it reaches more widely. We each have a responsibility to do what we can.

The part played by the criminal justice system is always of lesser importance than grassroots efforts to build and maintain a society of conscientious citizens. But, the criminal justice system can do much harm if it fails to play its part in this great endeavour of maintaining a free and just society. During the last 20-30 years, the police and courts have not always backed up members of the rank and file who were doing their bit to preserve the ordinary decencies of life in their localities.

Upholding standards of behaviour depends on consensus. In a consensual society, policing, for example, can be light, but in a torn society, where significant groups refuse to give full legitimacy to the prevailing standards, consensual policing becomes difficult. Wide public acceptance is especially important for traditional English policing, under which the police officer is considered to be a citizen in uniform. However, from the 1960s there was reduced agreement about some kinds of behaviour, including drug use, industrial violence, political protest and urban rioting. Marxists wanted to encourage trade union militancy and saw the police as the 'lackeys of capitalism', preventing the unions from intimidating opponents. For some intellectuals in the Labour movement, common criminals were the revolutionary vanguard. However this attitude was very unpopular with the bulk of Labour voters and abandoned by the Labour party in the mid-1990s.

More recently the importance of consensus has been acknowledged. Schemes such as neighbourhood watch have been formed to encourage mutual support and, on a grander scale, schemes like *Communities That Care* have been set up in the hope of rebuilding a sense of community.[1]

The family

The most important influence on socialisation is the family, followed at some distance by schools. Based on longitudinal and cross-sectional studies, four main influences can be identified.

The first and most important is parental neglect. Children raised by parents who fail to supervise them or spend much time with them are more likely to become criminals.

Second, family conflict can be important, especially when parents contradict each other—thereby providing no clear moral lead—or compete for affection by being lax with their children. Such conflict is more likely in broken families, whether one-parent or step-families.

Third, criminal parents or those who condone crime are much more likely to raise criminal offspring.

Fourth, disruption of the family is associated with crime. It may take the form of the absence of one parent, the casual arrival of new partners, or the appearance of a step-parent.[2]

John Graham and Trevor Bennett have usefully summarised the main forms of family intervention so far attempted by government agencies.

- Discouragement of teenage pregnancy. Children born to teenage mothers are at a high risk of becoming criminals due to parental neglect. However, effective programmes have been hard to come by in the UK.

- Pre- and post-natal care. Home visits by health visitors to give advice and discourage abuse have been found to help. The Government's Sure Start initiative is one example.

- Parent training. Erratic and inconsistent discipline is associated with offending and some schemes have found that parents can acquire improved skills by attending classes. Such training may also discourage parents from putting children into care, an even bigger risk factor for crime.

- Family support. This can include a wide range of services, including financial assistance, personal counselling, child care and after-school clubs. Social workers may also encourage family preservation in the hope that children will not need to be taken into care, where they are even less likely to receive the moral guidance necessary to keep them out of trouble.

- Pre-school education combined with home visits. The most famous of these schemes is the Perry Pre-School project which began in 1962 with 123 black children from families of low socio-economic status. About half were single-parent families. Fifty-eight were in the programme group and 65 in the control group. The scheme lasted two years until the children were aged three. The pre-school programme offered a high teacher/ pupil ratio and lasted for 2.5 hours per day for 30 weeks of the year. In addition the teachers visited mothers at home while the child was present for 1.5 hours once per week. Information was gathered as the children grew up: at age 11, 15, 19 and 27. Those in the programme group did better in school and teenage pregnancy was lower. At age 19, arrest rates were about half those for the control group. At age 27, one in three of the control group had been arrested, compared with one in 14 of the programme group.

These programmes for parent support or parental substitution are largely uncontroversial but, compared with the impact of family breakdown, they are able only to scratch the surface. It is unlikely that primary socialisation can be improved while over one-fifth of children are being raised by only one parent. The causes of family breakdown and how it might be reduced are the subject of separate Civitas studies.[3]

Public opinion and the raw material of public debate

If a new consensus is to have any hope of emerging we will need to improve the quality of public debate. One of the main obstacles is government control of information about crime. It is widely accepted that in a democracy there should be a free flow of information to create the possibility of public discussion and to allow citizens to hold the government to account. However, governments hoping to win the next election face a constant temptation to conceal information that would damage their reputation and to publicise only information that would put them in a good light. The preparation and publication of crime figures has increasingly fallen into the hands of people who see information as a weapon in a propaganda war.

This realisation led us to reflect on a new concern: how to create a more independent public statistical service, beyond the reach of party politics? But the manipulation of information is not the only concern. The ideal of democratic government is based on the belief that human understanding is fragile. Consequently, we should place our confidence, not in the truths contained in sacred texts, nor in the authority of experts, but in a co-operative process of mutual learning through discussion. The best safeguard against individual fallibility is, not to put our trust in a few individuals assumed not to be fallible, but to rely on a collective process of argument and counter-argument.

At the same time, acknowledgement of human fallibility is not a justification for relativism. There is an objective truth towards which we struggle through a collaborative process. It is at its most systematic in science, where contributors are expected to frame their hypotheses so that they can easily be tested. Over time we arrive at a body of knowledge in which reasonable confidence can be placed because it has survived criticism so far.

Free and open discussion requires that we let everyone speak out in the belief that we might learn from them. But any such process requires a degree of public spirit. Each must be open to contradiction, willing to be self-critical, and to learn from opponents. Facts should not be manipulated. Each should accept the ideal of disinterested study and debate. It is only rarely that public discussion gets anywhere near this ideal. Frequently only the facts that fit a particular case are published. Opponents are accused of having ulterior motives, when such claims cannot be proved one way or the other.

There is no prospect of democratic decision-making based on mutual learning through open discussion when the vital raw material—information—is under the control of one protagonist, especially one that has the power of government at its disposal. We urgently need to find a way of putting the public information service, and especially the statistical service, beyond the reach of party politics.

2. Reducing Net Benefits: through Situational Prevention

Many scholars advocate better management of the environment in which crimes might occur. Three approaches are often distinguished: increasing the effort required by criminals (e.g. better locks, and car immobilisers); increasing the risk of detection (e.g. improved street lighting, and CCTV); and reducing the rewards of offending (e.g. property marking to reduce the saleability of stolen goods). The underlying assumption is that crime is a chosen activity which can be reduced if it is made less attractive compared to the alternatives.

Measures to increase the effort involved include 'target hardening' measures such as fitting improved locks or adding security devices to cars, homes and offices. Improved fencing may discourage theft and the use of reinforced materials in street furniture such as bus shelters may reduce vandalism.

The risk of detection does not only depend on police activity. It has long been recognised that devices such as CCTV, good street lighting, and security guards can reduce crime in specific localities. It is common to distinguish between formal and informal surveillance. As the name implies, formal surveillance refers to organised systems such as patrols by security guards and nightwatchmen. Informal or natural surveillance refers to oversight by people going about their normal business. It is much assisted by the amount of 'defensible space', a concept associated with Oscar Newman, who drew attention to the importance of architectural design in avoiding no-go areas. The more an area is monitored by residents, the better.

Third, the net rewards of offending can be reduced by making stolen goods harder to sell. Property marking reduces the number of potential buyers, for instance, and redesigning car radios so that they cannot be easily removed in full working order lowers their resale value.

However, when there is a high propensity to commit crimes it has been found that such measures often displace crime to less well protected areas. Consequently, in the absence of other reforms, situational prevention may not reduce the overall crime rate. Nevertheless, as Professor Ken Pease has argued, it is unlikely that the displacement effect is total. Many offenders, for instance, ply their trade within a convenient travelling time of their homes, and if local opportunities are reduced, lawful alternatives may appear relatively more attractive.[4]

3. Reducing Net Benefits by Increasing the Risk of Punishment

Chapter 3 showed that there is convincing evidence that increasing the risk of punishment reduces crime. When changes in the net benefits of crime lead to adjustments in human behaviour, three main influences can be distinguished: the swiftness and certainty of punishment; the severity of punishment; and the attractiveness of alternatives to crime.

The likelihood of capture is mostly in the hands of the police and the likelihood of conviction depends on the performance of the prosecution service and the courts. Whether an unwanted punishment will follow is mainly in the hands of the courts, though lawmakers may limit judicial discretion.

Police action
Policing is the subject of a separate study by Norman Dennis,[5] but a proposed crime reduction strategy could hardly fail to mention it at all. Police action can reduce crime in two main ways. The first might be called primary prevention, and takes the form of patrolling on foot to maintain a presence and 'keep an eye on' known or potential offenders. A neglected element of the preventive role is the potential for police officers to set a personal example.

Secondary prevention takes the form of reacting to calls and detecting crimes after they have occurred. In recent years, the police have increasingly abandoned primary prevention in favour of secondary.

The study of policing by Norman Dennis draws on the experience of five major cities: London, New York, Chicago, Paris and Berlin. The evidence points to the value of two major changes. First, there should be a substantial increase in police numbers. And second, the style of policing should seek to prevent crime rather than to respond to it once it has happened: the 'prevention' model rather than the 'call-out' model. In the terminology of police reform, this suggests a move towards community policing and problem-oriented policing.

The courts, prison and probation

The five purposes of sentencing listed in the 2003 Criminal Justice Act can be accepted, though it would have been better to add 'moral reaffirmation' as an independent objective. The white paper *Justice for All* said that public protection was 'first and foremost' and should be 'paramount' but did not go on to give it priority in practice.

We propose that the aims of sentencing should be put in the following order of priority:

- Just retribution. A wrong has been done and balance should be restored by applying a punishment or a reparation order to fit the crime. Simultaneously, any such sanction is likely to have a deterrent effect.

- Moral reaffirmation. A moral principle has been infringed and should be reaffirmed through punishment or reparation to send a message to the wrongdoer and to re-assure the law-abiding majority that their restraint is respected and not to their disadvantage.

- Public protection. Serious offenders should be incapacitated through prison or effective alternatives to protect other people.

- Rehabilitation. If there is a prospect of personal change without weakening the previous objectives, the opportunity should be taken to encourage offenders to embrace the community's standards.

Above all, we should increase prison capacity. Incapacitation has been discussed in Chapter 3. There are two principal concerns. The first is that the utilitarian aim of reducing offending should not outweigh the requirement that a just punishment should be proportionate to the harm done or the harm threatened. A policy of 'three strikes and you're out', for instance, will often go too far in punishing individuals too severely for the offence committed.

Second, is the policy cost-effective? From a purely utilitarian vantage point, there would be little to be gained by imprisoning offenders who are unlikely to offend again or who commit petty offences only rarely. Incapacitation in the form of imprisonment is most cost-effective for persistent and serious offenders. Many offenders have short criminal careers and incapacitation should be aimed at those likely to have long careers. Past behaviour is the best predictor of who they are. The relative costs and benefits of such an approach are discussed below.

Costs and benefits of prison

There has been a long debate among US academics about how to calculate the costs and benefits of prison. In 1987 Edwin Zedlewski, an economist at the National Institute of Justice, published a cost-benefit analysis of prison. He estimated the annual cost per prisoner to be $25,000 and calculated that the average offender carried out 187 crimes per year. He found that the typical crime cost $2,300, taking into account property losses and human injuries and suffering. On these estimates the typical prisoner was responsible for $430,000 in social costs per year. This meant that the cost-benefit ratio was 17 (25,000:430,000).

His study was strongly criticised by some academics, who argued that offending should be based on the median offender, not the average. Zedlewski had used a RAND study of prisoners that reported that inmates averaged between 187 and 287 non-drug crimes per year. However, half the inmates committed fewer than 15 crimes per year. If the median of 15 crimes per year is used, the cost-benefit ratio is 1.38 not 17.

The debate was continued by John DiIulio and Anne Piehl, who also estimated the gain in reduced crime from imprisoning the median offender. They based their calculations on a self-report survey of prisoners in Wisconsin, and found that the median prisoner carried out 12 non-drug crimes per year. If the cost of prison continued to be $25,000 per year, then the social cost, according to the estimates of DiIulio and Piehl, of allowing the median offender to roam free would be $46,072. Using these figures, imprisoning 100 such people would cost $2.5 million, but leaving them on the streets would cost $4.6 million.[6]

In a later study (1997) DiIulio and Piehl used a self-report survey of prisoners in New Jersey to conclude that, at some point between the 10th and 25th percentile of prisoners, incarceration was uneconomic. If the cost of prison were $25,000 and the social cost of the median offender were $70,098, then the result is a cost-benefit ratio of 25,000:70,098 or 2.80. Put another way, for every dollar spent, $2.80 are saved. At the 25th percentile the social cost is only $19,509, which produces a ratio of 0.78. Hence, DiIulio and Piehl conclude that the public purse could benefit if between 10 and 25 per cent of prisoners were under a less costly form of sanction or supervision.[7]

Based on a similar estimate of the social and economic costs of crime, how many more prison places should be provided in England and Wales? In the 2001 document, *Criminal Justice: The Way Ahead* the Home Office estimated that there were about 100,000 persistent offenders who carried out about half of all crime.[8] It also estimated that about 20,000 might be in jail at any one time. We conclude that the Government's first priority should be to incarcerate the remaining 80,000.

The Home Office already recognises that the prison population is likely to increase and is projecting an increase in prison places of between 91,000 and 109,000 by 2009. Let us assume that an additional 80,000 places are needed. How much would it cost to provide them? According to a Parliamentary answer given on 15 December 2000 by Paul Boateng, 12,265 additional places were provided between 1995/96 and 2000-01 at a total cost of £1.287 billion.[9] This produces an average cost per place of £105,000. However, the cost for five private prisons is based on the 'net present value' of the PFI contracts which last for 25 years and include running costs. A more accurate estimate of the capital cost can be based on a parliamentary answer given by Mr Boateng on 27 January 2000 and the Home Office annual report and accounts for 1999/2000. Excluding running costs, the capital value of the five prisons built under the PFI was put at £212 million. These five prisons (Parc, Altcourse, Lowdham Grange, Ashfield and Forest Bank) provided an additional 3,504 places at an average cost per place of £60,502.[10]

The total cost of 80,000 places at £105,000 each would be £8.4 billion. The total annual cost of crime has been estimated by the Home Office to be £60 billion.[11] The building programme would need to proceed in stages, perhaps at a rate of 5,000 places per year, or £525 million, an easily manageable figure.

If the lower estimate of the cost is used, the total cost of 80,000 places at £60,502 each would be £4.8 billion. At a rate of 5,000 places per year, the cost would be £302.5 million.

What would the running costs be? The average cost of a prison place in 2002 was £38,753 per year. An additional 5,000 prisoners would therefore cost only £194m per year. On these figures, imprisoning the most serious and persistent offenders would be highly cost-effective. If 100,000 offenders commit half of all crime, then they impose costs on society of £30 billion, or £300,000 each for every year they are free. Even if the building costs are charged to a single financial year and added to the running costs we arrive at a total of £143,753, a saving of £156,247.

But all such estimates are based on assumptions and everyone knows that if you tweak the assumptions you can get the answer you want. How can we produce a more reliable estimate? Rather than opting for a single set of assumptions, let's explore a range. The first relies on a Home Office self-report survey of prisoners in 2000. The second is ultra-conservative, the third emulates Home Office calculations used to work out the crime-reducing effects of offending behaviour programmes, the fourth is based on a study by Cambridge University's Professor Farrington to discover the cost-effectiveness of youth custody, and the fifth is based on calculations made by the Government's Strategy Unit. The estimates of the total social and economic cost were made in 2000 at 1999 prices and should be compared with prison costs for a similar period. According to the Parliamentary answer given in June 2001, the average cost per prisoner place in a male closed Young Offender Institution (where the most persistent offenders might find themselves) was £23,063.

Prisoners' Self-Reports: The Home Office document, *Making Punishments Work*, reported the results of a survey of prisoners in 2000, which found that the average offender carried out 140 offences per year. The variation was large, and offenders who admitted to a drug problem were committing an average of 257 crimes per year.[12]

If we were to jail 5,000 criminals who would otherwise have committed 140 offences, then 700,000 offences against the public would be prevented by 12 months in jail. If they were high-rate offenders (257 crimes), the effect would be 1.3 million offences. According to a Home Office estimate in 2000, the average cost of crimes against individuals and households (excluding commercial crime) was £2,000. An offender committing 140 crimes per year would, therefore, impose costs on society of £280,000. If true, for every £1 spent on prison, we would save £12.14.

Ultra-conservative assumptions: Another method of calculating the crime-reducing effects of programmes has been used by Professor Farrington, also in a Home Office study. He estimated the relative cost-effectiveness of two military-style programmes for young offenders at Thorn Cross and Colchester. In 2002 he monitored for two years the reconvictions of a 'control group' of young offenders released from custody in 1997 and 1998. He then calculated the average cost to society of their crimes. Professor Farrington found that offenders were convicted on average 2.57 times per year and that the average cost of each crime was £1,923 each, a total cost of £4,942. He thought that to estimate the real rate of offending, this figure should be multiplied by at least five, producing 12.85 crimes at a total cost of £24,710. In this case, for every £1 spent we save £1.07 (£23,063:£24,710).

Home Office assumptions: In *Findings 161* the Home Office claimed that, based on the number of prisoners expected to complete cognitive skills courses in 2002-03, almost 21,000 crimes would be prevented. This estimate was based on the following assumptions, supplied by the Home Office.

In 2001 6,405 prisoners completed offending behaviour programmes.[13] At the time, the Home Office believed that offending behaviour programmes would produce a fall in reconvictions after two years of eight percentage points.[14] There were four steps to the calculation:

- Multiply the number of completions by eight per cent: 6,405 x 8/100 = 512.4.

- Multiply by five to reflect the Home Office estimate that for every conviction five other offences are recorded by the police: 512.4 x 5 = 2,562.

- Multiply by two because the effect is being measured over two years: 2,562 x 2 = 5,124.

- Multiply by 4.2 because police records do not reflect the larger number of crimes discovered by the British Crime Survey: 5,124 x 4.2 = 21,520.

This method produces a total number of 54 offences per year, which in turn produces a total cost of £103,842. For every £1 spent we save £4.50.

Professor Farrington's preferred assumptions: Professor Farrington has expressed doubts about the 'five' multiplier used by the Home Office and cited his own earlier study of 18-year-olds in South London, which had found that for six types of crime (burglary, taking vehicles, stealing from vehicles, shoplifting, theft from automatic machines and vandalism) only about one in 30 led to conviction. If there are 2.57 convictions per year, they should be multiplied by 30 to arrive at the number of offences, 77. This produces a total social cost of £148,071. For every £1 spent we save £6.42.

Government Strategy Unit assumptions: The Strategy Unit calculated the likely impact of prison on crime for the Carter report of 2003 by comparing three approaches and basing their estimate on a composite.[15] One method used was based on the assumption that there are 100,000 persistent offenders who committed half of all crime between 1997 and 2000.[16] In 1997 there were 16.798m BCS crimes and in 2000, 13.338m BCS crimes, a fall of 21 per cent.

The prison population increased by about 15,000 from 1997 to 2000 and, if all 15,000 were persistent offenders (as the Strategy Unit assumed), then half the fall would have been due to incarceration. The fall was 3.460m BCS crimes and half the fall was 1.730m BCS crimes. If imprisoning 15,000 criminals reduced crime by 1.730m, they would have carried out 115 crimes per year each, a figure consistent with average number of crimes per prisoner reported to the Prisoner Criminality Survey for 2000 (140 offences). The annual cost would be £230,000 (115 x £2,000), in which case we save £6.13 for every £1 spent on prison.

When the incapacitation effect only is taken into account, prison is good value. (Most people would accept that it is also worth paying something for deterrence and moral affirmation.)

So far we have compared prison with sentences served in the community, where we assume there is little or no incapacitation effect. This assumption applies to most community sentences, but electronic tagging does have an incapacitation effect, at least during the hours of monitoring (up to 12 hours per day). However, as Chapter 7 showed, the only Home Office evaluation so far found that there was no lasting impact on offending behaviour. Perhaps GPS tracking for 24 hours per day may prove to be a more cost-effective way of restraining offenders, but as yet it is an unproven technology.

4. Rehabilitation of Offenders

Belief in the possibility of rehabilitation became fashionable among criminologists who denied that offenders were responsible for their conduct. For psychologists, they were to be treated as if they had a medical condition which could be treated.

However, to speak of personal reform in prison does not necessarily imply a medical condition with a corresponding treatment. It also suggests an effort to overcome the failed moral education of the offender's early life. Just as some children may have to repeat a year at school because of a failure to meet an academic standard, so other youngsters are effectively repeating their moral education. When such schemes have worked, their aim has been to encourage offenders to refrain from crime through acts of self-control.

What is the record of success of schemes for personal change? As we have seen, much depends on the particular features of each programme. Therapies intended to alter the subjective state of an individual's mind tend not to work very well, especially 'encounter' groups or those relying on learning through group discussion, but behaviour modification programmes (Chapter 4), based on rewarding compliance with supervisors and sanctioning non-compliance, have sometimes produced modest but measurable effects. However, those behaviour modification programmes that worked while offenders were in custody appear not to have had a lasting effect once offenders were released. As we have seen, one of the major unmet challenges is to discover how best to follow offenders after the completion of their sentence to ensure that they do not simply return to old habits.

During the last thirty years of intensive research effort, our knowledge of how to bring about personal change has improved only slightly. The main lessons suggest that we should focus on getting the simple things right: get persistent offenders off the streets; and while they are in jail get them off drugs, and provide them with basic education and vocational skills. At present, both the prison service and the probation service fall a long way short of achieving even these modest aims.

Begin preparing prisoners for release immediately on entering prison

With the exception of a few criminals serving life sentences, and once the requirements of just desserts, moral reaffirmation and public protection have been met, a prison term should be seen as an opportunity for encouraging offenders to rejoin the community of law-abiding citizens on release. The key to success is careful assessment of each individual on admission, to appraise the prospects for personal reform. In particular, do they have a drug or alcohol problem? And do they possess workplace skills that would enable them to get a job, if they wanted one?

Perhaps 70 per cent of the prisoners in England and Wales have a drug problem which should be tackled, and many lack basic educational skills, quite apart from vocational qualifications. The Home Office has tried to improve the assessment of offenders. The Youth Justice Board has developed ASSET for juveniles and there is OASys for older offenders. These systems could no doubt be refined, but the real challenge is implementation.

Get prisoners off drugs

The first priority should be to get criminals off drugs. As Chapter 5 showed, the most effective schemes are in-prison therapeutic communities, with follow up in the form of halfway houses and continued supervision after that.

Prisons are supposed to test regularly for drug taking but, as the former chief inspector of prisons David Ramsbotham relates, testing is not always very rigorous. Each month, a proportion of prisoners are meant to be subject to random drugs tests and prisons are judged on a target that requires a reduction in the number testing positive. During a visit he found one prisoner with nine certificates on his wall for testing negative. The prisoner told Mr Ramsbotham that he was always picked for the 'random' drug test because he was known as a non-user.[17]

Provide basic and vocational skills

Efforts to provide education of all types should be stepped up. The evidence from the meta-analyses quoted in Chapter 4 was that schemes with a vocational element can have an effect. More significantly, as Chapter 6 revealed, US long-term studies confirm this conclusion. Efforts are already being made to improve education and the Prison Service is well aware of its deficiencies, but the present rate of progress is too slow.

As Chapter 4 showed, cognitive skills programmes have proved to be largely a waste of money. They should be abandoned and the resources transferred into basic and vocational education. However, for a small number of carefully selected offenders they may have a part to play, and it would be useful to carry out pilot schemes to identify who is capable of benefiting.

Make release dates conditional on good behaviour and extend supervision after release

Many prison governors already subscribe to the view that time in prison should be preparation for release, and Chapter 11 described some of the efforts already being made. However, there is a long way to go, especially in integrating the prison sentence with supervision after release.

The new National Offender Management Service (NOMS) is able to award contracts for the provision of parts of its service, and already makes use of private prison contractors. One possibility would be to award a contract combining prison management with aftercare so that the same organisation took responsibility at all stages. If such a scheme were piloted it might prove possible to integrate prison and probation, a hope often expressed but rarely achieved.

Vulnerable people, who live in unstable accommodation or none at all, who have spent time in care, who are mentally unstable, who have drug and alcohol dependencies, a low level of employable skills, low educational achievement, little competence in handling their finances and who are lacking in certain social skills, are hugely over-represented in prisons. Such disadvantages can make embarking on a law-abiding life after prison very difficult. One answer to this problem is to stave off release until professionals are fully confident that the prisoner is ready to adopt independent, law-abiding living arrangements.

Some offenders tend to be quite positive about their futures, but once on the outside, good intentions are often overridden by other factors beyond the remit of correctional agencies, such as re-admission to a criminal peer-group, the availability of drugs, money concerns, boredom, delays in finding employment and impetuousness fuelled by arguments or drinking.[18] Correctional services are keen to try to prevent any such relapse into criminal behaviour by providing help to offenders in areas such as drug rehabilitation, job-hunting and interview skills, and thinking skills courses (to help them to make appropriate decisions when feeling impetuous, for example) during their prison sentences, but these services classically stop at the prison gates, beyond which ex-prisoners are left to go it alone.

In theory, the responsibility for co-ordinating throughcare provision for an individual lies with his or her personal officer during internment, and his or her probation officer after release. In practice, however, personal officers are often ineffective, and probation officers tend to have minimal contact with their clients. Much of current throughcare provision is in fact managed by voluntary and community agencies.

Some small studies into the effectiveness of throughcare provision are currently available (e.g. NACRO's On-Side project run at HMYOI Portland and the Short-Term Prisoner Project at HMP Canterbury). These are, for the most part, not rigorous enough and based on samples too small to be conclusive. They do, however, point to areas in which throughcare can be improved.

The most fundamental problem encountered by people running pilot throughcare programmes was keeping in touch with the offenders once they left prison. Usually, responsibility for keeping in contact with throughcare agencies lay with the offenders themselves, who were expected to call their project workers whenever they felt like meeting up.[19]

A policy should include the following elements: establish firm contact between the offender and a trained, committed individual in good time prior to release, who will take on the role of the project worker once the offender is out; and ensure that any efforts begun on the inside to address the offender's needs are continued as seamlessly as possible on the outside.

How can effective contact be sustained? We can look to America for possible answers. Halfway houses are used quite extensively in the US, as a stepping stone from jail to independent living.[20] The system is similar to supported housing schemes led in the UK by voluntary organisations such as the St Giles Trust and NACRO, whereby vulnerable people (ex-offenders and people leaving prison among them) can move into sheltered accommodation, where they also have access to a doctor, benefits advice, job-hunting help, advice on procuring more independent accommodation, and many other services. However, demand always exceeds supply.

At the moment there is no state-led supported housing system in the UK, but our open prisons and (currently underused) resettlement prisons could provide a sensible starting point. Resettlement prisons are similar to open prisons, but they are aimed specifically at helping vulnerable offenders prepare themselves for successful release.

Ideally, however, offenders would not be released from prison until they are deemed to have sorted out any problems identified on admission to prison and they are seen to be fully capable of managing their own lives in the community. If this means lengthening sentences, then that must be an option. Many offenders need the time that prison allows them to think about their lives and futures, and often time away from peer groups can provide a much needed opportunity for an offender to dissociate him/herself from them.

After serving half of their full sentence in a regular prison, rather than being released as they would be under Automatic Conditional Release, they should be transferred to a resettlement prison or live in supported accommodation for a specified period.

The current system of early release at the halfway stage for all prisoners serving under four years should be scrapped. It should be replaced by a system that allows prisoners to earn time off their sentences for good behaviour and for demonstrating their capacity to lead a law-abiding life on release. In addition they would need to agree to be supervised in the community for the remainder of the original sentence, plus at least six months afterwards.

Juvenile offending

The American OJJDP recognises that a graduated approach is needed. Early efforts should be primarily educational in intent and aimed at re-integration into the law-abiding community.

The OJJDP approach rests on risk assessments that measure criminal history and social and personal stability. Most research indicates that both are strongly related to recidivism. The number of prior arrests or adjudications is an important indicator, as is age at first arrest. Measures of stability include substance abuse problems, history of running away, mental health problems and placements in care. The risk assessment instruments in Louisiana and Colorado reflect both the severity of the current offense and the probability of continued delinquency and both systems give the greatest weight to measures of the severity of current and prior offenses.[21]

The weights were designed to ensure that offenders committing the most serious crimes were automatically recommended for secure placement. Juveniles were put into one of three categories: high-risk and in need of secure placement; medium-risk and in need of short-term secure placement followed by community supervision; and low-risk and appropriate for intensive community-based placements.[22]

This approach is consistent with existing policy for first-time offenders in England and Wales. Reprimands and Final Warnings are a useful preliminary step and discourage some young people from further offending. Similarly, referral to a Youth Offender Panel may be beneficial and sound in principle.

Youth Offender Panels were intended to deal with young offenders at an early stage in the hope of diverting them from crime. They comprise members of the public and representatives of the local Youth Offending Team, generally a social worker or a probation officer. Our initial study found that in many localities a division of opinion emerged between volunteers on YOPs and YOT professional representatives. The volunteers felt that the YOP failed to confront youths with their wrongdoing and consequently had little effect. YOT professionals felt it was inappropriate to criticise offenders because it would involve 'stigmatisation'. Moreover, they often appeared to have no concept of re-integrative shaming. If this inconsistency continues YOPs are unlikely to be of much help in reducing crime, but it is too early to make a final judgement.

Another consideration, not really given full weight in risk-assessment formulae, is the extent to which the offender's family is a good or a bad influence. At present the Youth Justice Board has set a target to house young offenders in institutions within 50 miles of their home, presumably on the assumption that their family is a beneficial influence. However, it is often quite the opposite. As already mentioned, the Social Exclusion Unit report of 2002 found that 47 per cent of offenders had run away from home, 27 per cent had been in care, 35 per cent had a family member who had been in jail and 43 per cent a family member with a criminal conviction. All this suggests unstable family backgrounds.[23] In cases when the family is a criminogenic influence, children would be better off well away from it.

Despite repeated efforts to co-ordinate the child protection and juvenile justice systems—the latest through YOTs—the lack of co-operation remains a problem still to be overcome in England and Wales. In America, the OJJDP Guide concluded that most violent offending was not brought to the attention of the juvenile justice authorities and that 'in most cases' the system was intervening 'towards the end of self-reported offending careers'. It recommends that the authorities should intervene early.[24] In England this ideal is often expressed, but only rarely achieved.

If serious offences continue to be committed after a final warning or a YOP referral, the reaction of the authorities should escalate. The more recalcitrant the offender the more determined the response should be. Our system fails to react with sufficient resilience when dealing with persistent offenders.

The most common offence by 11-15 year-olds is fare dodging and it could easily be dealt with effectively by fines and community penalties. But burglary, robbery or violent assaults should result in custody, initially short-term, but for intractable offenders long-term. We suggest that once offenders have been convicted three times there is such overwhelming evidence that they are likely to spend the next several years committing offences, that they should be sent to secure institutions for a significant time with no possibility of early release without a prolonged period of demonstrated good behaviour.

The length of the sentence must be justified by the nature of the offences already committed, which rules out any policy resembling 'three-strikes and you're out'. However, courts should be able to take into account the likely danger to the public as demonstrated by past behaviour. Past conduct is the best predictor of future conduct. There was considerable logic to the old Borstal sentence, abolished in 1983, which provided for a minimum of one year and a maximum of three years, depending on the behaviour of the offender. Release was followed by six months supervision.

At present, persistent offenders are being given a series of short sentences. 82 per cent of males aged under 17 who were released from custody in 1999 were reconvicted within two years. Predictably, those with more previous convictions were found guilty of further offences more frequently. If they had no previous convictions, 42 per cent were reconvicted within two years; if they had one or two previous convictions, it was 77 per cent; if 3-6 previous offences, 91 per cent and if seven or more, 96 per cent. Those with three or more previous convictions are almost certain to continue offending at a high rate and are candidates for the revised DTO of between one and four years (below). The figures for offenders aged 18-20 are similar: 28 per cent of those with no previous convictions reoffended within two years, compared with 96 per cent of those with 11 or more. If older still, aged 21-24, 20 per cent of those with no previous convictions were reconvicted within two years, compared with 89 per cent of those with 11 or more. Current policies fail to protect the public. For example, only 67 per cent of males aged 18-20 released from prison in 1999 with 7-10 previous convictions were sent to prison when reconvicted.[25]

The main custodial sentence after three convictions (fewer for serious offences) should be a minimum of 12 months and a maximum of four years. Release after 12 months should depend on a prolonged period of demonstrated good behaviour. A variable sentence would be most appropriate for juveniles who ought to be most open to change. However, inadequate policies over the last few years mean that we now have a large number of offenders in their 20s regularly carrying out serious crimes. The variable sentence, from one to four years, could profitably be extended to this older age group.

Another approach would be to establish a pilot scheme in which a single agency took responsibility for children at risk of anti-social or criminal behaviour. The intention would be to discourage children from embarking on criminal careers by working closely with families, schools and local institutions to improve acceptance of community standards and respect for just treatment of other people.

YOTs were intended to bring together all agencies involved with young offenders. Their effectiveness is very patchy and it would be desirable to experiment with different structures. One such experiment could, for instance, give the police sole responsibility for crime reduction in an area. This would mean that probation officers and child welfare workers would work for the police to ensure a co-ordinated and graduated approach to child criminals. Perhaps it would be desirable for the police to take the lead in one area, the probation service in another, social services in a third, a voluntary agency in a fourth and a commercial agency in another. The results could then be compared.

15

Government Policy in 2005

This chapter focuses on existing public policies. So that it can be read as a self-contained discussion there is occasionally some overlap with earlier chapters, but we have tried to keep repetition to a minimum.

Prison

The Government frequently claims that it is 'tough' on crime. In his Foreword to the Home Office strategic plan for 2004-08, Tony Blair promised to 'toughen up every aspect of the criminal justice system'.[1] An earlier white paper, *Justice for All*, also contained some tough talking. The Government boasted that it had already increased prison capacity by 18 per cent and said that its sentencing policy would protect the public, punish offenders, and encourage them to make amends for their crime.[2]

So far so good, but it then went on to say that: 'Our aim is not to increase the prison population' but to make sure that people receive the right punishment.[3] Legislation, it said, 'will make it clear that custody should be used only when no other sentence would be adequate'.[4] The cost of prison appeared to be the main concern:

> Custody has an important role to play in punishing offenders and protecting the public. But it is an expensive resource which should be focused on dangerous, serious, seriously persistent offenders and those who have consistently breached community sentences.[5]

The use of the term 'seriously persistent' rather than just plain 'persistent' suggests that the Government is prepared to tolerate a certain amount of reoffending. And similarly, use of the phrase 'consistently breach community sentences' suggests that criminals will be allowed to ignore community sentences on more than one occasion before serious action is taken. That is certainly what happens now.

In addition to wanting to avoid the cost of new prisons, the Government also appears to believe that prison can make matters worse. *Justice for All* repeated some common mistakes about prison.

Short prison sentences increase offending: The white paper, *Justice for All*, noted that prisoners given short sentences were reconvicted at a higher rate than those who served longer sentences and concluded that short spells in prison, 'increase the chances of reoffending'.[6]

It is true that short sentences are associated with a higher re-conviction rate than longer sentences, but to claim that short sentences are the cause of this reoffending implies that a prisoner's subsequent conduct is determined by his short time in jail. Consider someone aged 20 who has been a regular offender and only just been caught. How likely is it that three months in jail will become the main cause of his later conduct? It is more likely that the attitudes acquired in the previous 20 years continue to exert a powerful influence.

It would be more true to say that the short prison sentence only provides the public with a short respite from persistent offenders. The pattern of repeat offending is not the result of prison, but rather the consequence of a failure to imprison habitual offenders for long enough to protect the public. The Government has ignored the findings of the Social Exclusion Unit's report on the consequences of repeat offending, which raised the possibility that failure to jail repeat offenders in the hope of reducing expenditure on prison could be a false economy. The SEU estimated that an unrepentant offender would cost the criminal justice system an additional £65,000 per year. To try an offender again at a Crown Court would alone cost on average £30,500.[7] The average full-year cost of keeping an adult offender in a local prison at the time was £23,700.[8]

Prison causes family break-up: *Justice for All* also claimed that prison can make matters worse in another respect. It can 'break up families, impede resettlement and place children at risk of an inter-generational cycle of crime'. Over 40 per cent of sentenced prisoners claim to have lost contact with their families since entering prison, yet, according to the white paper, 'Research shows that prisoners are six times less likely to reoffend if contact with their families is maintained'.[9]

There are two main problems with this statement. First, it is not true that simply reinstating family contacts will reduce offending. As shown earlier, 43 per cent of prisoners had other family members who had been convicted (compared with 16 per cent of the general population) and 35 per cent had a family member who had been in prison. In such cases the family is a bad influence. The Government's manner of reasoning has been called the 'ecological fallacy' by statisticians. This fallacy assumes that the average or predominant characteristics of a group apply to all the individual members. Thus, while it is true that people with strong family ties are less likely to be criminals, it does not follow that all people with strong family ties are law abiding. They are not. Moreover, to leave criminals in the community in the belief that they will automatically have stronger family ties will often lead to no change in their family circumstances, while leaving the public exposed to crime.

Second, it is not true that prison always causes the breakdown of family contacts. Many criminals had few, if any, close family ties before admission to prison. We have already referred to the SEU report, which showed that 47 per cent of male prisoners had run away from home as a child, and 27 per cent had been in care (compared with two per cent of the general population).[10] Some 81 per cent were unmarried prior to imprisonment (compared with 39 per cent for the general population), nearly five per cent were sleeping rough before admission, and 32 per cent were not living in permanent accommodation prior to their imprisonment.[11] Moreover, when their family disowns them or a wife leaves them, it is often because they disapprove of the prisoner's self-chosen conduct. The prisoner's law-breaking is the cause of the breakdown, not prison as such.

Many in the Home Office are hostile to prison and want to reduce its use, but their influence has been tempered by acknowledgement that community sentences do not adequately protect the public. This realism has led the Government to search for 'tough community sentences' that are a 'credible alternative to custody', including community sentences with multiple conditions like tagging, reparation and drug treatment and testing. It is imperative, according to the Government, that 'we have a correctional system which punishes but also reduces reoffending through the rehabilitation of the offender'.[12] Consequently, it says, a genuine third option is needed in addition to custody and community punishment.

The list of new sentences includes a modified suspended sentence called Custody Minus, under which offenders will be automatically imprisoned if they fail to comply with the conditions of the sentence. Custody Plus involves closer supervision by the Probation Service on release. The period of custody and supervision combined will be not more than 12 months in total. Intermittent Custody is designed for low-risk offenders and involves serving time at weekends or overnight, but working or training during the day.

However, the greater the time spent unsupervised, the longer the time offenders will have available for crime. And, however tough sounding the language used to describe community sentences, it is an inescapable fact that the Government is increasing the amount of time known offenders will be unsupervised. They may be tagged from 7.00 pm until 7.00 am, but this leaves them free to carry out crimes during the other 12 hours of each day, even if they are required to attend a training course or take a job.

The number of juveniles sentenced to custody increased from 3,700 in 1993 to 6,100 in 1997 but, despite the high level of juvenile crime, it has been held constant at just over 6,000 per year since then. In fact, the Youth Justice Board has set itself a target from 2003-04 to 2005-06 to secure a ten per cent reduction in the number of under-18s remanded and sentenced to secure facilities, compared with October 2003. However, at the end of November 2003 there were 2,254 juveniles aged 15-17 in custody, compared with 2,189 at the end of November 2002.[13] By the end of March 2004, there were 2,868.[14]

Does the Government's policy towards prison mean that serious offenders are being allowed to remain at large? Until the present government took office it was easier to gain an understanding of the extent to which the courts were protecting the public from persistent offenders, but we can get some insight from the 2001 Halliday report, *Making Punishments Work*. It found that many offenders with a long track record of previous convictions were not being sent to prison.[15] Taking all Standard List offences in 1998, the Home Office found that only 33 per cent of males over 21 were sentenced to immediate custody when they had ten or more previous convictions. And if they had 3-9 convictions, only 21 per cent were sent to jail. Put the other way round, two-thirds of males with ten or more previous convictions were given community sentences that enabled them to continue offending.

For males aged 18-20, the peak period of offending, eight per cent of those convicted for the first time were sent to jail; 30 per cent of those with 3-9 previous convictions; and 51 per cent of those with ten or more previous convictions.

Even for serious offences like burglary, males over 18 received a custodial sentence in only 70 per cent of cases when they had ten or more previous convictions.

We can use another Home Office figure to judge whether the courts are failing to protect the public. How many offenders classified by the Home Office as 'high-risk offenders' are jailed? The Home Office assigns criminals a score on the Offender Group Reconviction Scale (OGRS) and those with a risk of reoffending of over 70 per cent are classified 'high risk'. In 1998, the latest available figures, 23 per cent were given a community sentence and only 26 per cent were given immediate custody. In other words, about three-quarters of convicted criminals classified by the Home Office as 'high-risk offenders' were allowed to remain a risk to the public. It would be useful if the Home Office updated this information.

We can also look at sentence length. Logically an offender who posed a bigger threat to society would stand not only a higher chance of being imprisoned but also receive a longer sentence. However, for all Standard List offences, the more persistent the offender the shorter the sentence. Males aged 21 or more were given an average of 18.0 months on their first conviction; 12.6 months if they had 3-9 previous convictions: and 12.2 months if they had ten or more previous convictions.

However, for burglary the gradient was in a more logical direction. Males aged 18 or more received 16.4 months on their first conviction; 16.6 if they had 3-9 previous convictions; and 19.1 if they had ten or more. But, to add only three months to the average sentence of hardened offenders with long criminal careers ahead of them is a serious failure.[16]

Yet, according to *Reducing Crime—Changing Lives*, published in January 2004 by David Blunkett, the growth in the use of prison since 1991 is the result of increased severity in sentencing. In 1991, 15 per cent of offenders found guilty of an indictable offence were given custody, whereas in 2002 it was 25 per cent. He proposed to reduce the number of people being sent to prison and to induce the courts to impose either fines or more rigorous community penalties instead. Mr Blunkett implied that offenders convicted of burglary for the first time should not be given a custodial sentence. But, burglars have a very high reoffending rate of 76 per cent. Moreover, Mr Blunkett's distinction between serious and less serious offenders is not as clear cut as he seems to think. Car thieves are not just car thieves. Persistent offenders commit a mixture of offences. An analysis of the 1997 Offenders Index found that when the current offence was violence against the person, offenders with long careers (ten previous convictions) had been sentenced for property offences (burglary and theft) in 52 per cent of cases. If the current offence was sexual, offenders with five previous convictions had been found guilty of violence against the person in 11 per cent of cases, burglary in 17 per cent and theft in 23 per cent.

The upshot is that many criminals with a long track record of offending are not being jailed, despite being a major threat to the public.

The Intensive Supervision and Surveillance Programme (ISSP)

The most important of the 'third options' to be implemented so far is the Intensive Supervision and Surveillance Programme (ISSP) which began in April 2001 with an investment of £45m over three years. According to *Justice for All*, ISSP is the most rigorous, non-custodial intervention available for young offenders. It initially targeted 2,500 of the most serious and prolific young offenders (aged 10 to 17) per year. They were thought to be responsible for a quarter of all youth crime. Young offenders on ISSP can be subject to intensive monitoring for up to 24 hours a day, seven days a week, if necessary (although usually for a far shorter period). Electronic tagging and voice verification (telephone checking of an offender's 'voice print') can be used to monitor offenders, as well as intelligence-led policing and 'tracking' of their movements by case workers from the Youth Offending Team. The minimum requirement is for two surveillance checks per day.

They are also subject to a structured programme of activities for 25 hours a week for three months. Core elements include education and training, interventions to tackle offending behaviour and reparation to victims. It is available for convicted young offenders and to prevent persistent young offenders on bail from committing more crimes while awaiting trial. From April 2002 ISSP was available for the most serious and persistent offenders, defined as those who have been charged or convicted of an offence and have either been charged or warned for an imprisonable offence on four or more separate occasions within the past 12 months, or previously received at least one community or custodial penalty (the persistence criterion); were at risk of custody because the current charge or sentence related to an offence that could lead to an adult being sent down for 14 years or more (the serious-crime shortcut); or were at risk of custody because they had a history of repeat offending on bail, and were at risk of a secure remand (the repeat-offending-on-bail shortcut).

ISSP is not a sentence as such, but a condition attached to a sentence. Offenders could be serving a Detention and Training

Order (served partly in custody and partly in the community) when the non-custodial element would be under the ISSP. Or, they could have been sentenced to Supervision Orders or Community Rehabilitation Orders (collectively called community ISSP).[17] Offenders should spend six months on ISSP. The most intensive supervision (25 hours per week) lasts for the first three months of the programme, after which the supervision continues at a reduced intensity (a minimum of five hours per week) for a further three months.

The Youth Justice Board (YJB) claims that ISSP is based on the best evidence of what will reduce the frequency and seriousness of offending. It promises to bring structure to offenders' lifestyles, and to tackle the factors contributing to their offending behaviour, particularly lack of educational qualifications, weaknesses in thinking skills, or drug misuse. But what is the evidence suggesting that ISSP is likely to be successful? In January 2004 the National Audit Office concluded that it was too early to say, although its findings raised some doubts.[18] Early experience of ISSP in Swansea and Newcastle found that 60 per cent of participants failed to complete the sentence and, in 10/16 cases examined, offenders had been subject to breach proceedings.[19]

In September 2004 the YJB published a summary of the initial report on ISSP, produced by a team at Oxford University. The headline of the press release could hardly be more misleading. It said, 'New report shows positive start for bold and imaginative scheme to reform the worst young offenders'.[20] The text of the press release claims that reoffending was reduced:

> The report shows that there was a marked reduction in the frequency and seriousness of offending for young people on the programme. It found that in the 12 months before and after the start of ISSP the frequency of offending fell by 43 per cent and the seriousness dropped by 16 per cent.[21]

Rod Morgan, Chairman of the YJB, claims that the report 'shows a promising start for this groundbreaking programme'. The offenders were being supervised in a way that 'inspires the confidence' of sentencers, as well as the police and public.

The summary of the initial report[22] also reads in parts like a press release, instead of an independent appraisal. It highlights in large bold text taking up about a quarter of the page, the statement, 'When offending data in the 12 months before and after the start of ISSP are compared, there is a marked reduction both in the frequency and seriousness'. And, in a discussion of social costs, it highlights in large bold letters the statement 'it was found that, on the whole, ISSP paid handsome social dividends'.

In fact, as the full initial report shows, the two statements placed in huge bold letters are misleading. Compared with offenders serving alternative sentences, such as Supervision Orders, Community Rehabilitation Orders and Detention and Training Orders, those on ISSP reoffended more frequently. If ISSP caused their behaviour, as the Youth Justice Board claims, then it made them worse.

Reoffending: The study looks at the impact on reoffending by making two comparisons: offenders before and after ISSP; and offenders on ISSP and those eligible but not on it. Offenders were followed for 12 months 'at liberty' from the start of ISSP, or the end of the custody element of their Detention and Training Order (DTO). Reconvictions were based on the Police National Computer (PNC).[23]

The full initial report states that the 'key objective' of the YJB was, 'To reduce the rate of reoffending in the target group of offenders by five per cent and reduce the seriousness of any reoffending'. It declares that 'viewed simply, the objective above was met'.[24] But, it turns out that 'viewed simply' means 'viewed wrongly'. The authors of the full initial report do not think that the five per cent objective was a sufficiently exacting standard. Moreover, offending did not fall *because* of ISSP.

The success claimed by the YJB in its press release relies on a comparison between the reconviction rate of offenders in the 12 months before ISSP and the reconviction rate of the same offenders 12 months afterwards. However, in the full initial report, the authors made it clear that the reduction would have happened anyway and was not the result of ISSP. They said:

> Given the aims of ISSP, it is not possible to avoid this problem of regression to the mean. The way we have dealt with it is by using a comparison group with similar characteristics. We expect both groups to reduce in offending frequency and seriousness. The impact of ISSP is measured by whether the ISSP group outperforms the comparison group.[25]

The statistical term 'regression to the mean' is not as complicated as it might sound. It describes the well-established tendency for human behaviour to fluctuate over time. There may be an upward or downward trend over several years, but from one year to the next the results may go up or down. More specifically, individuals with high scores in one year will tend to have lower scores (nearer to the average) in the following year. This tendency is called regression to the mean (average). Candidates for ISSP were selected because they were the most frequent offenders in a given year. Any statistician would, therefore, expect that their offending behaviour in the following year would be less frequent. For this reason, no conclusions about the impact of a programme like ISSP can validly be drawn merely by observing that an expected fall had in fact occurred. Such a finding was a 'sure thing'.

What were the results? Comparing the 12 months before ISSP with the 12 months after, those on community ISSP were reconvicted on 43 per cent fewer occasions and those on DTO ISSP, 45 per cent fewer. However, members of the comparison group for community ISSP were convicted on 46 per cent fewer occasions and the DTO comparison on 62 per cent fewer.[26] The report calls this performing 'just as well or even slightly better', although a difference of 16 percentage points would not normally be considered a 'slight' change.

These results show that the 'before and after' change for offenders on ISSP cannot be considered to be the result of the programme. Yet, in its press release the YJB chose to claim that ISSP reduced the frequency of offending by 43 per cent.

What about the overall rate of offending after the start of ISSP? The only valid measure of the impact of ISSP is the comparison between the programme group and the control group. The findings were as follows:

Table 15.1
Percentage of offenders reconvicted 12 months after the start of ISSP

	Reconvictions (%)
Community ISSP	84
Community comparison	72
DTO ISSP	91
DTO comparison	82

The results unequivocally show that reoffending was lower for offenders serving Supervision Orders or Community Rehabilitation Orders without ISSP and for those serving Detention and Training Orders without ISSP.[27] The only valid conclusion is that ISSP is less effective than other (less costly) alternatives.

ISSP was also less effective than custody, despite the fact that the custody figures (produced annually in *Prison Statistics*) are for two years 'at liberty'. The overall reconviction rate within two years for all 14-17 year-old offenders who had been sentenced to custody was 80 per cent in 2002, and 79 per cent for 17-year-olds.[28] Of course, the two groups being compared are not matched. The ISSP group were the most prolific offenders, whereas 'all offenders sentenced to custody' would have a different offending profile. However, instead of concentrating its energy on finding better ways of protecting the public, the YJB published a press release on 14 September 2004 along with a misleading online summary.

The full initial report also reveals that over half of offenders (53 per cent) did not even complete the six-month programme. Of those sentenced to supervision orders, 58 per cent did not complete. Worse still, 35 per cent of offenders who 'completed' the course had breached their orders at least once. In some localities they were given several warnings, when in more rigorous localities they would have been breached and removed from the programme.

It is also relevant that tagging, in which the Home Office places so much confidence, was associated with a lower completion rate. Only 42 per cent of offenders who were tagged completed ISSP, compared with 56 per cent of those with personal 'trackers' who were in direct contact with offenders.[29]

Cost-Benefit Analysis: Given the findings in the previous chapter of the Oxford study, the cost-benefit analysis in Chapter 15 was academically indefensible. The authors admit that their results could be invalidated by regression to the mean:

> Ideally, the crime savings from lower reconviction rates should be calculated on the basis of some well-defined comparison group where the only difference between the two groups would be ISSP participation, so that the savings can be said to rise [sic] specifically from ISSP participation.[30]

Finding a comparison group, says the report, is 'not easy' and, as a result, the researchers found it difficult to 'ascertain whether any differences of reconviction rates between treatment and comparison group can be put down to ISSP alone'.[31] The report then ignores its own stipulations and carries out the analysis anyway.

The report compares both the frequency and gravity of offending. The average frequency of offending was 8.74 offences during the 12 months before ISSP and 5.07 in the 12 months after the start of ISSP. The gravity score was 5.10 before and 4.45 after.[32]

On page 342 the report says 'At first glance, it appears that ISSP paid handsome dividends to society'. But it then goes on to explain why the results do not tell us whether ISSP works because of regression to the mean. Yet, only three pages later, the conclusion (p. 345) says: 'It was found that, on the whole, ISSP paid handsome social dividends'. The average saving came to £40,000 per start, an average total saving of 'almost £4 million per scheme'. It then admits that the benefits are 'likely to be over-estimated' because no comparison with a control group was made.[33]

These passages are double-talk. It is not enough to say that there was an 'over-estimate'. The result was the exact opposite of the reported finding. If the authors had used the correct (though incomplete) figures on pages 304-05 of their own report, the results would have been reversed. There was no saving at all. In fact, there was a cost—in ordinary language, a waste of money.

Calculations based on the difference between the reoffending rates of the programme group and the control group are not made by the authors, and it is not possible to make them without the breakdown of offences for each offender. (The report does not give these figures.) However, we can take an educated guess using the incomplete figures given in their earlier chapter.

Table 15.2
Frequency and gravity of offending 12 months after the start of ISSP

	Frequency	Gravity
All ISSP	5.07	4.45
Community comparison	3.70	4.00
DTO comparison	3.90	4.60

Even if we take the worst case of the DTO comparison group with a lower frequency (3.9 compared with 5.07) but a slightly higher gravity (4.6 compared with 4.5), the result would have been a net loss. If we take the average of the community and DTO figures, both the frequency and gravity scores are lower.[34] It can, therefore, be validly inferred that the alternative schemes, Supervision Orders and Community Rehabilitation Orders plus DTOs without ISSP produced savings compared with ISSP.

It is revealing to compare ISSP with the cost of custody. The total cost of ISSP for 36 of the schemes was £1,097,064. The cost per completion was £31,865.[35] These figures for the six-month-long ISSP can be compared with the full 12-month cost of a male closed Young Offender Institution (YOI) of £29,721 per prisoner, or a male open YOI of £18,866.[36]

Having calculated the social benefit inaccurately the report goes on to repeat the process for the cost-benefit analysis. The average cost per start is put at about £12,000 and compared with the average saving (of about £40,000) based on the false attribution of falling frequency and gravity of offending entirely to ISSP.[37]

This section of the study draws attention to an underlying difficulty. How can the independence of external researchers heavily reliant on Home Office funding be guaranteed so that they are able to report results without fear or favour? The great majority of crime research in this country is funded by the government. University academics who fall out of favour risk losing their jobs. There is a hint of the pressure they face in the conclusion to the chapter on reoffending, where the authors make a revealing remark: 'Even though a number of methods have been used, it has proved difficult to establish that ISSP has a beneficial impact on offending'.[38] This sounds rather like an apology to their clients in government. It's almost as if they are saying: 'Sorry, we looked for the result you wanted but we're afraid it was impossible.'

To sum up: the Oxford University study found that ISSP failed to reduce offending during the 12 months following the start of the scheme. In fact, if the behaviour of offenders on the scheme is taken to have been entirely the result of ISSP (as the YJB assumes), then the scheme made offenders worse than they would have been. As Chapter 7 (above) revealed, this result could have been predicted from American experience.

Cognitive-Behavioural Skills: A central feature of ISSP is the use of cognitive skills courses to encourage offenders to alter their attitudes. Cognitive skills courses were first introduced in 1992 and have been stepped up under the Blair Government. They are based on the idea that criminals carry out crimes because of mistaken beliefs. They might tell themselves that no one gets hurt (they are all insured) or interpret innocent actions as aggressive (demanding to know 'what are you looking at' if you catch their eye in the street) or they may simply be unable to put themselves in other people's shoes. Psychologists claim to know how to alter these attitudes and the Home Office has been stepping up the number of offending behaviour programmes inspired by their theories. As Chapter 4 showed, these schemes have not been effective in the prison service. An evaluation of schemes initiated by the YJB between 1999 and 2001 found that only 59 per cent of all offenders completed the course and that under half (47 per cent) of persistent young offenders did so. The reconviction rate for persistent young offenders was 80 per cent within 12 months of the date of conviction.[39] The reconviction rate within two years for offenders under the age of 17 released from prison in 1998 was identical at 80 per cent, even though it covered a longer period following release from prison.[40]

The Government relies on tagging to protect the public from offenders serving some community sentences. However, as Chapter 7 revealed, the only study of tagging so far (Home Detention Curfew) to look at the impact on re-conviction rates found that it made no significant difference. Chapter 7 showed that HDC is at best neutral in its impact on reoffending. While they were tagged for up to 60 days it had a restraining effect on offenders, though not as powerful as prison, which prevented any offences being committed against members of the public. Moreover, as the ISSP initial report discovered, tagging was associated with a lower completion rate. Compared with offenders subject to 'tracking' by case workers, a higher proportion of tagged offenders had their ISSP terminated for reoffending.

Rehabilitation

The National Audit Office (NAO) concluded in January 2004 that efforts to rehabilitate juvenile offenders were often 'fragmented'.[41] The Youth Justice Board (YJB) is responsible for offenders under 18, for whom hopes that rehabilitation might work are highest. YJB policy is to reduce the number in custody, ostensibly to devote more resources to rehabilitation. However, the NAO remarked in January 2004 that if the policy were to succeed, the YJB needed to 'improve the credibility and effectiveness of higher tariff community sentences'.[42]

The majority of district judges and magistrates were reasonably satisfied with community sentences, but 34 per cent thought that offenders should be sent back to court more frequently following breaches. The National Audit Office was more sceptical. It examined case files and found that it could not always determine whether contact hours were being achieved by the Youth Offending Teams charged with supervising juveniles, nor could it tell the nature of the work undertaken during sessions.[43] Records were not always updated, and in some cases records of 'several weeks work' were not available. Staff shortages meant that in six YOTs examined by the NAO no case worker at all had been assigned to at least five offenders, and only 76 per cent of YOTs were able to say that every young offender had been allocated a case worker within five working days of sentence.[44]

Reconviction data were unconvincing. The NAO analysed Home Office data for community sentences served by juveniles in 2001 and found that the actual rate was close to the predicted rate (based on the age, sex and criminal history of offenders). In many cases it was worse.[45] For example, those sentenced to supervision orders, action plans, reparation orders and fines all exceeded the predicted reoffending rate. Offenders sentenced to community rehabilitation and community punishment orders had reoffending rates a percentage point or two lower than the predicted rate but in both cases between 60 per cent and 70 per cent were reconvicted within one year. The latest two-year reconviction rate for juveniles sent to custody was 84 per cent.[46]

The essential starting point for effective rehabilitation is a good understanding of a young offender's problems. However, the NAO found that YOTs had not made sufficient use of information about offenders gathered by ASSET (the assessment scheme used by the YJB).[47]

Worse still, the most elementary aims of providing 'purposeful activity' and education were not being achieved to a satisfactory standard. The YJB target for purposeful activity was 30 hours per week, including a minimum of 15 hours education. The Prison Service, which manages the Young Offender Institutions for the YJB, reported that it delivered an average of 35.6 hours of purposeful activity in 2002-03. However, the NAO remarked that this claim should be interpreted 'with caution'.[48] YOIs were in fact unable to provide information on the number of hours of education and training for 2002-03.[49] Moreover, the YJB and the Prison Service performance measures were not the same. Purposeful activity in the Prison Service included prison work like cleaning, whereas the YJB excluded it. Worse still, the YJB had adopted a rather undemanding definition, including association time such as playing board games, 'eating with staff' and watching TV documentaries.[50]

A fundamental aim of a detention and training order is to ensure that offenders keep up their education. Half the time is spent in custody, and half in the community continuing education or training begun inside. Custodial sentences were an opportunity 'to lead a more structured lifestyle and to return to education or training' and the YJB target was that YOTs should ensure that 80 per cent of offenders were in full-time education, training or employment by the end of December 2003 and 90 per cent by the end of 2004.[51] In 36/155 YOTs the 80 per cent target had been met by the end of March 2003 but 14 reported that less than 50 per cent were in full-time education, training or work.[52] The NAO also found that integration between YOTs and custody was inadequate. Only six per cent of YOTs said that young offenders were able to continue the education started while in custody.[53]

The NAO also looked at offending behaviour programmes and found that in 6/31 cases examined the course did not meet the needs identified by the YOT.[54]

Anti-social behaviour

One of the Government's main concerns since 1997 has been to reduce anti-social behaviour. Anti-Social Behaviour Orders (ASBOs) were introduced by the Crime and Disorder Act 1998, which defines 'anti-social behaviour' as conduct that 'causes or is likely to cause harassment, alarm or distress to one or more people who are not in the same household as the perpetrator'.[55] It includes behaviour that puts people in fear of crime and can take any of the following forms: graffiti, abusive and intimidating language, excessive noise, dealing in drugs, litter, and drunken behaviour in public places.

The objective in placing someone on an ASBO is to prevent them from 'exhibiting a particular type of behaviour in a particular location'.[56] In England and Wales, they are civil orders made in court and are effective for a minimum of two years. This contrasts with the practice in Scotland where the Sheriff Court[57] has the discretion to award an order for as long as they thought necessary, given the seriousness of the behaviour.[58]

Orders can be brought against anyone aged ten years or more. The agency applying for the order (local authorities and police forces acting together, British Transport Police or registered social landlords) must show that 'the defendant behaved in an anti-social manner and an order is necessary for the protection of persons from further anti-social behaviour by the defendant'. The breaching of an order is a criminal offence, which is arrestable and recordable.[59] In the magistrates' court, for an adult, the maximum penalty on conviction is five years in prison or £5,000; and in the crown court it is five years in prison or a fine, or both.

Acceptable Behaviour Contracts: Acceptable Behaviour Contracts (ABCs) are voluntary written agreements between 'a person who has been involved in anti-social behaviour and one or more local agencies whose role it is to prevent such behaviour'. The 'local agency' might be the local police department, housing department, a Youth Offending Team (YOT), a registered social landlord (RSL), or a school. The police and the council do not have to apply to a magistrate and the contracts are not legally binding. ABCs, if issued to a child under ten years old, are known as Parental Control Agreements (PCAs). In such cases, the agreement is signed by the parents rather than the child.[60]

Although an ABC may be used for a person of any age, it is most commonly used for children and young adults. When an agency has decided that an ABC is the most appropriate course to pursue, a meeting with the individual is arranged to which a parent or guardian of the child is invited,[61] and a contract is drawn up specifying the behaviour that the individual has agreed not to repeat. The consequence of a breach of the contract is often eviction, or the use of an ASBO if the individual lives in private property.

While both ASBOs and ABCs are aimed at pre-empting anti-social behaviour rather than punishing the perpetrator, there are differences between them. ASBOs are reactive measures while ABCs are preventive, and an ASBO is a legally-enforceable, formal process, whereas an ABC is informal.[62]

Between 1 April 1999 and 30 September 2003 a total of 1,623 ASBOs were issued in England and Wales, with 38 applications refused. This is a surprisingly low number, given the high number of reports of anti-social behaviour during the 'Anti-social Behaviour Day' count in September 2003, when there were 66,107 reports in a 24-hour period. Areas where low uptake has been identified may have been using different measures in preference to ASBOs to deal with anti-social behaviour, including the practice of holding problem-solving forums between partnership agencies.

In April 2002, from a sample of half the local authorities in England and Wales, a total of 173 ABC schemes were identified. A total of 1,868 contracts had been issued, but there was a large variation in the number of contracts used by each scheme - 24 schemes had issued no contracts, and one scheme had issued 200. More ABCs had been issued by April 2002 than ASBOs had been made by September 2003; this reflects the fact that ASBOs are generally used as secondary measures to persuade people to stick to terms agreed in an ABC. From the schemes tested, the most common reasons for issuing an ABC were to tackle harassment (93 per cent), verbal abuse (88 per cent) and criminal damage (81 per cent). Police, housing and the Youth Offending Team were the main agencies involved.

ASBOs and ABCs in England: The first full report on ASBOs in England and Wales[63] was based on evidence obtained from 94 case files from nine areas. The general perception in the areas studied was that the deterrent value continued up until the point an order was breached. If the offender was taken to court and given only a nominal sentence, behaviour worsened. Four main concerns emerged: delays, the burden of collecting evidence, weak follow-up, and the high cost.

ASBOs are a partnership approach to solving local problems and success depends on the level of co-operation between interested parties. However, Campbell found that the need to consult all agencies often caused delays. The average time taken was 13 weeks from summons to final hearing. In 56 per cent of cases more than three hearings occurred before the decision was made about whether to grant an ASBO. To overcome delays, interim ASBOs were introduced in December 2002. They have been used successfully all over the country, although there has been no official evaluation.

According to Campbell, too much evidence was collected, adding to delays. The delivery of an ASBO depends largely on local witnesses, often acquaintances of the perpetrator, but witnesses were sometimes too scared to come forward.

The orders were not credible if they were not enforced. However, many areas could not provide information about eventual outcomes of ASBOs they had issued. A third of local authorities and over a half of RSLs did not even keep records of complaints. Even when breaches were detected, individuals were not always punished or reprimanded. Many police forces considered it too trivial to prosecute someone for entering an exclusion area but not actually committing any acts. Some forces waited for several breaches to occur before the case was taken to court.

The costs associated with obtaining an ASBO differed greatly from area to area. The average cost of the ASBOs in the sample was £5,350. However, some areas thought that the benefits outweighed the cost. In one area, an ASBO placed on a single individual 'immeasurably' increased the income of local stores.[64]

Bethan Jones and Karen Bullock published an evaluation of ABCs in 2001, which was based on police and housing data for 95 children placed on the ABC scheme in Islington between 1999 and 2001. In most cases ABCs had been used with 10-18 year- olds. Most commonly, youths were reported by neighbours on housing estates (96 per cent), police intelligence (37 per cent), and police stop data

(44 per cent). Most lived in council accommodation, which their family had lived in for more than ten years. This finding contrasts with previous research[65] which suggested that anti-social behaviour corresponded with short tenancies. Many culprits were involved in criminal activity as well as anti-social behaviour, with 85 arrests having taken place among the cohort in the six months prior to the commencement of the ABC. The most common crimes were burglary, vehicle and motor bike theft.

In the first six months of the contract, only 43 per cent of the individuals came to the attention of the police and housing officers for anti-social behaviour, compared with 62 per cent in the six months immediately preceding the start of the contract. The actual number of anti-social acts committed by the sample of individuals on a contract decreased while they were on the contract (164 acts down to 80). Some of the young people who had committed criminal offences in the six months before the contract continued to do so but at a reduced rate (85 arrests before the contracts and 34 during).

Fifty-seven per cent of contracts were not breached, 19 per cent were breached once, 12 per cent were breached twice and 11 per cent were breached at least three times. However, where contracts were found to have been breached, there were concerns that punishments were not being enforced. For example, few notices seeking tenancy-possession were served following breaches, despite this being the agreed policy.[66]

Individuals subject to ABCs were not fully monitored, and so assessment of effectiveness is difficult. The contracts were mainly monitored by police and housing officers, who claimed that time and resources were insufficient to carry out effective monitoring. In only 19 per cent of contracts issued during phase one, was the monthly update of the intelligence system actually completed, and home visits were conducted for just 28 per cent of the contracts. Nevertheless, in some localities the authorities felt that ABCs had been useful.

It has proved difficult to assess the effectiveness of ASBOs and ABCs in reducing anti-social behaviour due to limited attempts to monitor the orders and contracts. Bethan Jones (co-author of the Islington ABC study) has confirmed that the Home Office only collects information about the number of ASBOs granted and refused. No information is collected centrally about breaches, although it is possibly collected in some localities. Jones confirmed that the bulk of the evidence concerning ASBOs is anecdotal.

Rehabilitation and drug use

One of the most urgent challenges is to get young offenders off drugs but the National Audit Office found only one YOT during its visits that had identified dealing with substance abuse as a priority in 2003-04. The YJB intends to set a target requiring all offenders to be screened and for those in need to receive specialist assessment within five days, with treatment following in a further ten days. However, the NAO found that YOTs did not provide appropriate treatment in most cases: only three per cent said they could 'always' access services, 54 per cent 'sometimes' and 25 per cent 'rarely'.[67] The Government has increased drug treatment places since 1997 and in July 2004 announced plans for an additional 60,000 places by 2008, but it remains to be seen whether significant inroads will be made.

The record of the Prison Service in controlling drug use is the least defensible. We have already referred to the experience of the former Chief Inspector of Prisons, David Ramsbotham, who found that prisoners who were known *not* to take drugs were given regular 'random' drug tests to boost the results. This kind of practice makes a mockery of targets. The subsequent Chief Inspector of Prisons has also noted that 'many prisons are not meeting their targets, are testing at inappropriate times, or are not carrying out targeted testing'.[68]

The inability of the system to control drug use is reflected in the somewhat chaotic history of official targets. For example, a target set in 1998, hoped to reduce the rate of positive random drug tests to 16 per cent of all random tests by 2002 and to provide voluntary drug testing for all prisoners by 2002. In 2000, this target had not been achieved, and instead of carrying the target forward, it was amalgamated with another target to produce a new target, which aimed to reduce by 25 per cent the levels of repeat offending among drug-misusing offenders by 2005, and to have produced a 50 per cent reduction by 2008. By 2002, this target had again been re-set to be less specific. The new target, numbered 6, was amalgamated with another target that had aimed to reduce the proportion of people under the age of 25 reporting the use of Class A drugs by 25 per cent by 2005, and similarly by 50 per cent come 2008. The new target 6 was a mere aspiration: to reduce the harm caused by drugs by: reducing the use of Class A drugs and the frequent use of any illicit drugs among people under 25; and to reduce drug-related crime, including the proportion of offenders testing positive at arrest.[69] The target is notable for its exclusion of the 'do-by' date, perhaps explained by the failure of efforts in 2002 to reduce either drug use or drug-related crime by any significant amount —in fact, drug use had increased marginally. Further revision followed in 2004: 'Reduce the harm caused by illegal drugs (as measured by the Drug Harm Index encompassing measures of availability of Class A drugs and drug-related crime) including substantially increasing the number of drug misusing offenders entering treatment through the Criminal Justice System.' The second part of the target is a measure of 'input' rather than outcomes. As earlier chapters revealed, increasing the number of people who are put through drug treatment programmes does not necessarily reduce drug taking or the crime associated with it. Policy needs to focus on increasing the use of the programmes that work best, notably in-prison therapeutic communities with intensive follow-through after release.

The adaptation of targets over the years to fit actual trends renders the setting of targets in the first place practically useless, and is likely to be seen as a cop-out. In general, the Government is failing to rise to challenges that it has set for itself.

Conclusions

In its 2002 white paper, *Justice For All*, the Government said that it wants to send the strongest possible message to criminals that the system will be effective in 'detecting, convicting and properly punishing them'. After many years of being opposed to prison and favouring community sentences, the Government now recognises that prison protects the public. However, the most recent independent survey of progress by the National Audit Office found that the youth justice system—where the prospects for steering offenders away from crime are at their best—was failing to perform even the simplest of tasks: many offenders were not in full-time education, training or work; drug treatment was often not available when needed; and 'purposeful activity' was defined so loosely that it was of little or no rehabilitative value. The same can be said of the whole system.

If the public-policy recommendations of this study could be summarised in a single sentence it would be this. Focus on getting the simple things right: increase the number of police; put all—not just some—of the persistent offenders in jail; while they are there get them off drugs and equip them with workplace skills; and finally, supervise them on release to reduce their chances of falling back into old habits.

Appendix 1

Langan and Farrington's Method

Langan and Farrington began with the total number of offences, drawing on both victim surveys and police records. They used 'offenders' rather than 'offences' because many crimes are committed by more than one person. Robberies in England and Wales, for example, are carried out by an average of 2.4 people, vehicle thefts by 2.1 people and burglaries by 1.8. They multiplied this average by the number of offences to calculate the total number of criminals at risk of punishment (called 'alleged offenders' in the text). For example, in America in 1994 there were 5,482,720 domestic burglaries. This figure was multiplied by the US average number of offenders in burglary cases (1.4) to arrive at 7,675,808 offenders at risk of conviction. They are not, of course, all different people.

Langan and Farrington then calculated how many alleged offenders were detected, convicted and imprisoned. For England and Wales, the definition of 'immediate imprisonment' is defined in Criminal Statistics England and Wales 2000. The main categories are sentences with no part suspended, referred to as 'unsuspended imprisonment', and for persons aged 21 and over, 'immediate custody'. For persons aged under 21, 'immediate custody' is equivalent to detention in a young offender institution from October 1988.

Appendix 2

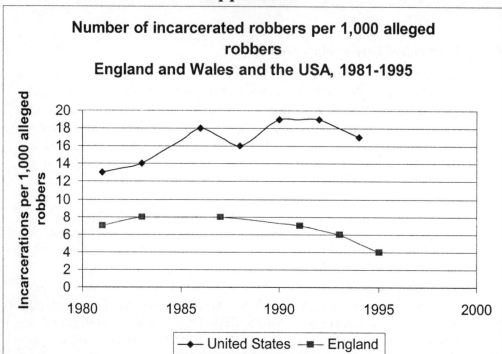

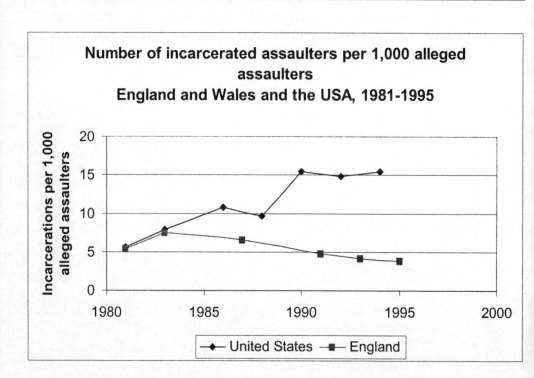

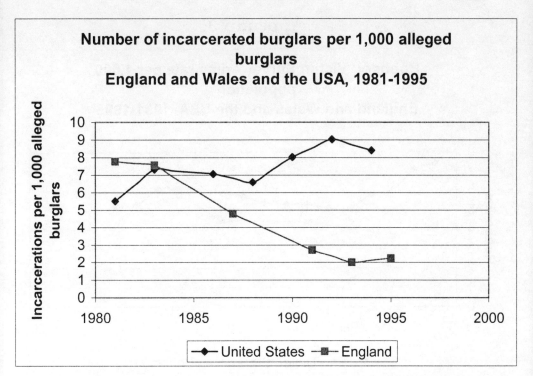

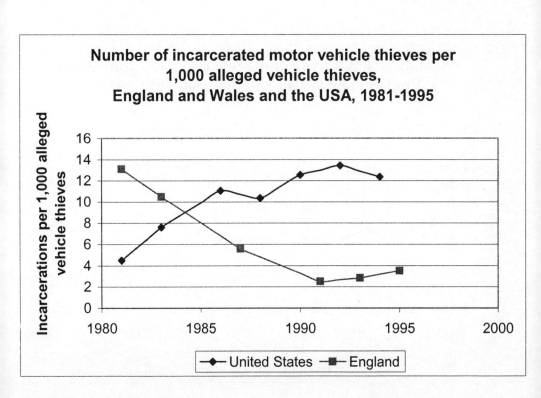

Appendix 3

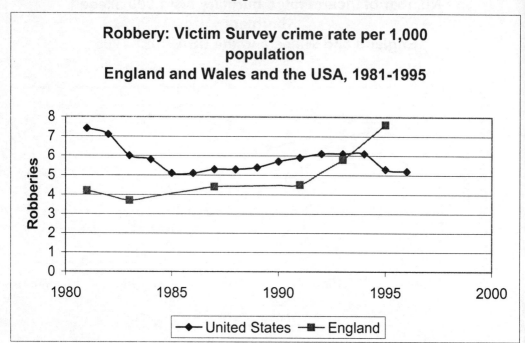

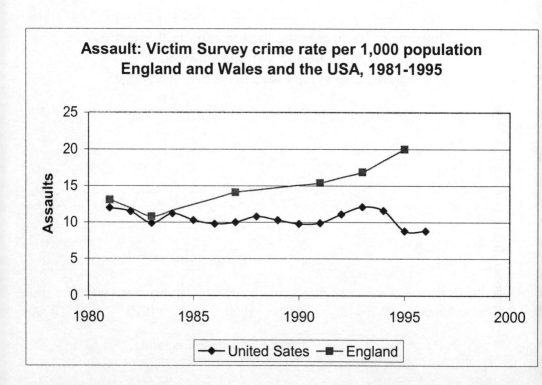

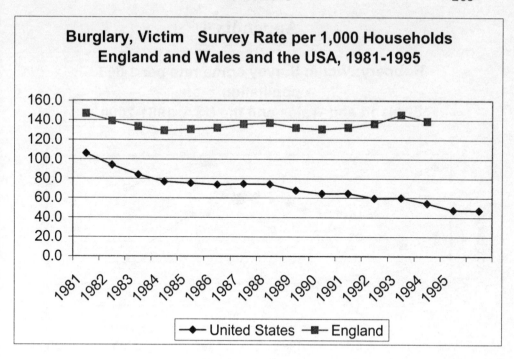

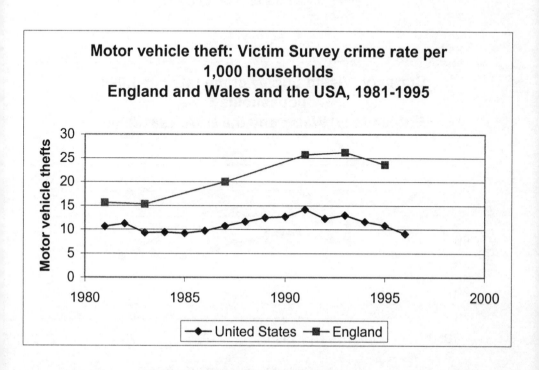

Appendix 4

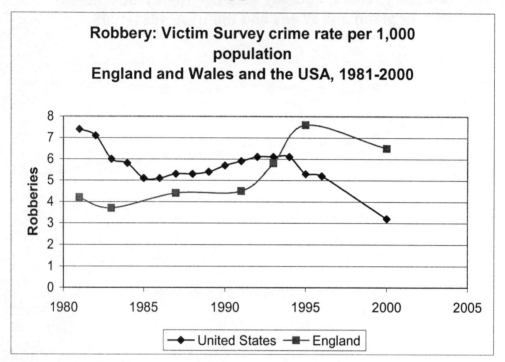

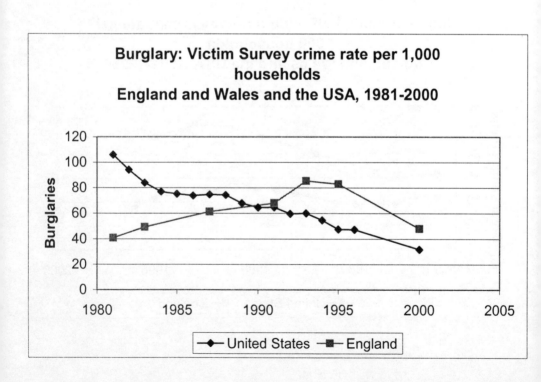

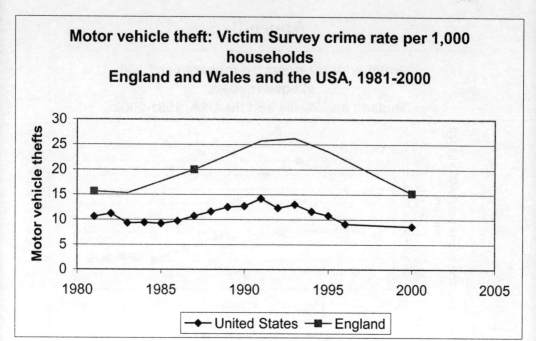

Appendix 5

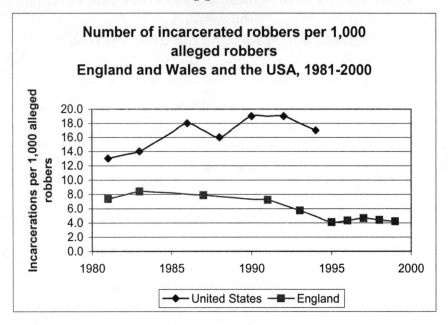

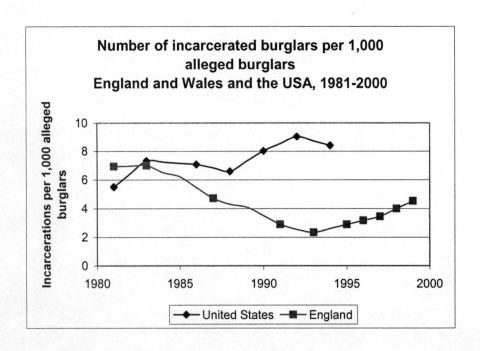

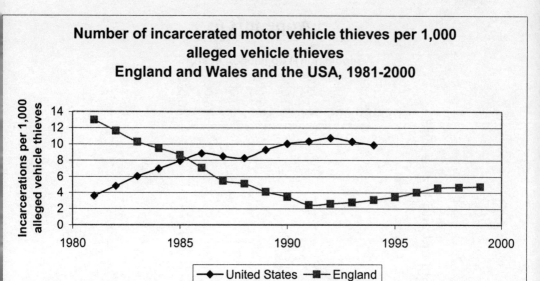

Number of incarcerated motor vehicle thieves per 1,000 alleged vehicle thieves
England and Wales and the USA, 1981-2000

Appendix 6

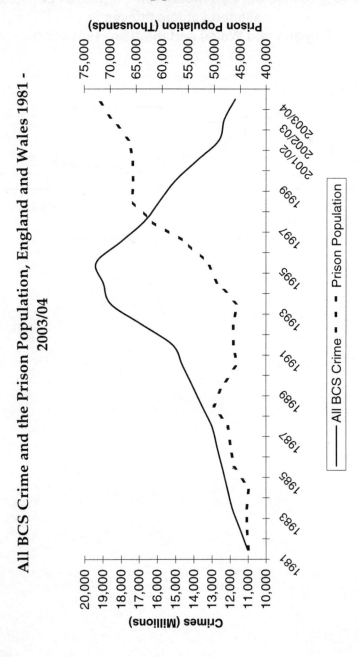

All BCS Crime and the Prison Population, England and Wales 1981 - 2003/04

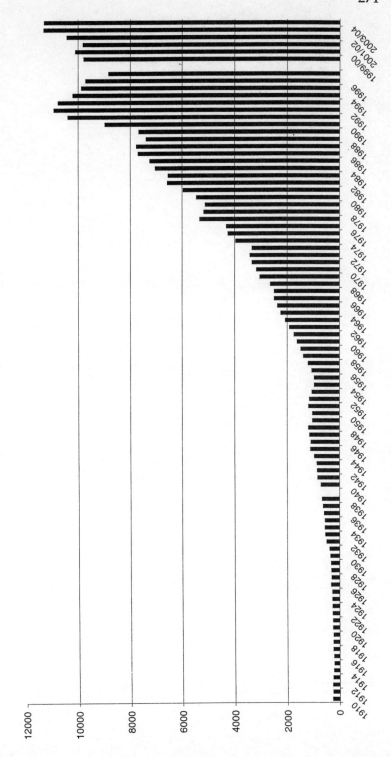

Appendix 7

Crimes Recorded by the Police Per 100,000 Population
England and Wales, 1910 - 2003/04

List of Abbreviations

ABC	Acceptable Behaviour Contract
ASBO	Anti-social Behaviour Order
ASBU	Anti-social Behaviour Unit
BCS	British Crime Survey
BESD	binomial effect size display
CCTV	closed circuit television
CDATE	Correctional Drug Abuse Treatment Effectiveness
CSO	Community Support Officer
CYTCIP	Comprehensive Youth Training and Community Involvement Programme
D2W	Dependency to Work
DfES	Department for Education and Skills
DTTO	Drug Treatment and Testing Order
DWI	driving while intoxicated
EM	electronic monitoring
ESF	European Social Fund
ESOL	English for Speakers of Other Languages
ETS	Enhanced Thinking Skills
FARE	Financial Assessment Related to Employability
GDPS	Glasgow Drug Problem Service
HDC	Home Detention Curfew
HIT	High Intensity Training
HMP	Her Majesty's Prison
HMSO	Her Majesty's Stationery Office
HMYOI	Her Majesty's Young Offender Institution
HORS	Home Office Research Study
HOSB	Home Office Statistical Bulletin
IAP	Intensive Aftercare Probation
ICCP	Intensive Control and Change Programme
ICVS	International Crime Victim Survey
IPU	Intensive Probation Unit
IPSP	Intensive Protective Supervision Project
ISSP	Intensive Supervision and Surveillance Programme
JAS	Jail Addiction Services
JSA	Job Seeker's Allowance
KPI	Key Performance Indicator
LIDS	Local Inmates Database System
MCTC	Military Corrective Training Centre
MHS	Michigan Human Services
NAO	National Audit Office

NCRS	National Crime Recording Standard
NIJ	National Institute of Justice
NOMS	National Offender Management Service
NYS	National Youth Survey
OI	Offenders Index
OJJDP	Office for Juvenile Justice and Delinquency Prevention
ONS	Office for National Statistics
PCYC	Paint Creek Youth Centre
PREP	Post-Release Employment Project
PRES	Prisoner Release Employment Scheme
PSI	pre-sentence investigation
R&R	Reasoning and Rehabilitation
RISSAP	Rotherham Intensive Supervision, Support and Advocacy Programme
RJ	restorative justice
RSL	registered social landlord
SEU	Social Exclusion Unit
SIR	statistical information on recidivism
SMS	scientific methods scale
SOTP	Sex Offenders Treatment Programme
SOVA	Society of Voluntary Associates
STOP	Straight Thinking On Probation
TASC	Treatment Alternatives to Street Crime
TC	therapeutic community
TICO	Training Institute for Central Ohio
TUC	Trades Union Congress
VDS	Vocational Delivery System
W2W	Welfare to Work
YDC	Youth Development Centre
YJB	Youth Justice Board
YLS	Youth Lifestyle Survey
YOI	Young Offender Institution
YOT	Youth Offending Team

Bibliography

A Second Chance: The employment and training of children with criminal records, conference report, London: Michael Sieff Foundation, 2000.(Online: www.btguk.org/graphics/sieff2.pdf).

Adams, K., Bennett, T., Flanagan, T.J., Marquart, J., Cuvelier, S., Fritsch, E.J., Gerber, J., Longmire, D. and Burton, V., 'A Large-scale Multidimensional Test of the Effect of Prison Education Programs on Offender Behavior', *The Prison Journal*, vol. 74, 1994, pp. 433-39.

Allnutt, D., *Review of Statistics on Efficacy of Sentencing: Report on a review for the Home Office*, London: Home Office, 2001. (http://www.statistics.gov.uk/about/consultation_by_theme/dow nloads/postconsdrft.pdf).

Alternatives to Prison Sentences, Session 1997-98, 3rd Report, HC486, July 1998, para 249 - 9.

Anderson, B., Beinart, S., Farrington, D., Longman, J., Sturgis, P. and Utting, D., 'Effective Risk Focused Interventions with Young Offenders', in *Risk and Protective Factors Associated with Youth Crime and Effective Interventions To Prevent It*, London: Youth Justice Board, 2001.

Andrews, D. and Bonta, J., *LSI-R: The Level of Service Inventory – Revised*, Toronto, Ontario: Multi-Health Systems, Inc., 1995.

Andrews, D. and Bonta, J., *The Psychology of Criminal Conduct*, Ohio: Anderson Publishing Co. 1994.

Andrews, D., Bonta, J. and Hoge, R., 'Classification for effective rehabilitation: Rediscovering psychology', in *Criminal Justice and Behaviour*, 1990, vol. 17:19-52.

Andrews, D.A., Zinger, L., Hoge, R.D., Bonta, J., Gendreau, P. and Cullen, F.T., 'Does correctional treatment work? A clinically relevant and psychologically informed meta-analysis', *Criminology*, vol. 28, 1990, pp. 369-04.

Anglin, M.D. and Maughn, T.H., 'Ensuring Success in Interventions with Drug-using Offenders', *Annals of the American Academy of Political and Social Science*, vol. 521, 1992, pp. 66-90.

Annual Report of HM Chief Inspector of Prisons for England and Wales 2001-2002, London: The Stationary Office, 2002. (Online: www.homeoffice.gov.uk/docs/annual_report02.pdf).

Annual Report of HM Chief Inspector of Prisons for England and Wales 2002-2003, London: The Stationary Office, 2004. (Online: http://www.homeoffice.gov.uk/docs2/hmcipannualreport2002-03.pdf).

Antonawitcz, D. H., Izzo, R. L. and Ross, R. R., 'Characteristics of Effective Offender Rehabilitation', in Ross *et al.* (eds), 1995.

Armitage, R., *Tackling Anti-social Behaviour–What Really Works*, London: Nacro, 2002.

Ashworth, A., 'Sentencing' in Maguire, M. *et al.* (eds), *The Oxford Handbook of Criminology*, 1994, p. 838.

Baker, M., 'Warrant Enforcement Services Born 12th November 2001', *Team Reliance Newsletter*, Spring 2002.

Barton, W.H. and Butts, J.A., 'Viable Options: Intensive Supervision Programs for Juvenile Delinquents', *Crime and Delinquency*, vol. 36, no. 2, 1990, pp. 238-56.

Baumer, T. L., and Mendelsohn, R. I., *The Electronic Monitoring of Non-violent convicted felons: An experiment in home detention, final report* (Final report from NIJ Grant No. 86-IJ-CX-0041), Indianapolis: Indiana University, School of Public and Environmental Affairs, 1990.

Baumer, T. L. and R. I. Mendelsohn, 'Electronically Monitored Home Confinement: Does it work?' in Byrne, J.M. *et al.*, 1992, pp. 54-67.

Bazemore, G. and Umbreit, M., *Boards and Mediations: Restorative justice and citizen involvement in the response to youth crime*, Florida Atlantic University: Balanced and Restorative Justice Project, Office of Juvenile Justice and Delinquency Prevention (OJJDP), 1998.

Belenko, S., *Research on Drug Courts: A Critical Review*, New York: The National Center on Addiction and Substance Abuse at Columbia University, June 2001.

Berriman, L., *The Role of Social Support within a Short-Term Prisoner Project Designed to Address Resettlement Needs and Recidivism*, Kent: University of Kent (unpublished; provided by Colin Gray, Head of Resttlement at HMP Canterbury), 2002.

Bloom, H.S., Orr, L.L., Cave, G., Bell, S.H. and Doolittle, F., *The National JTPA Study: Title IIA Impacts*, Research and Evaluation Report Series 93-C, Washington, DC: US Department of Labor, 1993.

Blumstein, A. and Wallman, J., *The Crime Drop in America*, Cambridge: Cambridge University Press, 2000.

Blunkett, D., *Reducing Crime – Changing Lives: The Government's Plans for Transforming the Management of Offenders*, London: Home Office, 2004.

Bonta, J., 'Offender Assessment: General Issues and Considerations', *Forum on Corrections Research*, vol. 12, no. 2, 2000, pp. 14-18.

Bonta, J., Wallace-Capretta, S., *Electronic Monitoring in Canada*, Public Works and Government Services Canada, 1999 (Online: http://www.sgc.gc.ca).

Bonta, J., and Gendreau, P., 'Re-examining the Cruel and Unusual Punishment of Prison Life', *Law and Human Behaviour*, vol. 14, 1990, pp. 347-72.

Bottoms, A., *Intensive Community Supervision for Young Offenders: Outcomes, Process and Costs*, University of Cambridge, Institute of Criminology, 1995.

Braithwaite, J., *Crime, Shame and Reintegration*, Cambridge: Cambridge University Press, 1989.

Brand, S. and Price, R., *The Economic and Social Costs of Crime*, HORS 217, London: Home Office, 2000.

Burnett, R., *Fitting Supervision to Offenders: Assessment and Allocation Decisions in the Probation Service*, Home Office Research Study No 153, London: Home Office, 1996, as discussed in Vennard *et al.*, 1997.

Burrows, J., Clark, A., Davison, T., Tarling, R. and Webb, S., *Research into the Nature and Effectiveness of Drugs Throughcare*, RDS Occasional Paper No. 68, London: Home Office, 2001.

Byrne, J.M., Lurigio, A.J. and Petersilia, J., *Smart Sentencing: The Emergence of Intermediate Sanctions*, Newbury Park, CA, Sage, 1992.

Campbell, S. *A Review of Anti-social Behaviour Orders*, HORS 236, London: Home Office, 2002(a).

Campbell, S., *Implementing Anti-social Behaviour Orders: Messages for Practitioners*, Findings 160, London: Home Office, 2002(b).

Carter, P., *Managing Offenders, Reducing Crime: A New Approach*, London: Home Office, 2003.

Castellano, T.C. and Soderstrom, I.R., 'Therapeutic Wilderness Programs and Juvenile Recidivism: A Program Evaluation', *Journal of Offender Rehabilitation*, vol. 17, no. 3, 1992, pp. 19-46.

Crawford, A. and Newburn, T., *Youth Offending and Restorative Justice*, Cullompton, UK: Willan, 2003.

Crime, Justice and Protecting the Public, White Paper Cm 965, Sessional papers 1989-90, London: Home Office, 1990.

Criminal Justice: The Way Ahead, White Paper Cm 5074, London: Home Office, 2001.

Crime Statistics: England and Wales 2002, London: Home Office (Accessible online February 2004: www.homeoffice.gov.uk/rds/crimestats02.html).

Criminal Statistics 1993, London: HMSO.

Coid, *et al.*, 'The Impact of Methadone Treatment on Drug Misuse and Crime', Home Office Research Findings No. 120, London: Home Office, 2000.

Comptroller and Auditor General of the National Audit Office, *The Drug Treatment and Testing Order: Early Lessons*, London: HMSO, 2004.

Cox, F. A., Gingerich, R. J., Harris, P., Magliolo, D. M. and White, B., 'Reasoning and Rehabilitation in Texas', in Ross *et al.* (eds), 1995.

Davies, M., Croall, H. and Tryer, J., *Criminal Justice: An Introduction to the Criminal Justice System in England and Wales*, second edn, Essex: Pearson Education Ltd, 1998.

Davies, W., *A Cognitive Approach to Working with Offenders*, Leicester: Association for Psychological Therapies, 1998.

Department for Education and Skills (DfES): Offenders' Learning and Skills Unit (Online: http://www.dfes.gov.uk/offenderlearning/)

Deschenes, E.P., Turner, S., Greenwood, P. and Chiesa, J., *An Experimental Evaluation of Drug Testing and Treatment Interventions for Probationers in Maricopa County*, Santa Monica, CA: RAND Corporation, 1996.

Ditchfield, J., *Family Ties and Recidivism: Main findings of the literature*, Home Office Research Bulletin No. 36, London: Home Office, 1994.

DiIulio, J. and Piehl, A., 'Does Prison Pay? The Stormy National Debate Over the Cost Effectiveness of Imprisonment', *Brookings Review*, fall issue, 1991, pp. 28-35.

DiIulio, J. and Piehl, A., 'Does Prison Pay? Revisited', *Brookings Review*, winter issue, 1995, pp. 21-25.

Dodgson, K., Goodwin, P., Howard, P., Llewellyn-Thomas, S., Mortimer, E., Russell, N. and Weiner, M., *Electronic Monitoring of Released Prisoners: An Evaluation of the Home Detention Curfew Scheme*, Home Office Research Study 222, London: Home Office, 2001.

Eley, S., Gallop, K., McIvor, G., Morgan, K. and Yates, R., 'Drug Treatment and Testing Orders: Evaluation of The Scottish Pilots', Edinburgh: Scottish Executive Social Research, 2002, (online: http://www.scotland.gov.uk/cru/kd01/green/dtts-00.asp).

Elliot, R., Airs, J., Easton, C. and Lewis, R., *Electronically Monitored Curfew for 10 to 15 Year Olds: Report of the pilot*, Home Office Occasional Paper, London: Home Office, 2000.

Employment and Ex-Offenders, London: Trades Union Congress, 2001, (www.tuc.org.uk).

Falshaw, L., Friendship, C., Travers, R., and Nugent, F., *An Evaluation of HM Prison Service Accredited Cognitive Skills Programmes*, Home Office Research Study No. 206, London: Home Office, 2003.

Farrington, D., and Nuttall, C., 'Prison Size, Overcrowding, Prison Violence, and Recidivism', *Journal of Criminal Justice*, vol. 8, 1980, pp. 221-231.

Farrington, D., *Understanding and Preventing Youth Crime*, York, UK: Joseph Rowntree Foundation, 1996.

Farrington, D., *Evaluation of Two Intensive Regimes for Young Offenders*, Home Office Research Findings No. 121, London: Home Office, 2000.

Farrington, D., Ditchfield, J., Hancock, G., Howard, P., Jolliffe, D., Livingston, M.S. and Painter, K.A., *Evaluation of Two Intensive Regimes for Young Offenders*, Home Office Research Study 239, London: Home Office, April 2002.

Flood-Page, C., Campbell, S., Harrington, V., and Miller, J., *Youth Crime: Findings from the 1998/99 Youth Lifestyles Survey*, Home Office Research Study 209, London: Home Office, 2000.

Friendship, C., Blud, L., Erikson, M. and Travers, R., *An Evaluation of Cognitive Behavioural Treatment for Prisoners*, Home Office Research Findings No. 161, London: Home Office, 2002.

Friendship, C., Falshaw, L. and Beech, A., 'Measuring the Real Impact of Accredited Offending Behaviour Programmes', *Legal and Criminal Psychology*, vol. 8, 2003, pp. 115-27.

Gaes, G.G., Flanagan, T.J., Motiuk, L. and Stewart, L., *Adult Correctional Treatment*, 1998, (published online: http://www.bop.gov/orepg/oreprcopyoftr.pdf).

Garland, D., *Punishment and Modern Society*, Oxford: Clarendon Press, 1990.

Genders, E. and Player E., *Grendon: A Study of a therapeutic prison*, London: Clarendon Press, 1995.

Gendreau, P., Cullen, F., and Bonta, J., 'Intensive Rehabilitation Supervision', *Federal Probation*, vol. 58, 1994, pp. 72-78.

Gendreau, P., Goggin, C., Cullen, F. T. and Andrews, D.A., 'The Effects of Community Sanctions and Incarceration on Recidivism', *Forum on Corrections Research*, vol. 12, no. 2, 2000, pp. 10-13.

Gendreau, P., Little, T. and Goggin, C., 'A Meta-Analysis of the Predictors of Adult Offender Recidivism: What works!', *Criminology*, vol. 34, no. 4, 1996, pp. 575-607.

Gendreau, P. and Ross, R.R., 'Effective Correctional Treatment: Bibliotherapy for Cynics', *Crime and Delinquency*, vol. 25, 1979, pp. 463-89.

Gerber, J. and Fritsch, E.J., *Prison Education Research Project: Final Report*, Hunstville, TX: Sam Houston State University, 1994.

Gesch, C.B., Hammond, S.M., Hampson, S.E., Eves, A. and Crowder, M.J., 'Influence of Supplementary Vitamins, Minerals and Essential Fatty Acids on the Antisocial Behaviour of Young Adult Prisoners: Randomised, Placebo-controlled Trial', *British Journal of Psychiatry*, vol. 181, 2002, pp. 22-28.

Ghate, D. and Ramella, M., 'Positive Parenting: The National Evaluation of the Youth Justice Board's Parenting Programme', London: Policy Research Bureau for the Youth Justice Board for England and Wales, September 2002.

Goldkamp, J.S., 'Miami's Treatment Drug Court for Felony Defendants: Some Implications of Assessment Findings', *The Prison Journal*, vol. 73, no. 2, 1994, pp. 110-66.

Goodwin, R. 'Merseyside Adelaide House R&R Project with Women', in Ross *et al.* (eds), 1995.

Gossop, M., Marsden, J. and Stewart, D., *National Treatment Outcome Research After Five Years*, London: Department of Health, 2001.

Gottfredson, D.C. and Barton, W.H., *A Short Term Outcome Evaluation of the Baltimore City Drug Treatment Program*, College Park, MD: Department of Criminology and Criminal Justice, University of Maryland, 1996.

Graham, J. and Bowling, B., *Young People and Crime*, HORS 145, London: Home Office, 1995.

Greenwood, P.W., Deschenes, E.P., and Adams, J., *Chronic Juvenile Offenders: Final results from the Skillman Aftercare Experiment*, Santa Monica, CA: RAND Corporation, 1993.

Greenwood, P.W. and Turner, S., 'Evaluation of the Paint Creek Youth Center: A Residential Program for Serious Delinquents', *Criminology*, vol.31, no. 2, 1993, pp. 263-79.

Grove, P.G., 'Report on the Study into Forecasting the Prison and Probation Populations', Consultation Draft 1, August 2001.

Guidance For Practitioners Involved In Drug Treatment and Testing Order Pilots, section, 5.3 (Online: http://www.homeoffice.gov.uk/cdact/dttguid.htm#TESTING AND ENFORCEMENT).

Hagell, A. and Newburn, T., *Persistent Young Offenders*, London: Policy Studies Institute, 1994.

Hagell, A., Hazel, N. and Shaw, C., *Evaluation of Medway Secure Training Centre*, London: Policy Research Bureau, on behalf of Home Office, July 2000.

Hanlon, T. and Nurco, D., 'The Relative Effects of Three Approaches to the Parole Supervision of Narcotic Addicts and Cocaine Abusers', *The Prison Journal*, vol. 79, no. 2, 1999, pp. 163-81.

Hanson, R.K., Steffy, R.A. and Gauthier, R., 'Long-Term Recidivism of Child Molesters', *Journal of Consulting and Clinical Psychology*, vol. 61, no. 4, 1993, pp. 646-52.

Harer, M.D. 'Recidivism Among Federal Prisoners Released in 1987', *Journal of Correctional Education*, vol. 46, 1995(a), pp. 98-127.

Harer, M.D., *Prison Education Program Participation and Recidivism: A Test of the Normalization Hypothesis*, Washington, DC: Federal Bureau of Prisons, Office of Research and Evaluation, 1995(b).

Hart, H.L.A., *Punishment and Responsibility: Essays in the Philosophy of Law*, Oxford: Oxford University Press, 1970.

Hawkins, J., Catalano, R. and Miller, J., 'Risk and Protective Factors for Alcohol and Other Drug Problems in Adolescence and Early Adulthood: Implications for Substance Abuse Prevention', *Psychological Bulletin*, vol. 112, no. 1, 1992, pp. 64-105.

Hedderman, C. and Sugg, D., 'Part I: The Influence of Cognitive Approaches: A Survey of Probation Programmes', *Changing Offenders' Attitudes and Behaviour: What works?*, Home Office Research Study, no. 171, London: Home Office, 1997.

Hillsman, S.T., 'Fines and Day Fines' in Tonry, M. and Morris, N. (eds), *Crime and Justice: A Review of Research*, vol. 12, Chicago, IL: University of Chicago Press, 1990.

Hollin, C. R. 'The Meaning and Implication of Programme Integrity', in McGuire, J. (ed.), 1995.

Hollin, C. R., 'Treatment Programs for Offenders: Meta-Analysis, "What Works," and Beyond', *International Journal of Law and Psychiatry*, vol. 22, nos. 3-4, 1999, pp. 361-72.

Hollin, C., McGuire, J., Palmer, E., Bilby, C., Hatcher, R. and Holmes, A., *Introducing Pathfinder Programmes into the Probation Service: An Interim Report*, Home Office Research Study 247, London: Home Office Research, Development and Statistics Directorate, July 2002.

Hollin, C., McGuire, J., Palmer, E., Bilby, C., Hatcher, R., Holmes, A., *Introducing Pathfinder Programmes into the Probation Service*, Home Office Research Findings no. 177, London: Home Office, 2002.

Home Office, *A Guide to Anti-Social Behaviour Orders and Acceptable Behaviour Contracts*, London: Home Office, November 2002.

Home Office, *Annual Report of HM Chief Inspector of Prisons for England and Wales 2001-2002*, London: HM Inspectorate of Prisons, 2002, (available online: www.homeoffice.gov.uk/docs/annual_report02.pdf).

Home Office, *Annual Report of HM Chief Inspector of Prisons for England and Wales 2002-2003*, London: HM Inspectorate of Prisons, 2004, (available online: http://www.homeoffice.gov.uk/justice/prisons/inspprisons).

Home Office, *Autumn Performance Report 2003*, Cm 6057, London: Home Office, 2003.

Home Office, *Departmental Report 2003*, London: Home Office, 2003.

Home Office, *Home Office Targets Delivery Report*, Cm 5754, London: Home Office, February 2003.

Hough, M., Clancy, A., McSweeney, T., Turnball, P.J., *The Impact of Drug Treatment and Testing Orders on Offending: Two-year Conviction Results*, Home Office Research Findings 184, 2003, (online: http://www.homeoffice.gov.uk/rds/pdfs2/r184.pdf).

Howell, J., and Bilchik, S., *Guide for Implementing the Comprehensive Strategy for Serious, Violent and Chronic Juvenile Offenders*, Washington: OJJDP, 1995.

Howells, K. and Day, A., 'The Rehabilitation of Offenders: International Perspectives Applied to Australian Correctional Systems', *Trends and Issues in Crime and Criminal Justice*, no. 112, Canberrra: Australian Institute of Criminology, 1999.

Inciardi, J., Martin, S.S., Butzin, C.A., Hooper, R.M. and Harrison, L.D., 'An Effective Model of Prison-based Treatment for Drug-involved Offenders', *Journal of Drug Issues*, vol. 27, 1997, pp. 261-78.

Introductory Guide to The Crime and Disorder Act, section 61-64 (online: http://www.homeoffice.gov.uk/cdact/cdaint19.htm).

Izzo, R.L. and Ross, R.R., 'Meta-analysis of Rehabilitation Programmes for Juvenile Delinquents: A Brief Report', *Criminal Justice and Behaviour*, vol. 17, 1990, pp.134-42.

Jackson, S., *A Study of the Needs of Short Term Prisoners at HM Prison Canterbury, Kent, Surrey and Sussex Area: Psychological Services*, (unpublished; provided by Colin Gray, Head of Resettlement at HMP Canterbury) 2000.

Justice for All, White Paper Cm 5563, London: Home Office, 2002.

Kemshall, H., *Risk Assessment and Management of Serious Violent and Sexual Offenders: A review of current issues*, Research Findings No. 64/2002, Crime and Criminal Justice Research Programme, Edinburgh: Scottish Executive, 2002, (online: www.scotland.gov.uk/cru/resfinds/crf64-00).

Kennedy, S.M., 'Treatment Responsivity: Reducing Recidivism by Enhancing Treatment Effectiveness', *Forum on Corrections Research*, vol. 12, no. 2, 2000, pp. 19-23.

Kershaw, C., Goodman, J. and White, S., *Reconvictions of Offenders Sentenced or Discharged from Prison in 1995, England and Wales*, issue 19/99, London: Home Office, 1999.

Knight, T., Mowlam, A., Woodfield, K., Lewis, J., Purdon, S., Kitchen, S., Roberts, C., 'Evaluation of the Community Sentences and Withdrawal of Benefits Pilots', Research Report No 198, London: Department for Work and Pensions, 2003, (online: http://www.dwp.gov.uk/asd/asd5/rports2003-2004/rport198/%Main.pdf).

Lab, S.P. and Whitehead, J.T., 'From "Nothing Works" to the "Appropriate Works": The Latest Step in the Search for the Secular Grail', *Criminology*, vol. 28, 1990, pp. 405-17.

Lambert, M.J. 'The Psychotherapist's Contribution to Psychiatry process and outcome', *Clinical Psychology Review*, vol. 9, 1989, pp. 469-85, cited in Davies, 1998.

Land, K.C., McCall, P.L. and Williams, J.R., 'Something that Works in Juvenile Justice: An Evaluation of the North Carolina Court Counsellors' Intensive Protective Supervision Randomised Experimental Project, 1987-1989', *Evaluation Review*, vol. 14, no. 6, 1990, pp. 574-606.

Langan, P. and Farrington, D., *Crime and Justice in the United States and in England and Wales, 1981-96*, Washington: US Department of Justice, 1998.

Lattimore, P.K., Witte, A.D. and Baker, J.R., 'Experimental Assessment of the Effect of Vocational Training on Youthful Property Offenders', *Evaluation Review*, vol. 14, no. 2, 1990, pp. 115-33.

Leukefeld, C.G. and Tims, F.M. (eds), *Drug Abuse Treatment in Prisons and Jails*, Research Monograph no. 118, Rockville, MD: US Department of Health and Human Services, Public Health Service, 1992.

Levitt, S.D., 'The Effect of Prison Population Size on Crime Rates: Evidence from Prison Overcrowding Litigation', *Quarterly Journal of Economics*, May 1996, pp. 319-51.

Lewis, R.V., 'Scared Straight – California Style: Evaluation of the San Quentin Squires Program', *Criminal Justice and Behaviour*, vol. 10, no. 2, 1983, pp. 209-26.

Lewis, S., Vennard, J., Maguire, M., Raynor, P., Vanstone, M., Raybould, S. and Rix, A., *The Resettlement of Short-term Prisoners: An Evaluation of Seven Pathfinders*, London: Home Office, 2003.

Lipsey, M.W., 'Juvenile Delinquency Treatment: A Meta-analytic Inquiry into the Variability of Treatment Effects', in Cook, T.D.,

Cooper, H., Cordray, D.S., Hartmann, H., Hedges, L.V., Light, R.J., Louis, T.A. and Mosteller, F., *Meta-Analysis for Explanation: A Casebook*, New York: Russell Sage Foundation, 1992.

Lipsey, M.W., 'What Do We Learn from 400 Research Studies on the Effectiveness of Treatment with Juvenile Delinquents?', in McGuire, J. (ed.), 1995.

Lipton, D.S., Martinson, R. and Wilks, J., *The Effectiveness of Correctional Treatment*, New York: Praeger, 1975.

Lipton, D.S., 'The Correctional Opportunity: Pathways to Drug Treatment for Offenders', *Journal of Drug Issues*, vol. 24, nos. 1- 2, 1994, pp. 331-48.

Lipton, D.S., 'Prison-based Therapeutic Communities: Their Success with Drug- abusing Offenders', *National Institute of Justice Journal*, February 1996, pp. 12-20.

Lipton, D.S., Pearson, F.S., Cleland, C.M. and Yee, D., 'The Effectiveness of Cognitive-Behavioural Treatment Methods on Offender Recidivism: Meta-analytic Outcomes from the CDATE Project', in McGuire, J. (ed.), 2002.

Lobley, D., Smith, D. and Stern, C., *Freagarrach: An Evaluation of a Project for Persistent Juvenile Offenders*, Crime and Criminal Justice Research Findings, no. 53, Edinburgh: Scottish Executive Central Research Unit, The Stationary Office, 2001.

Logan, C. and Gaes, G., 'Meta-analysis and the Rehabilitation of Punishment', *Justice Quarterly*, vol. 10, no. 2, June 1993.

Losel, F., 'The Effectiveness of Treatment in Institutional and Community Settings', *Criminal Behaviour and Mental Health*, vol. 3, 1993, pp. 416-37.

Losel, F., 'The Efficacy of Correctional Treatment: A Review and Synthesis of Meta-evaluations', in McGuire, J. (ed.), 1995.

Lucas, P. and Liabo, K. *One-to-one, Non-directive Mentoring Programmes have not been Shown to Improve Behaviour in Young People Involved in Offending or Anti-social Activities*, What Works for Children Group Evidence Nugget, 2003, (online: http://www.whatworksforchildren.org.uk/docs/Nuggets/pdfs/Mentoring230703.pdf).

Mackenzie, D.L., Brame, R., MacDowall, D. and Souryal, C., 'Boot Camp Prisons and Recidivism in Eight States', *Criminology*, vol. 33, no. 3, 1995, pp. 327-58.

Mackie, A., Raine, J, Burrows, J., Hopkins, M., and Dunstan, E., *Clearing the Debts: The Enforcement of Financial Penalties in Magistrates' Courts*, Home Office Online Report 09/03, 2003.

Maguire, K.E., Flanagan, T.J. and Thornbury, T.P., 'Prison Labor and Recidivism', *Journal of Quantitative Criminology*, vol. 4, no. 1, 1988, pp. 3-18.

Making Punishments Work: The Halliday Report, (Appendices and Correspondence), London: Home Office, July 2001.

Marques, J.K., Day, D.M., Nelson, C., West, M.A., 'Effects of Cognitive Behavioural Treatment on Sex Offender Recidivism: Preliminary Results of a Longitudinal Study', *Criminal Justice and Behaviour*, vol. 21, no. 1, 1994, pp. 28-54.

Marshall, P., *A Reconviction Study of HMP Grendon Therapeutic Community*, Research Findings 53, London: Home Office, 1997.

Martin, C. and Player, E., *Drug Treatment in Prison: An Evaluation of the RAPt Treatment Programme*, Winchester: Waterside Press, 2000.

Martin, S.S., Butzin, C.A. and Inciardi, J., 'Assessment of a Multistage Therapeutic Community for Drug Involved Offenders', *Journal of Psychoactive Drugs*, vol. 27, no. 1, 1995, pp. 109-16.

Martin, S.S., Butzin, C.A., Saum, C.A. and Inciardi, J., 'Three-year Outcomes of Therapeutic Community Treatment for Drug-involved Offenders in Delaware: From Prison to Work Release to Aftercare', *The Prison Journal*, vol. 79, no. 3, 1999, pp. 294-320.

Martinson, R., 'What Works: Questions and Answers about Prison Reform', *The Public Interest*, vol. 10, 1974, pp. 22-54.

Martinson, R., 'New Findings, New Views: A Note of Caution Regarding Sentencing Reform', *Hofstra Law Review*, vol. 7, 1979, pp. 243–58.

Matrix MHA and Nacro, *Evaluation of Drug Testing in the Criminal Justice System in Nine Pilot Areas*, Home Office Research Findings No. 180, London: Home Office 2003.

McGuire, J. (ed.), *What Works: Reducing Reoffending*, Chichester: John Wiley and Sons, 1995.

McGuire, J., 'Defining Correctional Programs', *Forum on Corrections Research*, vol. 12, issue 2, 2000(a), pp. 5-9.

McGuire, J., *Cognitive-behavioural Approaches: An Introduction to the Theory and Research*, London: Home Office, 2000(b).

McGuire, J. (ed.), *Offender Rehabilitation and Treatment*, England: Wiley and Sons, 2002.

McIvor, G., *Sanctions for Serious or Persistent Offenders: A Review of the Literature*, Stirling: Social Work Research Centre, University of Stirling, 1990.

Menninger, K., *The Crime of Punishment*, New York: Viking, 1968.

Merrington, S. and Hine, J. *A Handbook for Evaluating Probation Work with Offenders*, London: Home Office, 2001.

Mimms, A. 'Exercise for the Brain: Colorado's Adams County Probation Office', in Ross *et al.* (eds), 1995.

Misspent Youth: Young People and Crime, Oxon, UK: Audit Commission, 1996.

Nagin, D., 'Criminal Deterrence Research at the Outset of the Twenty-first Century', in Tonry, M. (ed.), *Crime and Justice: A Review of Research*, Chicago: University of Chicago Press, 1997.

Nagin, D.S., 'Deterrence and Incapacitation', in Tonry, M. (ed.), *The Handbook of Crime and Punishment*, New York: Oxford University Press, 1998.

National Audit Office, *Reducing Prisoner Reoffending*, Report by the Comptroller and Auditor General of General of HM Prison Service, London: HMSO, 2002.

National Audit Office/Lord Chancellor's Department, *Collection of Fines and Other Financial Penalties in the Criminal Justice System*, Report by the Comptroller and Auditor General, HC 672 session 2001-2002: 15 March 2002, London: HMSO, 2002.

NAO, *Youth Offending: the Delivery of Community and Custodial Sentences*, London: TSO, January 2004.

National Prison Survey *1991 – Main Findings*, Home Office Research Study No. 128, London: HMSO, 1992.

National Probation Service, *A New Choreography: An Integrated Strategy for the National Probation Service for England and Wales*, Strategic Framework 2001-2004, London: Home Office and National Probation Service for England and Wales, August 2001.

National Probation Service, *Performance Report 10*, November 2003.

National Standards for the Supervision of Offenders in the Community Revised, London: Home Office, 2002.

'National Standards Monitoring Performance Report: April 2002-March 2003', London: National Probation Service for England and Wales, Home Office.

'National Standards Monitoring Performance Report: October 2001-March 2002', London: National Probation Service for England and Wales, Home Office.

Nixon, J., Hunter, H., and Shayer, S., *The Use of Legal Remedies by Social Landlords to Deal with Neighbour Nuisance: Survey Report*, Centre for Regional Economic and Social Research Paper No. H8, Sheffield: Sheffield Hallam University, 1999.

Nurco, D., Hanlon, T., Bateman, R. and Kinlock, T., 'Drug Abuse Treatment in the Context of Correctional Surveillance', *Journal of Substance Abuse Treatment*, vol. 12, no. 1, 1995, pp. 19-27.

Nuttall, C., Goldblatt, P. and Lewis, C., *Reducing Offending: An Assessment of Research Evidence on Ways of Dealing with Offending Behaviour*, Home Office Research Study No. 187, London: Home Office, 1998.

OJP Drug Court Clearinghouse and Technical Assistance Project at American University: Summary of Drug Court Activity by State and County, September 8, 2003.

Oldfield, M., *From Welfare to Risk: Discourse, Power and Politics in the Probation Service*, Issues in Community and Criminal Justice: Monograph 1, London: NAPO, 2002.

Olson, S., *United Kingdom Drug Treatment Court: Promoting a Healthier Drug Free Lifestyle for Substance Misusing Acquisitive Crime Offenders*, Ottawa: Royal Canadian Mounted Police, 1999.

Parker, T., *The Frying Pan*, London: Hutchinson, 1970.

Pawson, R. and Tilley, N., *Realistic Evaluation*, London: Sage, 1997.

Petersilia, J. and Turner, S., *Prison versus Probation in California: Implications for Crime and Offender Recidivism*, Santa Monica, CA: RAND Corporation, 1986.

Petersilia, J. and Turner, S., 'Intensive Supervision Programs for Drug Offenders', in Byrne, J.M., Lurigio, A.J. and Petersilia, J. (eds), *Smart Sentencing: The Emergence of Intermediate Sanctions*, Newbury Park: Sage Publications, 1992, pp. 18-37.

Petersilia, J. and Turner, S., *Evaluating Intensive Supervision Probation/Parole: Results of a Nationwide Experiment*, Washington, DC: National Institute of Justice, 1993.

Petersilia, J. and Turner, S., *Day Fines in Four U.S. Jurisdictions*, DRU-1153-NIJ, Santa Monica, CA: RAND Corporation, 1996.

Petersilia, J., Turner, S., Kahan, J. and Peterson, J., *Granting Felons Probation: Public Risks and Alternatives*, Santa Monica, CA: RAND Corporation, 1985.

'Pioneer projects reduce reoffending', *Guardian*, 18 October 2000.

Porporino, F., Fabiano, E. and Robinson, D., 'Focusing on Successful Reintegration: Cognitive Skills Training for Offenders', Research and Statistics, Ottawa: Correctional Services Canada, 1991.

Porporino, F. and Robinson, D., 'An Evaluation of the Reasoning and Rehabilitation Program with Canadian Federal Offenders', in Ross *et al.* (eds), 1995.

Prime, J., *Progress Made against Home Office Public Service Agreement Target 10*, Home Office Online Report 16, London: Home Office, 2002.

Probation Offending Behaviour Programmes – Effective Practice Guide, Development and Practice Report 2, London: Home Office, 2002.

Probation Statistics England and Wales 2002, London: Home Office, 2004.

Probation Statistics England and Wales 1999, London: Home Office, 2001.

Pullen, S., *Evaluation of the Reasoning and Rehabilitation Cognitive Skills Development Program as Implemented in Juvenile ISP in Colorado–Final Report*, Washington, DC: United States Department of Justice, National Institute of Justice, 1996.

Punishment, Custody and the Community, Green Paper Cm 424, London: Home Office, 1998.

Pyle, D. and Deadman, D., 'Crime and the Business Cycle in Post-war Britain', *British Journal of Criminology*, vol. 34, no. 3, 1994, pp. 339-57.

Ramsbotham, D., *Prisongate*, London: Free Press, 2003.

Raynor, P., Kynch, J., Roberts, C. and Merrington, S., *Risk and Need Assessment in Probation Services: An Evaluation*, Home Office Research Study 211, London: RDS, Home Office, 2000.

Raynor, P. and Vanstone, M., 'STOP (Straight Thinking On Probation): The Mid-Glamorgan Experiment', *International Journal of Offender Therapy: Comparative Criminology*, vol. 40, 1996, pp. 272-84.

'Reducing Reconviction Rates', National Probation Service Briefing, issue 4, July 2002.

Reducing Re-offending by Ex-prisoners, London: Social Exclusion Unit, July 2002, (online: http://www.socialexclusionunit.gov.uk /reduce_reoff/rr_main.pdf).

Reinventing Probation Council, '"Broken Windows" Probation: The Next Step in Fighting Crime', *Civic Report*, No. 7, New York: Center for Civic Innovation, Manhattan Institute, August 1999.

Reinventing Probation Council, *Transforming Probation through Leadership: The "Broken Windows" Model*, New York: Center for Civic Innovation, Manhattan Institute, July 2002.

Reliance Security Website, http://www.reliancesecurity.co.uk

Report on a Full Announced Inspection of HMP Belmarsh, 26 May-

4 June 2003 by HM Chief Inspector of Prisons, London: Home Office.

Report on a Full Announced Inspection of HMYOI Aylesbury,

28 April - 2 May 2003 by HM Chief Inspector of Prisons, London: Home Office.

Restorative Justice: The Government's Strategy, A Consultation Document on the Government's Strategy on Restorative Justice, London: Home Office, 22 July 2003.

Review of Efficacy of Sentencing, National Statistics Quality Review Series Report No. 21, London: Home Office, 2003.

Rex, S., Gelsthorpe, L., Roberts, C. and Jordan, P., *Crime Reduction Programme An Evaluation of Community Service Pathfinder Projects Final Report 2002*, RDS Occasional Paper

No. 87, London: Home Office, 2003.

Robinson, D., *The Impact of Cognitive Skills Training on Post-Release Recidivism among Canadian Federal Offenders*, Research Reports, Ottawa: Correctional Services Canada, 1995.

Rosenthal,R. and Rubin, D.B., 'A Simple, General Purpose Display of Magnitude of Experimental Effect', *Journal of Educational Psychology*, vol. 74, issue 2, 1982, pp. 166-69.

Ross, R.R., and Fabiano, E.A., *Reasoning and Rehabilitation: A Handbook for Teaching Cognitive Skills,* Ottawa: T3 Associates, 1991, cited in Pullen, 1996.

Ross, R.R., Fabiano, E.A. and Ewles, C.D., 'The Pickering Project for High Risk Probationers', in Ross *et al.* (eds), 1995.

Ross, R. R. and Ross, R. D. (eds), *Thinking Straight: the Reasoning and Rehabilitation Programme for Delinquency Prevention and Offender Rehabilitation,* Ottawa: Air Training and Publications, 1995.

Ross, R.R., and Ross, R. D., 'In Search of a Program', in Ross *et al.* (eds), 1995(a).

Ross, R.R., and Ross, R. D., 'The R&R Program', in Ross *et al.* (eds), 1995(b).

Ross, R. R., and Ross, R. D., 'Offender Selection and Assessment', in Ross *et al.* (eds), 1995(c).

Rousseau, J-J., 'A Discourse on the Origin of Inequality', *The Social Contract and Discourses,* London: Dent (Everyman edition) 1973.

Saylor, W.G. and Gaes, G.G., *PREP: Training Inmates through Industrial Work Participation and Vocational and Apprenticeship Instruction,* Washington, DC: US Federal Bureau of Prisons, 1996.

Saylor, W.G. and Gaes, G.G., 'Training inmates through industrial work participation and vocational and apprenticeship instruction', *Corrections Management Quarterly,* vol. 1, no. 2, 1997, pp. 32-43.

Sechrest, L., White, S.O. and Brown, E.D. (eds), *The Rehabilitation of Criminal Offenders: Problems and Prospects,* Panel on Research and Rehabilitative Techniques, National Academy of Sciences, Washington, DC: National Academy of Sciences, 1979.

Shelter and Protection: An Inspection of the Langley House Trust Fresh Start Projects, London: HM Inspectorate of Probation, 2001.

Sherman, L.W., Farrington, D.P., Welsh, B.C. and Mackenzie, D.L., *Evidence-Based Crime Prevention,* London: Routledge, 2002.

Sherman, L.W., Strang, H. and Woods, D.J., *Recidivism Patterns in the Canberra Reintegrative Shaming Experiments (RISE),* Canberra: Centre for Restorative Justice Research School of Social Sciences, Australian National University, 2000,

(online: http://www.aic.gov.au/rjustice/rise/recidivism/).

Shinar, D. and Compton, R.P., 'Victim Impact Panels: Their Impact on DWI Recidivism', *Alcohol, Drugs and Driving*, vol. 11, no. 1, Los Angeles: UCLA Brain Information Service/Brain Research Institute, 1995.

Skills for Life: The National Strategy for Improving Adult Literacy and Numeracy Skills 'What Works' Early Findings from the Pathfinder Projects, Brief no. 342, London: DfEE, 2002.

Solanki, A-R., *On-Side Project: Full Evaluation Report – Final Draft*, London: Nacro, 2003.

Smartt, U., *Grendon Tales*, Winchester: Waterside Press, 2001.

Somander, L., *The Second Year of Intensive Supervision with Electronic Monitoring*, Swedish Prison and Probation Administration: Kriminalvården, 1996.

Sontheimer, H. and Goodstein, L., 'Evaluation of Juvenile Intensive Aftercare Probation: Aftercare System versus System Response Effects', *Justice Quarterly*, vol. 10, 1993, pp. 197-227.

Spelman, W., 'The Limited Importance of Prison Expansion', in Blumstein, A. and Wallman, J., *The Crime Drop in America*, Cambridge: Cambridge University Press, 2000.

Stewart, L. and Rowe, R., 'Problems of Self-regulation Among Adult Offenders', *Forum on Corrections Research*, vol. 12, issue 2, 2000, pp. 49-52.

Summary Probation Statistics England and Wales 1992, Home Office Statistical Bulletin, issue 17/93, 1993.

Sugg, D., Moore, L. and Howard, P., *Electronic Monitoring and Offending Behaviour: Reconviction Results for the Second Year of Trials of Curfew Orders*, Home Office Research Findings 141, London: Home Office, 2001.

Tagging Offenders: The Role of Electronic Monitoring in the Scottish Criminal Justice System, Consultation Document, Edinburgh: Scottish Executive, 2000, (online: http://www.scotland.gov.uk/consultations/justice/toem-00.asp).

Targeting Anti-social Behaviour – The Use of Anti-social Behaviour Orders in Scotland, October 2003.

Taxman, F.S. and Spinner, D.L., *The Jail Addiction Services (JAS) Project in Montgomery County, Maryland: Overview of Results from a 24 month Follow-up Study,* unpublished manuscript, University of Maryland, College Park, MD, 1996.

Taylor, R., *Predicting Reconvictions for Sexual and Violent Offences Using the Revised Offender Group Reconviction Scale,* Development and Statistics Directorate, London: Home Office, 1999.

Taylor, R., *A Seven-Year Reconviction Study of HMP Grendon Therapeutic Community,* Home Office Research Findings 115, London: Home Office, 2000.

'Tell Them So They Listen': Messages from Young People in Custody, Home Office Research Study 201, London: Home Office, 2000.

Thompson, B. and Cavadino, P., *The Role of Non-Governmental Agencies and the Resettlement of Prisoners,* conference paper, London: NACRO, 2000.

Through the Prison Gate: A Joint Thematic Review by HM Inspectorates of Prisons and Probation, London: Home Office, 2001.

Tripartite Group Report, *Throughcare: developing the service,* Edinburgh: Scottish Executive, 2003, (online: www.Scotland.gov.uk/library5/justice/tcds-02.asp).

Turnbull, P.J., *Drug Treatment and Testing Orders: Interim Evaluation,* Home Office Research Findings 106, London: Home Office, 1999.

Turnbull, P.J., McSweeney, and Hough,M., *Drug Treatment and Testing Orders: The 18-Month Evaluation,* Home Office Research Findings 128, London: Home Office, 2000.

Turnbull, P.J., McSweeney, T., Webster, R., Edmunds, M. and Hough, M., (October 2000) *Drug Treatment and Testing Orders: Final Evaluation Report,* Home Office Research Study 212, London: Home Office, October 2000, (online: http://www.homeoffice.gov.uk/rds/pdfs/hors212.pdf).

Turner, S. and Greene, J., *The Fare Probation Experiment: Implementation and Outcomes of Day Fines for Felony Offenders in Maricopa County,* Santa Monica, CA: RAND Corporation, 2000.

Turner, S. and Petersilia, J., 'Work Release in Washington: Effects on Recidivism and Corrections Costs' *The Prison Journal,* vol. 76, no. 2, June, 1996, pp. 138-64.

Underdown, A., *Strategies for Effective Offender Supervision Report of the HMIP What Works Project,* London: Home Office, 1998, (available online: http://www.homeoffice.gov.uk/docs2/seos.html).

Underdown, A., *Strategies for Effective Offender Supervision: Report of the HMIP What Works Project*, London: Home Office, 2000.

Vennard, J., Sugg, D., and Hedderman, C., 'The Use of Cognitive-behaviour Approaches with Offenders: Messages from the Research', *Changing Offenders' Attitudes and Behaviour: What Works?*, Home Office Research Study 171, London: Home Office, 1997.

von Hirsch, A., *Doing Justice: The Choice of Punishments*, New York: Hill and Wang, 1976.

von Hirsch, A., Bottoms, A.E., Burney, E. and Wikstrom, P-O., *Criminal Deterrence and Sentence Severity: An Analysis of Recent Research*, Oxford: Hart, 1999.

Walsh, A., 'An Evaluation of the Effects of Adult Basic Education on Rearrest Rates Among Probationers', *Journal of Offender Counseling, Services and Rehabilitation*, vol. 9, 1985,

pp. 69-76.

Weaver, C. and Bensted, J., 'R&R in a Probation Centre: Avon Probation Service, Bristol', in Ross *et al.* (eds), 1995.

Webster, R., Hedderman, C., Turnbull, P. J. and May, T., *Building Bridges to Employment for Prisoners: Summary and Survey of Interventions*, Home Office Research Study 226, London: Home Office, 2001.

Welsh, B.C., Farrington, D.P. and Sherman, L.W., *Costs and Benefits of Preventing Crime*, Boulder, Colorado: Westview Press, 2001.

Wexler, H.K., Falkin, G.P. and Lipton, D.S., 'Outcome Evaluation of a Prison Therapeutic Community for Substance Abuse Treatment', in Leukefeld, C.G. and Tims, F.M. (eds), *Drug Abuse Treatment in Prisons and Jails*, Research Monograph no. 118, Rockville, MD: US Department of Health and Human Services, Public Health Service, 1992, pp. 156-75.

Wexler, H.K., Melnick, G., Lowe, L. and Peters, J., '3-Year Rein-carceration Outcomes for Amity In-prison Therapeutic Community and Aftercare in California', *The Prison Journal*, vol. 79, no. 3, 1999, pp. 321-36.

What Works (2000-2001), Second Report from the Joint Prison/Probation Accreditation Panel.

What Works (2001-2002), Third Report from the Joint Prison/Probation Accreditation Panel.

Wexler, H.K., Falkin, G.P. and Lipton, D.S., 'Outcome Evaluation of a Prison Therapeutic Community for Substance Abuse Treatment', in Leukefeld, C.G. and Tims, F.M. (eds), *Drug Abuse Treatment in Prisons and Jails*, Research Monograph no. 118, Rockville, MD: US Department of Health and Human Services, Public Health Service, 1992, pp. 156-75.

Wexler, H.K., Melnick, G., Lowe, L. and Peters, J., '3-Year Reincarceration Outcomes for Amity In-prison Therapeutic Community and Aftercare in California', *The Prison Journal* , vol. 79, no. 3, 1999, pp. 321-36.

What Works (2000-2001), Second Report from the Joint Prison/Probation Accreditation Panel.

What Works (2001-2002), Third Report from the Joint Prison/Probation Accreditation Panel.

What Works in Prison Strategy, London: What Works in Prisons Unit, 2002.

Whitehead, J.T. and Lab, S.P., 'A Meta-analysis of Juvenile Correctional Treatment', *Journal of Research in Crime and Delinquency*, vol. 26, 1989, pp. 276-95.

Wilson, D. and Ashton, J., *What Everyone in Britain Should Know about Crime and Punishment*, London: Blackstone Press, 1998.

Wilson, J.Q., *Thinking about Crime*, New York: Basic Books, 1975.

Wilson, J.Q., 'Criminal justice in England and America', *The Public Interest*, vol. 126, 1997, pp. 3-14.

Wilson, J.Q. and Herrnstein, R., *Crime and Human Nature*, New York: Simon and Shuster, 1985.

Witt, R., *et al.*, 'Crime and Economic Activity: A Panel Data Approach', British Journal of Criminology, vol. 39, no. 3, 1999, pp. 391-400.

Zimring, F.E. and Hawkins, G., *Incapacitation: Penal Confinement and Restraint of Crime*, Oxford: Oxford University Press, 1995.

Notes

Preface

1   Dennis, N. and Erdos, G., *Cultures and Crimes: policing in four nations*, London: Civitas, January 2005.

Understanding and the Social Sciences

1   Farringdon, D.P., Gottfredson, D.C., Sherman, L.W. and Welsh, B.C., 'The Maryland Scientific Methods Scale', in Sherman, L.W., Farringdon, D.P., Welsh, B.C. and MacKenzie, D.L., *Evidence Based Crime Prevention*, London: Routledge, 2002.

2   McConnell, B., *Evil Empire: the rise and fall of the brothers Kray*, London: Minerva, 1969. McConnell was a reporter with the *Daily Mirror*. The *Daily Mirror* had to pay large libel damages for making allegations that later proved to be true.

3   Marks, H., *Mr Nice: an Autobiography*, London: Minerva, 1997.

4   Edwards, G., 'The background', in Edwards, G. and Busch, C. (eds), *Drug Problems in Britain*, London: Academic Press, 1981, pp. 9-10. *Report of the Departmental Committee on Drug Dependence* (Rolleston), London: HMSO, 1926.

5   Condon, J. and Smith, N., *Prevalence of Drug Use: key findings from the 2002-2003 British Crime Survey*, London: Home Office, 2003, p. 5.

6   Burke, E., *Reflections on the Revolution in France and Other Writings* (1790-91), London: OUP, 1907, pp. 8 and 9.

7   Dennis, N., *Rising Crime and the Dismembered Family: how conformist intellectuals have campaigned against common sense*, London: Institute of Economic Affairs, Health and Welfare Unit, 1993.

8   Arnold, M., *Culture and Anarchy: an essay in social and political criticism* (1869), Cambridge, CUP, 1960, p. 47 and p. 70.

9   Anton Markarenko's account of the work of his young offenders' institute in the late 1920s and early 1930s , the Maxim Gorky colony, is entitled in Russian *The Smithy of the New Man*. The two volumes were published with the English title of *The Road to Life*. Makarenko, A.S., *The Road to Life: an epic of education*, Moscow: Foreign Languages Publishing House, 1955.

10 Boyers, R. and Orill, R. (eds), *R.D. Laing and Anti-Psychiatry*, Harmondsworth: Penguin, 1972.

Introduction

1   *Guardian*, 27 February 2003.

2   *Guardian*, 5 February 2001.

3   Some official statistics are for the UK, some for Great Britain, but the crime figures are for England and Wales, largely because Scotland has different laws.

4   027/2004, 22 January 2004.

5   206/2003, 17 July 2003.

6   *Crime, Justice and Protecting the Public*, 1990, p. 6.

7   *Crime, Justice and Protecting the Public*, 1990, p. 6.

8   Ashworth, A., 'Sentencing' in Maguire, M. *et al* (eds), *The Oxford Handbook of Criminology*, 1994, p. 838.

9   Research Findings 52, 1997.

10 Research Findings 52.

11 Research Findings 52.

12 Langan, P. and Farrington, D., *Crime and Justice in the United States and in England and Wales, 1981-96*, Washington: US Department of Justice. 1998, p. 43.

13 Home Office, *Criminal Statistics 1993*, Table 6.2.

14 From Ashworth, A., 'Sentencing' in Maguire, M. *et al* (eds), *The Oxford Handbook of Criminology*, 1994, p. 842.

15 The calculation is 120,000 x 2 x 150 = 36 million. See, Brand, S. and Price, R., *The Economic and Social Costs of Crime*, HORS 217, London: Home Office, 2000, p. 16, note 17.

16 Civitas wishes to record its thanks to the Home Office for checking and confirming the accuracy of the comparisons between the BCS and recorded crime in 2001-02.

17 *Misspent Youth: young people and crime*, Oxon, UK: Audit Commission, 1996, p. 5.

18 *Misspent Youth*, 1996, p. 12.

19 *Misspent Youth*, p. 22.

20 *Misspent Youth*, p. 26.

21 *Misspent Youth*, pp. 29-30.

22 *Misspent Youth*, p. 33.

23 *Misspent Youth*, p. 35.

24 *Misspent Youth*, p. 42.

25 Newburn, T. and Hagel, A., *Persistent Young Offenders*, Policy Studies Institute, 1994, p. 8.

26 Newburn and Hagel, *Persistent Young Offenders*, 1994, p. 11.

27 Crawford, A. and Newburn, T., *Youth Offending and Restorative Justice*, Cullompton, UK: Willan. Crawford and Newburn, 2003, p. 8.

28 Davies, M., Croall, H. and Tryer, J., *Criminal Justice: an introduction to the criminal justice system in England and Wales*, 2nd Edition, Essex: Pearson Education Ltd, 1998, pp. 157-8.

29 Newburn and Hagel, *Persistent Young Offenders*, 1994, p. 21.

30 Preface by the Home Secretary, *No More Excuses: a new approach to tackling youth crime in England and Wales*, Cm 3809, London: Home Office, November 1997.

31 Hughes, G., Leisten, R. and Pilkington, A., 'An Independent Evaluation of the Northamptonshire Diversion Unit', unpublished report, Northampton: Nene College, 1996, pp. 46-47.

32 Sherman, L., Farrington, D.P., Welsh, B.C. and Mackenzie, D.L., *Evidence-Based Crime Prevention*, London: Routledge, 2002.

33 Sherman *et al.*, *Evidence-Based Crime Prevention*, 2002, p. 10.

34 Sherman *et al.*, *Evidence-Based Crime Prevention*, 2002, pp. 9-10.

2: Rival Explanations of Crime

1 Farrington, D., *Understanding and Preventing Youth Crime*, York: Joseph Rowntree Foundation, 1996, p. 5.

2 Pyle, D. and Deadman, D., 'Crime and the business cycle in post-war Britain', *British Journal of Criminology*, vol. 34, no. 3, Summer 1994, pp. 339-357.

3 Witt, R. *et al.*, 'Crime and economic activity: a panel data approach', *British Journal of Criminology*, vol. 39, no. 3, Summer 1999, pp. 391-400.

4 Field, S., *Trends in Crime and Their Interpretation: a study of recorded crime in post-war England and Wales*, HORS 119, London: HMSO, 1990.

5 Farrington, D., Langan, P.A. and Tonry, M. (eds), *England and Wales Cross-National Studies in Crime and Justice*, US Department of Justice, 2004. www.ojp.usdoj.gov/bjs/abstract/cnscj.htm

6 Wilson, D. and Ashton, J., *What Everyone in Britain Should Know About Crime and Punishment*, London: Blackstone Press, 1998, p. 8.

7 Wilson and Ashton, *What Everyone in Britain Should Know About Crime and Punishment*, 1998, p. 11.

8 Rousseau, J-J., 'A Discourse on the Origin of Inequality', in *The Social Contract and Discourses*, London: Dent (Everyman edn), 1973, p. 68.

9 Rousseau, J-J., *Émile*, London: Dent (Everyman edn), 1993, p. 11.

10 Wilson, James Q. and Herrnstein, R., *Crime and Human Nature: the definitive study of the causes of crime*, New York: Simon and Shuster, 1985.

11 Andrews, D.A. and Bonta, J., *The Psychology of Criminal Conduct*, Cincinatti, Ohio: Anderson, 1994, p. 228.

12 See discussion in von Hirsch, A., *Doing Justice: the choice of punishments*, New York: Hill and Wang,1976; and Wilson and Herrnstein, *Crime and Human Nature*, 1985.

13 Laws may also serve narrow interests and Hart's argument only applies when law is in the common good.

14 Hart, H.L.A., *Punishment and Responsibility: essays in the philosophy of law*, Oxford: Oxford University Press, 1970, pp. 22-23.

15 Hart, *Punishment and Responsibility* 1970, p. 23.

16 Hart, *Punishment and Responsibility*, 1970, p. 26.

17 Hart, *Punishment and Responsibility*, 1970, p. 27.

18 Gaylin, W., *The Killing of Bonnie Garland*, 1982. Quoted in Wilson and Herrnstein, 1985, p. 490.

19 Menninger, K., *The Crime of Punishment*, New York: Viking, 1968, pp. 254, 261-62.

3: Incapacitation and Deterrence

1 Nagin, D.S., 'Deterrence and incapacitation', in Tonry, M. (ed.), *The Handbook of Crime and Punishment*, New York: Oxford University Press, 1998, p. 346.

2 Nagin, 'Deterrence and incapacitation', in Tonry, 1998, p. 346.

3 Nagin, 'Deterrence and incapacitation', in Tonry, 1998, p. 347.

4 Nagin, 'Deterrence and incapacitation', in Tonry, 1998, p. 348.

5 They were asked: 'And generally speaking, how likely is it that someone like you would be caught taking something from a shop worth £20 without paying for it?'. Five answers were possible: very likely, quite likely, not very likely, not at all likely, it depends, *Criminal Statistics England and Wales, 1999*, p. 42.

6 They were asked: 'And generally speaking, how likely is it that someone like you would be caught burgling a house and stealing a video recorder?'. Five answers were possible: very likely, quite likely, not very likely, not at all likely, it depends, *Criminal Statistics England and Wales, 1999*, p. 42.

7 The National Prison Survey *1991*, Main Findings, HORS 128, London: HMSO, 1992.

8 *Reducing Reoffending by Ex-prisoners: summary of the Social Exclusion Unit report* London: Social Exclusion Unit, 2002. (www.socialexclusionunit.gov.uk)

9 von Hirsch, A. *et al.*, *Criminal Deterrence and Sentence Severity: an analysis of recent research*, Oxford: Hart, 1999, p. 47. See also Nagin, D., 1997, 'Criminal deterrence research at the outset of the twenty-first century', in Tonry, M. (ed.), *Crime and Justice: a review of research*, Chicago: University of Chicago Press, 1997.

10 Kershaw, C., Goodman, J. and White, S., *Reconvictions of Offenders Sentenced or Discharged from Prison in 1995, England and Wales*, issue 19/99, London: Home Office, 1999.

11 Sherman *et al.*, *Evidence-Based Crime Prevention*, 2002, p. 335.

12 Zimring, F.E. and Hawkins, G., *Incapacitation: penal confinement and restraint of crime*, Oxford: Oxford University Press, 1995, p. ix.

13 Zimring and Hawkins, *Incapacitation*, 1995, pp. vii and 126.

14 Zimring and Hawkins, *Incapacitation*, 1995, p. 121.

15 Zimring and Hawkins, *Incapacitation*, 1995, p. 108.

16 Zimring and Hawkins, *Incapacitation*, 1995, p. 172.

17 Zimring and Hawkins, *Incapacitation*, 1995, pp. 126-27.

18 Langan, P. and Farrington, D., *Crime and Justice in the United States and in England and Wales, 1981-96,* Washington: US Department of Justice, 1998, p. 43.

19 *Criminal Statistics 1993,* London: HMSO, Table 6.2.

20 Langan and Farrington, *Crime and Justice in the United States and in England and Wales, 1981-96,* 1998, p. 38.

21 Langan and Farrington, *Crime and Justice in the United States and in England and Wales, 1981-96,* 1998, p. 38.

22 Levitt, S.D., 'The effect of prison population size on crime rates: evidence from prison overcrowding litigation', *Quarterly Journal of Economics,* May 1996, pp. 319-51.

23 Levitt, 'The effect of prison population size on crime rates', 1996, p. 323.

24 Nagin, D.S., 1998, 'Criminal deterrence research at the outset of the twenty-first century', in Tonry, M. (ed.), *Crime and Justice: a review of research,* Chicago: University of Chicago Press, 1998, p. 27.

25 Spelman, W., 2000, 'The limited importance of prison expansion', in Blumstein, A. and Wallman, J., *The Crime Drop in America,* Cambridge: Cambridge University Press, 2000, p. 123.

26 Spelman, 'The limited importance of prison expansion' in Blumstein *et al.,* 2000, p. 124.

27 Spelman, 'The limited importance of prison expansion' in Blumstein *et al.,* 2000, p. 125.

28 Nagin, 'Deterrence and incapacitation', in Tonry, 1998, p. 362.

29 Nagin, 'Deterrence and incapacitation', in Tonry, 1998, p. 365.

30 Nagin, 'Deterrence and incapacitation', in Tonry, 1998, p. 366.

4: Rehabilitation

1   Davies, M., Croall, H. & Tyrer, J., *Criminal Justice: an introduction to the criminal justice system in England and Wales,* 2nd edn, Essex: Pearson Education Ltd., 1998, p. 278.

2   Davies *et al., Criminal Justice,* 1998, p. 279.

3   Davies *et al., Criminal Justice,* 1998, p. 280

4   Davies *et al., Criminal Justice,* 1998, Fig. 9.2, p. 281

5   Wilson, J. Q. (1975) *Thinking about Crime,* New York: Basic Books, p. 172.

6   von Hirsch, A., *Doing Justice: the choice of punishments,* New York: Hill and Wang, 1976.

7   von Hirsch, A., *Doing Justice,* 1976, p. 51.

8   Wilson, *Thinking about Crime,* 1975, p. 172.

9 Wilson, *Thinking about Crime*, 1975, p. 173.

10 *Punishment, Custody and the Community*, White Paper Cm 424, London: HMSO, 1988.

11 *Crime, Justice and Protecting the Public*, White Paper Cm 965, Sessional papers 1989-90, London: HMSO, 1990.

12 McGuire, J. (ed.), *What Works: reducing reoffending*, Chichester: Wiley, 1995.

13 *Misspent Youth: young people and crime*, Oxon, UK: Audit Commission, 1996, Appendix 1.

14 *Alternatives to Prison Sentences*, Session 1997-98, 3rd Report, HC486, July 1998, para 249 - 9.
http://www.publications.parliament.uk/pa/cm199798/cmselect/cmhaff/486/48615.htm

15 Underdown, A., *Strategies for Effective Offender Supervision Report of the HMIP What Works Project*, London: Home Office, 1998 (available online: http://www.homeoffice.gov.uk/docs2/seos.html).

16 *Misspent Youth*, 1996, p. 111.

17 Evidence to the Home Affairs Select Committee, 1998.

18 Quoted in Gaes, G.G., Flanagan, T.J., Motiuk, L. and Stewart, L., *Adult Correctional Treatment*, (published on-line) 1998, pp. 36-37.

19 Raynor, P. and Vanstone, M., STOP (Straight Thinking On Probation): The Mid-Glamorgan Experiment, *International Journal of Offender Therapy: comparative criminology*, vol. 40, 1996, pp. 272-84.

20 Gaes *et al.*, *Adult Correctional Treatment*, 1998, pp. 35-36.

21 Friendship, C., Blud, L., Erikson, M. and Travers, R., 'An Evaluation of Cognitive Behavioural Treatment for Prisoners', Home Office, Findings 161, 2002.

22 Friendship, C., Falshaw, L. and Beech, A., 'Measuring the Real Impact of Accredited Offending Behaviour Programmes', *Legal and Criminal Psychology*, vol. 8, 2003, pp. 115-27.

23 Andrews, D.A., Zinger, L., Hoge, R.D., Bonta, J., Gendreau, P. and Cullen, F.T., 'Does correctional treatment work? A clinically relevant and psychologically informed meta-analysis', *Criminology*, vol. 28, 1990, p. 374.

24 Andrews, D. and Bonta, J., *The Psychology of Criminal Conduct*, Ohio: Anderson Publishing Co., 1994, p. 175.

25 Falshaw, L., Friendship, C., Travers, R., and Nugent, F., 'Searching for 'What Works': an evaluation of cognitive skills programmes', Findings 206, 2003.

26 Falshaw *et al.*, 'Searching for "What Works"', 2003.

27 McGuire and Priestly in McGuire, J. (ed.), *What Works*, 1995.

28 McGuire, J. *Cognitive-behavioural Approaches: an introduction to the theory and research*, London: Home Office, 2000b, p. 97.

29 For an explanation see Sherman, L.W., Farrington, D.P., Welsh, B.C. and Mackenzie, D.L., *Evidence-Based Crime Prevention*, London: Routledge, 2002, p. 69.

30 Rosenthal, R. and Rubin, D.B., 'A Simple, General Purpose Display of Magnitude of Experimental Effect', *Journal of Educational Psychology*, vol. 74, issue 2, 1982, pp. 166-69.

31 For a fuller discussion see Gaes *et al.*, *Adult Correctional Treatment*, 1998, p. 17.

32 Quoted in Gaes *et al.*, *Adult Correctional Treatment*, 1998, p. 18.

33 Lipsey, M.W., 'What do we learn from 400 research studies on the effectiveness of treatment with juvenile delinquents?', in McGuire, J. (ed.), *What Works*, 1995, p. 67.

34 Lipsey, 'What do we learn from 400 research studies on the effectiveness of treatment with juvenile delinquents?' 1995, p. 73.

35 Lipsey, 'What do we learn from 400 research studies on the effectiveness of treatment with juvenile delinquents?' 1995, p. 73.

36 Lipsey, 'What do we learn from 400 research studies on the effectiveness of treatment with juvenile delinquents?' 1995, pp. 74-75.

37 Lipsey, 'What do we learn from 400 research studies on the effectiveness of treatment with juvenile delinquents?' 1995, p. 76.

38 Lipsey, 'What do we learn from 400 research studies on the effectiveness of treatment with juvenile delinquents?' 1995, p. 76.

39 Lipsey, 'What do we learn from 400 research studies on the effectiveness of treatment with juvenile delinquents?' 1995, p. 76.

40 Lipsey, 'What do we learn from 400 research studies on the effectiveness of treatment with juvenile delinquents?' 1995, p. 41.

41 Logan, C. and Gaes, G., 'Meta-analysis and the rehabilitation of punishment', *Justice Quarterly*, vol. 10, no. 2, June 1993.

42 Pawson, R. and Tilley, N., *Realistic Evaluation*, London: Sage 1997.

43 Pawson and Tilley, *Realistic Evaluation*, 1997, p. 33.

44 Pawson and Tilley, *Realistic Evaluation*, 1997, p. 123.

45 Gaes *et al.*, *Adult Correctional Treatment*, 1998, p. 30.

46 Andrews *et al.*, 'Does correctional treatment work? A clinically relevant and psychologically informed meta-analysis', 1990; Losel in McGuire, 1995, p. 94.

47 Gaes *et al.*, *Adult Correctional Treatment*, 1998, p. 31.

48 Gaes *et al.*, *Adult Correctional Treatment*, 1998, p. 32.

49 Gaes *et al.*, *Adult Correctional Treatment*, 1998, p.78.

50 At the 0.05 level.

51 Gesch, B.C., Hammond, S.M., Hampson, S.E., Eves, A. and Crowder, M.J., 'Influence of supplementary vitamins, minerals and essential fatty acids on the antisocial behaviour of young adult prisoners: Randomised, placebo-controlled trial', *British Journal of Psychiatry*, Vol. 181, 2002, pp. 22-28, p. 22.

52 Gesch *et al.*, 'Influence of supplementary vitamins, minerals and essential fatty acids on the antisocial behaviour of young adult prisoners', 2002, p. 23.

53 Gesch *et al.* did not include an average number of disciplinary incidents for the placebo group after treatment and only cited the percentage change from pre-treatment measures as indicated, Gesch *et al.*, 'Influence of supplementary vitamins, minerals and essential fatty acids on the antisocial behaviour of young adult prisoners, 2002, p. 26.

54 Gesch *et al.*, 'Influence of supplementary vitamins, minerals and essential fatty acids on the antisocial behaviour of young adult prisoners, 2002, p. 26.

55 Gesch *et al.*, 'Influence of supplementary vitamins, minerals and essential fatty acids on the antisocial behaviour of young adult prisoners, 2002, p. 27.

56 Martinson, R. 'What Works? Questions and Answers about Prison Reform', *The Public Interest*, vol. 10, 1974, pp. 22–54.

57 See Martinson, R. 'New Findings, New Views: A Note of Caution Regarding Sentencing Reform', *Hofstra Law Review*, vol. 7, 1979, pp. 243–58.

58 Lipton, D.S. 'Prison-based therapeutic communities: Their success with drug-abusing offenders', *National Institute of Justice Journal*, note 21, February 1996, p. 19.

59 The full study was Lipton, D.S., Martinson, R. and Wilks, J., *The Effectiveness of Correctional Treatment*, New York: Praeger, 1975.

60 Sherman *et al.*, *Evidence-Based Crime Prevention*, 2002, p. 385.

61 Sherman *et al.*, *Evidence-Based Crime Prevention*, 2002, p. 351.

62 *Criminal Statistics England and Wales* 2002.

63 Allnutt, D. *Review of Statistics on Efficacy of Sentencing: report on a review for the Home Office*, London: Home Office, 2001. (http://www.statistics.gov.uk/about/consultation_by_theme/downloads/po stconsdrft.pdf)

64 Allnutt, *Review of Statistics on Efficacy of Sentencing*, 2001, p. 9.

65 Allnutt, *Review of Statistics on Efficacy of Sentencing*, 2001, p. 4.

66 Allnutt, *Review of Statistics on Efficacy of Sentencing*, 2001, p. 8.

67 Allnutt, *Review of Statistics on Efficacy of Sentencing*, 2001, p. 11.

68 Allnutt, *Review of Statistics on Efficacy of Sentencing*, 2001, p. 8.

5: Prison-Based Therapeutic Communities

1 Wexler, H.K., Falkin, G.P. and Lipton, D.S. 'Outcome Evaluation of a Prison Therapeutic Community for Substance Abuse Treatment', in Leukefeld, C.G. and Tims, F.M. (eds), *Drug Abuse Treatment in Prisons and Jails*, Research

Monograph no. 118, Rockville, MD: US Department of Health and Human Services, Public Health Service, 1992, pp. 156–75. For a good summary also see Lipton, D.S., 'Prison-based therapeutic communities: their success with drug-abusing offenders', *National Institute of Justice Journal*, 1996, pp. 12-20.

2 Wexler, H.K., Melnick, G., Lowe, L. and Peters, J., '3-Year reincarceration outcomes for Amity in-prison therapeutic community and aftercare in California', *The Prison Journal*, vol. 79, no. 3, 1999, pp. 321-36.

3 Wexler *et al.*, '3-Year reincarceration outcomes for Amity in-prison therapeutic community and aftercare in California', 1999, pp. 7-8.

4 Wexler *et al.* '3-Year reincarceration outcomes for Amity in-prison therapeutic community and aftercare in California', 1999, p. 14.

5 Wexler *et al.* '3-Year reincarceration outcomes for Amity in-prison therapeutic community and aftercare in California', 1999, p. 14.

6 Martin, S.S., Butzin, C.A. and Inciardi, J., 'Assessment of a multistage therapeutic community for drug involved offenders', *Journal of Psychoactive Drugs*, vol. 27, no. 1, 1995, pp. 109-116; Inciardi, J., Martin, S.S., Butzin, C.A., Hooper, R.M. and Harrison, L.D. 'An effective model of prison-based treatment for drug-involved offenders', *Journal of Drug Issues*, vol. 27, 1997, pp. 261-278.

7 Martin, S.S., Butzin, C.A., Saum, C.A. and Inciardi, J., 'Three-year outcomes of therapeutic community treatment for drug-involved offenders in Delaware: from prison to work release to aftercare', *The Prison Journal*, vol. 79, no. 3, 1999, pp. 294-320.

8 Martin *et al.*, 'Three-year outcomes of therapeutic community treatment for drug-involved offenders in Delaware', 1999, p. 314.

9 Martin *et al.*, 'Three-year outcomes of therapeutic community treatment for drug-involved offenders in Delaware', 1999, p. 311.

10 Martin *et al.*, 'Three-year outcomes of therapeutic community treatment for drug-involved offenders in Delaware', 1999, p. 314.

11 The other offenders were either still in prison, had not been released for more than 24 months or had left the region.

12 This was to be expected as the comparison sample were selected on the basis of self-reported drug problems or a desire for substance abuse treatment, and so they were more likely to affirm a drug problem.

13 At the 0.05 level there is a less than five per cent chance that this difference is due to chance.

14 This is statistically significant at the 0.01 level.

15 Martin, C. and Player, E., *Drug Treatment in Prison: an evaluation of the RAPt Treatment Programme*, Winchester: Waterside Press, 2000.

16 Martin and Player, *Drug Treatment in Prison*, 2000, p. 19.

17 Martin and Player, *Drug Treatment in Prison*, 2000, p. 43.

18 Martin and Player, *Drug Treatment in Prison*, 2000, p. 61.

19 One hundred and ninety-seven inmates constitute all of those for whom conclusions were drawn on reconviction levels at the end of the study. The entire original sample included 230 prisoners.

20 Hanson, R.K., Steffy, R.A. and Gauthier, R., 'Long-Term Recidivism of Child Molesters', *Journal of Consulting and Clinical Psychology*, vol. 61, no. 4, 1993, pp. 646-52 p. 648.

21 Hanson *et al.*, 'Long-Term Recidivism of Child Molesters', 1993, p. 648.

22 Hanson *et al.*, 'Long-Term Recidivism of Child Molesters', 1993, pp. 648-69.

23 It was not possible to classify one of the treatment group subjects according to these categories, as sufficient information was unavailable.

24 Hanson *et al.*, 'Long-Term Recidivism of Child Molesters', 1993, pp. 649-50.

25 Hanson *et al.*, 'Long-Term Recidivism of Child Molesters', 1993, p. 651.

26 Marshall, P., *A Reconviction Study of HMP Grendon Therapeutic Community*, Research Findings 53, London: Home Office, 1997.

27 Marshall, *A Reconviction Study of HMP Grendon Therapeutic Community*, 1997.

28 Taylor, R., *A Seven-Year Reconviction Study of HMP Grendon Therapeutic Community*, Research Findings No.115, London: Home Office, 2000. See also Genders, E. and Player, E., *Grendon: a study of a therapeutic prison*, London: Clarendon Press, 1995; Parker, T., *The Frying Pan*, London: Hutchinson, 1970, (the classic interview study); for a more recent set of interviews in the vein of Parker's work, see Smartt, U., *Grendon Tales*, Winchester: Waterside Press, 2001.

6: Prison Education and Work

1 *Prison Statistics, England and Wales 2001*, London: Home Office, Table 11.5.

2 Harer, M.D., 'Recidivism Among Federal Prisoners Released in 1987', *Journal of Correctional Education*, vol. 46, 1995, pp. 98-127; and also Harer, M.D., *Prison Education Program Participation and Recidivism: a test of the normalization hypothesis*, Washington, DC: Federal Bureau of Prisons, Office of Research and Evaluation, 1995.

3 When these two levels of education (no education and at least half a course per six months) were compared to the middle level (those who had taken more than zero courses but less than half a course per sixth month period), the results were statistically less significant; thus, Harer considered education to mean at least half a course of any kind per six month period in his conclusions. Only 13 inmates constituted 'college graduates', of which one reoffended (he had taken zero to less than half a course), a result on which Harer was unable to draw any conclusions.

4 Harer, *Prison Education Program Participation and Recidivism*, 1995, p. 14.

5 Harer, *Prison Education Program Participation and Recidivism*, 1995, p. 12.

6   Adams, K., Bennett, T., Flanagan, T.J., Marquart, J., Cuvelier, S., Fritsch, E.J., Gerber, J., Longmire, D. and Burton, V., 'A Large-scale Multidimensional Test of the Effect of Prison Education Programs on Offender Behavior', *The Prison Journal*, vol. 74, 1994, pp. 433-39.

7   Adams *et al.*, 'A Large-scale Multidimensional Test of the Effect of Prison Education Programs on Offender Behavior', 1994, p. 442; Gaes, G.C., Flanagan, T.J., Motiuk, L. and Stewart, L., *Adult Correctional Treatment*, (published online- see bibliography) 1998, p. 62.

8   Walsh, A., 'An Evaluation of the Effects of Adult Basic Education on Re-arrest Rates Among Probationers', *Journal of Offender Counselling, Services and Rehabilitation*, vol. 9, 1985, pp. 69-76.

9   Too few females enrolled for the GED programme to consider them for the study.

10 Walsh considered misdemeanor-one and felony arrests only in measuring prior criminal histories.

11 Twenty-two of the non-participants were arrested at least once as compared to twelve of the participants; Walsh, 'An Evaluation of the Effects of Adult Basic Education on Re-arrest Rates Among Probationers', 1985, pp. 72-73.

12 Walsh, 'An Evaluation of the Effects of Adult Basic Education on Re-arrest Rates Among Probationers', 1985, pp. 74-75.

13 Walsh, 'An Evaluation of the Effects of Adult Basic Education on Re-arrest Rates Among Probationers', 1985, p. 75.

14 Walsh, 'An Evaluation of the Effects of Adult Basic Education on Re-arrest Rates Among Probationers', 1985, Table 2, p. 73; and Sherman, L.W., Farrington, D.P., Welsh, B.C. and Mackenzie, D.L., *Evidence-Based Crime Prevention*, London: Routledge, 2002, p. 358.

15 Pawson, R. and Tilley, N., *Realistic Evaluation*, London: Sag, 1997, p. 104.

16 Pawson and Tilley, *Realistic Evaluation*, 1997, p. 110.

17 Pawson and Tilley, *Realistic Evaluation*, 1997, pp. 112-13.

18 Gerber, J. and Fritsch, E.J., *Prison Education Research Project: Final Report*, Hunstville, Texas: Sam Houston State University, 1994, p. 6.

19 Lattimore, P.K., Witte, A.D. and Baker, J.R., 'Experimental Assessment of the Effect of Vocational Training on Youthful Property Offenders', Evaluation Review, vol. 14, no. 2, 1990, pp. 115-33; reference on p. 117.

20 Lattimore *et al.*, 'Experimental Assessment of the Effect of Vocational Training on Youthful Property Offenders', 1990, p. 119.

21 Lattimore *et al.*, 'Experimental Assessment of the Effect of Vocational Training on Youthful Property Offenders', 1990, pp. 123-24.

22 Lattimore *et al.*, 'Experimental Assessment of the Effect of Vocational Training on Youthful Property Offenders', 1990, p. 131.

23 While Saylor and Gaes only consulted federal prison records, there is no reason to believe that the percentage difference between the experiment group's and control group's recidivism rates would differ if non-federal prison records had also been considered.

24 Gaes, G.G., Flanagan, T.J., Motiuk, L. and Stewart, L., *Adult Correctional Treatment* (online publication – see bibliography), 1998, p. 67.

25 Gerber and Frisch, Gerber, J. and Fritsch, E.J., *Prison Education Research Project: Final Report*, 1994, p. 8.

7: Intensive Supervision in the Community

1 *Justice for All*, White Paper Cm 5563, London: Home Office, 2002, p. 87.

2 www.crimereduction.gov.uk

3 'Intensive Supervision and Surveillance Programmes': http://www.youth-justice-board.gov.uk/NR/rdonlyres/6C269732-E2FF-4DFD-9265-552A68990702/398/ISSPvsshortDTObriefing1Jan03.doc

4 Bonta, J. and Wallace-Capretta, S., *Electronic Monitoring in Canada*, 1999, Public Works and Government Services Canada (published online- see bibliography), pp. 46-47.

5 Bonta and Wallace-Capretta, *Electronic Monitoring in Canada*, 1999, pp. 47-48.

6 Bonta and Wallace-Capretta, *Electronic Monitoring in Canada*, 1999, p. 54.

7 Bonta and Wallace-Capretta, *Electronic Monitoring in Canada*, 1999, p. 52.

8 Bonta and Wallace-Capretta, *Electronic Monitoring in Canada*, 1999, p. 16.

9 Dodgson, K., Goodwin, P., Howard, P., Llewellyn-Thomas, S., Mortimer, E., Russell, N. and Weiner, M., *Electronic Monitoring of Released Prisoners: an evaluation of the Home Detention Curfew scheme*, Home Office Research Study 222, London: Home Office, 2001.

10 Dodgson *et al.*, *Electronic Monitoring of Released Prisoners*, 2001, p. 52.

11 Dodgson *et al.*, *Electronic Monitoring of Released Prisoners*, 2001, p. 54.

12 Dodgson *et al.*, *Electronic Monitoring of Released Prisoners*, 2001, p. 60.

13 Dodgson *et al.*, *Electronic Monitoring of Released Prisoners*, 2001, pp. 54 and 61.

14 Petersilia, J. and Turner, S., *Evaluating Intensive Supervision Probation/Parole: results of a nationwide experiment*, Washington, DC: National Institute of Justice, 1993.

15 A delinquent offence is an act committed by a juvenile that would be a crime if committed by an adult. A status offence is only applicable to children, as defined earlier.

16 'Success' on the course was judged by the individual counsellors, and was based not only on whether the participant had reoffended or not, but also on measures of co-operation and progress made during the period of supervision.

17 Sontheimer, H. and Goodstein, L., 'Evaluation of Juvenile Intensive Aftercare Probation: Aftercare system versus system response effects', *Justice Quarterly*, vol. 10, 1993, pp. 197-227.

18 Barton, W.H. and Butts, J.A., 'Viable Options: Intensive supervision programs for juvenile delinquents', *Crime and Delinquency*, vol. 36, no. 2, 1990, pp. 238-56.

19 Baumer, T.L. and Mendelsohn, R.I., *The Electronic Monitoring of Non-violent Convicted Felons: an experiment in home detention, final report* (Final report from NIJ Grant No. 86-IJ-CX-0041). Indianapolis: Indiana University, School of Public and Environmental Affairs, 1990.

20 Baumer, T.L. and Mendelsohn, R.I., 'Electronically Monitored Home Confinement: Does It Work?', in Byrne, J.M., Lurigio, A.J. and Petersilia, J., *Smart Sentencing: the emergence of intermediate sanctions*, Newbury Park, CA: Sage, 1992, pp. 54-67.

21 Baumer and Mendelsohn 'Electronically Monitored Home Confinement: Does It Work?', 1992.

22 Baumer and Mendelsohn, *The Electronic Monitoring of Non-violent Convicted Felons*, 1990.

23 Baumer and Mendelsohn 'Electronically Monitored Home Confinement: Does It Work?', 1992, p. 63.

24 Baumer and Mendelsohn 'Electronically Monitored Home Confinement: Does It Work?', 1992, p. 61.

25 Baumer and Mendelsohn, *The Electronic Monitoring of Non-violent Convicted Felons*, 1990.

26 Baumer and Mendelsohn 'Electronically Monitored Home Confinement: Does It Work?', 1992, p. 62.

27 From:
http://inventors.about.com/gi/dynamic/offsite.htm?site=http://www.trimble.com/gps/

28 From: http://www.dc.state.fl.us/pub/gpsrf/2003/index.html

29 From: http://www.dc.state.fl.us/pub/gpsrf/2003/index.html

30 From: http://www.dc.state.fl.us/pub/annual/9899/sec.html

31 From: http://www.dc.state.fl.us/pub/gpsrf/2002/tab3a.html

8: Community-Based Drug Treatment

1 Nurco, D., Hanlon, T., Bateman, R., and Kinlock, T., 'Drug Abuse Treatment in the Context of Correctional Surveillance', *Journal of Substance Abuse Treatment*, vol. 12, no. 1, 1995, pp. 19-27.

2 Hepburn, J.R. and Albonetti, C.A., 'Recidivism Among Drug Offenders: A Survival Analysis of the Effects of Offender Characteristics', *Journal of Quantitative Criminology*, vol. 10 , issue 2, 1994, pp. 159-79.

3   Anglin, M.D., Longshore, D., Turner, S., McBride, D., Inciardi, J. and Pendergast, M., *Studies of Functioning and Effectiveness of Treatment Alternatives to Street Crime (TASC) Programs: final report*, Washington DC: National Institute on Drug Abuse, 1996.

4   Taxman, F.S. and Spinner, D.L., *The Jail Addiction Services (JAS) Project in Montgomery County, Maryland: Overview of results from a 24 month follow-up study*, unpublished manuscript, University of Maryland, College Park, MD, 1996.

5   Nurco, *et al.*, 'Drug Abuse Treatment in the Context of Correctional Surveillance', 1995, pp. 19-27.

6   Nurco *et al.*, 'Drug Abuse Treatment in the Context of Correctional Surveillance', 1995, pp. 19-27.

7   Petersilia, J. and Turner, S., 'Intensive Supervision Programs for Drug Offenders', in Byrne, J.M., Lurigio, A.J. and Petersilia, J. (eds), *Smart Sentencing: the emergence of intermediate sanctions*, Newbury Park: Sage Publications, 1992, pp. 18-37.

8   *OJP Drug Court Clearinghouse and Technical Assistance Project at American University: summary of drug court activity by state and county*, (September 8, 2003).

9   Deschenes, E.P., Turner, S., Greenwood, P. and Chiesa, J., *An Experimental Evaluation of Drug Testing and Treatment Interventions for Probationers in Maricopa County*, Sanata Monica, CA: RAND Corporation, 1996.

10 Gottfredson, D.C. and Barton, W.H., *A Short Term Outcome Evaluation of the Baltimore City Drug Treatment Program*, College Park, MD: Department of Criminology and Criminal Justice, University of Maryland, 1996.

11 Goldkamp, J.S., 'Miami's treatment drug court for felony defendants: Some implications of assessment findings', *The Prison Journal*, vol. 73, no. 2, 1994, pp. 110-66.

12 A felony is a serious crime punishable by imprisonment for more than one year or death; a misdemeanour is a less serious crime punishable by less than one year in prison, or some form of diversionary sentence (ISP etc.). In Florida, for example, there are five degrees of felony (third, second, first, life and capital) and two degrees of misdemeanour (first and second), depending on the seriousness of the offence and each with different maximum tariff. Aggravated assault or battery, for example, is a second degree felony and carries with it a maximum sentence of 15 years. Aggravated stalking or incest are third degree felonies, and carry a five-year maximum sentence.

13 As the programme had been up and running for some time it was not possible for a random assignment study to be set up.

14 Gottfredson, D.M., Coblentz, K. and Harmon, M.A., *A Short Term Outcome Evaluation of the Baltimore City Drug Treatment Court Program*, Colleg park, MD: Department of Criminology and Criminal Justice, University of Maryland, 1996. The relative percentages are not given by Sherman.

15 The relative percentages are not given by Sherman.

16 Belenko, S., *Research on Drug Courts: a critical review*, New York: The National Center on Addiction and Substance Abuse at Columbia University, June 2001. (1998, updated in 1999 and 2001.)

17 Turnbull, P.J., McSweeney, T. and Hough, M., *Drug Treatment and Testing Orders: the 18-month evaluation*, Home Office Research Findings, no. 128, London Home Office, 2000.

18 *Guidance For Practitioners Involved In Drug Treatment and Testing Order Pilots*, section, 5.3. http://www.homeoffice.gov.uk/docs/dttguid.html

19 *Guidance For Practitioners Involved In Drug Treatment and Testing Order Pilots*, section, 5.3. http://www.homeoffice.gov.uk/docs/dttguid.html

20 Gottfredson, D. and Exum, M., *The Baltimore City Drug Treatment Court: one-year results from a randomised study*, University of Maryland, Department of Criminology and Criminal Justice, 2000.

21 Breckenridge, J.F., Winfree, L.T., Maupin, J.R. and Clason, D.L., 'Drunk drivers, DWI "drug court" treatment, and recidivism: who fails?', *Justice Research and Policy*, University of New Mexico, 2000.

22 Dickie, J.L., *Summit County Juvenile Court Drug Court Evaluation Report: 1 July 1999 - 30 June 2000*, University of Akron, The Institute for Health and Social Policy, 2000.

23 Lipton, D.S., Martinson, R. and Wilks, J., *The Effectiveness of Correctional Treatment*, New York: Praeger, 1975.

24 *Introductory Guide to The Crime and Disorder Act*, section 61-64 (Online: http://www.homeoffice.gov.uk/cdact/cdaint19.htm)

25 Turnbull, McSweeney and Hough, M., *Drug Treatment and Testing Orders: The 18-Month Evaluation*, 2000.

26 *Guidance For Practitioners Involved In Drug Treatment and Testing Order Pilots*, section, 5.3 (Online: http://www.homeoffice.gov.uk/cdact/dttguid. htm#TESTING AND ENFORCEMENT).

27 *Guidance For Practitioners Involved In Drug Treatment and Testing Order Pilots*.

28 *Guidance For Practitioners Involved In Drug Treatment and Testing Order Pilots*.

29 Turnbull, P.J., McSweeney, T., Webster, R., Edmunds, M. and Hough, M., *Drug Treatment and Testing Orders: final evaluation report*, Home Office Research Study 212, October 2000. (Online: http://www.homeoffice.gov.uk/rds/pdfs/hors212.pdf)

30 Turnbull *et al.*, *Drug Treatment and Testing Orders: final evaluation report*, October 2000.

31 Turnbull *et al.*, *Drug Treatment and Testing Orders: final evaluation report*, October 2000.

32 Turnbull *et al.*, *Drug Treatment and Testing Orders: final evaluation report*, October 2000.

33 Hough, M., Clancy, A., McSweeney, T., Turnball, P.J. *The Impact of Drug Treatment and Testing Orders on Offending: two-year conviction results,* Home Office Research Findings 184, 2003. (Online:http://www.homeoffice. gov.uk/rds/pdfs2/r184.pdf).

34 Comptroller and Auditor General of the National Audit Office, *The Drug Treatment and Testing Order: early lessons,* London: HMSO, 2004, p. 23.

35 Comptroller and Auditor General of the National Audit Office, *The Drug Treatment and Testing Order: early lessons,,* 2004, p. 4.

36 Comptroller and Auditor General of the National Audit Office, *The Drug Treatment and Testing Order: early lessons,* 2004, p. 31.

37 Hough *et al., The impact of Drug Treatment and Testing Orders on Offending: two-year conviction results,* Home Office Research Findings 184, 2003; Offenders in the pilot group on the Drug Treatment and Testing Order had an average of 42 previous convictions.

38 Hough *et al., The impact of Drug Treatment and Testing Orders on Offending: two-year conviction results,* Home Office Research Findings 184, 2003.

39 *Prisoners' Drug Use and Treatment: seven studies,* Home Office Research Study 267. Offenders completing the RAPt programme who were followed up had an average of 22 previous convictions.

40 Gossop, M., Marsden, J. and Stewart, D., *National Treatment Outcome Research After Five Years,* London: Department of Health, 2001.

41 Hough *et al., The impact of Drug Treatment and Testing Orders on Offending: two-year conviction results,* Home Office Research Findings 184, 2003.

9: Boot Camps and Shock Tactics

1 Mackenzie, D.L., Brame, R., MacDowall, D. and Souryal, C., 'Boot camp prisons and recidivism in eight states', *Criminology,* vol. 33, no. 3, 1995, p. 330.

2 Mackenzie *et al.,* 'Boot camp prisons and recidivism in eight states', 1995.

3 Mackenzie *et al.,* 'Boot camp prisons and recidivism in eight states', 1995, p. 331.

4 Mackenzie *et al.,* 'Boot camp prisons and recidivism in eight states', 1995, p. 350.

5 Mackenzie *et al.,* 'Boot camp prisons and recidivism in eight states', 1995, p. 350.

6 Mackenzie *et al.,* 'Boot camp prisons and recidivism in eight states', 1995, p. 352.

7 Mackenzie *et al.,* 'Boot camp prisons and recidivism in eight states', 1995, p. 350.

8 MacKenzie, D.L., Wilson, D.B. and Kider, S.B., 'Effects of correctional boot camps on offending', *Annals of the American Academy of Political and Social Sciences,* Part 578, 2001, pp. 126-43.

9   The overall weighted average odds ratio was 1.02. The odds ratio means the odds of a member of the experimental group reoffending compared to the odds of a member of the control group reoffending. An odds ratio of one means that the treatment group are just as likely to reoffend as the control group. Higher than one is a positive result in favour of the treatment group, lower than one a negative result for the experimental group.

10 The predicted rate was based on the same principles as the revised Offender Group Reconviction Scale (OGRS) used by the Home Office. This is a statistical risk score which provides an estimate of the probability that a convicted offender will be reconvicted at least once within two years of release from custody or from the start of a community sentence. The scores are based on a logistic regression analysis of a large sample of offenders whose history of reconvictions has been tracked through the Home Office Offenders Index. Using these data, the relative significance of a large number of factors known to be correlated with criminal behaviour, such as age, gender, offending history etc., can be estimated. This is then used to give a predicted reconviction score of offenders with similar characteristics. The researchers used their own data to test the accuracy of the predictive scores.

11 This was in spite of evidence from America that the military aspects of boot camps did little to reduce recidivism.

12 Lewis, R.V., 'Scared straight—California style: evaluation of the San Quentin Squires Program' in *Criminal Justice and Behaviour*, vol. 10, no. 2, 1983, pp. 209-26.

10: Financial Penalties

1   Petersilia, J. and Turner, S., *Day Fines in Four U.S. Jurisdictions*, DRU-1153-NIJ, Santa Monica, CA: RAND Corporation, 1996. Gordon, M.A. and Glaser, D., 'The use and effects of financial penalties in municipal courts', *Criminology*, vol. 29, no. 4, 1991.

2   Hillsman, S.T., 'Fines and day fines' in Tonry, M. and Morris, N. (eds), *Crime and Justice: a review of research*, vol. 12, Chicago, IL: University of Chicago Press, 1990.

3   Glaser, D. and Gordon, M.A., *Use and Effectiveness of Fines, Jail, and Probation*, Los Angeles: University of Southern California, Social Sciences Research Institute, 1988.

4   This shift in sentencing towards fines and away from incarceration is apparent since the 1880s in West Germany, the 1920s in Sweden, and between the 1930s and 1960s in England and Wales; Hillsman, 'Fines and Day Fines', 1990, pp. 75-76.

5   Gordon and Glaser, 'The use and effects of financial penalties in municipal courts', 1991.

6   The cases were first divided into six types of offences and then the random sample of offenders was drawn from each of them. Cases with a conviction for indecent exposure were later disregarded for the purposes of Gordon and Glaser as the cases 'are strikingly dissimilar to those in other offence groups',

as explained in Gordon and Glaser, 'The use and effects of financial penalties in municipal courts', 1991, footnote 1, p. 654.

7   Gordon and Glaser, 'The use and effects of financial penalties in municipal courts', 1991, pp. 660-61.

8   Gordon and Glaser, 'The use and effects of financial penalties in municipal courts', 1991, p. 672.

9   Gordon and Glaser, 'The use and effects of financial penalties in municipal courts', 1991, Table 1, p. 656.

10 Gordon and Glaser, 'The use and effects of financial penalties in municipal courts', 1991.

11 Petersilia, J. and Turner, S., *Day Fines in Four U.S. Jurisdictions*, DRU-1153-NIJ, Santa Monica, CA: RAND Corporation, 1996.

12 Turner and Greene published the findings additionally, as 'The FARE Probation Experiment: Implementation and Outcomes of Day Fines for Felony Offenders in Maricopa County'.

13 Petersilia and Turner, *Day Fines in Four U.S. Jurisdictions*, 1996, Table 4.11, p. 34.

14 Turner, S. and Greene, J., *The Fare Probation Experiment: implementation and outcomes of day fines for felony offenders in Maricopa County*, Santa Monica, CA: RAND Corporation, 2000, p. 11.

15 Turner and Greene, *The Fare Probation Experiment*, 2000, p. 11.

16 Turner and Greene, *The Fare Probation Experiment*, 2000, p. 11.

17 Turner and Greene, *The Fare Probation Experiment*, 2000, p. 12.

18 Turner and Greene, *The Fare Probation Experiment*, 2000, p. 13.

19 What happened to those who neither paid in full nor were still on probation is not clear.

20 Turner and Greene, *The Fare Probation Experiment*, 2000, p. 14.

21 Turner and Greene, *The Fare Probation Experiment*, 2000, p. 19.

22 Turner and Greene, *The Fare Probation Experiment*, 2000, p. 14, Table 5.

23 Turner and Greene, *The Fare Probation Experiment*, 2000, p. 14, Table 5.

24 Turner and Greene, *The Fare Probation Experiment*, 2000, p. 19.

25 National Audit Office /Lord Chancellor's Department, *Collection of Fines and Other Financial Penalties in the Criminal Justice System*, Report by the Comptroller and Auditor General, HC 672 session 2001-2002, London: HMSO, 15 March 2002.

26 These figures include both criminal and civil impositions as the accounting systems of many of the courts do not distinguish the two; from National Audit Office /Lord Chancellor's Department, *Collection of Fines and Other Financial Penalties in the Criminal Justice System*, 2002, London: HMSO, p. 3.

27 National Audit Office, *Collection of Fines and Other Financial Penalties in the Criminal Justice System*, 2002, p. 4.

28 National Audit Office, *Collection of Fines and Other Financial Penalties in the Criminal Justice System*, 2002, p. 10.

29 National Audit Office, *Collection of Fines and Other Financial Penalties in the Criminal Justice System*, 2002, p. 10.

30 Mackie, A., Raine, J, Burrows, J., Hopkins, M., and Dunstan, E., *Clearing the Debts: the enforcement of financial penalties in Magistrates' courts*, Home Office Online Report 09/03, 2003, p. 25.

31 Mackie *et al.*, *Clearing the Debts*, 2003, p. 15. The pilot projects were initiated at 20 magistrates' courts, but two (Leeds and Plymouth) withdrew because of shortages in local resources.

32 Mackie *et al.*, *Clearing the Debts*, 2003, p. 53.

33 Mackie *et al.*, *Clearing the Debts*, 2003, p. 77.

34 Mackie *et al.*, *Clearing the Debts*, 2003, p. 55.

35 Mackie *et al.*, *Clearing the Debts*, 2003, p. 58.

36 Mackie *et al.*, *Clearing the Debts*, 2003, p. 60.

37 Mackie *et al.*, *Clearing the Debts*, 2003, p. 60.

38 Mackie *et al.*, *Clearing the Debts*, 2003, p. 64.

39 Mackie *et al.*, *Clearing the Debts*, 2003, p. 66.

40 Mackie *et al.*, *Clearing the Debts*, 2003, p. 66.

41 Due to the unusual method of calculation used by the researchers, these figures seem improbable, but they are presented here as reported in the original; Mackie *et al.*, *Clearing the Debts*, 2003, p. 68.

42 Only two defaulters attended the clinic in Grimsby, Mackie *et al.*, *Clearing the Debts*, 2003, pp. 69-70.

43 Mackie *et al.*, *Clearing the Debts*, 2003, p. 70.

44 Mackie *et al.*, *Clearing the Debts*, 2003, p. 72.

45 Mackie *et al.*, *Clearing the Debts*, 2003, p. 72.

46 Mackie *et al.*, *Clearing the Debts*, 2003, p. 76.

47 As referred to here, the 'payment rate' is the money collected during the year, divided by the number of fines imposed during the year net of penalties transferred to or from other magistrates' courts committees, National Audit Office, *Collection of Fines and Other Financial Penalties in the Criminal Justice System*, 2002, Appendix 1, pp. 26-27.

48 Telephone interview with Mike Baker by Nadia Martin, 5th February 2004.

49 Blunkett, D., *Reducing Crime – Changing Lives: the Government's plans for transforming the management of offenders*, London: Home Office, 2004, p. 12.

11: Post-Release Support of Prisoners—Throughcare

1   *Through the Prison Gate: a joint thematic review by HM Inspectorates of prisons and probation,* London: Home Office, 2001, p. 12.

2   Tripartite Group Report, *Throughcare: developing the service,* Edinburgh: Scottish Executive, part 1, 2003.

3   Sentence plans are constructed for adult offenders; training plans, incorporating education and training, are constructed for juveniles.

4   *Report on a full announced inspection of HMP Belmarsh,* 26 May- 4 June 2003 by HM Chief Inspector of Prisons, London: Home Office, p. 119.

5   *Report on a full announced inspection of HMYOI Aylesbury,* 28 April – 2 May 2003 by HM Chief Inspector of Prisons, London: Home Office, p. 101.

6   *Annual Report of HM Chief Inspector of Prisons for England and Wales 2002-2003* London: Home Office, 2004, p. 34.

7   Webster, R., Hedderman, C., Turnbull, P. J. and May, T., *Building Bridges to Employment for Prisoners: summary and survey of interventions,* Home Office Research Study 226, London: Home Office, 2001, p. iii.

8   *Reducing re-offending by ex-prisoners: summary of the Social Exclusion Unit report,* London: Social Exclusion Unit, 2002.

9   Webster *et al., Building Bridges to Employment for Prisoners,* 2001, p. v.

10 Carter, P., *Managing Offenders, Reducing Crime: a new approach,* London: Home Office, 2003, p. 19.

11 From: http://www.dfes.gov.uk/offenderlearning/init-p.cfm?ID=17

12 *Annual Report of HM Chief Inspector of Prisons for England and Wales 2002-2003,* 2004, p. 21.

13 From: http://www.dfes.gov.uk/offenderlearning/init_p.cfm?ID=17

14 Lewis, S., Vennard, J., Maguire, M., Raynor, P., Vanstone, M., Raybould, S. and Rix, A., *The Resettlement of Short-term Prisoners: an evaluation of seven pathfinders,* London: Home Office, 2003.

15 Webster *et al., Building Bridges to Employment for Prisoners,* 2001, p. vi.

16 Sontheimer, H. and Goodstein, L., 'Evaluation of Juvenile Intensive Aftercare Probation: aftercare system versus system response effects', *Justice Quarterly,* Vol.10, 1993, pp. 197-227.

17 Greenwood, P.W., Deschenes, E.P., and Adams, J., *Chronic Juvenile Offenders: final results from the Skillman Aftercare Experiment,* Santa Monica, CA: RAND Corporation, 1993.

18 Minor, K.I. and Elrod, H.P., 'The Effects of a Multi-faceted Intervention on the Offense Activities of Juvenile Probationers', *Journal of Offender Counseling, Service and Rehabilitation,* 1 (2), pp. 87-108. Also Minor, K.I. and Elrod, P., 'The Effects of a Probation Intervention on Juvenile Offenders Self-concepts, Loci of Control, and Perceptions of Juvenile Justice, *Youth and Society,* 25 (4), 1994, pp. 490-511.

19 Turner, S. and Petersilia, J., 'Work Release in Washington: effects on recidivism and corrections costs', *The Prison Journal*, Volume 76, No. 2, June, 1996, pp. 138-64.

20 Multiplying 56 per cent by 40 per cent yields 22.4 per cent, which Turner and Petersilia define as 'almost one in four', in Turner and Petersilia, 'Work Release in Washington', 1996, p. 147.

21 'Unsuccessful' participants remained in prison until they were released directly to the community; Turner and Petersilia, 'Work Release in Washington', 1996, p. 147.

22 Turner and Petersilia, 'Work Release in Washington', 1996, Table 1, p. 148.

23 Turner and Petersilia, 'Work Release in Washington', 1996, p. 148.

24 The other eight candidates of each group of ten were placed in work release schemes as deemed appropriate by the DOC, so as to avoid disrupting the correctional measures deemed appropriate by the state. Turner and Petersilia did not consider these eight, as they would have disrupted the balance of their study.

25 Turner and Petersilia, 'Work Release in Washington', 1996, p. 157.

26 Turner and Petersilia, 'Work Release in Washington', 1996, p. 157.

27 Turner and Petersilia, 'Work Release in Washington', 1996, p. 161.

28 Turner and Petersilia, 'Work Release in Washington', 1996.

29 Solanki, A., *On-Side Project: Full Evaluation Report (Final Draft)*, London: Nacro, 2003.

30 Berriman, L., *The Role of Social Support within a Short-Term Prisoner Project Designed to Address Resettlement Needs and Recidivism*, Kent: University of Kent (unpublished; provided by Colin Gray, Head of Resttlement at HMP Canterbury), 2002.

31 Solanki, A., *On-Side Project: Full Evaluation Report (Final Draft)*, London: Nacro, 2003.

32 Jackson, S., *A Study of the Needs of Short Term Prisoners at HM Prison Canterbury*, Kent, Surrey and Sussex Area: Psychological Services (unpublished; provided by Colin Gray, Head of Resettlement at HMP Canterbury), 2000.

33 Berriman, *The Role of Social Support within a Short-Term Prisoner Project Designed to Address Resettlement Needs and Recidivism*, 2002, p. 38: Jackson reported that these were the most poignant factors associated with reoffending despite her findings actually showing that 'peer pressure', 'financial pressures', the need for 'drug money' and 'reputation', tied with 'other', were the four most compelling reasons reported for reoffending (Jackson, p. 11).

34 Berriman, *The Role of Social Support within a Short-Term Prisoner Project Designed to Address Resettlement Needs and Recidivism*, 2002.

35 Berriman, *The Role of Social Support within a Short-Term Prisoner Project Designed to Address Resettlement Needs and Recidivism*, 2002, p. 12-13.

36 It is not clear whether the researcher is referring here to reconviction data alone, or data encompassing both arrests and reconvictions. This is the only point in the report (p. 24) at which she suggests that the study used any data other than 'reoffending data'. When discussing the number of people who had 'reoffended', we given no indication of whether they had been arrested or actually been reconvicted. Since, though, the researcher measures the level of seriousness of new offences by examining the type of punishment resulting from the charge and the length of sentence imposed (p. 31), it is fair to suggest that 'new offences' are arrests, some of which did not result in a conviction.

37 Personal communication, 26/1/04.

38 Personal communication during visit to Wormwood Scrubs, 3/02/04.

12: Probation and Restorative Justice

1 *Probation Statistics, England and Wales 2002*, London: Home Office, 2004, p. 8.

2 *Probation Statistics, England and Wales 2002*, 2004,

3 *Probation Statistics, England and Wales 2002*, 2004, Tables 3.2, 5.2, 5.3

4 *Probation Statistics, England and Wales 2002*, 2004, Table 3.1.

5 Carter, P., *Managing Offenders, Reducing Crime*, London: Home Office, 2003.

6 *Probation Statistics, England and Wales 2002*, 2004, Table 8.16.

7 Kershaw, C. *et al.*, *Reconvictions of Offenders Sentenced or Discharged from Prison in 1995, England and Wales*, Statistical Bulletin, Issue 19/99, 1999, p. 2.

8 Reinventing Probation Council, *Transforming Probation through Leadership: the 'broken windows' model*, New York: Center for Civic Innovation, Manhattan Institute, July 2002, p. 3.

9 Bonczar and Glaze (1999), as cited in Reinventing Probation Council *Transforming Probation through Leadership*, 2002, p. 3.

10 Reinventing Probation Council *Transforming Probation through Leadership*, 2002, p. 3.

11 Cited in Petersilia, J., 'Probation in the United States', *Crime and Justice: a review of the research*, Chicago IL: University of Chicago Press, 1997, p. 163.

12 Petersilia, 'Probation in the United States', 1997, p. 167.

13 Petersilia, 'Probation in the United States', 1997, p. 167.

14 Petersilia, 'Probation in the United States', 1997, p. 168.

15 Probationers on 'automated' supervision were typically required to send in a pre-addressed postcard, indicating their movements, once or twice a month; Petersilia, 'Probation in the United States', 1997, p. 169.

16 Petersilia, 'Probation in the United States', 1997, p. 169.

17 Petersilia, 'Probation in the United States', 1997, p. 161.

18 Petersilia, 'Probation in the United States', 1997, p. 164.

19 Petersilia and Turner (1993) cited in Petersilia, 'Probation in the United States', 1997, p. 165.

20 Langan (1996), cited in Petersilia, 'Probation in the United States', 1997, p. 165.

21 When a judge suspends a prison sentence, the offender is actually put on probation. However, if the offender breaches the conditions of probation, he/she will be taken back to the courts, at which stage the judge may impose the original prison sentence, choosing either to deduct time for the duration of the probationary period or not; Petersilia, 'Probation in the United States', 1997, p. 165.

22 Cited from Langan (1994) in Petersilia, 'Probation in the United States', 1997, p. 165.

23 Cited from Parent *et al.* (1994) in Petersilia, 'Probation in the United States', 1997, p. 166.

24 Cited from Maguire and Pastore (1995) in Petersilia, 'Probation in the United States', 1997, p. 179.

25 Petersilia, 'Probation in the United States', 1997, p. 181.

26 Petersilia, J., Turner, S., Kahan, J. and Peterson, J., *Granting Felons Probation: public risks and alternatives*, Santa Monica, CA: RAND Corporation. 1985, p. 20; Petersilia, J. and Turner, S., *Prison versus Probation in California: implications for crime and offender recidivism*, Santa Monica, CA: RAND Corporation, 1986, p. v; and Petersilia, 'Probation in the United States', 1997, p. 181.

27 Petersilia, 'Probation in the United States', 1997, p. 181.

28 A split sentence includes a period spent in jail that is followed by regular probation. For the probationary group in the Petersilia and Turner (1986) study, 3.3 months was the average time spent in jail; Petersilia and Turner, *Prison versus Probation in California*, 1986, p. 13.

29 Petersilia and Turner, *Prison versus Probation in California*, 1986, pp. 10-11, 13.

30 Petersilia and Turner, *Prison versus Probation in California*, 1986, p. 13 and Table A.2, p., 49.

31 Petersilia and Turner, *Prison versus Probation in California*, 1986, p. 16.

32 Petersilia and Turner, *Prison versus Probation in California*, 1986, p. 19.

33 Petersilia and Turner use the word 'estimated' because the rates provided are not the *actual* number of crimes committed by offenders, which would be the best way to measure the incapacitation effect for the sample, but reflect the number of crimes that resulted in arrest rather than conviction. Actual offending rates are probably higher; Petersilia and Turner, *Prison versus Probation in California*, 1986, pp. 28-29.

34 Petersilia and Turner, *Prison versus Probation in California*, 1986, p. 36.

35 Petersilia and Turner, *Prison versus Probation in California*, 1986, p. 36.

36 Petersilia and Turner, *Prison versus Probation in California*, 1986, p. 24.

37 Petersilia and Turner, *Prison versus Probation in California*, 1986, p. 25.

38 The word estimate is used here as in note 33.

39 Petersilia and Turner, *Prison versus Probation in California*, 1986, Table 4.1, p. 25.

40 Petersilia and Turner, *Prison versus Probation in California*, 1986, p, 26.

41 Petersilia and Turner, *Prison versus Probation in California*, 1986, p, 36.

42 Reinventing Probation Council *Transforming Probation through Leadership*, 2002, p. 15.

43 Reinventing Probation Council *Transforming Probation through Leadership*, 2002, p. 16.

44 Reinventing Probation Council *Transforming Probation through Leadership*, 2002, pp. 17-18.

45 Reinventing Probation Council *Transforming Probation through Leadership*, 2002, p. 19.

46 Reinventing Probation Council *Transforming Probation through Leadership*, 2002, p. 20.

47 Reinventing Probation Council *Transforming Probation through Leadership*, 2002, p. 22.

48 Reinventing Probation Council *Transforming Probation through Leadership*, 2002, p. 24.

49 Reinventing Probation Council *Transforming Probation through Leadership*, 2002, p. 26.

50 Reinventing Probation Council *Transforming Probation through Leadership*, 2002, p. 29.

51 Reinventing Probation Council *Transforming Probation through Leadership*, 2002, p. 31.

52 Knight, T., Mowlam, A., Woodfield, K., Lewis, J., Purdon, S., Kitchen, S. and Roberts, C., *Evaluation of the Community Sentences and Withdrawal of Benefits Pilots*, Research Report No 198, London: Department for Work and Pensions, 2003, p. 16.

53 Jobcentre Plus is part of the DWP. It is the government sector that deals with all applications for help with finding employment and/or job seekers' allowance and income support claims.

54 Knight *et al.*, *Evaluation of the Community Sentences and Withdrawal of Benefits Pilots*, 2003, p. 12.

55 Knight *et al.*, *Evaluation of the Community Sentences and Withdrawal of Benefits Pilots*, 2003, p. 3.

56 Knight *et al.*, *Evaluation of the Community Sentences and Withdrawal of Benefits Pilots*, 2003, p. 37.

57 Knight *et al.*, *Evaluation of the Community Sentences and Withdrawal of Benefits Pilots*, 2003, p. 3

58 Knight *et al.*, *Evaluation of the Community Sentences and Withdrawal of Benefits Pilots*, 2003, p. 29

59 Telephone discussion with Sharon Ward, media relations manager for London Probation Head Office, February 2004.

60 Rex, S., Gelsthorpe, L., Roberts, C. and Jordan, P., *Crime Reduction Programme: an Evaluation of community service pathfinder projects final report 2002*, RDS Occasional Paper No. 87, London: Home Office, 2003, pp. 1-2.

61 Richard Ford of *The Times* reported on the performance of evaluated cognitive skills-based probation programmes and claimed that they were proven not to work. At the end of February 2004, he was still unchallenged in his claims, though the government has not published any evaluations of the programme that include reoffending rates.

62 Elliott Robin, e-mail sent to Nadia Martin on 26 February 2004, RDS, Home Office.

63 Shinar, D. and Compton, R.P., 'Victim Impact Panels: their impact on DWI recidivism', *Alcohol, Drugs and Driving*, vol. 11, no. 1, Los Angeles: UCLA Brain Information Service/Brain Research Institute, 1995.

64 Shinar and Compton, 'Victim Impact Panels', 1995, p. 79.

65 Sherman, L., Farrington, D.P., Welsh, B.C. and Mackenzie, D.L., *Evidence-Based Crime Prevention*, London: Routledge, 2002, Table 9.9, p. 374.

66 Shinar and Compton, 'Victim Impact Panels', 1995, pp. 79-80.

67 Shinar and Compton, 'Victim Impact Panels', 1995, p. 80.

68 Shinar and Compton, 'Victim Impact Panels', 1995, Table 5, p. 81.

69 Shinar and Compton, 'Victim Impact Panels', 1995, p. 81.

70 Shinar and Compton, 'Victim Impact Panels', 1995, p. 82.

71 Sherman, L.W., Strang, H. and Woods, D.J., *Recidivism Patterns in the Canberra Reintegrative Shaming Experiments (RISE)*, Canberra: Centre for Restorative Justice Research School of Social Sciences, Australian National University, 2000.

72 Sherman *et al.* chose cases rather than offenders for unit measurements, as RJ rests on the premise that every offender involved in a crime is equally responsible and blameworthy; thus, the method was to have all of the offenders known to the victims and courts present at the conference, Sherman, Strang and Woods, *Recidivism Patterns in the Canberra Reintegrative Shaming Experiments (RISE)*, 2000, p. 10.

73 Sherman, Strang and Woods, *Recidivism Patterns in the Canberra Reintegrative Shaming Experiments (RISE)*, 2000, p.4.

74 Sherman, Strang and Woods, *Recidivism Patterns in the Canberra Reintegrative Shaming Experiments (RISE)*, 2000, p. 6.

75 Sherman, Strang and Woods, *Recidivism Patterns in the Canberra Reintegrative Shaming Experiments (RISE)*, 2000, p. 7.

76 Sherman, Strang and Woods, *Recidivism Patterns in the Canberra Reintegrative Shaming Experiments (RISE)*, 2000, p. 8.

77 Sherman, Strang and Woods, *Recidivism Patterns in the Canberra Reintegrative Shaming Experiments (RISE)*, 2000, p. 12 and Figure 1.

78 Sherman, Strang and Woods, *Recidivism Patterns in the Canberra Reintegrative Shaming Experiments (RISE)*, 2000, p. 13 and Figure 3.

79 Sherman, Strang and Woods, *Recidivism Patterns in the Canberra Reintegrative Shaming Experiments (RISE)*, 2000, pp. 14-15 and Figure 7.

80 Sherman, Strang and Woods, *Recidivism Patterns in the Canberra Reintegrative Shaming Experiments (RISE)*, 2000, p. 15 and Figure 9.

81 From:
http://www.homeoffice.gov.uk/justice/victims/restorative/index.html

82 The Criminal Justice System, *Restorative Justice: The Government's Strategy*, Consultation Document, 22 July 2002.

13: Can We Learn from America?

1 Howell, J., and Bilchik, S., *Guide for Implementing the Comprehensive Strategy for Serious, Violent and Chronic Juvenile Offenders*, Washington: OJJDP, 1995, pp. 7-8.

2 Howell and Bilchik, *Guide for Implementing the Comprehensive Strategy for Serious, Violent and Chronic Juvenile Offenders*, 1995, p. 2.

3 Graham, J. and Bowling, B., *Young People and Crime*, HORS 145, London: Home Office, 1995.

4 *No More Excuses: a new approach to tackling youth crime in England and Wales*, Cm 3809, London: Home Office, 1997, p. 5.

5 Flood-Page, C., Campbell, S., Harrington, V., and Miller, J., *Youth crime: findings from the 1998/99 Youth Lifestyles Survey*, Home Office Research Study 209, London: Home Office, 2000, p. 13.

6 Howell and Bilchik, *Guide for Implementing the Comprehensive Strategy for Serious, Violent and Chronic Juvenile Offenders*, 1995, p. 3.

7 Howell and Bilchik, *Guide for Implementing the Comprehensive Strategy for Serious, Violent and Chronic Juvenile Offenders*, 1995, p. 4.

8 Home Office Statistical Bulletin 4/01, March 2001.

9 Prime, J., White, S., Liriano, S. and Patel, K., *Criminal Careers of those Born Between 1953 and 1978*, HOSB 401, London: Home Office, 2001.

10 Flood-Page *et al.*, *Youth Crime*, cited in Farrington, D. and Painter, K.A., *Evaluation of Two Intensive Regimes for Young Offenders*, Home Office Research Study 239, London: Home Office, 2002, p. 5.

11 Flood-Page *et al.*, *Youth Crime*, 2000, Figure 3.7.

12 Howell and Bilchik, *Guide for Implementing the Comprehensive Strategy for Serious, Violent and Chronic Juvenile Offenders*, 1995, p. 18.

13 Howell and Bilchik, *Guide for Implementing the Comprehensive Strategy for Serious, Violent and Chronic Juvenile Offenders*, 1995, p. 20.

14 Flood-Page *et al.*, *Youth Crime*, 2000.

15 Farrington *et al.*, *Evaluation of Two Intensive Regimes for Young Offenders*, 2002 p. 21.

16 Howell and Bilchik, *Guide for Implementing the Comprehensive Strategy for Serious, Violent and Chronic Juvenile Offenders*, 1995, p. 22.

17 Howell and Bilchik, *Guide for Implementing the Comprehensive Strategy for Serious, Violent and Chronic Juvenile Offenders*, 1995, p. 22.

18 Howell and Bilchik, *Guide for Implementing the Comprehensive Strategy for Serious, Violent and Chronic Juvenile Offenders*, 1995, p. 26.

19 *Reducing Reoffending by Ex-prisoners: Social Exclusion Unit report*, London: Social Exclusion Unit, 2002, p. 18.

20 *Reducing Reoffending by Ex-Prisoners*, 2002, p. 18.

21 *Sunday Times*, 16 November 2003.

22 Howell and Bilchik, *Guide for Implementing the Comprehensive Strategy for Serious, Violent and Chronic Juvenile Offenders*, 1995, p. 23.

23 Rowntree has funded a UK pilot scheme, but it is too early to judge its impact.

14: Guiding Principles for Public Policy

1 France, A. and Crow, I., *CTC – the story so far*. York: Joseph Rowntree Foundation, 2001.

2 For a useful summary see Graham, J. and Bennett, T., *Crime Prevention Strategies in Europe and North America*, Helsinki: European Institute for Crime Prevention and Control, 1995, p. 15.

3 Dennis, N. and Erdos, G., *Families Without Fatherhood*, 3rd edn, London: Civitas, 2000.

4 Pease, K., 'Crime prevention', in Maguire, M. *et al.* (eds), *The Oxford Handbook of Criminology*, Oxford: Clarendon Press, 1994, p. 677.

5 Dennis, N. and Erdos, G., *Cultures and Crimes: policing in four nations*, London: Civitas, 2004.

6 DiIulio, J. and Piehl, A., 'Does prison pay?', *Brookings Review*, vol. 3, 1991, pp. 28-35.

7 DiIulio, J. and Piehl, A., 'Does prison pay? Revisited', *Brookings Review*, 1995, pp. 21-25.

8 *Criminal Justice: the way ahead*, White Paper Cm 5074, 2001, pp. 20-21. The Carter Report of 2003 estimated that 15,000 were in jail at any one time. Carter, P., *Managing Offenders, Reducing Crime: a new approach*, London: Home Office, 2003, p. 15.

9 Hansard, column 312W, *Home Office Annual Report and Accounts 1999-2000*.

10 Hansard, column 234W, *Home Office Annual Report and Accounts 1999-2000*. These figures are also consistent with estimates of the building cost in the *Contract Journal* (www.contractjournal.com).

11 Brand, S. and Price, R., *The Economic and Social Costs of Crime*, HORS 217, London: Home Office, 2000.

12 *Making Punishments Work: the Halliday report*, (Appendices and Correspondence), London: Home Office, July 2001, Appendix 6, p. 130.

13 *Prison Statistics, England and Wales 2001*, London: Home Office, 2001.

14 Civitas is grateful to the Home Office for supplying the method of calculating the estimated fall in crime.

15 We are grateful to the Strategy Unit for explaining the method of calculation used.

16 *Criminal Justice: The Way Ahead*, p. 20.

17 Ramsbotham, D., *Prisongate*, London: Free Press, 2003, p. 84.

18 Solanki, A-R., *On-Side Project: full evaluation report – final draft*, London: Nacro, 2003, pp. 61-65.

19 Although 43 per cent of those who were included as Pathfinders participants had some kind of contact with the project after release, only 35 per cent continued to receive useful services (Lewis, S., Vennard, J., Maguire, M., Raynor, P., Vanstone, M., Raybould, S. and Rix, A., *The Resettlement of Short-term Prisoners: an evaluation of seven pathfinders*, London: Home Office, 2003, p. 58). The interviewer for the On-Side project managed to contact 50 per cent of participants six months after release, a reasonable proportion, but after 18 months the researcher could no longer get in contact with any (Solanki, *On-Side Project*, 2003, p. 32).

20 A halfway house for drug-involved offenders is studied by Martin *et al.* as one of a series of community-based treatments for drug offenders. See Martin, S.S., Butzin, C.A., and Inciardi, J., 'Assessment of a multistage therapeutic community for drug involved offenders', *Journal of Psychoactive Drugs*, vol. 27, no. 1, 1995, pp. 109-16; Inciardi, J., Martin, S.S., Butzin, C.A., Hooper, R.M. and Harrison, L.D., 'An effective model of prison-based treatment for drug-involved offenders', *Journal of Drug Issues*, vol. 27, 1997, pp. 261-78.

21 Howell, J., and Bilchik, S., *Guide for Implementing the Comprehensive Strategy for Serious, Violent and Chronic Juvenile Offenders*, Washington: OJJDP, 1995, p. 31.

22 Howell and Bilchik, *Guide for Implementing the Comprehensive Strategy for Serious, Violent and Chronic Juvenile Offenders*, 1995, p. 31.

23 *Reducing Reoffending by Ex-prisoners: Social Exclusion Unit report*, London: Social Exclusion Unit, 2002, p. 18.

24 Howell and Bilchik, *Guide for Implementing the Comprehensive Strategy for Serious, Violent and Chronic Juvenile Offenders*, 1995, pp. 5-6.

25 *Prison Statistics 2002*, Table 9.10.

15: Government Policy in 2005

1 *Confident Communities in a Secure Britain: the Home Office Strategic Plan 2004-08*, Home Office, Cm 6287, July 2004.

2 *Justice for All*, White Paper Cm 5563, London: Home Office, 2002, p. 18.

3 *Justice for All*, 2002, p. 33.

4 *Justice for All*, 2002, p. 88.

5 *Justice for All*, 2002, p. 87.

6 *Justice for All*, 2002, p. 102.

7 *Reducing Re-offending by Ex-prisoners*, London: Social Exclusion Unit, July 2002, p. 5.

8 *Reducing Re-offending by Ex-prisoners*, 2002, p. 31.

9 *Reducing Re-offending by Ex-prisoners*, 2002, p. 85, p. 106.

10 *Reducing Re-offending by Ex-prisoners*, 2002, p. 18.

11 *Reducing Re-offending by Ex-prisoners*, 2002, p. 19, p. 21.

12 *Justice for All*, 2002, p. 87.

13 YJB, Corporate and Business Plan 2003-04 - 2005-06; *Prison Population Brief*, November 2003.

14 YJB press release, 20 May 2004.

15 Based on all Standard List offences in 1998. *Making Punishments Work: The Halliday Report*, (Appendices and Correspondence), London: Home Office, July 2001, Appendix 3.

16 *Making Punishments Work*, 2001, Appendix 3.

17 A Detention and Training Order involves a period in custody and a period in the community, theoretically continuing the education and training begun in the Young Offender Institution. When in the community, an offender can be required to take part in the ISSP.

18 NAO, *Youth Offending: the delivery of community and custodial sentences*. London: TSO, January 2004, p. 5.

19 NAO, *Youth Offending*, 2004, p. 31.

20 YJB press release, 14 September 2004.

21 YJB press release, 14 September 2004.

22 Moore, R. *et al.*, *ISSP: the Initial Report, Summary*, London: YJB, September 2004.

23 The researchers were only able to match 85 per cent of the sample. The study did not count offenders jailed during the follow-up, which led to the exclusion of about 30 per cent of the sample. As the report admits, 'This is likely to have made the remaining sample unrepresentative by removing some of the most

troublesome offenders'. Moore, R. *et al.*, *ISSP: the Initial Report* (Full version) London: YJB, 2004, p. 298.

24 Moore, *ISSP: the Initial Report* (Full version), 2004, p. 28.

25 Moore, *ISSP: the Initial Report* (Full version), 2004, p. 299.

26 Moore, *ISSP: the Initial Report* (Full version), 2004, pp. 304-05.

27 Moore, *ISSP: the Initial Report* (Full version), 2004, p. 301.

28 *Prison Statistics 2002.*

29 Moore, *ISSP: the Initial Report* (Full version), 2004, p. 276.

30 Moore, *ISSP: the Initial Report* (Full version), 2004, p. 342.

31 Moore, *ISSP: the Initial Report* (Full version), 2004, p. 342.

32 They differ slightly from the earlier figures on pages 304 and 307, presumably because the cost-benefit analysis covers 36 schemes and the main report covers 41.

33 Moore, *ISSP: the Initial Report* (Full version), 2004, p. 345.

34 Moore, *ISSP: the Initial Report* (Full version), 2004, pp. 305, 308.

35 Moore, *ISSP: the Initial Report* (Full version), 2004, p. 334.

36 Prison Service Annual Report and Accounts 2002-03.

37 Moore, *ISSP: the Initial Report* (Full version), 2004, pp. 344-45.

38 Moore, *ISSP: the Initial Report* (Full version), 2004, p. 321.

39 Feilzer, M., with Appleton, C., Roberts, C. and Hoyle, C., *The National Evaluation of the Youth Justice Board's Cognitive Behaviour Projects*, YJB, 2004, p. 53.

40 *Prison Statistics 2001*, p. 165.

41 NAO, *Youth Offending*, 2004, p. 2.

42 NAO, *Youth Offending*, 2004, p. 2.

43 NAO, *Youth Offending*, 2004, p. 38.

44 NAO, *Youth Offending*, 2004, p. 38.

45 NAO, *Youth Offending*, 2004, Figure 12, p. 30.

46 Quoted in NAO, *Youth Offending*, 2004, p. 29.

47 NAO, *Youth Offending*, 2004, p. 3.

48 NAO, *Youth Offending*, 2004, p. 21.

49 NAO, *Youth Offending*, 2004, pp. 20-21.

50 NAO, *Youth Offending*, 2004, pp. 19-20.

51 NAO, *Youth Offending*, 2004, p. 3.

52 NAO, *Youth Offending*, 2004, p. 33.

53 NAO, *Youth Offending*, 2004, p. 34.

54 NAO, *Youth Offending*, 2004, p. 23.

55 Campbell, S., *A review of anti-social behaviour orders*, HORS 236, London: Home Office, 2002.

56 *Targeting Anti-social behaviour – the use of anti-social behaviour orders in Scotland*, October 2003.

57 The Sheriff Court in Scotland is the equivalent of the Magistrate Court in England and Wales.

58 Scottish Executive, *Targeting Anti-social Behaviour*, Scotland: Chartered Institute of Housing in Scotland, 2003.

59 Campbell, S., *Implementing Anti-social Behaviour Orders: messages for Practitioners*, Findings 160, London: Home Office, 2002.

60 Armitage, R., *Tackling anti-social behaviour - What really works*, London: Nacro, 2002.

61 Home Office, *A Guide to Anti-Social Behaviour Orders and Acceptable Behaviour Contracts*, London: Home Office, November 2002.

62 Home Office (November 2002).

63 Campbell, *A review of anti-social behaviour orders*, HORS 236, 2002.

64 Campbell, *A review of anti-social behaviour orders*, HORS 236, 2002.

65 Nixon, J., Hunter, H., and Shayer, S., *The use of legal remedies by social landlords to deal with neighbour nuisance: Survey Report*, Centre for Regional Economic and Social Research Paper No. H8, Sheffield: Sheffield Hallam University, 1999.

66 The number of individuals who had committed no acts of anti-social behaviour in the six months before they were put on the contract was 36. Having committing 'no anti-social acts' means no *police recorded* acts, i.e. there was no hard data that they had committed anti-social acts. There was, how-ever, more informal evidence such as complaints from residents and local authorities, which had allowed these individuals to be identified and put on an ABC. Bethan Jones, co-author of the study, commented that this itself highlights the general monitoring problem—the authorities were aware who the trouble makers were but there was a failure to formally record the incidents.

67 NAO, *Youth Offending*, 2004, p. 37.

68 *Annual Report by HM Chief Inspector of Prisons*, London: Home Office, 2002.

69 *Home Office Targets Delivery Report*, London: Home Office, February 2003, p. 16.